Cisco CCDP ARCH
Simplified

Study Guide

Daniel Gheorghe

ISBN: 978-0-9569892-8-4

Published by:
Reality Press Ltd.
Midsummer Court
314 Midsummer Blvd.
Milton Keynes
MK9 2UB
help@reality-press.com

LEGAL NOTICE
The advice in this book is designed to help you achieve the standard of the Cisco Certified Design Professional (CCDP), which is Cisco's advanced internetworking examination. Cisco Certified Design Professional (CCDP) validates knowledge required to design a Cisco converged network. With a CCDP certification, a network professional demonstrates the skills required to design routed and switched network infrastructures and services involving LAN, WAN, and broadband access for businesses and organizations. The CCDP curriculum includes designing advanced campus, data center, security, and voice networks.

The practical scenarios in this book are meant to illustrate a technical point only and should be used only on your privately owned equipment, never on a live network.

PREFACE

Cisco Systems are the market leader in providing robust and scaleable IT infrastructure solutions. For this reason, every year many tens of thousands of engineers study to pass one of their many certifications exams, from core routing and switching to voice, security, service provider, wireless, and beyond.

One subject area which is just as important as hands-on skill, and yet often neglected, is that of a network design engineer. Without a designer, there would be no network installed in the first place. The network designer is often referred to as the network architect and Cisco recognise this fact through their design certification programs, starting with CCDA and progressing onto the CCDP and CCDE. Cisco CCNP-qualified engineers can, in fact, qualify as a CCDP by taking only one additional exam, the CCDP ARCH exam which is the subject of this study guide.

According to Cisco:

> 'Cisco Certified Design Professional (CCDP) certification is for senior network design engineers, senior analysts, and principal systems engineers, who discuss, design, and create advanced addressing and routing, security, data center, and IP multicast multi-layered enterprise architectures. This includes virtual private networking and wireless domains and it focuses on the design components of larger networks. The CCDP curriculum includes building scalable internetworks and multilayer-switched networks, and designing network service architecture.'

You can attain the CCDP qualification by passing three exams, the ROUTE, SWITCH and ARCH.

Achieving the CCDP qualification will set you apart from other IT engineers, especially those with only hands-on skill. It means you have a clear understanding of network design principles from the ground up and can apply these principles to the needs of a company, offering them cost-effective and scaleable solutions to their network requirements.

Cisco CCDP ARCH Simplifed has been written to answer the same problem as all of the Simplified range. How do you learn what you need to know to understand the concepts, pass the exam, and then apply your skills in the real world of internetworking?

I hope you enjoy this guide and your career as a design engineer.

Amazon Reviews

We sell many thousands of books on Amazon but people are so busy nowadays that they often forget to post a positive review. If you can take a couple of minutes to do this for us on Amazon, we will send you a free CCDP exam by way of a thank you. Please post a screen shot of your review in an e-mail and send it to us at:

howtonetworkhelp@gmail.com

INTRODUCTION

Advanced network design has become a challenge in the last few years because modern networks are complex and they are critical to business operations. The challenge for design engineers is maintaining the skills necessary in response to the internetworking industry's constant and rapid changes, one of which is designing robust, reliable, and scalable networks.

The Designing Cisco Network Service Architectures (ARCH) exam is the core exam required for Cisco Certified Design Professional (CCDP) certification, along with the Implementing Cisco IP Routing (ROUTE) and Implementing Cisco IP Switched Networks (SWITCH) exams. This book provides the latest developments in network design and technologies, including network infrastructure, intelligent network services, and converged network solutions. Objectives for the ARCH exam, according to the official blueprint, include the following:

Designing advanced Enterprise Campus networks
- Design high availability for Enterprise networks
- Design Layer 2 and Layer 3 Campus infrastructures using best practices
- Describe Enterprise network virtualization considerations
- Design infrastructure services, including voice, video, and QoS
- Identify network management capabilities in Cisco IOS software

Designing advanced IP addressing and routing solutions for Enterprise networks
- Create summarizable and structured addressing designs
- Create stable and scalable routing designs for EIGRP, OSPF, and BGP for IPv4
- Describe IPv4 multicast routing
- Create IPv4 multicast services and security designs
- Describe IPv6 for Campus design considerations

Designing WAN services for Enterprise networks
- Describe Layer 1, Layer 2, and Layer 3 WAN connectivity options, including optical networking, Metro Ethernet, VPLS, and MPLS VPNs
- Describe IPsec VPN technology options
- Evaluate WAN service provider design considerations, including features, SLAs, and WAN backup
- Create site-to-site VPN designs with appropriate technologies, scaling, and topologies

Designing an Enterprise Data Center
- Describe Enterprise Data Center best practices
- Describe the components and technologies of a SAN network

- Describe integrated fabric designs using Nexus technology
- Describe network and server virtualization technologies for the Enterprise Data Center
- Create an effective e-commerce design
- Design a high availability Data Center network that is modular and flexible

Designing security services
- Create firewall designs
- Create NAC appliance designs
- Create IPS/IDS designs
- Create remote access VPN designs for the teleworker

The major objective of this book is to introduce the Cisco Borderless Network architectural framework in the context of meeting the Enterprise network's needs for performance, scalability, availability, and security. This book also explains how to create detailed Enterprise Campus, Enterprise Edge, and remote infrastructure designs that offer effective functionality, performance, scalability, and availability, as well as how to create detailed intelligent network services and Virtual Private Network designs.

ABOUT THE AUTHOR

Daniel Gheorghe

Daniel Gheorghe is a CCIE in Routing and Switching. He is currently preparing for his second CCIE certification (in Security) and he is developing his skills in system penetration testing. He also holds numerous certifications in networking and security, from Cisco and other vendors, including CCNA, CCDA, CCNA Security, CCNP, CCDP, CCIP, FCNSA, FCNSP, and CEH. He took an interest in IT at an early age and soon developed a passion for computer networking, which made him study hard in order to reach an expert level.

Daniel worked for different Cisco Partners and System Integrators in Romania in system design, implementation, and troubleshooting for enterprise-level networks. He is also involved in several international freelance consulting projects in his area of expertise.

Daniel is a very dynamic person and in his spare time, he likes to travel and participate in all kinds of sports.

TABLE OF CONTENTS

Chapter 1: The Cisco Enterprise Architecture Model 1

Cisco Intelligent Information Network 2

Service-Oriented Network Architecture 3

PPDIOO Lifecycle Methodology 5

Design Phase Methodology 9

Identifying Network Requirements 10

Characterizing the Existing Network 14

Designing the Network Topology and Solutions 19

Design Process: Final Steps 21

Cisco Hierarchical Network Model 24

The Core Layer 27

The Distribution Layer 28

The Access Layer 29

Cisco Enterprise Architecture Model 30

Enterprise Campus Module 31

Enterprise Edge Module 33

Service Provider Edge Module 37

Remote Modules 38

Summary 38

End of Chapter Quiz 44

Chapter 2: Advanced Enterprise Architecture Model 49

Layer 2 Campus Infrastructure Best Practices 50

Collapsing the Core Layer 50

Cisco Non-Stop Forwarding with Stateful Switchover 52

Cisco IOS Software Modularity 54

Spanning Tree Protocol Best Practices 55

Trunking Best Practices 57

EtherChannel Recommendations 58

Layer 3 Campus Infrastructure Best Practices 59

Managing Oversubscription 59

Cisco Express Forwarding Polarization 60

Routing Protocols 61

First Hop Redundancy Protocols 63

Designing the Layer 2 to Layer 3 Boundary 66

Virtualization Design Considerations 68

Designing a Wireless Network 72

802.11 Protocol Family 73

Collision Avoidance 74

WLAN Service Set Identifiers 74

Wireless Association 75

WLAN Topologies 76

Designing WLAN Security 78

Cisco Unified Wireless Solution 80

CUWN Roaming and Mobility 85

WLAN Design Recommendations 86

Designing Quality of Service 88

Congestion Management 88

Congestion Avoidance 92

Shaping and Policing 93

Link Efficiency Mechanisms 93

QoS Design Recommendations for Voice Transport 94

Network Management 96

Simple Network Management Protocol 96

Remote Network Monitoring 98

NetFlow 99

Cisco Discovery Protocol 100

Network-Based Application Recognition 101

IP Service Level Agreement 103

Summary 104

End of Chapter Quiz 110

Chapter 3: Designing Advanced IP Addressing 115

Importance of IP Addressing 116

Subnet Design Recommendations 117

Summarization 118

Routing Protocols and Summarization 121

Variable Length Subnet Masking and Structured Addressing 123

Private versus Public Addressing 125

Address Planning 128

Role-Based Addressing 129

Network Address Translation Applications 130

Designing IPv6 Addressing 131

Address Representation 132

IPv6 Mechanisms 136

Transitioning from IPv4 to IPv6 139

IPv6 Compared to IPv4 141

Summary 141

End of Chapter Quiz 145

Chapter 4: Designing Advanced IP Multicast 149

Defining the Concept of IP Multicast 150

IP Multicast Functionality 153

Protocol Independent Multicast Deployment Methods 157

PIM Sparse Mode and RP Design Considerations 160

Ethernet Multicasting 164

Multicast in Switched Environments 164

IP Multicast Security and Optimization 166

IPv6 Multicast 169

Summary 171

End of Chapter Quiz 175

Chapter 5: Designing Advanced Routing Solutions 179

Concepts of Routing Protocols 180

Static Routing 180

Dynamic Routing 180

Other Considerations for Routing Protocols 186

Routing Problems and Avoidance Mechanisms 187

Route Summarization and Filtering 188

Default Routing 189

Default Routes and OSPF Stub Areas 189

Route Filtering 190

Routing Protocol Migration 192

Advanced EIGRP 193

EIGRP Operations 193

Scalable EIGRP 194

Advanced OSPF 196

OSPF Functionality 196

OSPF Router Types 197

Virtual Links 198

Link-State Advertisements 199

OSPF Area Types 200

Scalable OSPF 201

Advanced BGP 206

Necessity of BGP 206

BGP Functionality 208

BGP Path Vector Attributes 209

Scalable BGP 210

IPv6 Routing 213

Summary 215

End of Chapter Quiz 219

Chapter 6: Designing Advanced WAN Services 223

   Wide Area Network Design Overview 224

      WAN Categories 225

      WAN Topologies 226

   Optical Networking 228

      Synchronous Optical Network and Synchronous Digital Hierarchy 228

      Coarse Wave Division Multiplexing and Dense Wave Division Multiplexing ... 229

      Resilient Packet Ring 230

   Metro Ethernet 231

      General Considerations for Metro Ethernet 231

      The Cisco Metro Ethernet Solution 232

   Virtual Private LAN Service 236

      General Considerations for VPLS 236

      Hierarchical VPLS 236

   Virtual Private Network Design 238

   IP Security for VPNs 239

      IPsec VPN Functionality 239

      Site-to-Site IPsec VPN Design 242

   Multiprotocol Label Switching VPN Technology 245

      General Considerations for MPLS 245

      MPLS VPN Operation and Design 246

      Layer 2 versus Layer 3 MPLS VPN 248

      Advanced MPLS VPN 249

   WAN Design Methodologies 251

   Selection Considerations for WAN Services 252

   Service Level Agreement 253

      General Considerations for SLAs 253

      SLA Monitoring 254

   Summary 255

   End of Chapter Quiz 260

Chapter 7: Designing the Enterprise Data Center 265

   General Considerations for the Enterprise Data Center 266

      Enterprise Data Center Components 267

      Server Considerations 269

      Enterprise Data Center Facility and Spacing Considerations 269

      Enterprise Data Center Power Considerations 270

      Enterprise Data Center Cooling Considerations 271

      Enterprise Data Center Cabling Considerations 272

   Enterprise Data Center Architecture 273

      Enterprise Data Center Architecture Overview 273

Enterprise Data Center Routing Protocol Design Recommendations 278

Aggregation Layer Design Recommendations 279

Access Layer Design Recommendations 281

Designing Blade Servers 289

Enterprise Data Center Scalability 291

Enterprise Data Center High Availability 292

Storage Area Networks 293

SAN Technology Overview 293

SAN Design Considerations 296

Cisco Nexus 298

Virtualization 302

Virtualization Considerations 302

Server Virtualization 303

Summary 304

End of Chapter Quiz 310

Chapter 8: Designing the E-Commerce Submodule 315

General Considerations for the E-Commerce Submodule 316

E-Commerce High Availability 318

Redundancy 319

Technology 319

People 320

Processes 321

Tools 322

E-Commerce Security Design 322

E-Commerce Server Load Balancing 325

Server Load Balancing Design Models 327

SLB Router Mode 327

SLB Bridge Mode 328

SLB One-Armed/Two-Armed Modes 328

ISP Multi-Homing Design 329

One Firewall per ISP 329

Stateful Failover Design 330

Distributed Data Centers Design 331

Integrated Designs for the E-Commerce Submodule 332

E-Commerce Base Design 332

E-Commerce Dual Layer Firewall Design 333

E-Commerce SLB One-Armed Mode with Dual Layer Firewall Design 334

E-Commerce SLB One-Armed Mode with Security Contexts 334

E-Commerce Submodule Optimization 335

Summary 337

End of Chapter Quiz 340

Chapter 9: Designing Advanced Security Services 345

  Network Attacks and Countermeasures 346

    Threats to Confidentiality, Integrity, and Availability 347

    Network Device Vulnerabilities 351

    Network Infrastructure Vulnerabilities 351

    Application Vulnerabilities 352

  Designing Firewalls 353

    Virtual Firewalls 353

    Active/Active Failover Firewalls 354

    Private VLANs 355

    Zone-Based Firewalls 357

  NAC Services 358

  Designing Intrusion Prevention Systems and Intrusion Detection Systems 361

  Advanced VPN 364

    Secure Sockets Layer VPN 364

    Site-to-Site IPsec VPN 367

    Dynamic Multipoint Virtual Private Network Design 370

    Group Encrypted Transport VPN Design 372

  Security Management 373

    Security Threats and Risks 373

    Security Policy Mechanisms 375

    Network Security System Lifecycle 377

    Trust and Identity Management 383

    Secure Connectivity 384

    Threat Defense Best Practices 384

  Summary 385

  End of Chapter Quiz 391

Quiz Answers 395

CHAPTER 1

The Cisco Enterprise Architecture Model

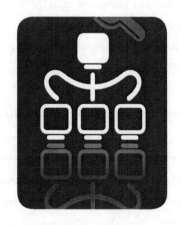

Network design is becoming more complex, with the increasing development of technology and the different types of traffic being added to the network backbone. As a result, having knowledge in the methodologies, processes, and architectures involved in network design plans will support a company's business goals. The following factors are driving the new network architectures:

- The growth in different types of applications
- The evolution of IT, from basic network connectivity to converged intelligent systems
- Increased business expectations from networks

Two network models will be analyzed in this chapter: (1) the Cisco Hierarchical Network model, a classic model with a long history in Cisco instruction; and (2) the Cisco Enterprise Architecture model, an expanded and evolved new and improved model.

CISCO INTELLIGENT INFORMATION NETWORK

The Cisco Intelligent Information Network (IIN) is a multi-phased architecture that injects intelligence into a network's infrastructure. This multi-phased approach integrates the network with applications, software, servers, and services, using a single integrated system to provide intelligence across multiple layers and to align the network infrastructure with the rest of the IT infrastructure. In other words, the network becomes an active participant in the total delivery of applications and services. Cisco considers this an evolving environment (or ecosystem) that responds to constantly changing business requirements. The IIN has three main capabilities:

- **Integrated system:** The network is integrated with the applications and services.
- **Active delivery:** The network fully participates in the monitoring, the management, and the optimization of service delivery and applications.
- **Policy enforcement:** The network enforces policies that allow it to reach business goals and that link business processes and network rules and procedures.

The IIN is a three-phase evolutionary approach that includes the following:

1. **Integrated transport:** This is the convergence of data, voice, and video in a single transport network. An example of this is Cisco's Unified Communications platform. As new applications are delivered, they are placed into the infrastructure for integrated transport. For example, unified messaging integrates voice messaging, e-mail, text, and voice recording.
2. **Integrated services:** These represent the merger of common components, such as data center server capacity or storage, and virtualization technologies that allow the integration of servers, storage, and network components. By virtualizing systems with redundant resourc-

es, the network infrastructure can offer services if the local network fails, as well as enhance disaster recovery and business continuity.

3. **Integrated applications:** At this level the network becomes fully application-aware and it can proactively optimize application performance by integrating application message handling, application security, and application optimization. Cisco calls this integrated application technology Application-Oriented Networking (AON).

SERVICE-ORIENTED NETWORK ARCHITECTURE

Service-Oriented Network Architecture (SONA) is an ongoing architectural framework that supports emerging technologies, IT strategies, and initiatives. As shown below in Figure 1.1, SONA is a three-layer model:

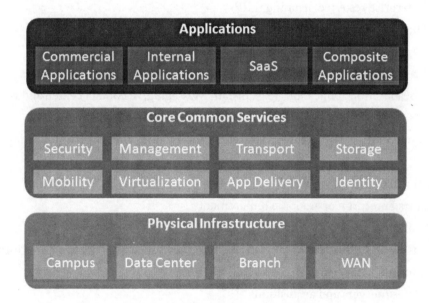

Figure 1.1 – SONA Three-Layer Model

The physical infrastructure, which is also referred to as the network infrastructure layer, is the bottom layer. This is where the servers, storage, and clients are located and it includes different modular design areas (e.g., WAN, Enterprise Edge, Enterprise Campus, branch, data center, and teleworker). The middle layer, which consists of an interactive services layer and management of the services, houses common core services:

- Real-time communications
- Mobility services
- Storage services
- Application delivery

- Management services
- Virtualization technology
- Transport services

The top layer forms the middleware and applications platform, which includes the following:

- Commercial applications
- In-house developed applications
- Software as a service (SaaS)
- Composite applications:
    - Product lifecycle management (PLM)
    - Customer relationship management (CRM)
    - Enterprise resource planning (ERP)
    - Human capital management (HCM)
    - Supply chain management (SCM)
    - Procurement applications
    - Collaboration applications (e.g., Instant Messaging, IP contact center, and video delivery)

All of these components work together as an architectural framework, with the following advantages:

- Functionality
- Supports Enterprise operational requirements
- Scalability
- Expansion and growth of organizational tasks, as it separates the functions into layers and components
- Facilitates mergers and acquisitions
- Modularity
- Hierarchical design that allows network resources to be easily added during times of growth
- Availability of services from any location in the Enterprise, at any time.

The SONA network is built from the ground up with redundancy and resiliency to prevent network downtime. The goal of SONA is to provide high performance, fast response times, and throughput by ensuring Quality of Service (QoS) on an application-by-application basis. The SONA network is configured to maximize the throughput of all critical applications, such as voice and video. SONA also provides built-in manageability, configuration management, performance monitoring, fault detection, and analysis tools, in addition to an efficient design with the goals of reducing the total cost of ownership (TCO) and maximizing the company's existing resources when the application demands increase.

PPDIOO LIFECYCLE METHODOLOGY

In addition to knowing the essential features of a flexible network, a network designer should also follow a methodology that guides the entire lifecycle of the design process. In this regard, Cisco developed the PPDIOO methodology. PPDIOO is a succession of phases that every network implementation will experience during its operational lifetime.

From a business perspective, one common goal of the PPDIOO lifecycle and SONA is lowering the TCO. This can be achieved in the early phases of the process, in which technology requirements are evaluated and validated, and changes in the infrastructure and requirements for resources are properly planned. These early phases also improve network availability by using a solid network design and validating network operations. This process makes the business more agile as it establishes business requirements and technology strategies and adjusts them on a regular basis. It also speeds access to applications and services by improving the following features:

- Availability
- Scalability
- Performance
- Reliability
- Security

PPDIOO is a six-phase model:

1. Prepare
2. Plan
3. Design
4. Implement
5. Operate
6. Optimize

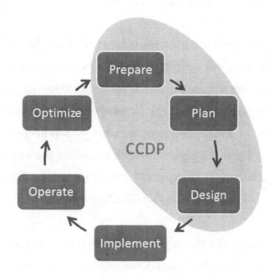

Figure 1.2 – PPDIOO Model

The network lifecycle might not go through all of these six phases in the order shown in Figure 1.2 above without some type of iterative process, where the flowchart can be modified based on changing technologies, budget, infrastructure, business needs, or business structure. For example, after the implement phase, the network designer might need to go back to the Plan phase or the Design phase and make changes at that level. Unplanned actions can happen, especially in the Operate phase. The following sections offer a more detailed description of each phase in the PPDIOO lifecycle:

- **Prepare phase:** The first phase of the PPDIOO lifecycle is the Prepare phase, in which business requirements and goals are established. The IT and the network/security infrastructure must always be in line with these business requirements and goals. In this phase a network strategy and high-level architecture to support that strategy are developed, and possible technologies that can support the architecture are identified. A business case must also be established to justify the budget for the overall network strategy. Representatives from the company's board of directors (i.e., CIO, COO, etc.) might be involved in this phase.

- **Plan phase:** The Plan phase, which includes identifying the decision makers and policy makers and determining the fundamental network requirements (i.e., who needs what services and when), is the most underutilized phase in the PPDIOO process. This phase involves information gathering and identifying the network/security requirements and the legislation to which the company or its customers must adhere (e.g., SOX, HIPAA, etc.). The network security system lifecycle must be carefully analyzed. This includes evaluating the company's needs, risk analysis, security policies, guidelines and processes, the security system that is in place, and possible security system acquisitions in the future, such as a Cisco ASA device. The Plan phase also includes examining best practices and case studies and establishing security and response operations, monitoring, and compliance.

The network management processes must be considered in this phase because they are closely related to the network infrastructure. These processes include fault management, which detects and corrects specific problems; configuration management, which establishes a network baseline and develops a configuration tracking process (for networking appliances and devices); accounting management, which keeps track of circuits for billing of services; performance management, which monitors the network's effectiveness in delivering packets; and security management, which includes Authentication, Authorization, and Accounting (AAA) and RADIUS/TACACS protocols.

The Plan phase characterizes the network and performs an analysis against best-practice architectures, and it looks at the operational environment overall. A project plan must be created to help manage tasks, identify responsible parties or individuals, set milestones, and identify the resources needed for the design and implementation of the project. This generated project plan must be followed through the remaining phases of the PPDIOO lifecycle.

NOTE: Remember, security is a top-priority consideration in every phase.

- **Design phase:** The next phase involves designing the network according to the company's policies, procedures, goals, available budget, and technologies. The design phase also might entail meeting with the policy makers, team leaders, and end-users to gather and analyze data and audit all of the key activities. Results from the Design phase are the basis for the approach taken in the next phase, which is implementing the network infrastructure. The focus of the Cisco design blueprint is on the first three PPDIOO phases – Prepare, Plan, and Design – among which the Design phase is the most complex; as such, this phase will be examined in detail in this chapter and in the rest of the book.

- **Implement phase:** The competitive nature of business and the rush to market products and services forces many organizations to skip the first two phases and start with the Implement phase. Many times those companies get stuck in this phase because of the lack of planning and design. The Implement phase involves constructing the network infrastructure with the best affordable technologies based on all of the design specifications.

The Implement phase includes configuring the network using the Command Line Interface (CLI) or graphical tools (e.g., SDM, ASDM, etc.), installing new equipment, maintenance, and so on. Old devices might be replaced with new devices or some components (e.g., memory, operating systems, etc.) might be upgraded. The project plan must be followed during the Implement phase. Planned network changes should occur here and they should be communicated through control channels in meetings and receive the appropriate approvals.

Each step in the Implement phase should have a description, detailed implementation guidelines, a time estimate, and instructions for falling back to a previous state in case something goes wrong. The Implement phase will also combine additional reference information from RFCs, white papers, case studies, or other Cisco documentation. Any changes implemented in this phase should be tested before moving to the Operate phase, which is next in the PPDIOO lifecycle.

- **Operate phase:** The Operate phase is the final proof that the network design was implemented properly. Performance monitoring, fault detection, and operational parameters will be confirmed in this phase. This will also provide the data used for the last phase.

  This phase involves maintaining the day-to-day operational maintenance and health of the network infrastructure. This includes managing and monitoring the network components, analyzing and creating reports, routine maintenance, managing system upgrades (hardware, software, or firmware), managing the network's performance, and identifying and correcting any network faults or security incidences. In analyzing the actual operations of the implemented network system, this is the final test of the design process. Network management stations (NMSs) should monitor the network's health parameters through Simple Network Management Protocol (SNMP) traps (and certain thresholds reached) or other real-time monitoring solutions.

- **Optimize phase:** Optimizing involves proactive and aggressive management and control over the network. Problems need to be identified quickly so troubleshooting can be engaged for fault detection. This phase is crucial because it is often followed by another planning or design session to redesign the implementation. This makes the first two phases all the more important. Much time and money could be spent in the Optimize phase if failures occur in the initial Plan and Design phases.

  Optimization entails identifying and resolving issues before they move throughout the entire network. The Optimize phase might also generate a modified network design if too many problems appear in the Implement and Operate phases, which may require going back to the Design phase to solve those problems and implement new solutions.

  The next section will focus on the primary goals of a network designer in terms of the Design phase and will analyze some of the design methodologies used in the PPDIOO process.

NOTE: A seventh phase actually exists in the PPDIOO lifecycle: the retirement phase. This phase is implemented when equipment needs to be taken out of production.

A proven method for network design is necessary because it provides consistency to the design process, it offers a framework to work within, and it assures the network designer that no steps will be left out of the design process.

Design Phase Methodology

Like the other phases in the PPDIOO lifecycle, the Design phase is based on the requirements of the company as they align with the technical requirements. The Design phase includes the following features:

- High availability
- Assurance of redundancy
- Failover and fallback mechanisms, both at the software level and the hardware level under network-enabled devices
- Scalability (i.e., the ability to grow the project based on future growth models)
- Security
- Performance models and goals

These features can also be considered the goals of the network design phase. In this particular phase the team involved in the design process might request input from different areas of the company, from security professionals, or from various department leaders. The information gathered will be compiled, logical and physical diagrams will be created, and analysis and reports will be generated based on the conclusions. The initiated project plan will be modified, updated, and eventually finalized during the Design phase, as the next phase involves implantation and no more modifications should be made to the plan during that phase.

The design methodology is comprised of three steps:

- **Identifying network requirements:** This will be done with the help of the decision makers, the stakeholders, or the steering committee. Proposals for the conceptual architecture must be defined, followed by another Prepare phase.
- **Characterizing the existing network:** The existing network must be assessed to determine the necessary infrastructure and to meet the requirements defined previously. This step will define what resources exist and what resources need to be procured to meet the goals of the project plan. The network should be assessed based on functionality, performance, and quality.
7. **Designing the network topology and solutions:** The network topology should be designed to meet all the business and technical requirements. A detailed design document will be generated in this phase, based on the project plan. This will include design solutions for the network infrastructure, Voice over IP (VoIP), security, content networking, and intelligent network services (e.g., Cisco NetFlow).

As mentioned earlier, the methodology in the Design phase focuses on the first three phases of the PPDIOO process: Prepare, Plan, and Design.

Identifying Network Requirements

Step one of the design phase methodology is to define the network requirements. This process can be carried out for a company or for a customer, and it is part of the Prepare phase in the PPDIOO lifecycle. This phase will identify both current and future applications and their importance in the organization. For example, e-mail is considered a critical system, but different applications have different priorities in the organization. These applications and services must be analyzed, along with the data plane traffic (i.e., traffic that moves from client to client or client to server, not traffic destined to network devices).

The next step is to see how the identified network applications and services map to the organization's goals. These goals must align with the IT infrastructure, and they should include improving customer support in the case of Internet service providers (ISPs) or improving service desk support if internal users are served. Among the objectives that must be analyzed in this phase are decreasing costs and increasing competitiveness in a specific field or industry.

Next, the network designer must define the possible constraints to meeting the organization's goals, including the following:

- Budget constraints
- Personnel constraints (the Prepare, Plan, and Design phases might have less resources allocated to them compared to the Implement and Operate phases)
- Organizational policy constraints
- Security policy constraints (open source solutions may be preferred to proprietary solutions, such as EIGRP)
- Need for external contractors and consultants
- Scheduling constraints (i.e., timeframe)

NOTE: The Design phase is one of the most commonly overlooked phases in the PPDIOO lifecycle. Failing to complete this phase might result in a waste of time and money in the end.

After defining the constraints, the technical goals must be defined. These should be aligned with the organization's goals and they typically consist of the hardware and software needed to meet those goals. The response and throughput of the network should be improved while decreasing network failures and downtime that can affect corporate productivity. Network management should be simplified so results and analysis can be obtained quicker and more time can be allocated to incidents and troubleshooting instead of wasting it on management. The network security, availability, and reliability of mission-critical applications (e.g., e-mail or database) should also be improved. Outdated technologies should be updated according to a well-defined plan that should include milestones. Network scalability should also be improved as the system evolves and grows.

The technical goals mentioned above have some constraints, such as a lack of proper wiring capacity to support all of the applications and the lack of bandwidth (e.g., FastEthernet links instead of GigabitEthernet or 10-GigabitEthernet links). Other constraints would be having legacy equipment that does not support newer features or legacy applications that cannot be replaced and need to be accommodated within the network infrastructure. The following techniques must be mastered in the design process:

- **Scope assessment:** The network designer must decide whether to start with a new network implementation or to build upon an existing network infrastructure. If the network implementation is new, step two of the design phase methodology (i.e., characterizing the existing network) can be skipped. Another important aspect is to decide whether to design the entire Enterprise Network or just a subset of it (e.g., specific departments), which is a modular network design concept. The technologies used must also be determined (e.g., LAN, WAN, VoIP, and security). The scope assessment technique is closely related to analyzing the Open Systems Interconnection (OSI) model because it must be determined whether the scope will cover just the Physical Layer, Layer 3 technologies (i.e., addressing, NAT, routing, etc.), or the Application Layer.

- **Gathering the necessary data:** Design information is generally extracted from certain documents called RFPs (requests for proposals) or RFIs (requests for information). An RFP is a more formal document sent to vendors, suppliers, or strategic partners to ask them for proposals to help meet the organization's needs by using their products or services. On the other hand, the RFI is a more informal document used to gather ideas and information from vendors and partners about a specific project or a specific area of implementation. These different proposals and requests are used for different reasons, including gathering information from existing and potential customers (initial requirements) and creating draft documentation that will describe the initial design requirements. This information must be verified by customers, management, and vendors. This data gathering process will be revised as necessary as things change within the organization. All of the documents (i.e., RFPs, RFIs, customer queries, etc.) can be modified based on the feedback received from the stakeholders.

- **Identifying the organization's goals:** Identifying the organization's goals must always precede the process of establishing the technical goals and means. A network designer must understand what the management considers a success and a failure. In addition, customer expectations must be determined, along with the organization's short-term and long-term goals. Most companies want to use IT and networking tools to lower their expenses, increase their applications and services, and obtain a competitive advantage. From a business standpoint, the infrastructure must be as flexible and as reliable as possible. Some of the common goals most companies have, no matter their size, are as follows:

- Utilizing available resources efficiently
- Maximizing profits and revenue
- Reducing development and production cycles
- Increasing competitiveness
- Improving availability of data
- Enhancing interdepartmental communications
- Boosting customer support and customer satisfaction
- Broadening the information infrastructure to stakeholders

- **Identifying the organization's limits:** This step usually covers four different categories:
  - Budget
  - Personnel
  - Policies
  - Timeframe

Unfortunately, network designers are often forced to find the most affordable solution instead of the optimal technical solution. This means that certain features might need to be compromised, such as scalability, manageability, performance, or availability. The available budget should include all the purchases, equipment, licenses, and training needed for the project. Budgets should be the final decision, but in most cases it is the primary consideration. Network designers must find areas in which they can make compromises to improve the overall goals of a specific project and obtain an effective solution.

Another limitation concerns the personnel involved in the project and what kind of expertise they have. Additional training might be necessary if they are not very technically skilled. The number of contractors and the level of outsourcing in the project should also be analyzed. For implementation and maintenance, an adequately trained technical staff must exist to fulfill the organization's goals.

The organization's limits are also dictated by its policies and procedures. This includes what vendors are being used, what standards are in place (open standards or closed standards), policies about protocols, and different applications.

The last category is the timeframe, particularly the deadlines that must be met. This limitation can make the network designer's job either easier or more complicated. This includes how long it will take to deploy applications and to train users. This category is typically the concern of the project manager, who must create milestones for the design and implementation processes.

- **Identifying applications and services:** The next phase is finding out what applications and services will be used. After discussions with key decision makers, a detailed analysis must be made that will take into consideration the following aspects:
    - Application category (e-mail, productivity, database, security, Web browsers, management, etc.)
    - Application choices for each category (low, medium, high, critical)
    - The application's or service's level of importance

All of this information can be identified during a brainstorming session with the stakeholders or team leaders to determine the necessary applications and their level of importance.

- **Reaching technical goals:** This technique involves isolating and reaching the technical goals. The network designer should be an expert in determining what these goals should be and how to achieve them under the limitations of budget, personnel, time, procedures, and policies. Common technical goals include the following:
    - Maximize performance and productivity
    - Enhance security
    - Achieve reliability for critical core applications (99.9% for most organization)
    - Reduce downtime
    - Update obsolete hardware and software (depending on budget constraints)
    - Boost network scalability (modular solutions)
    - Simplify network management

- **Identifying technical restraints:** A successful design engineer must recognize the technical obstacles and restraints in the network design. This usually falls under the following categories:
    - Limitations of existing equipment (updates might be required)
    - Availability of bandwidth (mostly related to WAN connections)
    - Compatibility of applications (the use of a single vendor might be required)
    - Adequacy of trained personnel (more training might be required)

Characterizing the Existing Network

Step two in the design phase methodology is characterizing or classifying the network. This is where the network designer identifies the major features and characteristics of the network and defines the tools used to analyze, audit, and monitor network traffic. Information gathering always occurs in an early phase in any multi-step process, such as developing applications or designing the security model. The information gathering process consists of three steps:

1. Compile all existing information and documentation.
2. Conduct a network audit.
3. Perform traffic analysis.

Information gathering involves compiling all of the existing information in any form of documentation. This must happen first to avoid duplicating tasks, especially those that have already been completed by somebody else.

The second step is conducting a network audit with as much pre-information as possible. The network audit might need to be performed by a Certified Information System Auditor (CISA) or other certified professionals. Network auditing tools should be used along with the necessary documentation and network management tools (e.g., Cisco Prime Tivoli) that will provide information about the network's device inventory, configuration, and status. The audit must provide information about the version of the software used, the Internetwork Operation System (IOS), the management software (e.g., ASDM, SDM, etc.), the configuration on the devices, Layer 1 and Layer 2 information and topologies, interface speeds, CPU and memory utilization, Wide Area Network (WAN) types, and Virtual Private Network (VPN) types. Manual auditing of the network devices will involve using a wide variety of "show" commands on Cisco devices, such as "show tech-support" (which will generate a huge report on individual systems), "show version", or "show running-config". Other tools that might be used in the auditing phase are as follows:

- Packet sniffers (e.g., Wireshark)
- SNMP tools
- Network analysis tools:
    - Network-Based Application Recognition (NBAR) from Cisco, an IOS tool that helps identify well-known applications, protocols, and services
    - NetFlow (a very popular solution that runs on Cisco and third-party devices), a reporting tool that records information about traffic patterns that cross devices

A network checklist is useful in the auditing phase. This should include available topology segments, IP addressing schemes, and WAN connections.

All of the tools presented above can be used in the third step of the information gathering phase, which is performing traffic analysis. In this phase the designer should investigate the following:

- Network response time
- Available bandwidth
- QoS mechanisms used, especially when using VoIP
- Security features implemented, such as segmenting the network using Virtual Local Area Networks (VLANs)

Network designers are often in a situation where the network infrastructure is already in place and the new design will cover only the restructuring or the upgrading of the existing network. The network designer must review the existing network documentation and diagrams that the company has, get input from different IT personnel, perform some kind of network auditing, define and describe the existing topology, and analyze the traffic. Five different components that describe the network are as follows:

- Layer 3 topology
- Layer 2 topology
- Network services
- Applications
- Network modules

The first step in the process is to obtain a Layer 3 topology of the network from the existing documentation or diagrams. Analyzing Figure 1.3 below, the Core Layer (backbone) of the network is made up of high-end routers. Other network areas include the internal server zone, the network management area, the WAN connection, the Public Switched Telephone Network (PSTN) connection, the Internet connection, and the Demilitarized Zone (DMZ, for Web servers).

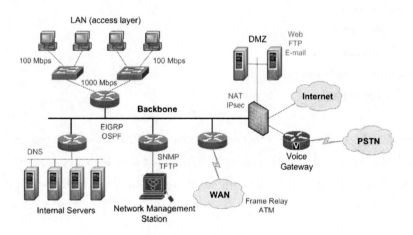

Figure 1.3 – Network Components

Important information that can be gathered at Layer 3 are the routing protocols (e.g., Enhanced Interior Gateway Routing Protocol – EIGRP and Open Shortest Path First – OSPF) used in the network core or at the edge, the Internet connection capacity, and applications that are accessed through the Internet.

The Layer 2 topology can be a separate map or it can be built by adding elements onto the existing Layer 3 topology. The recommendation is to isolate and document the network areas based on the shared bandwidth capacity (e.g., GigabitEthernet, FastEthernet, etc.) and the switching infrastructure used at different layers (Access, Distribution, or Core). Layer 2 technologies also include the WAN connections (e.g., Frame Relay or Asynchronous Transfer Mode – ATM) that connect the company's branch offices.

The next step is to isolate the network services and map them onto a separate document that should include the following:

- Domain name services (Domain Name System – DNS)
- Network management services (SNMP, Trivial File Transfer Protocol – TFTP)
- Security services (*Terminal Access Controller Access Control System* – TACACS, Access Control Lists – ACLs – on the routers, IP Security – IPsec, Network Address Translation – NAT)
- Routed protocols (Internet Protocol – IP, Internet Packet Exchange – IPX)
- Routing protocols (EIGRP, OSPF)
- Quality of Service
- Multicast services

The fourth aspect includes the applications that run on the network:

- File sharing applications (File Transfer Protocol – FTP)
- Web applications
- E-mail applications
- Instant Messaging
- Unified Communications
- Microsoft Exchange

Once the Layer 2 and Layer 3 network topologies, the network services, and the applications have been identified, the information gathered must be divided into logical submodules to obtain a modular design. Based on Figure 1.4 below, the following submodules might be of interest:

- Backbone
- Network management
- PSTN access
- Corporate Internet
- Public access
- WAN
- Internal server farm
- LAN (Access Layer)

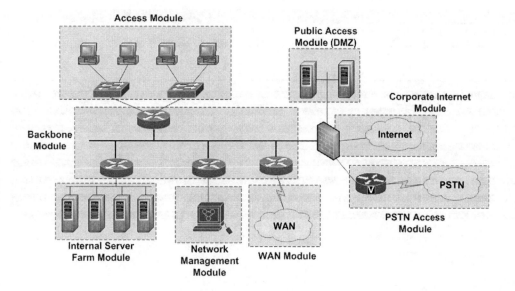

Figure 1.4 – Modular Network Map

The next step is identifying the components and properties for each network device (e.g., router, switch, firewall, etc.), such as the following:

- Device model
- CPU/memory
- Resource utilization
- IOS version
- Device configuration
- Routing tables
- Interfaces
- Modules/slots

This information can be obtained from the IT staff or it can be gathered individually by accessing the NMS and connecting to each network device in the topology.

NOTE: The process of gathering configuration and performance information about a specific network device is also called device auditing. The Cisco solution for network auditing and monitoring is called CiscoWorks.

A network designer might also need to use network analysis tools to find information about traffic flows, Quality of Services techniques, security information, traffic profiles, and the way certain applications and protocols use the available traffic. Some of the tools that can be used in this regard are Cisco NetFlow analyzer tools or the Wireshark packet capturing tool (sniffer). The screenshot below is an example of a Wireshark FTP capture session:

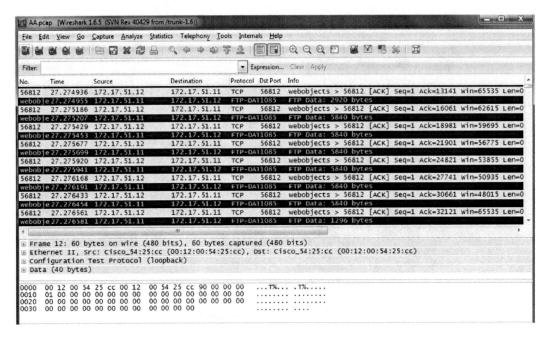

Figure 1.5 – FTP Packet Capture Session

The last step in describing the existing network is combining the created Layer 2 and Layer 3 topology maps with the discovered services and applications and creating a summary report that can be presented to key decision makers and policy makers within the organization. This document can include the following:

- Number and types of devices
- IOS version used
- Memory capacity and upgrade recommendations
- Discovered points of congestion and recommendations
- Suboptimal paths and recommendations
- Routed and routing protocols and upgrade recommendations
- Survey of applications and services
- Impact assessment (cost, personnel, time)

Designing the Network Topology and Solutions

The third step of the design phase methodology is designing the network topology and solutions. An effective approach for this step is a structured design (see Figure 1.6 below) that allows the development of a complete system, with optimum design at the lowest cost, while meeting all the company's requirements in the following areas:

- Performance
- Functionality
- Flexibility
- Capacity
- Availability
- Scalability

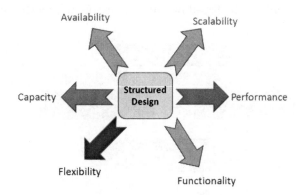

Figure 1.6 – Designing the Network Topology and Solutions

The network designer's goal in this phase should be to develop a systematic approach that takes into consideration the organization's needs, goals, policies and procedures, technical goals and constraints, and the existing and future network infrastructure. This includes physical models, logical models, and functional models.

The best approach in this phase, and the one recommended by Cisco for a medium-sized network to a large Enterprise Campus design, is the top-down approach. Using this approach presents an overview of the design before getting down to the design details. This entails beginning with the Application Layer (Layer 7) of the OSI model and then moving down through the Presentation Layer, the Session Layer, the Transport Layer, the Network Layer, the Data-link Layer, and, finally, the Physical Layer (Layer 1).

The network and physical infrastructure should be adapted to the needs of the network applications and services. In other words, do not choose network devices or hardware and software technologies until the requirements for the applications are fully analyzed and met. The concepts of SONA and IIN should also be incorporated into the design process, combined with the organization's requirements. This includes considering organizational and technical constraints.

The top-down approach is usually a very time-consuming process and is a bit more costly, but it is preferred over bottom-up solutions, where typically the design is based on previous experience and a quick fix or solution. The problem with the bottom-up approach is an inappropriate design in the medium to long term, and the organization's requirements and constraints are not included. This would cause trouble and possible process rollback during later project phases.

NOTE: To learn more about the Cisco top-down network design approach, read *Top-Down Network Design*, 3rd Edition, published by Cisco Press (2010).

Figure 1.7 below is an example of the top-down network approach methodology:

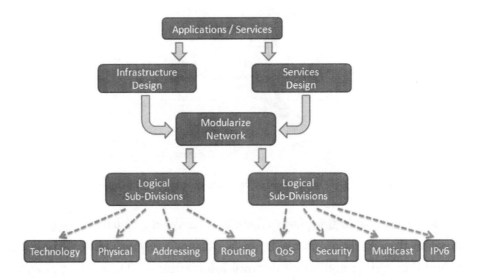

Figure 1.7 – Example of the Top-Down Approach

Figure 1.7 starts at the top with the applications and services, which includes the Application, Presentation, and Session Layers. Based on the requirements for the applications and the way they match the organization's goals, a network infrastructure design and an infrastructure services design to meet the application requirements of the organization should be applied. This includes the data, the types of traffic and services, and what types of design and network services will meet the needs of those applications.

Once the goals are met, the network should be modularized, taking a modular approach and including the Core, Distribution, and Access Layers of the network, the data center, the server farm, the branches, and the Internet connectivity layer. Next, apply the decisions made for the infrastructure and services to different modular areas of the network by dealing with certain segments of the network at a time.

The next step is to take this modular implementation and create logical subdivisions that will be addressed on a project-by-project basis. Looking at them from a project management or steering committee standpoint, these will be logical subprojects. Different subprojects might exist for the following circumstances:

- Choosing the technology, acquisitions, and provisioning
- Physical topology design (implementing the design in different layers)
- Addressing the design scheme, including NAT solutions
- Routing selection and design
- Quality of Service design (traffic management)
- Security design
- IP multicast design (for video and audio streaming)
- IPv6 provisioning design

Design Process: Final Steps

The final steps of the design process within the PPDIOO lifecycle include the following:

- **Plan the network implementation process:** This step involves a high degree of documentation and diagramming. A step-by-step procedure must be established for each aspect of the modular design. This must be well documented and detailed, must describe every step (with references to the different documents, diagrams, or reports created), and must include a detailed guideline for the implementation of the network. In case of a pitfall or a design failure, the network designer must have a rollback plan in place. In addition, an estimation of the time needed for the implementation process should be provided, and project managers and other staff members must be consulted. Testing should be performed at every step in the process, and complex procedures must be broken down into smaller pieces using teams of people. This might be the case when implementing complex technologies like IP Telephony.

- **Pilot and prototype testing:** The network designer must be sure to verify the design once this step is completed. This can be done with a prototype or a pilot network, meaning a sample implementation that will help test the solution. Depending on the solution, some organizations might implement both pilot and the prototype testing, or just one of them.

  A pilot site is a live location that serves as a test site before the solution is deployed. This is a real-world approach to discovering problems before deploying the network design solution to the rest of the internetwork. A pilot network is used to test and verify the design before the network is implemented or launched. The design should also be tested on a subset of the existing network infrastructure. The pilot test might be done within a particular module or a particular building or access area before extending the network to other areas.

A prototype is a subset of the full design tested in an isolated environment, unlike the pilot test, which is implemented in the production network. The benefit of using a prototype is that it allows full testing of the network design before it is deployed, without having any negative effects on the production network. A prototype test is often used before applying a redesign to an existing network. The results of the pilot or prototype tests will be documented in a proof of concept section in the final design document.

Like in other phases, the company's requirements must always be at the top of the priority list. The prototype or pilot network implementation has two possible results: it is either successful or it fails the design goals. If the prototype does not meet all of the objectives, corrections must be made. A success means it is proving the concept of the actual network design.

Successful testing will prove that the Plan, Preparation, and Design phases are on target and will facilitate moving on to the Implement phase. Sometimes a success in this step concludes the network designer's job, who will then hand over the project to the personnel or outside consultants who will handle the implementation of the hardware and software solutions.

A failure in this phase does not mean the entire project has failed. It simply means that some corrections must be made to the actual design, after which the prototype/pilot test must be repeated until it is considered a success. Any failures that happen during the testing phase require going back to the iterative process and correcting the planning, preparation, or design aspects and repeating the pilot/prototype test to correct any weaknesses that might have a negative effect on the implementation process.

- **Fully document the design:** The design document, which is complementary to the planning document, is the final document that will be created. The design document should include the following components:
  - Introduction (description of project goals)
  - Design requirements, including the organizational and technical constraints
  - Existing network infrastructure (logical Layer 3 topology diagram, physical topology diagram, audit and analysis results, routing protocols, applications and services summary, device list, configuration, and description of any issues identified)

- Design section (specific design information, logical topology design, physical topology design, IPv4 and IPv6 design, routing protocols, and security configurations)
- Proof of concept (conclusion of the pilot/prototype testing phase)
- Implementation plan (useful in the next phase of the PPDIOO process; presents the steps that must be followed by the implementation team to successfully implement the new system or the network upgrade)
- Appendix (white papers, case studies, additional information, and configurations)

An example of the design document structure is presented below:

1. Introduction
2. Requirements for the Design
3. Existing Infrastructure
    3.1 Layer 1 Topology
    3.2 Layer 2 Topology
    3.3 Layer 3 Topology
    3.4 Audit Results
    3.5 Recommendations
4. Intelligence Services
    4.1 Applications
    4.2 Services
    4.3 Analysis
    4.4 Recommendations
5. Solution Design
    5.1 Design Summary
    5.2 Design Details
    5.3 Implementation Details
    5.4 Recommendations
6. Prototype Network
    6.1 Prototype Details
    6.2 Prototype Results
    6.3 Recommendations
7. Implementation Plan

This document might be cross-referenced with other documents used during the design process to fully describe the proposed solution.

To summarize, the design steps presented below in Figure 1.8 are structured as an eight-step methodology:

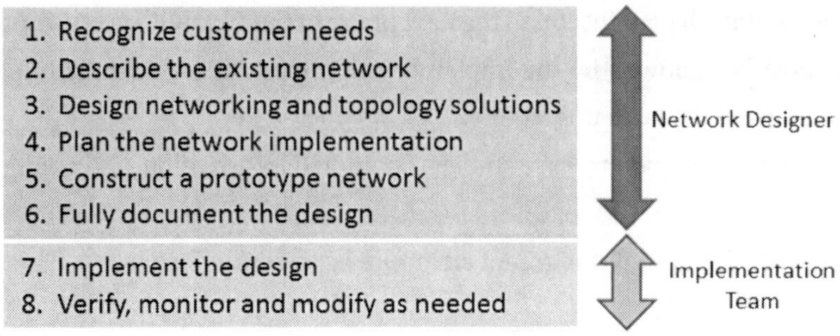

1. Recognize customer needs
2. Describe the existing network
3. Design networking and topology solutions
4. Plan the network implementation
5. Construct a prototype network
6. Fully document the design

Network Designer

7. Implement the design
8. Verify, monitor and modify as needed

Implementation Team

Figure 1.8 – Eight-Step Design Methodology

From a technical standpoint, in the eight-step design methodology, step 6 and step 7 represent the separation between the network designers and the network engineers who will take care of the network implementation process. In context of the CCDP, only the first six steps are of interest. Step 7 and step 8 should be of interest for implementation engineers, not for network designers.

CISCO HIERARCHICAL NETWORK MODEL

The most important idea concerning the Cisco Hierarchical Network model is the construction of the network step by step, implementing one module at a time, starting with the foundation. The implementation of each module can be supervised by the network architect, but the details are covered by specialized teams (e.g., routing, security, voice, etc.). This modular approach is the key to making implementation simple. The main advantages of the Cisco Hierarchical Network model are as follows:

- Easy to understand and implement
- Flexibility
- Cost savings
- Modular
- Easily modified
- Easy network growth
- Facilitates summarization
- Fault isolation

This model was created so that the construction of the IIN would be easier to understand. Cisco has always tried to make efficient and cost-effective networks that have a modular structure so they can be easily divided into building blocks. The modular network design facilitates modifications in certain modules, after implementation, and makes it easy to track faults in the network.

A special feature promoted by the Cisco Hierarchical Network model is summarization. This allows for smaller routing tables and smaller convergence domains, which leads to many advantages, such as summarizing routes from an OSPF area as they enter the backbone or having a more stable network by not advertising specific network changes to other areas or domains. For example, a network failure or modification in an OSPF area means a specific prefix will not be advertised within that area, but this does not impact the rest of the network because that prefix is part of a larger, summarized network that does not change. This behavior enhances efficiency in the network's functionality and allows for optimal network design.

NOTE: Depending on the situation, summarization can also have some disadvantages, including making troubleshooting more difficult and allowing traffic black holes.

The Cisco Hierarchical Network model (see Figure 1.9 below) is defined by the following three layers:

- The Core (backbone) Layer
- The Distribution Layer
- The Access Layer

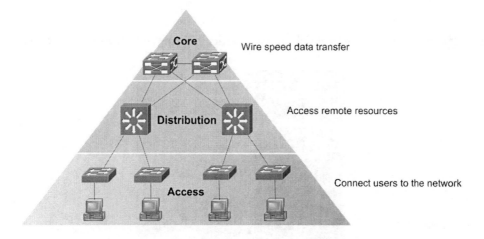

Figure 1.9 – Cisco Hierarchical Network Model Layers

These three layers might sometimes collapse into each other to make networking easier, especially in small networks. For example, a network might have two real layers: an Access Layer and a collapsed Distribution and Core Layer. Although the Distribution and Core Layers may be considered united in this scenario, there is a clear difference between the functionalities of the Distribution Layer and the functionalities of the Core Layer within the compressed layer.

The Core Layer is the backbone of the network and its main purpose is to move data as fast as possible through Core Layer devices. The design purpose in the Core Layer is providing high bandwidth and obtaining a low overhead. The Core Layer contains Layer 3 switches or high-speed routers, which are used to obtain wire speed. For example, if the Core Layer devices have 10 Gbps interfaces, the devices should send data at 10 Gbps without delay on those interfaces.

It is not possible to connect to all of the necessary resources through the LAN because some resources are remotely located. A legacy network concept, the 80/20 rule, states that 80% of the network resources are local and 20% are remote. In modern networks this rule is inverted, meaning 20% of the network resources are local and 80% are accessible remotely. The Distribution Layer is the layer that provides access to these remote resources, as fast as possible, usually using Layer 2 switches. This layer facilitates speedy access to resources located in other networks (different locations) or on the Internet.

The Access Layer connects users to the network using Layer 2 and Layer 3 switches. This layer is often called the desktop or workstation layer because it connects user stations to the network infrastructure. The Access Layer also connects other type of devices, including servers, printers, and access points.

The Cisco Hierarchical Network model can be generically mapped to the OSI model, as follows:

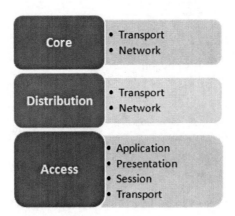

Figure 1.10 – Cisco Hierarchical Network Model Mapped to the OSI Model

As shown in Figure 1.10 above, each layer has physical and data-link processes, but the higher OSI layers used in the Access, Distribution, and Core Layers might be different. The Core Layer mainly uses transport and network services and there is some overlap between the Core and Distribution

Layers in this regard. The Distribution Layer also handles transport and network services but with more emphasis on the Network Layer (Layer 3). The Access Layer is involved with the upper layer protocols, namely Transport, Session, Presentation, and Application Layers. This makes sense, as speed decreases going from the Core Layer to the Access Layer because of the addition of more layers of protocols, applications, and services.

To summarize, users connect to the network through the Access Layer, access remote resources through the Distribution Layer, and move data through the network as fast as possible through the Core Layer.

The Core Layer

The Core Layer of the network involves the following aspects:

- High speed
- Reliability and availability
- Redundancy
- Fault tolerance
- Manageable and scalable
- No filters, packet handling, or other overhead
- Limited, consistent diameter
- Quality of Service (low latency)

High speed refers to ports operating close to true wire speed on the Core Layer devices, with minimal delay. Reliability is another important issue when defining how often equipment functions at normal parameters. Redundancy and fault tolerance are intertwined, and they influence the recovery time when a network device or service stops functioning. Sometimes the network is back up and running seamlessly (transparently) because of redundancy technologies, so when something crashes in the network, users are not impacted and can continue working.

Another feature of the Core Layer operations is it does not influence the traffic in any way, as its main goal is fast traffic switching. To avoid overhead and to move traffic through the Core Layer as quickly as possible, complex security features and filtering are not configured on Core Layer devices; instead, they are configured in the Access and Distribution Layers. One important aspect that should be monitored carefully is the growth of the Core Layer. The network backbone usually consists of a limited but consistent diameter, and a solid network design should support Distribution and Access Layer expansions without impacting the Core Layer.

A very powerful feature used in the Core Layer is called Quality of Service (QoS); however, the QoS parameters implemented in the Core Layer are different from the QoS parameters used at the network edge, as they are focused on ensuring low-latency packet switching. Quality of Service is a complex and sophisticated topic that will be covered in detail later in this book. However, to preview, the major QoS techniques are as follows:

- **Best effort:** This implies sending traffic without the guarantee of assurance or reliability.

- **Integrated Services approach (IntServ):** IntServ is based on the admission control concept on the network devices. For example, when someone uses a VoIP telephone, all of the devices in the path to the destination can communicate with each other and reserve the amount of bandwidth necessary for that call. To achieve this, IntServ uses protocols like the Resource Reservation Protocol (RSVP).

- **Differentiated Services (DiffServ):** This is the most modern and popular QoS approach in that it classifies and marks traffic on a hop-by-hop basis. The DiffServ approach is comprised of the following disciplines:
  - Classification
  - Marking
  - Congestion management
  - Congestion avoidance
  - Traffic compression
  - Link Fragmentation and Interleaving (LFI)

  When using DiffServ, each layer is assigned specific QoS mechanisms that integrate and work together with the QoS mechanisms at other layers.

NOTE: The QoS features presented above are not specific to the Core Layer. Instead, they are generic concepts that are applied to all three layers and are presented in this section as a reference.

The Distribution Layer

Unlike the Core Layer, the Distribution Layer includes features that involve some kind of traffic processing, since this is where policies are implemented in a network, for example, which user can access what resources from outside of the network. This is also where many of the security features are implemented in response to the growing number of attacks from the Internet. The Distribution Layer shares some common features with the Core Layer, like QoS techniques and redundancy features. Except for these commonalities, the Distribution Layer performs a unique and completely different set of functions, such as the following:

- Access control to the Core Layer
- Redundancy to Access Layer devices
- Routing protocol boundaries
- Redistribution
- Filtering
- Route summarization
- Policy routing
- Security
- Separate multicast and broadcast domains
- Routing between VLANs
- Media translation and boundaries (e.g., FastEthernet to GigabitEthernet)
- Aggregation

The value of this separation of functions is easier to understand, troubleshoot, and manage when there are different jobs occurring in these hierarchical network layers.

The Access Layer

In an Enterprise Campus design, the Access Layer is characterized by a shared LAN, a switched LAN, and VLANs to the workstations and servers. This layer provides high availability and flexible security features, like port security, Address Resolution Protocol (ARP) inspection, and VLAN Access Control Lists (VACLs). These security features will be covered in detail in the dedicated security chapter later in this book.

Other functions of the Access Layer involve port security, 802.1x, broadcast control, and defining QoS trust boundaries (i.e., what devices are trusted based on the QoS settings or the distance to the actual desktop stations before classification and marking takes place). In addition, to mitigate the threat of users trying to deploy Denial of Service (DoS) attacks on the network, rate limiting techniques can be implemented.

Other features implemented in the Access Layer include the Spanning Tree Protocol (STP – to ensure that the Layer 2 logical topology is loop-free) and Power over Ethernet (PoE) or voice VLAN settings (if the network functionality requires them). Examples of the latter would be automatically placing the voice traffic in a voice VLAN when plugging an IP phone into a Cisco switch, and powering IP phones using an Ethernet cable when using PoE-capable Cisco Catalyst switches. From a WAN standpoint, the Access Layer can provide access to PSTN, Frame Relay, or ATM networks and ISDN, DSL, or cable services.

CISCO ENTERPRISE ARCHITECTURE MODEL

The Cisco Hierarchical Network model presented previously will not be abandoned in the remainder of this chapter. In fact, the legacy three-layer model must be mastered to understand the changes that led to the creation of the new and improved Cisco Enterprise Architecture model, which extends the three-layer Hierarchical Network model.

The Cisco Enterprise Architecture model leveraged the Hierarchical Network model, added new components, and made the network more modular. The key aspect regarding this model is modularity. This defines new models that have different functions in the network and facilitates the convenient building block approach when building an IIN. The modules included in the Cisco Enterprise Architecture model include the following:

- Enterprise Campus
- Enterprise Edge
- Enterprise WAN
- Enterprise Data Center
- Enterprise Branch
- Enterprise Teleworker
- Service Provider Edge

The purpose of using this model is to build modules that coordinate with the typical components of the IIN. The three-layer Hierarchical Network model is often fully included in the Enterprise Campus module, as shown in Figure 1.11 below:

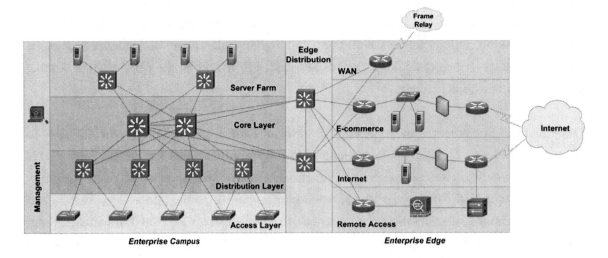

Figure 1.11 – Cisco Enterprise Architecture Model Components

In addition to the Enterprise Campus, which includes the Access, Distribution, and Core Layers, there is also an Edge Distribution module that provides a connection between the Enterprise Campus module and other submodules (e.g., WAN, e-commerce, remote access, etc). Different networks will require different modules and submodules based on their particular role and function. The Service Provider Edge module provides external connectivity services to the Enterprise Edge module; however, it is not included in the figure above because it is not considered a part of the organization's network.

The following sections will briefly describe each module, while the rest of this book will cover all of the technologies used in each of these building blocks.

Enterprise Campus Module

The Enterprise Campus module is often referred to as the LAN and it consists of the Core Layer, the Distribution Layer, and the Access Layer. Sometimes the Core and Distribution Layers collapse into a single layer. An important submodule of the Enterprise Campus module is the edge distribution submodule, which allows connectivity to the Enterprise Edge and Service Provider Edge modules. Modern networks contain a server farm or a data center block (depending on the size and complexity of the network environment) inside the Enterprise Campus module, as depicted in Figure 1.12 below:

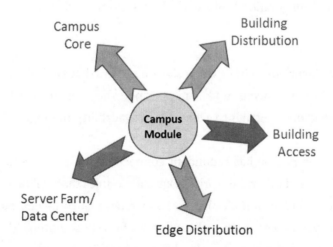

Figure 1.12 – Enterprise Campus Module Components

The Campus Core, Distribution, and Access Layers form the Enterprise Campus infrastructure block. The Access Layer submodule consists of workstations, IP telephones, and Layer 2 Access Layer switches. The Distribution Layer submodule is the central location that connects all of the modules together and it includes a high degree of routing and switching operations, ACLs, QoS techniques and filtering, redundancy, load balancing, and multiple equal cost paths. The Core (backbone) Layer submodule provides high-speed connectivity and fast convergence between other submodules (e.g., the server farm and the Edge Distribution submodules), typically using high-end Layer 3 switches. The Core Layer module might also have some QoS or security techniques implemented but caution must be taken with these features to avoid significant overhead. Remember, traffic must be switched at wire speed in the Core Layer.

The Enterprise Campus module might also include the network management submodule that interfaces with all of the other modules and submodules in the network design. This is where SNMP management, logging, and monitoring and configuration management (using applications and tools like CiscoWorks or TACACS+/RADIUS services, which are part of a larger AAA solution) can be found. Another submodule in the Enterprise Campus module is the server farm or data center. A common technology implemented in the server farm submodule is the Storage Area Network (SAN). The server farm submodule includes the following components:

- Database services (Oracle, SQL)
- E-mail or other collaboration systems
- Application services
- File services
- DNS services
- Dynamic Host Configuration Protocol (DHCP) servers
- Other servers

Generally, the services mentioned above will reside on servers that are linked to different switches for full redundancy, load balancing, and load sharing. They might also be cross-linked with Enterprise Campus backbone switches to achieve high availability and high reliability.

The edge distribution submodule has redundant connections to the Core Layer submodule, the Enterprise Edge module, and other Enterprise Edge submodules that will be presented in the next section. This is composed of one or multiple Layer 3 switches that connect redundantly to the Core Layer, Cisco Access Layer servers, high-end routers, or firewall solutions. The Edge Distribution module is the aggregation point for all of the different links in the Enterprise modules, and the demarcation point between the Enterprise Campus and the Enterprise Edge, as shown in Figure 1.11 above.

Enterprise Campus design best practices can be summarized as follows:

- Choose modules that map to different buildings/floors with Distribution Layer and Access Layer functionality.

- Count the number of Access Layer switches to Distribution Layer switches. Implement two or more Distribution Layer switches for redundancy and availability, and have at least two uplinks from each Access Layer switch.
- Design the server farm submodule.
- Design the network management submodule
- Locate and implement the edge distribution submodule.
- Design the Enterprise Campus infrastructure, including the Campus backbone, and link all of the modules to the Campus backbone redundantly.

Enterprise Edge Module

The Enterprise Edge module (see Figure 1.13 below) might consist of particular submodules. Depending on the particular network, one or more of these submodules might be of interest:

- E-commerce
- Internet and DMZ
- Remote access and VPN
- Enterprise WAN

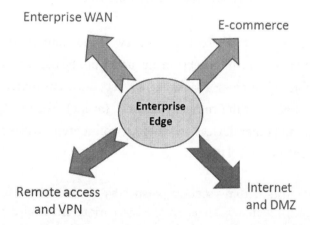

Figure 1.13 – Enterprise Edge Components

The following best practices should be taken into consideration when designing the Enterprise Edge module:

- Isolate permanent links to remote offices first.
- Count the number of connections from the corporate network to the Internet connectivity submodule.
- Design the remote access/VPN submodules.
- Create and implement the e-commerce submodule, if needed.

DMZ Submodule

One of the most interesting and often misunderstood concepts in the Enterprise Edge module is the Demilitarized Zone (DMZ). Figure 1.14 below and the text that follows briefly explain this concept:

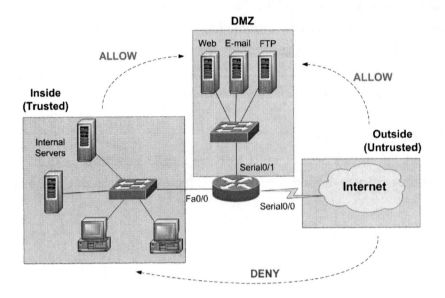

Figure 1.14 – Example of a DMZ

Suppose a company has a router that also acts as a firewall and connects to the Internet (outside) through the Serial0/0 interface. The Internet is an untrusted, public network because it is impossible to control and it is capable of launching attacks against networks. The router has another interface, FastEthernet0/0, that connects to the company network (inside). The inside network is made up of workstations, servers, and other devices and they are considered a trusted network because the company owns it and has full control over it.

> **NOTE:** According to statistics, from a security perspective, the majority of network attacks come from inside the network, initiated by angry employees, curious employees, or users who are not very technically trained and initiate attacks by mistake. Despite this consideration, for security design purposes consider the inside network a trusted network.

In addition to devices located on the Internet and inside the network, other resources might include:

- The company's Web server
- The company's e-mail server
- An FTP server so users can download information by accessing the company from the outside
- Network devices (firewalls, routers, etc.)

All of these devices and services can be organized on a separate interface (Serial0/1 in this example) that connects to a separate area called the DMZ. Notice that the DMZ is not on the inside of the network because people from the outside can access resources in this area. From a security standpoint, the DMZ is in the middle of the inside and the outside areas, as it is part of the company but it does not offer the security provided to inside devices. DMZ devices can be accessed either from inside users or from outside users, but the outside users still cannot connect to the inside network, which enforces the security policies regarding critical and confidential resources.

E-Commerce Submodule

The e-commerce submodule is used when electronic commerce is an important function in the organization. This submodule includes the following devices:

- Web servers
- Application servers
- Firewalls
- Intrusion Detection Systems (IDSs)
- Intrusion Prevention Systems (IPSs)
- Database servers

An IDS notifies administrators that there is some common security attack happening. For example, if it detects that someone is trying to get into the network with a "ping of death" attack, IDS will generate alarms that will notify administrators that this specific attack has been initiated in the network. IDSs do not prevent attacks, they just detect them. An IPS is more powerful than an IDS because in addition to the alarming functionality, it can also prevent attacks.

Internet Submodule

The Enterprise Edge module might have an Internet submodule because most companies today require Internet access. This submodule includes the following devices:

- Firewalls
- Internet routers
- FTP servers
- HTTP servers
- SMTP servers
- DNS servers

Regarding the firewall devices, Cisco implements this functionality in both routers running IOS and dedicated firewall appliances, like the modern Cisco ASA (Adaptive Security Appliance), which evolved from Cisco PIX firewalls.

The Internet submodule might have redundancy capabilities but this depends on two factors:

- The available budget for implementing redundancy
- How critical the Internet is for the organization

The importance of the Internet to the organization's functionality will depend on the level of Internet connectivity that it has:

- Single router, single link
- Single router, dual links to one ISP
- Single router, dual links to two ISPs
- Dual routers, dual links to one ISP
- Dual routers, dual links to two ISPs

The scenario in which the organization has links to two Internet Service Providers (ISPs) is called a dual-homed scenario. This provides a high degree of redundancy because a link or an ISP can be lost without losing Internet connectivity. The most advanced and safe dual-homed redundancy is comprised of multiple routers with multiple links to multiple ISPs. This is the connectivity model that must be chosen if Internet access is critical to the organization's functionality.

VPN/Remote Access Submodule

The remote access submodule can contain the following devices:

- Firewalls
- VPN concentrators
- Dial-in access concentrators
- IDSs/IPSs

An interesting aspect of the VPN concentrators is that they are no longer available as independent devices because their functionality has been integrated and enhanced in the sophisticated Cisco ASA security device. In addition to firewalls and VPN concentrators, this submodule also contains attack prevention systems, like IDS and IPS.

WAN Submodule

A WAN is typically part of a network, hence, the WAN submodule feature found in the Enterprise Edge module. This submodule connects to the Service Provider Edge module. A company's WAN connections may consist of different types and use different technologies (these will be covered in the appropriate sections of this book), including:

- MPLS
- Metro Ethernet
- Leased lines
- SONET and SDH
- PPP
- Frame Relay
- ATM
- Cable
- DSL
- Wireless

Service Provider Edge Module

The Service Provider Edge module shown in Figure 1.15 below contains the actual connections to the ISPs and offers the following services:

- Internet connectivity (primary ISP, secondary ISP)
- WAN services (Frame Relay/ATM)
- PSTN services

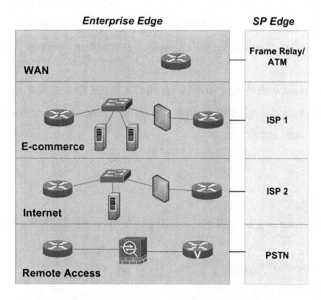

Figure 1.15 – Service Provider Edge Module

In modern networks, the PSTN technology is often replaced with the VoIP approach. Some of the best practices that should be taken into consideration when designing the Service Provider Edge module are as follows:

- Try to get two ISPs for redundancy or at least two links to a single ISP.
- Select the mobile/remote/dial-up technology.
- For slow WAN links use Frame Relay or leased lines.

Remote Modules

Depending on how much remote access there is to the network, remote modules might include the following:

- Enterprise Branch
  - Site-to-site VPNs
- Enterprise Data Center
  - High-speed LAN
  - Data Center management
- Enterprise Teleworker
  - Remote access VPNs

The Enterprise Branch module typically creates site-to-site VPNs that connect branch offices to the headquarters. The Enterprise Data Center is where various network blocks access data. This module features high-speed LAN capabilities and sophisticated Data Center management software. Some companies have a large number of telecommuters (i.e., people that work from home). This would necessitate an Enterprise Teleworker module that features remote access VPN technologies.

The next chapter will analyze different solutions that a large Enterprise network can use to take advantage of emerging technologies like high availability, intelligent network services, security, voice transport, and content networking.

SUMMARY

The Cisco approach to designing an IIN is the SONA framework. SONA contains three layers:

- Network infrastructure layer
- Infrastructure services layer
- Application layer

SONA offers the following benefits to the network design process:

- Functionality
- Scalability

- Availability
- Performance
- Manageability
- Efficiency

Cisco categorizes the network lifecycle into six phases identified within the PPDIOO concept:

Prepare	This phase involves determining the network's requirements, formulating a network strategy, and suggesting a conceptual architecture of the network.
Plan	This phase compares the existing network with the proposed network to help identify tasks, responsibilities, milestones, and resources required to implement the design.
Design	This phase clearly articulates the detailed design requirements.
Implement	This phase integrates equipment into the existing network (without disrupting the existing network) to meet design requirements.
Operate	This phase entails the day-to-day operation of the network, while responding to any issues that arise.
Optimize	This phase gathers feedback from the Operate phase to potentially make adjustments to the existing network. Changes might be implemented to address ongoing network support issues.

PPDIOO's lifecycle approach offers the following benefits:

- Reduces total cost of ownership (TCO)
- Improves network availability
- Allows business networks to respond to changing needs quickly
- Accelerates access to network applications and services

Designing a network in conjunction with the PPDIOO approach involves the following steps:

1. **Identifying network requirements:** To identify network requirements, the following information must be obtained:
   - Network applications
   - Network services
   - Business goals
   - Constraints imposed by the customer
   - Technical goals
   - Constraints imposed by technical limitations

2. **Characterizing the existing network**: To identify characteristics of the current network, the following tasks must be completed:

- Collect existing network documentation (with the understanding that the documentation might be somewhat dated and unreliable) and interview the organization's representatives to uncover information not available in the documentation.

- Conduct a network audit to identify information such as network traffic types, congestion points, and suboptimal routes.

- Supplement the information collected during the two previous tasks by performing network traffic analysis with tools such as Cisco Discovery Protocol (CDP), Network-Based Application Recognition (NBAR), NetFlow, Network General Sniffer, Wireshark, and Remote Monitoring (RMON) probes.

3. **Designing the network topology**: Using information collected in steps 1 and 2, the network's design can be completed. Although designing a network can be a daunting task, Cisco's recommended top-down design approach assists the designer by breaking down the design process into smaller and more manageable steps. The term top-down refers to beginning at the top of the OSI reference model (the Application Layer) and working down through the underlying layers.

Using a top-down design strategy, as opposed to a bottom-up design strategy (i.e., where the design begins at the Physical Layer of the OSI model and works its way up), provides the following benefits:

- Does a better job of including specific company requirements
- Offers a more clearly articulated "big picture" of the desired network for both the company and the designer
- Lays the foundation for a network that not only meets existing design requirements but also provides scalability to meet future network enhancements

When using the OSI reference model in the top-down design approach, the designer should determine what design decisions, if any, are required for each of the seven layers. For example, when considering the Application Layer, the designer might determine that voice applications such as the Cisco IP Contact Center and the Cisco Unity messaging system are applications needed for the design.

Network Layer design decisions might include the selection of a routing protocol, for example, the Enhanced Interior Gateway Routing Protocol (EIGRP) or the Open Shortest Path First Protocol (OSPF). In addition, when analyzing the Network Layer, the designer might need to determine an appropriate IP addressing scheme for the network (e.g., the use of private versus public IP addresses and the subnet masks to be used) to provide for future network scalability.

Physical Layer and Data-link Layer design decisions might involve the selection of LAN/WAN technologies (e.g., GigabitEthernet, FastEthernet, Frame Relay, ATM, or PPP) to provide for media transport. With the multitude of design decisions required in larger networks, network designers often benefit from network design tools, such as the following:

- **Network modeling tools:** These tools generate suggested configurations based on input information, which can then be further customized (e.g., adding redundancy or support for additional sites).
- **Strategic analysis tools:** These tools enable a network designer to experiment with various "what-if" scenarios and observe the resulting network effects.
- **Decision tables:** These tables record design decisions based on network requirements.
- **Simulation and verification tools/services:** These verify design decisions in a simulated environment to reduce the need to implement a pilot network.

Even with the availability of simulation tools, some network designs still benefit from building a small prototype network to serve as a proof of concept. An alternative to prototype networks, which are usually implemented in an isolated environment, is building a pilot network within a specific network module.

For many years, Cisco recommended the Hierarchical Network model, a three-layer network design model that included the Access Layer, the Distribution Layer, and the Core Layer:

- **Access Layer:** Typically, wiring closet switches connecting to end-user stations.
- **Distribution Layer:** An aggregation point for wiring closet switches, where routing and packet manipulation occurs.
- **Core Layer:** The network backbone, where high-speed traffic transport is the main priority.

However, to provide for enhanced scalability and flexibility, Cisco later introduced the Cisco Enterprise Architecture model, which categorizes Enterprise networks into six modules. The three layers of SONA can be found in each of these modules. Specifically, each module can contain its own network infrastructure, services, and applications. The functional areas that comprise the Enterprise Architecture model include the following:

- **Enterprise Campus:** The portion of the network design that provides performance, scalability, and availability and that defines the operations within the main campus.

- **Enterprise Edge:** An aggregation point for components at the edge of the network (e.g., Internet and MAN/WAN connectivity) that routes traffic to and from the Enterprise Campus functional areas.
- **WAN and Internet:** The portion of the network made available by an ISP (e.g., Frame Relay or ATM).
- **Enterprise Branch:** Remote network locations that benefit from extended network services, such as security.
- **Enterprise Data Center:** A consolidation of applications, servers, and storage solutions (similar to a Campus data center).
- **Enterprise Teleworker:** A collection of small office/home office (SOHO) locations securely connected to the Enterprise Edge via an ISP or PSTN.

When designing the Enterprise Campus module, four primary areas need to be addressed:

- **Access Layer:** Connects end-user devices to the network.
- **Distribution Layer:** Aggregates Access Layer switches and performs Layer 3 switching (i.e., routing) functions.
- **Core Layer (backbone):** Provides high-speed, redundant connectivity between buildings.
- **Server farm or data center:** Consolidates application servers, e-mail servers, domain name servers, file servers, and network management applications.

The edge distribution submodule connects the Enterprise Campus with the Enterprise Edge module, which contains the following four submodules:

- **E-commerce:** Contains the servers used to provide an e-commerce presence for an organization, including the following:
  - Web servers
  - Application servers
  - Database servers
  - Security servers

- **Internet connectivity:** Provides Internet-related services, including the following:
  - E-mail servers
  - Domain Name System (DNS) servers
  - Public Web servers
  - Security servers
  - Edge routers

- **WAN and site-to-site VPNs:** Interconnects a main office with remote offices over various transport technologies, such as the following:
  - Frame Relay
  - ATM
  - PPP
  - SONET

- **Remote access and VPN:** Provides secure access for remote workers (e.g., telecommuters) or remote offices and includes components such as the following:
  - Dial-in access concentrators
  - VPN concentrators
  - Cisco Adaptive Security Appliances (ASAs)
  - Firewalls
  - Intrusion Detection/Protection System (IDSs and IPSs) appliances

The WAN and Internet submodules are sometimes referred to as the Service Provider Edge module. These submodules are not explicitly designed because the Service Provider Edge module is designed, owned, and operated by an ISP. However, the Enterprise network designer can specify the type of connection to use in connecting to the ISP(s). Specifically, the Service Provider Edge module includes the following types of connectivity:

- Frame Relay
- ATM
- Point-to-point leased line
- SONET and SDH
- Cable modem
- Digital subscriber line (DSL)
- Wireless bridging

Enterprise locations are supported via the following previously described modules:

- Enterprise Branch
- Enterprise Data Center
- Enterprise Teleworker

END OF CHAPTER QUIZ

1. Which of the following comprise the three layers defined by the Cisco Hierarchical Network model (choose three)?
    a. Campus
    b. Distribution
    c. Access
    d. Internet
    e. Core
    f. WAN

2. Wire speed transmission is one of the characteristics of which layer?
    a. Access
    b. Distribution
    c. Core

3. Modern networks respect the 20/80 rule, meaning 80% of the destinations are accessed remotely.
    a. True
    b. False

4. Which layer is responsible for connecting workstations to the network?
    a. Distribution Layer
    b. Campus Layer
    c. Core Layer
    d. Access Layer

5. The Core and Distribution Layers usually operate at which OSI layer (choose all that apply)?
    a. Physical
    b. Data-link
    c. Network
    d. Transport
    e. Session
    f. Presentation
    g. Application

6. The main duty of the Core Layer devices is:
   a. Performing QoS
   b. Connecting users to the network
   c. High-speed transmission
   d. Implementing network security

7. SONA represents a:
   a. Security feature
   b. Architectural framework
   c. Testing procedure
   d. Network management protocol

8. What is the most underutilized phase in the PPDIOO methodology?
   a. Plan
   b. Design
   c. Operate
   d. Implement

9. What are the most important steps in the network design methodology (choose all that apply)?
   a. Characterizing the existing network
   b. Optimizing the network
   c. Identifying network requirements
   d. Designing the network topology and solutions
   e. Identifying the competitors
   f. Implementing security features

10. The most important aspect to keep in mind when designing a network is:
    a. Budget constraints
    b. Security policies
    c. Employee feedback
    d. Network manageability
    e. Business needs

11. The most critical organizational limitation in identifying the network requirements phase is:
    a. Number of users
    b. Budget
    c. Network size
    d. Network bandwidth

12. A network audit is recommended in which phase of the design methodology?
    a. Identifying network requirements
    b. Characterizing the existing network
    c. Designing the network topology
    d. Implementing a pilot network
    e. Writing the design document

13. An example of a packet sniffer software application is:
    a. NetFlow
    b. CiscoWorks
    c. Wireshark
    d. CDP

14. The Cisco software solution for network management is called:
    a. CiscoWorks
    b. Cisco Discovery
    c. NetFlow
    d. SDM

15. The recommended approach to designing the network topology phase is:
    a. The horizontal approach
    b. The vertical approach
    c. SONA
    d. The top-down approach
    e. The bottom-up approach

16. What is the difference between a pilot and a prototype implementation?
    a. Prototypes are used when building a network from scratch
    b. A prototype is a subset of the full design tested in an isolated environment
    c. A pilot site is an isolated site
    d. There is no different between a pilot and a prototype implementation

17. Which submodule does not belong in the Enterprise Edge module?

    a. Distribution Layer

    b. E-commerce

    c. WAN

    d. Internet connectivity

    e. Remote access

18. Which network area is exposed to both internal and external traffic and usually hosts services accessed from the Internet, like websites or e-mail?

    a. Data center

    b. Network access

    c. DMZ

    d. Network management

19. What is the highest level of Internet connectivity?

    a. Single router, dual links to one ISP

    b. Dual routers, dual links to two ISPs

    c. Dual routers, dual links to one ISP

    d. Single router, dual links to two ISPs

20. Which of the following are WAN technologies (choose all that apply)?

    a. ATM

    b. CEF

    c. Frame Relay

    d. EIGRP

    e. DMZ

CHAPTER 2

Advanced Enterprise Architecture Model

This chapter covers the following topics:

- High availability for Enterprise networks
- Layer 2 and Layer 3 Campus infrastructures using best practices
- Enterprise network virtualization considerations
- Infrastructure services, including voice, video, and QoS
- Network management capabilities of Cisco IOS software

This chapter will begin by analyzing the design of the Enterprise Campus network infrastructure in terms of Layer 2 and Layer 3 best practices and it will continue with details on network virtualization, infrastructure services (with emphasis on Quality of Service), and Cisco IOS management capabilities.

LAYER 2 CAMPUS INFRASTRUCTURE BEST PRACTICES

Campus infrastructure best practices are aimed at designing highly available modular mechanisms that make networks easier to scale, easier to comprehend, and easier to troubleshoot. This is usually accomplished by delivering deterministic traffic patterns.

Collapsing the Core Layer

The process of collapsing the Core Layer implies combining it with the Distribution Layer and this is one of the first decisions small and medium Enterprises make when analyzing the Enterprise Campus design. The Core Layer is the aggregation point for all of the other layers and modules in the Enterprise Campus architecture. The main technology features required inside the Core Layer include a high level of redundancy, high-speed switching, and high reliability.

Core Layer devices should be able to implement scalable protocols and technologies and they should support advanced load balancing mechanisms. Typically, the Core Layer infrastructure is based on Layer 3 high-speed switching and uses hardware-accelerated network services. Not all Enterprise Campus environments need a dedicated Core Layer, so in some situations it may be combined with the Distribution Layer to form a collapsed Core Layer architecture, as shown in Figure 2.1 below:

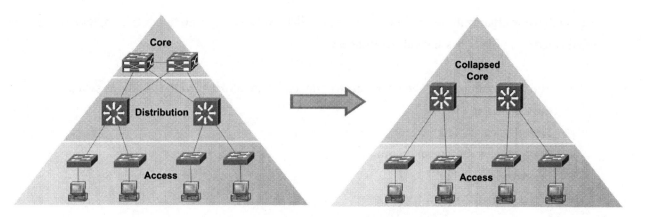

Figure 2.1 – Collapsed Core Layer Architecture

Another frequently used scenario is the one in which an organization has multiple buildings or areas that are composed of an Access Layer and a Distribution Layer. Instead of aggregating the connections through a Core Layer, the Distribution Layer switches are connected in a full-mesh topology. In this full-mesh collapsed Core Layer scenario, a number of connections are needed (n*(n-1), where "n" equals the number of Distribution Layer devices), as illustrated in Figure 2.2 below:

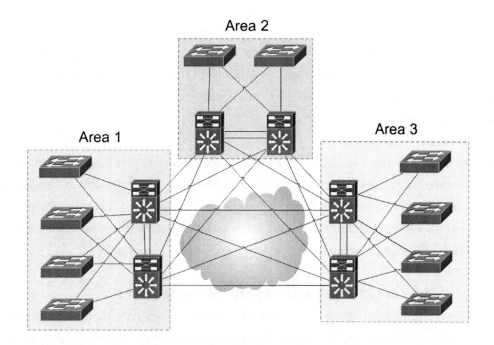

Figure 2.2 – Full-Mesh Distribution Layer

NOTE: All of the Distribution Layer (collapsed Core Layer) devices in a single area should have at least dual connections to achieve high availability.

Although some organizations can choose to use a collapsed Core Layer architecture, implementing a dedicated Core Layer has several advantages:

- The Distribution Layer switches can be connected hierarchically to the backbone switches in the Core Layer
- Less physical cabling
- Less complex routing environment
- Improved scalability
- Easier data and voice integration
- Easier to converge LAN and WAN
- Improved fault isolation
- Improved summarization capabilities
- Allows for identifiable boundaries

Using a collapsed Core Layer and full-mesh architecture requires increasing port density because each Distribution Layer switch would need to connect to other Distribution Layer switches. Alternatives to this issue include having a Layer 2 Core Layer with discrete VLANs on each Core Layer switch, so only two ports per Distribution Layer switch are needed. However this option is not very common in modern networks because of the use of multilayer switches.

Another downside of collapsing the Core Layer is the complexity of adding another network building or area. The new Distribution Layer switches would have to be connected to the full-mesh topology, so the total number of links would increase greatly. This problem can be avoided by using a dedicated Core Layer.

Considering all of the facts presented, large Enterprises that use a collapsed Core Layer model should upgrade to a three-layer network model with a dedicated Core Layer as soon as the appropriate expertise and resources are available. Cisco recommends having redundant connections between the Access Layer switches and the Distribution Layer switches, and between the Distribution Layer switches and the Core Layer switches.

Cisco Non-Stop Forwarding with Stateful Switchover

Cisco Non-Stop Forwarding (NSF) with Stateful Switchover (SSO) is another high availability feature (see Figure 2.3 below), and this can be implemented as a supervisor redundancy mechanism (within a Catalyst 6500 switch). One of the main objectives when implementing this feature is avoiding the interruption of Transmission Control Protocol (TCP) sessions (e.g., Border Gateway Protocol (BGP) neighbor relationships). The integrity of these sessions should be maintained to provide seamless convergence. In Layer 2 environments, SSO can be used on its own, while NSF with SSO can be used in Layer 3 environments.

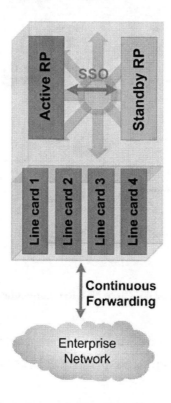

Figure 2.3 – Cisco NSF with SSO

When this feature is activated, the standby Route Processor (RP) will take control of the router after a hardware or software fault on the active RP. Cisco NSF will continue to forward packets until route convergence is complete, and SSO allows the standby RP to take immediate control and maintain connectivity protocols (e.g., BGP sessions).

Cisco NSF is supported by a wide variety of routing protocols, including the following:

- EIGRP
- OSPF
- IS-IS
- BGP

A router or a multilayer switch that runs one of these protocols can detect internal switchover and take the proper actions to continue forwarding the network traffic, using and leveraging Cisco Express Forwarding (CEF) while recovering route information from other devices, so forwarding continues and no link flapping occurs.

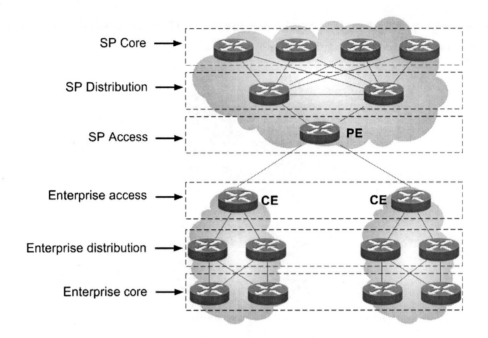

Figure 2.4 – Cisco NSF Recommendations

Analyzing Figure 2.4 above, Cisco provides some recommendations for each layer in the Service Provider Edge module and the Campus Enterprise module, as follows:

- **Service Provider Core Layer:** The Cisco NSF with SSO feature may provide some benefits, but usually it is not required.
- **Service Provider Distribution Layer:** This is a good position for NSF-aware routers.
- **Service Provider Access Layer:** This is the primary deployment position for Cisco NSF with SSO-capable routers.
- **Campus Enterprise Access Layer:** This is the secondary deployment position for Cisco NSF with SSO-capable routers.
- **Campus Enterprise Distribution Layer:** This is a good position for NSF-aware routers.
- **Campus Enterprise Core Layer:** SSO may provide some benefits.

Cisco IOS Software Modularity

To add extra functionality to Cisco 6500 IOS non-modular software (e.g., to patch a router), the new image must be loaded on the active and backup supervisors and a reload must occur before the new software patch can take effect. With Cisco IOS software modularity, this is no longer necessary. The most important advantages Cisco IOS software provides are as follows:

- It minimizes unplanned downtime.
- It makes software modifications much easier to accomplish.

- It can be integrated with the change control policy.
- It allows for process-level policy control.

To fully understand the Cisco IOS software modularity features, it is necessary to understand the different services that can be implemented and its different distributed subsystems, as follows:

- **The control plane:** Routing and multicast protocols.
- **The data plane:** ACLs, CEF FIB (Forwarding Information Base), or QoS.
- **The management plane:** CLI, SNMP, NetFlow, or SSH (Secure Shell).

A Cisco Catalyst 6500 switch that has IOS software modularity features allows several IOS control subsystems to operate in independent processes. To achieve process-level automated policy control, the Cisco Embedded Event Manager (EEM) can be integrated. This allows the offload of time-consuming processes to the network and the acceleration of resolutions for troubleshooting problems. EEM is a combination of processes and its goal is to allow critical system parameters monitoring, such as CPU utilization, SNMP alarms, Syslog events, and interface counters. The key benefits of the IOS software modularity feature include the following:

- **Operational consistency:** New CLI commands are added.
- **Memory protection:** Cisco IOS software modularity offers a memory architecture where subprocesses use protected address space only. (Every process and its associated subsystem has its own individual memory space, so memory corruption across the boundaries of the processes are avoided.)
- **Fault containment:** This increases availability, as issues that occur within one process do not affect other parts of the system.
- **Process restartability:** The modular processes can be restarted individually (using the "process restart" command).
- **Process modularization:** Each process is modularized.
- **Subsystem ISSUs (In-Service Software Upgrades):** Selective system maintenance during runtime is available through individual patches (i.e., versioning and patch management functionality, where patches can be installed and activated without restarting the system).

Spanning Tree Protocol Best Practices

The Spanning Tree Protocol (STP), defined by IEEE 802.1d, is a loop-prevention protocol that allows switches to communicate with each other to discover physical loops in a network. If a loop is found, STP specifies an algorithm that switches can use to create a loop-free logical topology. This algorithm creates a tree structure of loop-free leaves and branches that spans across the Layer 2 topology.

Implementing STP is another key issue when considering Layer 2 Campus infrastructure best practices. Although many designers disable STP at the network edge, Cisco does not recommend this because the loss of connectivity without STP is a much bigger issue than any information that might be revealed through STP to the outside world. The most important issues a network designer should take into consideration when working with STP are when to implement STP and which version of STP should be used.

There are several recommendations for STP implementation. First, if a VLAN spans multiple Access Layer switches to support business applications, STP might be necessary prevent loops. Second, STP could be implemented to support data center applications on server farms or to protect against user-side loops, which can occur in multiple ways:

- Workstation misconfiguration
- Malicious users
- Wiring misconfiguration

When considering the appropriate STP version, Cisco recommends Rapid Per VLAN Spanning Tree+ (RPVST+). In addition, network designers should take advantage of the Cisco STP toolkit, which includes the following features:

- **PortFast:** This is used to configure a LAN interface as an access port to enter the forwarding state immediately, bypassing the listening and learning states. PortFast should be used when connecting a single end-station to a Layer 2 access port or when dealing with trunks to servers in a data center.
- **UplinkFast:** This feature offers a 3- to 5-second convergence after a direct link failure and allows load balancing between redundant Layer 2 links using "uplink groups."
- **BackboneFast:** This will reduce convergence time and will be activated when a Root port or a blocked port on a network device receives inferior Bridge Protocol Data Units (BPDUs) from its designated switch.
- **Loop Guard:** This feature moves a non-designated port into the STP loop-inconsistent blocking state if it receives a BPDU. This prevents the port from assuming the designated role and forwarding packets, thus creating a loop.
- **Root Guard:** This is used to enforce the Root Bridge placement in the network by ensuring the port on which Root Guard is enabled is the designated port. If a switch receives a superior BPDU on a Root-Guard protected port, that specific port is placed into a root-inconsistent state.

- **BPDU Guard:** When BPDU Guard is enabled on a non-trunking port, it places it into an errdisabled state if it receives a BPDU. When enabling BPDU Guard globally, it shuts down ports in the operational PortFast state that receive BPDUs.
- **BPDU Filter:** BPDU filtering is used to avoid transmitting BPDUs on a PortFast-enabled port that connects to end systems.
- **UDLD:** UniDirectional Link Detection (UDLD) permits devices to monitor the physical cable and act when a unidirectional link exists by shutting down the affected LAN port. It is often configured on ports that are linking switches together. UDLD is most often implemented on optical fiber links, but it also supports copper Ethernet technology. Cisco recommends enabling UDLD in the "aggressive" mode, instead of the "normal" mode, in all environments that have optical fiber links because it actively tries to re-establish the state of the port once the connection is down.

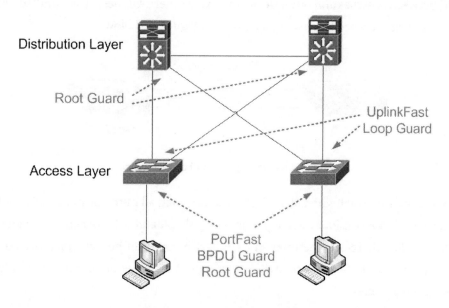

Figure 2.5 – Cisco STP Features

NOTE: All of the STP features in Figure 2.5 above are covered in detail in the CCNP Switch exam study materials.

Trunking Best Practices

Some of the most important recommendations when using trunking include the following:

- Use 802.1Q instead of Inter-Switch Link (ISL) for encapsulation, because in this case, the VLAN tag is internal to the Ethernet frame and the frame size is not affected.
- Set the native VLAN to an unused VLAN.

- Place all of the unused ports in a non-functional VLAN to increase network security.
- Use VLAN Trunk Protocol (VTP) "transparent" mode.
- Set Dynamic Trunking Protocol (DTP) to "desirable" mode with encapsulation "negotiate" when configuring switch-to-switch links that will carry multiple VLANs.
- Manually prune unused VLANs from the trunk interface to avoid the propagation of broadcasts.
- Hard code all of the access ports (disable trunks on host ports) as a security countermeasure to VLAN hopping.

EtherChannel Recommendations

A very common technology used to achieve media redundancy and increase bandwidth is EtherChannel. This is a Layer 2 or Layer 3 logical bundling or channel aggregation technique that can be used between switches and other devices (usually other switches). The bundled links appear as one logical link on the specific devices, as shown in Figure 2.6 below:

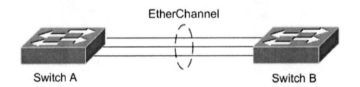

Figure 2.6 – Example of an EtherChannel

EtherChannels are important when using STP because when all of the physical links look like one logical link, STP will not consider them a possible loop threat and will not shut down any link from that specific bundle. Therefore, the links in an EtherChannel can be dynamically load balanced, without interference from STP. Cisco switches support two implementation options (protocols) when using EtherChannels:

- Port Aggregation Protocol (PagP) – a Cisco proprietary protocol
- Link Aggregation Control Protocol (LACP) – an open standard protocol

EtherChannel is a very popular technology and is typically deployed between the Distribution Layer and the Core Layer or between Core Layer devices where increased availability and scalability is needed. However, port aggregation is usually disabled on interfaces that are facing end-users. The recommended configuration when using PagP for Layer 2 EtherChannels is to set the port modes to "desirable" on all of the members of the bundle to ensure that individual link failures will not lead to an STP failure. The recommended practice for LACP is to configure both sides of the link in the "active" mode.

LAYER 3 CAMPUS INFRASTRUCTURE BEST PRACTICES

Continuing with the Enterprise Campus design, the process of Layer 3 design optimization, including managing oversubscriptions, CEF polarization, routing protocol design, First Hop Redundancy Protocols (FHRPs), and Layer 2 to Layer 3 boundary design, will be analyzed.

Managing Oversubscription

In any network environment, situations will seldom be found in which all of the users access the same servers at the same time. The concept of data oversubscription is usually applied at the Access and Distribution layers and implies understanding that not everyone will be accessing the bandwidth at the same time.

Data oversubscription recommendations often imply a 20:1 ratio for the access ports on the Access Layer to Distribution Layer uplinks. Some congestion might exist but this will not happen very often and usually can be solved by applying QoS techniques. If the network experiences frequent congestion, then the design does not have enough uplink bandwidth. When experiencing congestion, the goal is to increase the bandwidth, not to lower the oversubscription ratio.

The recommendation for the Distribution Layer to Core Layer link is a 4:1 ratio. If the bandwidth capacity on the Access Layer links is increased, for example to 1 Gbps (or multiples of 1 Gbps through aggregation techniques), then techniques for the Distribution Layer to Core Layer links will have to be investigated (e.g., additional EtherChannel links or 10 Gbps links).

When the bandwidth for the Distribution Layer to Core Layer link starts to grow, oversubscription at the Access Layer must be controlled and key design decisions must be made. To accommodate for greater needs at the Access Layer for the end-stations, the solution would seem to be to increase the number of uplinks between the Distribution Layer and the Core Layer, but the problem with this is that it adds extra peer relationships, which will lead to extra management overhead.

Another solution involves using EtherChannels, which reduces the number of peers because a single logical interface is created. This solution has some caveats. For example, when dealing with OSPF on an IOS-based device, the link failure event will increase the link cost and this will force traffic to be rerouted, which might lead to convergence issues. To mitigate this issue, consider manually configuring OSPF interface costs. If OSPF is running on a hybrid-based switch, the link cost will not increase because of the use of EtherChannels, and this can result in an overload on the other links in the bundle, as OSPF keeps partitioning the traffic equally along the channels with different bandwidths. When using EIGRP, the link costs will not be modified at link failures because this routing protocol considers end-to-end costs.

An important configuration aspect when using EtherChannels with LACP involves the "min-links" feature, which defines the minimum number of member ports that must be in the "link up" state and bundled in the EtherChannel for that interface to transition to the "up" state. The goal of using this feature is to prevent low-bandwidth LACP EtherChannels from becoming active.

Another technique to support the greater needs for bandwidth is to use 10 Gbps links. This is recommended instead of using EtherChannels because it has the advantage of not adding to routing complexity and not increasing the number of routing peers. In addition, routing protocols can deterministically find the best path between the Distribution Layer and the Core Layer.

Cisco Express Forwarding Polarization

CEF polarization, illustrated below in Figure 2.7, is part of the link load balancing methodology:

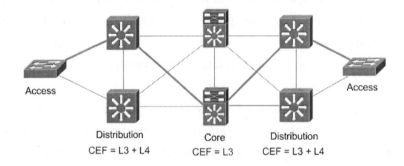

Figure 2.7 – CEF Polarization

CEF operates on all of the multilayer switches in the figure above and it has a deterministic behavior. As packets initiate from the left Access Layer switch and traverse the network toward the right Access Layer switch, they all use the same input value for the CEF hash and this implies using the same path. This has the negative effect of not utilizing some of the redundant links in the topology, which is known as CEF polarization.

This can be avoided by tuning the CEF algorithm across the infrastructure layers. The default input hash value in Layer 3 is based on the source and destination values. If this input is changed to Layer 3 plus Layer 4, adding port number values to the calculation, the output hash value will also change.

Cisco recommends using alternating hashes in the Core and Distribution Layers to avoid ignoring or underutilizing redundant links. In the Core Layer, the default hashes based on Layer 3 information (i.e., source and destination addresses) should be used, but in the Distribution Layer, Layer 3 plus Layer 4 information should be used as input for the CEF hashing algorithm. This can be accomplished by using the "mls ip cef load-sharing full" command in global configuration mode on all Distribution Layer switches. This will force the CEF algorithm to use Layer 3 plus Layer 4 information to calculate the hash values. Doing this will eliminate the static path effect in the CEF decision-making process and will help to better balance the traffic across equal cost redundant links in the network.

To achieve the best EtherChannel load balancing scenario, use two, four, or eight ports in the port-channel bundle. In addition, tune the hashing algorithm that is implemented to select the certain EtherChannel link that will transmit a packet. By default, Layer 3 source and destination information will be used, but an additional level of load balancing can be provided by implementing Layer 4 TCP port information as the input for the algorithm. This can be accomplished with the "port-channel load-balance src-dst-port" command in global configuration mode. This command forces the EtherChannel algorithm to add Layer 4 port information as the input and this is the recommended practice.

Routing Protocols

Routing protocols are usually used in the Distribution Layer to Core Layer and the Core Layer to Core Layer connections. An alternative would be moving Layer 3 routing implementation to the Access Layer. This solution is becoming more popular because it avoids the complexity of implementing STP and lowers re-convergence times in large-scale deployments.

Three methods can be used to quickly re-route around failed links and failed multilayer switches to provide load balancing with redundant paths:

- Build redundant triangle topologies for deterministic convergence (avoid using squares).
- Control unnecessary peering across the Access Layer by peering only on transit links.
- Summarize at the Distribution Layer to Core Layer for optimal results (limit the EIGRP query diameter and propagation of OSPF Link-State Advertisements).

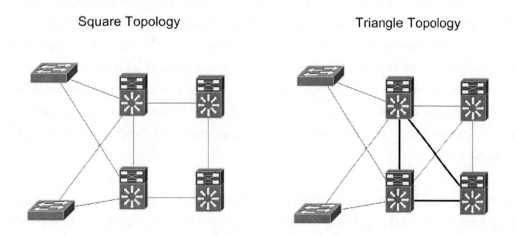

Figure 2.8 – Square versus Triangle Topologies

Analyzing Figure 2.8 above, it is usually the Access Layer devices that have redundant links to the upstream multilayer switches. Avoid using square topologies because this will lead to a higher degree of routing protocol convergence if there is a link failure. In other words, OSPF or EIGRP will have to take more time to calculate new paths using their specific route calculation algorithms. When using the triangle design, each node is directly connected to every other mode, so the convergence time is lower.

It is important to build the network Distribution Layer and Core Layer design based on triangles so that there are equal cost paths to all of the redundant nodes. This will avoid non-deterministic convergence, depending on the timers that come with the Layer 3 routing protocols. Another important routing protocol design consideration is to limit unnecessary peering across the Access Layer.

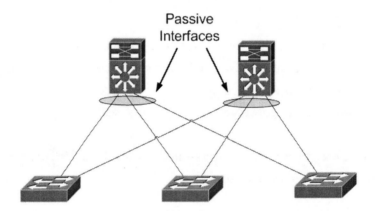

Figure 2.9 – Limiting Unnecessary Peering

Having Layer 3 peering across the different Access Layer switches (i.e., having multiple hosts on different switches across switch blocks) adds memory load, routing protocol update overhead, and more complexity. In addition, if there is a link failure, the traffic may transit through a neighboring Access Layer switch to get to another VLAN member. The goal is to eliminate unnecessary routing peering adjacencies (see Figure 2.9 above) and to configure the ports toward the Layer 2 switches as passive interfaces to suppress routing update advertisements. If a Distribution Layer switch does not receive a routing update from a potential peer on one of these interfaces, it will not process the updates and will not form a neighbor adjacency across that interface. The command for accomplishing this is usually "passive-interface [interface number]" in the routing process configuration mode.

The third method is to summarize at the Distribution Layer (i.e., toward the Core Layer but not sending queries beyond that point). By summarizing to the Core Layer, the EIGRP and OSPF re-convergence processes are simplified so the re-routing process is optimized. For example, when an Access Layer link goes down, the return traffic at the Distribution Layer to that device will be dropped until there is a convergence of OSPF or EIGRP and traffic is routed across another link.

When summarization is used at the Distribution Layer, summarizing toward the Core Layer, the individual distribution nodes will not advertise this failure of the Access Layer switch or loss of connectivity to a single VLAN or subnet. The Core Layer does not know that it cannot send traffic to the Distribution Layer switch where the Access Layer link failed, so the summarization toward the Core Layer limits the number of peers the EIGRP router must query or the number of OSPF Link-State Advertisements (LSAs) that must be processed, and this speeds up the re-routing process. This process can be accomplished by using the "ip summary-address eigrp" command for EIGRP or using an area border boundary for OSPF. To implement an efficient summarization scheme, an excellent hierarchical network addressing design and a contiguous address space is necessary.

First Hop Redundancy Protocols

Another critical aspect of convergence and high availability in the network design is the ability to have redundancy on behalf of the end-user in the Access Layer to the first hop (or the default gateway). With Layer 2 switches at the Access Layer and with Layer 3 switches at the Distribution Layer, the default gateway is usually the interface on the Distribution Layer switch that connects to the Access Layer.

> **NOTE:** Only FHRPs are needed if operating at Layer 2 in the Access Layer and Layer 3 in the Distribution Layer. If Layer 3 is extended to Access Layer switches, then these switches will be the default gateways for the end-stations.

To recover from a failure of the devices that are performing as the default gateway for the end-stations, there are three FHRPs to choose from:

- **Hot Standby Router Protocol (HSRP):** This is a Cisco proprietary protocol, the most common and preferred option when using Cisco equipment.
- **Virtual Router Redundancy Protocol (VRRP):** This is an IETF standard.
- **Gateway Load Balancing Protocol (GLBP):** This is the most recent protocol (again, a Cisco invention) and the most sophisticated FHRP.

HSRP and Cisco-enhanced VRRP are the most common and robust options. VRRP is usually used in a multi-vendor environment, when interoperability with other vendor devices is needed. HSRP and GLBP can help achieve a convergence of less than 800 ms, and the parameters can be tuned to achieve fast convergence if there is a node or link failure at the Layer 2 to Layer 3 boundary.

Hot Standby Router Protocol

Analyzing Figure 2.10 below, there are two gateway routers that connect to one Layer 2 switch that aggregates the network hosts:

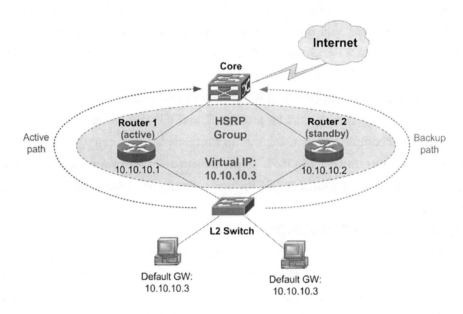

Figure 2.10 – Hot Standby Router Protocol

Router 1 is a potential default gateway (10.10.10.1) and Router 2 is another potential default gateway (10.10.10.2). The two routers will be configured in an HSRP group and they will serve clients with a virtual default gateway address of 10.10.10.3, although it is not assigned to any router interface and is only a virtual address.

In this example, Router 1 is the active gateway, as it is the one that is forwarding traffic for the 10.10.10.3 virtual address, while Router 2 is the standby gateway. The two routers exchange HSRP messages to each other to check on each other's status. For instance, if Router 2 no longer hears from Router 1, it realizes that Router 1 is down and it will take over as the active HSRP device (if preemption is enabled on Router 2). These devices are transparently providing access for the clients, as they are transparently serving the clients as default gateways.

Virtual Router Redundancy Protocol

The way VRRP works is similar to that of HSRP. The difference is that two routers are configured in a VRRP group. In this case, Router 1 is the master (instead of the active) and it forwards all of the traffic, while Router 2 is the slave (backup) (instead of the standby) since it can have more than one device. An example of a VRRP configuration is illustrated in Figure 2.11 below:

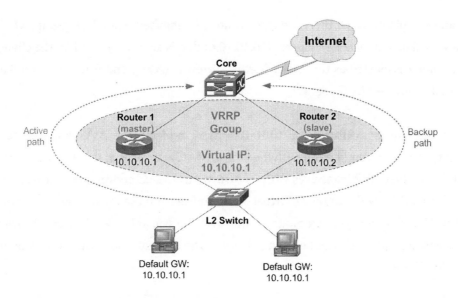

Figure 2.11 – Virtual Router Redundancy Protocol

As is the case for HSRP, the VRRP group presents a virtual IP address to its clients. An interesting aspect about VRRP is that it can utilize, as the virtual IP address, the same address that is on the master device. For example, in the figure above, the virtual address is configured as 10.10.10.1, identical to the address on the Router 1 interface.

Gateway Load Balancing Protocol

GLBP is the most unique of the FHRPs, as it not only has the ability to achieve redundancy but also has the ability to accomplish load sharing. In addition, it is much easier to use more than two devices. Figure 2.12 below illustrates a GLBP configuration:

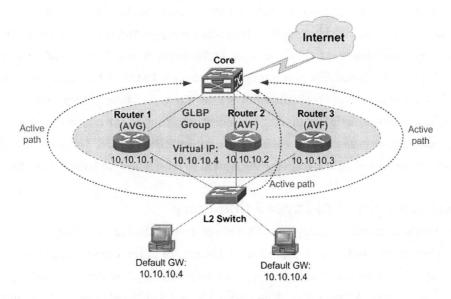

Figure 2.12 – Gateway Load Balancing Protocol

Consider an example in which there are three routers configured in a GLBP group, which will be assigned a virtual default gateway address (10.10.10.4) that is also configured on the clients. In this example, Router 1 is elected as the Active Virtual Gateway (AVG) and Routers 2 and 3 are in the Active Virtual Forwarder (AVF) state.

When the hosts request ARPs for the 10.10.10.4 MAC address, the AVG responds to the ARP requests and performs a round robin with the virtual MAC addresses of the AVF machines. Router 1 responds to the first ARP it receives with its own virtual MAC address, then it responds to the second ARP it receives with Router 2's virtual MAC address and then with Router 3's virtual MAC address. The AVG can then round robin the traffic over the available AVF devices. The round robin simplistic balancing approach can be changed within the configuration with other load balancing techniques for GLBP.

NOTE: The AVG can also function as an AVF and it usually does so.

FHRPs and Preemption

An important aspect when dealing with FHRPs is their preemptive behavior. This allows an HSRP router to assume the primary role when its FHRP priority is higher than the current active router. If preemption is not used and the primary router fails, the standby router will assume the active role and it will maintain this role even if the other router comes back up. Preemption should be enabled because the HSRP active device is often also the STP Root, and a best practice is to set these functions on the same device.

Because of the HSRP preemptive behavior, it is important to know how long it will take for the device to reboot and get connected to the rest of the network. Knowing this time will allow proper timers configuration. If the HSRP neighbor relationships form and preemption occurs before the primary device has Layer 3 connectivity to the Core Layer, traffic to the Access Layer could be dropped until full connectivity is established. The recommended practice is to take into account the system boot time and all of the other factors that will influence the amount of time a device will not be able to forward traffic and to set the HSRP preemption delay accordingly. The command to achieve this is "standby preempt delay minimum" in the interface configuration mode. This value should be 50% greater than the amount of time it takes for the system to reboot and for convergence to happen.

Designing the Layer 2 to Layer 3 Boundary

Depending on the network topology and the devices used, different design models for the Layer 2 to Layer 3 boundary can be used. If the Access Layer uses Layer 2 devices and the Distribution Layer uses Layer 3 devices, the links between the Distribution Layer switches can be Layer 2 trunks to support Layer 2 at the Access Layer. When using Layer 2 trunks between the Distribution Layer switches, a best practice would be to use the Rapid Spanning Tree Protocol (RSTP) as the STP version and place the HSRP active device and the primary STP Root Bridge on the same Distribution Layer switch. This design is more complex than the one that uses Layer 3 interconnections between Distribution Layer devices because STP convergence must be taken into consideration.

Layer 3 interconnection design at the Distribution Layer is the recommended design and some of its advantages include the following:

- STP convergence is not an issue if there is an uplink failure.
- Layer 3 VLAN numbers can be mapped to Layer 3 subnets, reducing the management overhead.

Layer 3 interconnection design is often used with GLBP at the Distribution Layer to allow full utilization of the Access Layer uplinks. Even though GLBP has the advantage of offering full link utilization, the downside is it is less deterministic compared to HSRP.

The next design involves using Layer 3 at the Access and Distribution Layers in a routed network design model. This allows for faster convergence and easier implementation because only Layer 3 links are used. A routing protocol is used across the topology, such as EIGRP or OSPF. The most important advantages of a full Layer 3 environment are as follows:

- Simplified implementation
- Faster convergence
- Equal cost load balancing on all of the links
- Eliminates the need for STP
- FHRP configurations are not necessary
- The convergence time to reroute around a failed link is around 200 ms, unlike the 700 to 900 ms in previous scenarios (Layer 2 to Layer 3 boundaries)

However, the one downside to this design is that it does not support VLANs spanning the Distribution Layer switches; however, overall, it is a best practice to keep the VLANs in isolated blocks at the Access Layer. Since both EIGRP and OSPF load share across equal cost paths, this scenario offers a convergence benefit similar to using GLBP. Some of the key actions to perform when using a full Layer 3 topology with EIGRP to the edge include the following:

- Use EIGRP to the edge (to the Access Layer submodule, the WAN submodule, the Internet submodule, and to other submodules).

- Summarize at the Distribution Layer to the Core Layer, like in a traditional Layer 2 to Layer 3 design.
- Configure all the edge switches as EIGRP stub nodes to avoid queries sent in that direction.
- Control route propagation to the edge switches using distribution lists.
- Set the appropriate hello and dead timers to protect against failures where the physical links are active but the route processing has terminated.

Some of the key actions to perform when using OSPF to the edge include the following:

- Configure each Distribution Layer block as a separate totally stubby OSPF area. The distribution switches will become Area Border Routers (ABRs) and their core-facing interfaces will belong to Area 0 (the OSPF backbone).
- Avoid extending Area 0 to the edge switches because the Access Layer should not be a transit area in the Enterprise Campus environment. Each Access Layer switch should be configured to be a unique totally stubby area.
- The OSPF timers (including hello and dead intervals) should be tuned to improve convergence.

Other general recommendations include the following:

- Avoid daisy-chaining the Layer 2 switches together to prevent black holes if there is a link or node failure.
- Consider using Cisco StackWise technology to eliminate the danger of black holes in the Access Layer.
- A balance of redundancy should be determined, as too much redundancy (too many links from the Access Layer to the Distribution Layer) will cause design issues and will increase troubleshooting efforts. On the other hand, too little redundancy might lead to traffic being black holed and might severely affect convergence effects.
- Avoid VLANs spanning across Access Layer switches to prevent asymmetric routing.

VIRTUALIZATION DESIGN CONSIDERATIONS

The official definition of computer virtualization is the pooling and abstraction of resources and services in a way that masks the physical nature and boundaries of those resources and services. A VLAN is a great example of this definition because it masks the physical nature of resources. The concept of virtualization dates back to the 1970s, with IBM mainframes. These mainframes were separated into virtual machines so that different tasks could run separately and to prevent a process failure that could affect the entire system.

One of the issues IT departments face today is called "server sprawl." This concept implies that each application is installed on its own server, and every time another server is added, issues such as power, space, and cooling must be addressed. With server sprawl, the infrastructure is not efficiently utilized so the concept of virtualization can enhance the utilization rate. This approach is similar to the bandwidth oversubscription method used instead of applying QoS techniques and properly optimizing the network traffic. This is not very efficient because the purchased links are not being properly utilized and this leads to increased costs.

Another issue with the scenario in which a server hosts a single application is that high availability implies high costs because all of the servers must be purchased in a redundant configuration. In addition, provisioning new applications is difficult and security is usually accomplished through physical isolation. All of these issues are not very cost effective. However, these IT challenges can be mitigated with server virtualization that allows the partitioning of a physical server to work with multiple operating systems and application instances. The most important advantages are as follows:

- Improved failover capabilities
- Better utilization of resources
- Smaller footprint

Virtualization is a concept that applies to many areas in modern IT infrastructures, including:

- Servers
- Networks
- Storage (Virtual SANs, Unified I/O)
- Applications
- Desktop (Virtual Desktop Infrastructure)

Network virtualization refers to one physical network supporting a wide array of logical topologies. This allows actions such as outsourcing by the IT department, where a logical topology can be created that can be accessed by an external IT professional. Another example is creating a dedicated logical topology for quality assurance or various tests. In the network security world, virtualization is present in firewall devices, under the form of virtual contexts. Network virtualization with Cisco products is typically classified into four different areas:

- **Control plane virtualization:** Implies making sure processes like routing are separate and distinct so any routing process failure will not affect the entire device.
- **Data plane virtualization:** This is done every time different streams of data traffic are multiplexed (i.e., different forms of traffic are placed into the same medium). The simplest example

of data plane virtualization is a trunk link between two devices. This allows multiplexing the traffic of different VLANs on a single data link.

- **Management plane virtualization:** This implies the ability to make a software upgrade on a device without rebooting the device and without losing its capabilities to communicate on the network.
- **Pooling and clustering:** This is used in the Cisco Catalyst 6500 Virtual Switching System (VSS) and it works by creating pools of devices that act a single device. Another technology example is the Nexus vPC (Virtual Port Channel), which allows EtherChannels to be created that span across multiple devices.

A great example of data and control plane virtualization is the concept of Virtual Routing and Forwarding (VRF) instances. VRF allows an interface to have multiple routing tables associated with it and this is very useful, for example, in ISP Multiprotocol Label Switching (MPLS) environments where they must serve and isolate multiple customers. Virtualization has become a critical component in most Enterprise networks because of the modern demands in IT, including increasing efficiency while reducing capital and operational costs. Virtualization is a critical component of the Cisco Network Architecture for the Enterprise.

Virtualization can represent a variety of technologies but the general idea is to abstract the logical components from hardware or networks and implement them into a virtual environment. Some of advantages of virtualization include the following:

- Flexibility in managing system resources
- Better use of computing resources
- Consolidating low-performance devices into high-performance devices
- Providing flexible security policies

Some of the drivers behind implementing a virtualized environment include the following:

- The need to reduce the number of physical devices that perform individual tasks
- The need to reduce operational costs
- The need to increase productivity
- The need for flexible connectivity
- The need to eliminate underutilized hardware

Virtualization can be implemented at both the network and the device level. Network virtualization implies the creation of network partitions that run on the physical infrastructure, with each logical partition acting as an independent network. Network virtualization can include VLANs, VSANs,

VPNs, or VRF. On the other hand, device virtualization allows logical devices to run independently of each other on a single physical machine. Virtual hardware devices are created in software and have the same functionality as real hardware devices. The possibility of combining multiple physical devices into a single logical unit also exists.

The Cisco Network Architecture for the Enterprise contains multiple forms of network and device virtualization:

- Virtual machines
- Virtual switches
- Virtual Local Area Networks
- Virtual Private Networks
- Virtual Storage Area Networks
- Virtual switching systems
- Virtual Routing and Forwarding
- Virtual port channels
- Virtual device contexts

Device contexts allow partitioning a single partition into multiple virtual devices called contexts. A context acts as an independent device with its own set of policies. The majority of features implemented on the real device are also functional on the virtual context. Some of the devices in the Cisco portfolio that support virtual contexts include the following:

- Cisco Adaptive Security Appliance (ASA)
- Cisco Application Control Engine (ACE)
- Cisco Intrusion Prevention System (IPS)
- Cisco Nexus series

Server virtualization allows servers' resources to be abstracted to offer flexibility and usage optimization on the infrastructure. The result is that data center applications are no longer tied to specific hardware resources, making the application unaware of the underlying hardware. Server virtualization solutions are produced by companies such as VMware (ESX), Microsoft (Hyper-V), and Citrix (XenServer).

The network virtualization design process must take into consideration the preservation of high-availability, scalability, and security in the data center submodule. Access control issues must be considered to ensure legitimate user access and protection from external threats. Proper path isolation ensures that users and devices are mapped to the correct secure set of resources and implies the creation of independent logical traffic paths over a shared physical infrastructure.

DESIGNING A WIRELESS NETWORK

Wireless technologies are rapidly advancing in Enterprise Networks and Cisco is a major player in this area due to their own internal developments and series of strategic acquisitions. Network designers should understand basic wireless LAN concepts to be prepared for possible network upgrades, even if the network is not initially designed to integrate wireless technologies. Wireless networks can include a wide variety of technologies:

- Mobile wireless that allows data to be sent via mobile phones:
  - GSM – low data rates, 9600 bps
  - GPRS – up to 128 kbps
  - 3G/UMTS – several Mbps
- Wireless Local Area Network (WLAN) technologies
- Wireless Bridges (point-to-point)

Bridging wireless networks involves a simple design of setting up two antennas on two different building that are pointing at each other to bridge the two LANs together. This technology can usually scale up to 50 Mbps.

WLAN technologies replace endpoint access physical wiring and the Layer 2 transport technologies with wireless mechanisms. One advantage to this replacement is that upper layer protocols are usually not directly affected. The wireless issues most often encountered include signal interference and obstruction, which is uncommon in wired environments.

Wireless networks also have many similarities to legacy Ethernet solutions, like Layer 2 addressing that uses MAC addresses and WLANs that are shared media. The reason for these similarities is that WLAN access points (APs) act like hub devices that use the same Radio Frequencies (RFs) to transmit and receive packets, which causes communication to be half-duplex and allows collisions to occur.

NOTE: WLAN technologies are based on a set of standards called IEEE 802.11 and they define computer communication in the 2.4, 3.6, and 5 GHz frequency bands.

802.11 Protocol Family

The original 802.11 standard was defined in 1997 by the IEEE, and it uses two different types of RF technologies operating in the 2.4 GHz range:

- Frequency Hopping Spread Spectrum (FHSS), which operates only at 1 or 2 Mbps
- Direct Sequence Spread Spectrum (DSSS), also operating at 1 or 2 Mbps

Modern enterprise environments usually use the 802.11a, 802.11b, 802.11g, and 802.11n standards. The 802.11b standard was defined in 1999 and its major features include the following:

- It can use DSSS in the 2.4 GHz range.
- It uses Barker 11 and Complementary Code Keying (CCK) encoding.
- It uses the Differential Binary Phase-Shift Keying (DBPSK) and Differential Quadrature Phase-Shift Keying (DQPSK) modulation types.
- It supports data rates of 1, 2, 5.5, and 11 Mbps (the 5.5 and 11 Mbps rates use CCK and DQPSK).
- It offers three non-overlapping channels: 1, 6, and 11.

The 802.11g standard was defined in 2001, is backward compatible, and can be used in the same 802.11b environment. The downside in this scenario is that interoperability demands the use of the lower level 802.11b. The main features offered by 802.11g include the following:

- It uses DSSS RF technology and operates in the 2.4 GHz spectrum for low rates (1, 2, 5.5, and 11 Mbps).
- It uses Orthogonal Frequency Division Multiplexing (OFDM) modulation technology for high data rates (6, 9, 12, 18, 24, 36, 48, and 54 Mbps).
- It offers three non-overlapping channels: 1, 6, and 11.

The 802.11a was defined in 1999 and it is not as widely deployed as 802.11b and 802.11g. It has the following characteristics:

- It operates in the 5 GHz range; therefore, it is incompatible with 802.11, 802.11b, and 802.11g. This allows it to avoid interference with devices that use those protocols, as well as microwaves, Bluetooth devices, and cordless phones.
- It supports 12 to 23 non-overlapping channels (as opposed to the 3 non-overlapping channels supported by 802.11b and 802.11g) because it uses OFDM, where subchannels can overlap.
- It uses several modulation types: BPSK, QPSK, 16-QAM, or 64-QAM.
- It supports a wide range of data rates: 6, 9, 12, 18, 24, 36, 48, and 54 Mbps.

802.11n is an amendment that improves upon the previous 802.11 standards by adding multiple-input-multiple-output (MIMO) antennas, with a significant increase in the maximum data rate, from 54 Mbps to 600 Mbps. 802.11n operates on both the 2.4 GHz and the lesser-used 5 GHz bands. The IEEE has approved the amendment and it was published in October 2009. MIMO comes in three types: pre-coding, spatial multiplexing, and diversity coding.

> NOTE: The data rate offered is influenced by the number of hosts served by the specific AP and by the distance between the host and the AP (high distances reduce the signal and the data rate).

Collision Avoidance

WLAN technologies do not allow collisions to be detected like they are in Ethernet environments. Stations cannot hear jam signals because they cannot listen and send at the same time (i.e., they have half-duplex functionality). To suppress the negative effects of half-duplex transmission, WLANs rely on the Carrier Sense Multiple Access with Collision Avoidance (CSMA/CA) mechanism. Stations in the WLAN attempt to avoid collisions before they happen by using a Distributed Coordinated Function (DCF) that utilizes random backoff timers.

DCF requires a station wishing to transmit to listen for the channel's status for a predefined interval. If the channel is busy during that interval, the station defers its transmission. In a network where a number of stations contend for the wireless medium, if multiple stations sense that the channel is busy and defer their access, they will also virtually find, simultaneously, that the channel has been released and they all will try to seize the channel. As a result, collisions may occur. To avoid such collisions, DCF also specifies random backoff timers, which forces a station to defer its access to the channel for an extra period. The AP is responsible for acknowledging client data and responds to successful transmissions by sending ACK packets.

WLAN Service Set Identifiers

Wireless network designers must fully understand the concept of Service Set Identifiers (SSIDs). This concept defines an identifier for the logical WLAN and is similar in some ways to the concept of Ethernet VLANs, which defines who can talk to each other in a LAN based on the broadcast domain. With WLANs, everyone is in the same collision and broadcast domain, so stations can receive everyone's traffic. This situation generated the need for SSID usage that logically splits WLANs. Two devices that are in different SSIDs will ignore each other's traffic, but this does not affect the collision domain.

One major misconception about wireless area networking that exists is that the SSID logical structures are similar to collision domains. This is not true because every device is in the same collision and broadcast domain with other devices in the same signal range. SSIDs cause the different stations to ignore the frames received from different SSIDs.

When considering the SSID concept, the infrastructure can be built using two modes over three different categories, based on who participates in the WLAN:

- Independent Basic Service Set (IBSS)
- Basic Service Set (BSS)
- Extended Service Set (ESS)

The IBSS, which is not used very much in modern networks, uses the ad-hoc mode, whereas wireless uses Wi-Fi capability without the use of any APs. An example of an ad-hoc network would be two workstations establishing a direct wireless connection without the use of an intermediary AP (the equivalent of directly connecting two workstations through an Ethernet path cord). The BSS approach, also called wireless infrastructure mode, is much more common. It involves the use of APs that act as traffic hubs, as described earlier. The ESS approach (also operating in infrastructure mode) involves the use of multiple APs that service the same SSID. This allows individuals to cover a larger distance with their wireless devices in a transparent and seamless manner. Thus, users can move from AP to AP, keeping the same SSIDs.

Wireless Association

Devices go through a wireless negotiation process, called association, with an AP to participate on a Wi-Fi network in infrastructure mode, as illustrated in Figure 2.13 below:

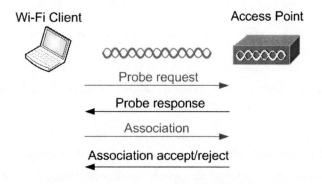

Figure 2.13 – Wireless Association Process

To accomplish this association, the client device sends a Probe request on the network to find the AP. The access probe that receives the Probe request will send a Probe response, and then the client will initiate the association, which will be accepted or rejected by the AP. If the association is successful, the AP will install the MAC address of the client. The wireless association process is very similar to a DCHP handshake.

WLAN Topologies

Once the association is complete, the AP's main job is to bridge traffic, either wired to wireless or wireless to wireless. WLANs, like non-broadcast multi-access (NBMA) technologies, can be implemented and configured under many different topologies. In WLAN environments, APs can perform the following roles:

- Bridges
- Repeaters
- Mesh topologies

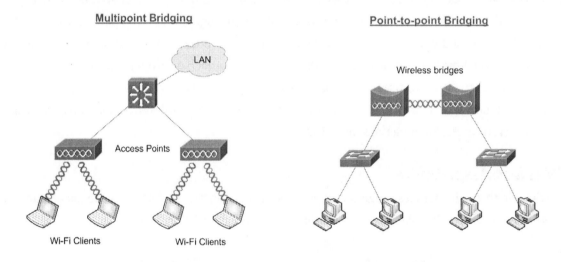

Figure 2.14 – WLAN Bridge Topology

An example of a WLAN bridge topology is shown above in Figure 2.14. Wireless bridges function in several ways:

- They accept traffic from traditional LANs and forward it to wireless clients. This is the process of translation between wired and wireless networks called multipoint bridging.
- They can work in point-to-point mode to connect two buildings (LANs).
- They can work in point-to-multipoint mode to connect multiple buildings.

NOTE: When using wireless bridging functionality in a point-to-point mode, the two buildings/areas must have line-of-sight connectivity.

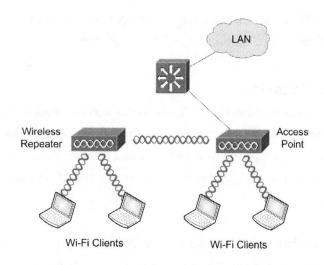

Figure 2.15 – WLAN Repeaters Topology

Access points can function as repeaters (see Figure 2.15 above), accepting a weak RF signal, strengthening (amplifying) it, and resending it. This operation is used to extend the range of wireless networks.

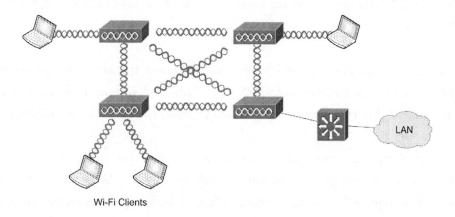

Figure 2.16 – WLAN Mesh Topology

The WLAN mesh topology (see Figure 2.16 above) is the most sophisticated and most used wireless topology. When used in this type of topology, the AP can function as a repeater or as a bridge, as needed, based on the RFs. This technology allows designers to use wireless technologies to cover large geographical areas and ensures features such as:

- Fault tolerance
- Load distribution
- Transparent roaming

NOTE: In addition to their use in the Enterprise sector, wireless mesh technologies are also used in the public sector to ensure Wi-Fi-access in certain urban areas.

Designing WLAN Security

Security is one of the essential aspects of WLAN that a network designer should consider. The original 802.11 standard was not built with great security features in mind. The first WLAN security mechanism was Wireless Equivalent Privacy (WEP) and it emerged with the 802.11b standard. WEP is a faulty security mechanism, as it is vulnerable to several attacks because it is built on the RC4 protocol.

Wi-Fi Protected Access (WPA) became available in 2003 and was intended as an intermediate measure in anticipation of the availability of the more secure and complex WPA2. The recommended WLAN security protocol is WPA2, based on the 802.11i architecture. WPA2 can be integrated with the 802.1x architecture that can work on top of either an 802.3 (wired) or an 802.11 (wireless) environment. This allows individual users and devices to authenticate using the Extensible Authentication Protocol (EAP) and an authentication server (RADIUS or TACACS+). The authentication server can be an open standard solution or the Cisco Access Control Server (ACS). WPA2 and 802.11i also involve the Robust Security Network (RSN) concept that is used to keep track of the associations to the APs.

To ensure confidentiality, integrity, and origin authentication, the network designer should go beyond the Data Encryption Standard (DES) algorithm and instead consider the Advanced Encryption Standard (AES) for strong encryption at the Enterprise level (128 bit, 256 bit, or beyond).

Another security design issue is unauthorized access. In wireless networks there are no physical boundaries, so attackers can gain access from outside of the physical security perimeter, where they can introduce rogue APs or soft APs that can breach security policies on laptops or handheld devices. Because wireless signals are not easily controlled or contained, this could create security issues for the network designer.

MAC address security can be used to allow only certain devices to associate with the APs, but this cannot prevent MAC address spoofing techniques. Another solution would involve MAC address filtering, but this is not very scalable when dealing with a large number of wireless clients. The most efficient solution to this problem is using 802.1x port-based authentication, which is an authentication standard for both wired and wireless LANs.

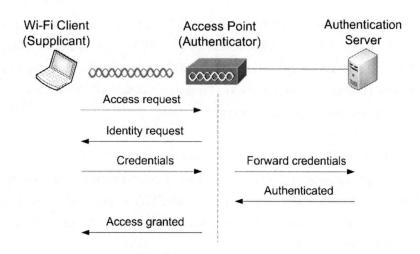

Figure 2.17 – 802.1x Functionality

As illustrated in Figure 2.17 above, 802.1x works by authenticating the user before receiving access to the network and this involves three components:

- Supplicant (client)
- Authenticator (access point or switch)
- Authentication server (Cisco ACS)

The client workstation can run client software known as a supplicant, which can be a Windows client or a Cisco client. The client software requests access to different services and it uses EAP to communicate with the AP (or LAN switch), which is the authenticator. The authenticator will then verify the client information against an authentication server (Cisco ACS). EAP encompasses five major types:

- EAP-Transport Layer Security (EAP-TLS)
- Protected Extensible Authentication Protocol (PEAP)
- EAP-Tunneled Transport Layer Security (EAP-TTLS)
- Lightweight EAP (LEAP)
- EAP-Flexible Authentication via Secure Tunneling (EAP-FAST)

EAP-TLS is a commonly used EAP method in wireless solutions that requires a certificate to be installed on both the supplicant and the authentication server. The key pairs must first be generated and then signed by a local or remote Certificate Authority (CA) server. The key communication process used by EAP-TLS is similar to Secure Socket Layer (SSL) encryption, in that the user certificate is sent through an encrypted tunnel. EAP-TLS is one of the most secure authentication methods, but it is also very expensive and difficult to implement.

PEAP requires only a server-side certificate that will be used to create the encrypted tunnel. The authentication process takes place inside that tunnel. PEAP was jointly developed by Cisco, Microsoft, and RSA, so it is heavily used in Microsoft Windows environments. PEAP uses the Microsoft Challenge Handshake Authentication Protocol (MS-CHAPv2) or Generic Token Card (GTC) to authenticate the user inside the encrypted tunnel.

EAP-TTLS is much like PEAP, as it uses a TLS tunnel to protect the less secure authentication mechanisms. This might include protocols like Password Authentication Protocol (PAP), CHAP, MS-CHAPv2, or EAP Message Digest 5 (MD5). EAP-TTLS is not widely used in Enterprise Networks; however, it can be found in legacy environments that contain older authentication systems (e.g., Windows NT).

LEAP was created by Cisco as a proprietary solution for their equipment and systems. It is still supported by a variety of operating systems, such as Windows and Linux, but it is no longer considered secure because a series of vulnerabilities that affect it were identified.

EAP-FAST is also a Cisco-developed EAP type that aimed to address the weaknesses in LEAP. When using EAP-FAST, server certificates are optional but it offers a lower cost implementation than a full-blown PEAP or EAP-TTLS. EAP-FAST uses a Protected Access Credential (PAC) technique to establish the TLS tunnel for the protection of the credential tunnel. PAC is a strong shared secret key that is unique for every client.

> **NOTE:** The most commonly used EAP solutions are PEAP and EAP-FAST for small business networks and EAP-TLS for large Enterprise Network solutions.

Another important security aspect in WLANs involves controlling WLAN access to servers. Just as DNS servers that are accessible from the Internet are placed into a DMZ segment, the same strategy should be applied to the RADIUS/TACACS+ and DHCP servers used in the WLAN solution. These servers should be placed into their own VLAN that has a strictly controlled network access policy. These servers should also be protected against DoS attacks by using IPS solutions.

Cisco Unified Wireless Solution

The Cisco Unified Wireless Network (CUWN) concept includes the following elements:

- **Wireless clients:** The wireless clients' components include laptops, workstations, PDAs, IP phones, smartphones, tablets, and manufacturing devices that have embedded wireless technology.

- **Access points:** The APs' components provide access to the wireless network, and they should be strategically placed in the right locations to achieve the best performance with minimal interference.

- **Network management:** This is accomplished through the network wireless control system, the central management tool that allows for the design, control, and monitoring of wireless networks.

- **Network unification:** The WLAN system should be able to support wireless applications by offering unified security policies, QoS, IPS, and RF management. Cisco Wireless LAN Controllers (WLC) offer this unified functionality integration in all of its major switching and routing platforms.

- **Network services:** Wireless network services are also referred to as mobility services and include things like guest access, voice services, location services, and threat detection and mitigation.

One of the advantages of using the CUWN solution is that it provides a centralized control architecture that offers reduced TCO, improved visibility, dynamic RF management, enhanced WLAN security, enterprise mobility, and improved productivity and collaboration.

Standalone APs, also known as autonomous access points, are easy to install but they can be difficult to manage in large deployments. They are not as desirable as the lightweight APs (LWAPs) from Cisco because they must be managed individually. In addition, different parameters must be manually configured on each device and this includes the SSID, VLAN information, and security features.

CUWN introduced the concept of LWAPs and WLCs. These two types of wireless devices divide the responsibilities and the functionalities that an autonomous AP would perform itself. This technology adds scalability by separating the WLAN data plane from the control plane, resulting in a "split MAC" design, as shown in Figure 2.18 below:

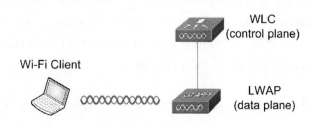

Figure 2.18 – WLAN Split MAC Operation

LWAPs only focus on the actual RF transmissions and the necessary real-time control operations, such as beaconing, probing, and buffering. At the same time, WLCs can manage all the non-real-time tasks, such as:

- SSID management
- VLAN management
- Access point association management
- Authentication
- Wireless QoS

Modern LWAPs have plug-and-play capabilities and require WLC for operation. They can be directly connected to the network without the need for additional configuration. The management logic and the way it functions are dictated by the WLC configuration. This makes the implementation process much easier than would be the case if autonomous access points were used. When using LWAPs, all RF traffic they receive must first go to the WLC device that manages the specific AP. This changes the way in which traditional WLAN communications work, even for hosts associated to the same AP.

The RF communication between LWAPs and WLCs is handled (tunneled) using the Lightweight Access Point Protocol (LWAPP). The LWAPP tunnel can operate either in Layer 2 or Layer 3 mode. Layer 2 mode implies that the AP and the WLC share the same VLAN, subnet, and functions with the LWAP receiving 802.11 frames and encapsulating them inside Ethernet toward the WLC. When the LWAPP tunnel operates in Layer 3 mode, the LWAP receives 802.11 frames and encapsulates them inside the User Datagram Protocol (UDP) toward the WLC. This implies that the WLC can be anywhere as long it is reachable by the AP.

LWAPP allows intelligence to move away from the AP and shares it with WLCs. WLCs handle the wireless policies, the control messaging setup, authentication, and wireless operations. WLCs are also the bridge between wireless networks and wired networks. WLC devices can manage multiple APs, providing configuration information as well as firmware updates on an ad-hoc basis. LWAPP is an IETF draft standard for WLC messaging between APs and WLCs. It can operate at both Layer 2 and Layer 3, but the Layer 3 LWAPP is far more popular.

NOTE: The APs and the WLCs exchange control messages over the wired backbone network.

LWAPP Layer 2 functions include:

- 802.11 beacons and Probe responses
- Packet control
- Packet acknowledgement and transmission
- Frame queuing and packet prioritization
- 802.11i MAC Layer data encryption and decryption

WLC Layer 2 functions include:

- 802.11 MAC management
- 802.11e resource reservation
- 802.11e authentication and key management

Layer 3 LWAPP tunnels are used between APs and WLCs to transmit control messages. They use UDP port 12223 for control and UDP port 12222 for data messages. Cisco LWAPPs can operate in six different modes:

- Local mode
- Remote Edge Access Point (REAP) mode
- Monitor mode
- Rogue Detector (RD) mode
- Sniffer mode
- Bridge mode

Local mode is the default mode of operation in the LWAPP. Every 180 seconds, the AP spends 60 ms on channels it does not operate on. During the 60 ms time period, the APs perform noise and interference measurements and scan for intrusion detection events.

REAP mode allows the LWAPP to reside across a LAN link and still be able to communicate with the WLC and provide the functionality of a regular LWAP. REAP mode is not supported on all LWAPP models.

Monitor mode is a special feature that allows LWAPP-enabled APs to exclude themselves from dealing with data traffic between clients and the infrastructure. Instead, they act as dedicated sensors for location-based services, rogue AP detection, and IDSs. APs in monitor mode cannot serve clients but they continuously cycle through all available channels, listening for each channel for approximately 60 ms.

In RD mode, the LWAPP monitors for rogue APs. The RD's goal is to see all of the VLANs in the network because rogue APs can be connected to any of these VLANs. The switch sends all of the rogue APs' client MAC address lists to the RD access point, which forwards these to the WLC to compare them with the MAC addresses of legitimate clients. If MAC addresses are matched, the controller knows that the rogue AP that deals with those clients is on the wired network.

Sniffer mode allows the LWAPP to capture and forward all of the packets on a particular channel to a remote machine that is running a packet capturing and analysis software. These packets include timestamps, packet size, and signal strength information.

The bridge mode typically operates on outdoor APs that function in a mesh topology. This is a cost-effective high-bandwidth wireless-bridging connectivity mechanism and it includes point-to-point or point-to-multipoint bridging.

WLCs have three major components:

- WLANs
- Interfaces
- Ports

The WLAN is basically the SSID network name. Every WLAN is assigned to an interface in the WLC, and each WLAN is configured with policies for RF, QoS, and other WLAN attributes. The WLC interfaces are logical connections that map to a VLAN on the wired network. Every interface is configured with a unique IP address, a default gateway, physical ports, VLAN tagging, and a DHCP server. WLCs support the following five interface types:

- **Management interface:** Used for in-band management, connectivity to an AAA server, and Layer 2 discovery and association.
- **Optional service port interface:** Used for out-of-band management that is statically configured.
- **AP manager interface:** Used for Layer 3 discovery and association (the static WLC IP address will be configured on this interface).
- **Dynamic interfaces:** These are the VLANs designated for WLAN clients' data.
- **Virtual interfaces:** These are used for Layer 3 security authentication, DHCP relay support, and management of mobility features.

The port is a physical connection to a neighboring switch or router, and by default each port is a .1Q trunk port. WLCs might have multiple ports that go into a single port-channel interface (link aggregation can be applied to these ports). Some WLCs also have a service port that is used for out-of-band management.

> **NOTE:** Different WLC platforms can support a different number of APs, up to several hundred.

CUWN Roaming and Mobility

One of the main features of a WLAN solution is allowing users the ability to access network resources from different areas, including zones where it is difficult to install cables. Another reason for using WLANs would be organizational policies that allow guest access only wirelessly. Sometimes a WLAN solution is built as a transition network until the complete wired network is implemented.

Considering the scenarios mentioned above, the end-users will most likely move from one location to another. The solution to this issue is the roaming and mobility features that give users the ability to access the network from different locations. Roaming occurs when wireless clients change their association from one LWAP to another without losing connectivity. Network designers should carefully scale the wireless network to allow for the client roaming process. Wireless roaming can be divided into two categories:

- Intra-controller roaming
- Inter-controller roaming (Layer 2 or Layer 3)

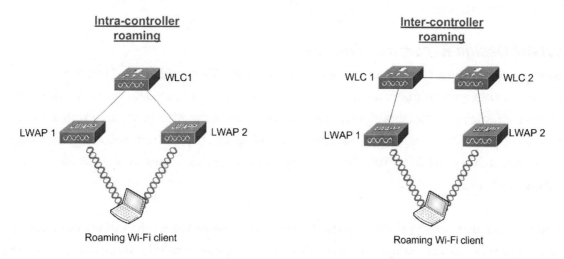

Figure 2.19 – WLAN Mobility

As illustrated in Figure 2.19 above, intra-controller roaming occurs when a client moves its association from one AP to another AP controlled by the same WLC. At that moment, the WLC will update the client database with the new association and it will not change the client's IP address. Inter-controller roaming can operate in either Layer 2 or Layer 3. Layer 2 inter-controller roaming implies that users move from AP to AP and from WLC to WLC, but at the same time they remain in the same subnet. Layer 3 inter-controller roaming is more difficult to implement, as users move from AP to AP, from WLC to WLC, and from subnet to subnet. In this scenario, WLCs must be configured with mobility groups to closely communicate and exchange information about the roaming user's status.

A very important advantage of Layer 3 inter-controller roaming is that the users can maintain their original IP address. The two WLCs are connected through an IP connection, and the traffic is bridged into a different IP subnet. When clients associate with the new AP, the new WLC exchanges mobility information with the old WLC. The original client database is not moved to the new WLC. Instead, the old WLC will mark the clients in its database entry (anchor entry) and this entry will be copied to the new WLC database entry (foreign entry). Wireless client keeps their original IP address and it is re-authenticated as soon as a new security session is established.

WLCs are assigned to mobility groups to exchange mobility messages dynamically and tunnel data over the IP connection. Mobility groups use the following ports to exchange data:

- LWAPP control: UDP 12223
- LWAPP data: UDP 12222
- WLC exchange un-encrypt messages: UDP 16666
- WLC exchange encrypt messages: UDP 16667

WLAN Design Recommendations

Some key issues must be considered when designing a WLAN environment. First, the controller redundancy design should be carefully analyzed. WLCs can be configured for dynamic redundancy or deterministic redundancy. With deterministic redundancy, the AP is configured with a primary controller, a secondary controller, and a tertiary controller. This requires much planning but it offers good predictability and faster failover times. Dynamic redundancy uses LWAPP to load balance APs across WLCs.

Another issue that must be analyzed in the design process involves radio channel management and radio groups (RGs). For example, the 802.11b and 802.11g standards offer three non-overlapping channels (1, 6, and 11), so Cisco Radio Resource Management (RRM) can be used to manage AP radio frequency channels and power configurations. WLCs use the RRM algorithm for automatic configuration and optimization. RGs are clusters of WLCs that coordinate their RRM calculations. When a WLC is placed in an RG, the RRM calculation will scale up from a single WLC to multiple floors, buildings, or even a campus.

An RF site survey should be accomplished by certified wireless professionals in the WLAN design phase. The RF site survey is comprised of five steps:

1. Define the company's requirements.
2. Identify coverage areas and user density.
3. Determine the preliminary locations and requirements of the APs (including necessary antenna types and wired connections).
4. Accomplish the actual survey and identify elements that might interfere with the WLAN signal and components.
5. Document the process (including AP location, data, and signal rates).

From a design standpoint, a network designer might also be in a situation of having to configure and plan an outdoor wireless mesh configuration. This includes several components:

- The wireless control system
- WLCs
- External AP bridge (rooftop AP)
- Outdoor mesh APs

An important design for outdoor wireless mesh scenarios refers to the existence of a 2 to 3 ms latency value per hop, so the recommendation is to have fewer than four hops to ensure a good level of performance. Another recommendation is to have no more than 20 mesh AP nodes per external AP bridge for best performance. The most important wireless campus design considerations are as follows:

- **The number of APs:** Sufficient APs should be included to ensure RF coverage for all of the wireless clients in all enterprise areas. Cisco recommends 20 data devices per AP.
- **The placement of APs:** Access points should be placed in central locations of different Enterprise areas to ensure proper user connectivity.
- **Power options for APs:** Access points can be powered by traditional methods or by using PoE capabilities.
- **The number of WLCs:** This depends on the chosen redundancy model and (based on the client's requirements) the number of APs. The recommended redundancy model is deterministic redundancy.
- **The placement of WLCs:** Wireless LAN controllers should be placed in secured wiring closets, server rooms, or data centers. WLCs can be placed in a central location or they can be distributed throughout the Enterprise Campus Distribution Layer block. Inter-controller roaming should be minimized.

DESIGNING QUALITY OF SERVICE

One of the key aspects that must be considered when designing Enterprise Campus solutions is Quality of Service. There are many different categories of the QoS approach, including:

- Shaping
- Policing
- Congestion management
- Congestion avoidance
- Link efficiency mechanisms

QoS involves a wide variety of techniques, especially in networks that offer multimedia services (voice and/or video), because these services are usually delay sensitive and require low latency and low jitter. Traffic generated by these applications must be prioritized using QoS techniques.

Congestion Management

Congestion happens for many different reasons in modern networks. In situations where a specific link is constantly congested, the link may need to be upgraded, but when experiencing occasional congestion on a particular link, QoS congestion management techniques can be used to take care of the problem.

The approach used for congestion management is called queuing. Applying queuing techniques means using techniques other than the default First In First Out (FIFO) method. An interface consists of two different queuing areas (see Figure 2.20 below):

- Hardware queue (or Transmit Ring – TX Ring)
- Software queue

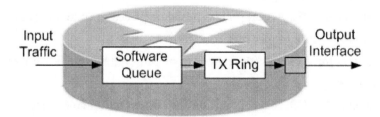

Figure 2.20 – Interface Queue Types

The hardware queue on the interface always uses the FIFO method for packet treatment. This mode of operation ensures that the first packet in the hardware queue is the first packet that will leave the interface. The only TX Ring parameter that can be modified on most Cisco devices is the queue length.

The software queue is the place where most of the congestion management manipulations occur. The software queue is used to order packets before they use the hardware queue, and they can be configured with different queuing strategies.

Congestion might occur because of the high-speed LAN connections that aggregate into the lower speed WAN connections. Aggregation refers to being able to support the cumulative effect of all the users wanting to use the connection.

There are many different approaches (queuing strategies) that can be used in congestion management, such as the following:

- First In First Out (FIFO)
- Priority Queuing (PQ)
- Round Robin (RR)
- Weighted Round Robin (WRR)
- Deficit Round Robin (DRR)
- Modified Deficit Round Robin (MDRR)
- Shaped Round Robin (SRR)
- Custom Queuing (CQ)
- Fair Queuing (FQ)
- Weighted Fair Queuing (WFQ)
- Class Based Weighted Fair Queuing (CBWFQ)
- Low Latency Queuing (LLQ)

NOTE: All of the techniques mentioned above are used in the interface software queue. The hardware queue always uses FIFO.

FIFO is the least complex method of queuing. It operates by giving priority to the first packets received. This is also the default queuing mechanism for software queues in high-speed Cisco interfaces. Having a sufficient budget to overprovision the congested links will allow the use of FIFO on all of the interfaces (hardware and software queues). However, in most situations, this is not possible, so some other kinds of advanced queuing techniques, such as WFQ, CBWFQ, or LLQ, will have to be employed. These are the most modern queuing strategies that will ensure that important packets receive priority during times of congestion.

FIFO used in the software queue will not make a determination on packet priority that is usually signaled using QoS markings. Relying on FIFO but still experiencing congestion means the traffic could be affected by situations like delay or jitter, and important traffic might be starved and might not reach its destination.

WFQ is a Cisco default technique used on slow-speed interfaces (less than 2 Mbps) because it is considered more efficient than FIFO in this case. WFQ functions by dynamically sorting the traffic into flows, and then dedicating a queue for each flow while trying to allocate the bandwidth fairly. It will do this by inspecting the QoS markings and giving priority to higher priority traffic.

WFQ is not the best solution in every scenario because it does not provide enough control in the configuration (it does everything automatically), but it is far better than the FIFO approach because interactive traffic flows that generally use small packets (e.g., VoIP) get prioritized to the front of the software queue. This ensures that high-volume talkers do not use all of the interface bandwidth. The WFQ fairness aspect also makes sure that high-priority interactive conversations do not get starved by high-volume traffic flows.

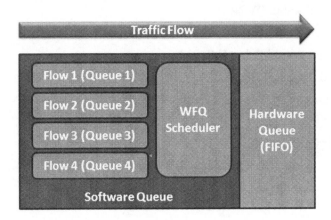

Figure 2.21 – Weighted Fair Queuing Logic

As illustrated in Figure 2.21 above, the different WFQ traffic flows are placed into different queues before entering the WFQ scheduler, which will allow them to pass to the hardware queue based on the defined logic. If one queue fills, the packets will be dropped, but this will also be based on a WFQ approach (lower priority packets are dropped first), as opposed to the FIFO approach of tail dropping.

Because WFQ lacks a certain level of control, another congestion management technology called Custom Queuing (CQ) was created. Even though CQ is a legacy technology, it is still implemented in some environments. CQ is similar to WFQ but it operates by manually defining the 16 static queues and the allocation of the number of bytes or packets for each queue. The network designer can assign a byte count for each queue (i.e., the number of bytes that are to be sent from each queue). Queue number 0 is reserved for the system to avoid starvation of key router messages.

Even though Custom Queuing provides flexible congestion management, this does not work well with VoIP implementations because of the round robin nature of CQ. For example, four queues are allocated a different number of packets (Q1=10 packets, Q2=20 packets, Q3=50 packets, and Q4=100 packets) over a time interval. Even though Q4 has priority, the interface is still using a round robin approach (Q4-Q3-Q2-Q1-Q4...and so on). This is not appropriate for VoIP scenarios because voice traffic needs strict priority for a constant traffic flow that will minimize jitter. As a result, another legacy technology called Priority Queuing (PQ) was invented. PQ places packets into four priority queues:

- Low
- Normal
- Medium
- High

As mentioned, VoIP traffic is placed in the high-priority queue to ensure absolute priority. However, this can lead to the starvation of other queues, so PQ is not recommended for use in modern networks.

If VoIP is not used in the network, the most recommended congestion management technique is CBWFQ, which defines the amount of bandwidth that the various forms of traffic will receive. Minimum bandwidth reservations are defined for different classes of traffic.

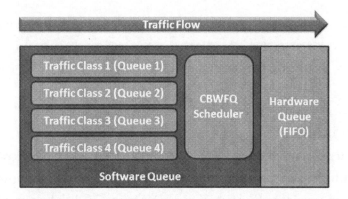

Figure 2.22 – Class Based Weighted Fair Queuing Logic

As illustrated above in Figure 2.22, CBWFQ logic is based on a CBWFQ scheduler that receives information from queues defined for different forms of traffic. The traffic that does not fit any manually defined queue automatically falls into the "class-default" queue. These queues can be assigned minimum bandwidth guarantees for all traffic classes. CBWFQ offers powerful methodologies for controlling exactly how much bandwidth these various classifications will receive. If it contains more than one traffic type, each individual queue will use the FIFO method inside the hardware queue, so the network designer should not combine too many forms of traffic inside a single queue.

Considering the inefficiency of CBWFQ when using VoIP, another QoS technique was developed: LLQ. As shown in Figure 2.23 below, this adds a priority queue (usually for voice traffic) to the CBWFQ system, so LLQ is often referred to as an extension of CBWFQ (i.e., LLQ=PQ-CBWFQ).

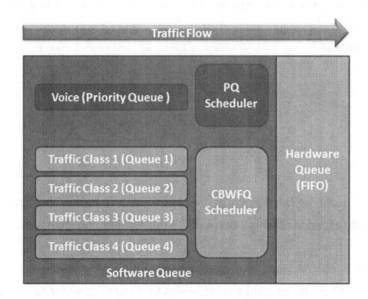

Figure 2.23 – Low Latency Queuing Logic

Adding a priority queue to CBWFQ will not lead to starvation because this queue is policed so that the amount of bandwidth guaranteed for voice cannot exceed a particular value. Since voice traffic gets its own priority treatment, the remaining traffic forms will use WFQ based on bandwidth reservation values.

Congestion Avoidance

Congestion avoidance is another category of Differentiated Services QoS often deploys in WANs. When both the hardware and the software queues fill up, they are tail dropped at the end of the queue, which can lead to voice traffic starvation and/or to the TCP global synchronization process described earlier. Using congestion avoidance techniques can guard against global synchronization problems. The most popular congestion avoidance mechanism is called Random Early Detection (RED). Cisco's implementation is called Weighted Random Early Detection (WRED). These QoS tools try to prevent congestion from occurring by randomly dropping unimportant traffic before the queue gets full.

Shaping and Policing

Shaping and policing are not the same technique, but many people think they are. Shaping is the process that controls the way traffic is sent (i.e., it buffers excess packets). Policing, on the other hand, will drop or re-mark (penalize) packets that exceed a given rate. Policing might be used to prevent certain applications from using all of the connection resources in a fast WAN or from offering only as many resources as certain applications with clear bandwidth requirements need.

Shaping is often used to prevent congestion in situations where there is asymmetric bandwidth. An example of this is a headquarters router that connects to a branch office router that has a lower bandwidth connection. In this type of environment, shaping can be employed when the headquarters router sends data so that it does not overwhelm the branch office router. Many times the contract between an ISP and its customer specifies a Committed Information Rate (CIR) value. This represents the amount of bandwidth purchased from the ISP. Shaping can be used to ensure that the data sent conforms to the specified CIR.

When comparing shaping and policing, shaping can be used only in the egress direction, while policing can be used in both the ingress and the egress directions. Another key distinction is that policing will drop or re-mark the packet, while shaping will queue the excess traffic. Because of this behavior, policing uses less buffering. Finally, shaping has the advantage of supporting Frame Relay congestion indicators by responding to Forward Explicit Congestion Notification (FECN) and Backward Explicit Congestion Notification (BECN) messages.

Link Efficiency Mechanisms

Link efficiency mechanisms include compression and Link Fragmentation and Interleaving (LFI). Compression involves reducing the size of certain packets to increase the available bandwidth and decrease delay and includes the following types:

- Transmission Control Protocol (TCP) header compression (compresses the IP and TCP headers, reducing the overhead from 40 bytes to 3 to 5 bytes)
- Real-time Transport Protocol (RTP) header compression (compresses the IP, UDP, and RTP headers of voice packets, reducing the overhead to 2 to 4 bytes)

LFI techniques are efficient on slow links, where certain problems might appear even when applying congestion management features. These problems are generated by big data packets that arrive at the interface before other small, more important packets. If a big packet enters the FIFO TX Ring before a small VoIP packet arrives at the software queue, the VoIP packet will get stuck behind the data packet and might have to wait a long time before its transmission is finished. To solve this problem, LFI splits the large data packet into smaller pieces (fragments). The voice packets are then interleaved between these fragments, so they do not have to wait for the large packet to be completely transmitted first. This process is illustrated in Figure 2.24 below:

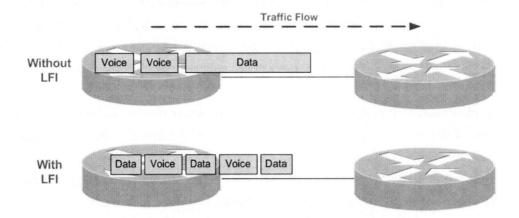

Figure 2.24 – Link Fragmentation and Interleaving

There are three different flavors of LFI used today:

- Multilink Point-to-Point Protocol (PPP) with interleaving (used in PPP environments)
- FRF.12 (used with Frame Relay data connections)
- FRF.11 Annex C (used with Voice over Frame Relay – VoFR)

QoS Design Recommendations for Voice Transport

Network designers should use some general guidelines for designing Quality of Service for voice transport. These QoS techniques are applied when using WAN connections equal to T1 or lower. When using high-bandwidth connections, QoS techniques do not need to be considered because congestion is less likely to occur.

QoS techniques are most effective on bursty connections, typically in Frame Relay environments where CIRs and burst rates are usually specified in the contract. Traffic bursts occur when sending large packets over the network or when the network is very busy during certain periods of the day. QoS techniques should be mandatory if the Enterprise Network uses any kind of delay-sensitive applications (e.g., applications that must function in real time, such as presentations over the Internet or video training sessions) and other traffic on that connection might affect the user's experience.

Congestion management should be considered only when the network experiences congestion, and this should be planned for by analyzing the organization's policies and goals and following the network design steps (PPDIOO). Before applying any QoS configuration, traffic should be carefully analyzed to detect congestion problems. The best QoS mechanism should be chosen based on the specific situation, and this can include packet classification and marking, queuing techniques, congestion avoidance techniques, or bandwidth reservation mechanisms (RSVPs).

Network designers should also be familiar with the most important QoS mechanisms available for IP Telephony, such as the following:

- Compressed RTP (cRTP)
- LFI
- PQ-WFQ
- LLQ
- AutoQoS

cRTP is a compression mechanisms that reduces the size of the IP, UDP, and RTP headers from 40 bytes to 2 or 4 bytes. cRTP is configured on a link-by-link basis, and Cisco recommends using this technique for links that are slower than 768 kbps.

> **NOTE:** cRTP should not be configured on devices that have high processor utilization (above 75%).

LFI is a QoS mechanisms used to reduce serialization delays. PQ is also referred to as IP RTP priority. This adds a single priority queue to the WFQ technique, which is used for VoIP traffic. All the other traffic is queued based on the WFQ algorithm. When using PQ, the router places VoIP RTP packets in a strict priority queue that is always serviced first.

LLQ (a.k.a. PQ-CBWFQ) also provides a single priority queue but it is preferred over the PQ-WFQ technique because it guarantees bandwidth for different classes of traffic. All voice traffic is assigned to the priority queue, while VoIP signaling and video traffic is assigned to its own traffic class. For example, FTP can be assigned to a low-priority traffic class and all other data traffic can be assigned to a regular traffic class.

AutoQoS is a Cisco IOS feature that uses a very simple CLI to enable Quality of Service for VoIP in WAN and LAN environments. This is a great feature to use on Cisco Integrated Services Routers (ISRs) (routers that integrate data and media collaboration features) because it provides many capabilities to control the transport VoIP protocols. AutoQoS inspects the device capabilities and automatically enables LFI and RTP where necessary and it is usually used in small- to medium-sized businesses that need to deploy IP Telephony fast but do not have experienced staff that can plan and deploy complex QoS features. Large companies can also deploy IPT using AutoQoS, but the auto-generated configuration should be carefully revised, tested, and tuned to meet the organization's needs.

> **NOTE:** QoS techniques should be carefully configured on all of the devices involved in voice transport, not just on individual devices.

NETWORK MANAGEMENT

Network management is an intelligent network service that allows the management and monitoring of the server farm, network devices in different network modules, or WAN connections. This involves system administration for the servers, with software tools specific to each operating system provider (e.g., Microsoft) or third-party tools (e.g., Tivoli, HP, etc.). Network management also includes logging, usually through a Syslog server implementation or security features like OTP (One Time Password). OTP represents a two-factor security mechanism (i.e., something one knows, like a password, and something one has, like a card or a token) that allows for a high-security environment. Cisco IOS software allows for the implementation of flexible network management features, some of which are described in the following sections.

Simple Network Management Protocol

The network management system is usually based on the Simple Network Management Protocol (SNMP), which is a TCP/IP Application Layer protocol that uses IP within UDP. SNMP, illustrated below in Figure 2.25, is used to share management information between network devices, usually between a management workstation and routers, switches, or other devices.

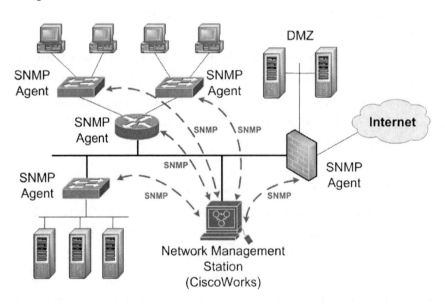

Figure 2.25 – Network Management Using SNMP

SNMP has evolved during the years and has now reached version 3 (SNMPv3). Network designers should demand that every environment uses SNMPv3, and not the older, unsecured SNMP versions (1 and 2), because of the advanced security features it presents. SNMP is used by network administrators and engineers to perform the following tasks:

- Monitoring the performance of network devices
- Troubleshooting
- Planning scalable enterprise solutions and intelligent services

SNMP accesses detailed information in Management Information Bases (MIBs) and it uses SNMP agents, as shown in Figure 2.25. An MIB is an object-oriented hierarchical database system stored locally on the network device. An example of an MIB entry is 1.3.6.1.2.1.2.2.1.20.0, with 1 being the root of the MIB tree and 0 being the final leaf.

The SNMP agent is used to send and receive information from the device to the Network Management Station (NMS) and the other way around. To do that, different types of SNMP messages are used. The NMS will run some kind of network management software (e.g., CiscoWorks) that retrieves and displays the SNMP information in a Graphical User Interface (GUI) format. The displayed information is used for controlling, troubleshooting, and planning.

Another SNMP concept is represented by community strings, also known as the access control method. A community is a password that controls what group of people has access to certain information on the device. The concept of community strings presented in earlier versions of SNMP evolved to the username/password authentication method used in SNMPv3.

The managed device contains SNMP agents and an MIB that stores all the information. Different types of messages are used to get information from the NMS to and from the managed device (or the monitored device), as shown in Figure 2.26 below:

NMS
(CiscoWorks)

Managed
device

Get Request
Get Next Request
Get Bulk
Set Request
Get Response
Trap
Inform Request

Figure 2.26 – SNMP Messages

The first message is called the Get Request. This is sent to the managed device when the NMS wants to get a specific MIB variable from the SNMP agent that runs on that device. The Get Next Request information is used to return the next object in the list after the Get Request message returned a value. The Get Bulk message works only in SNMPv3 environments and it can be used to retrieve a big chunk of data (e.g., an entire table); it also reduces the need to use many Get Request and Get Next Request messages. This reduces the overhead on bandwidth utilization on the link.

The Set Request message is also sent by the NMS and is used to set an MIB variable on the agent. The Get Response message is the response from the SNMP agent to the NMS Get Request, Get Next Request, or Get Bulk messages. A Trap is used by the SNMP agent to transmit unsolicited alarms to the NMS when certain conditions occur (e.g., device failure, state change, or parameter modifications). Different thresholds can be configured on the managed device for different parameters (e.g., disk space, CPU utilization, memory utilization, or bandwidth utilization) and Trap messages are sent when the defined thresholds are reached.

SNMPv3 introduced another message called the Inform Request. This is similar to a Trap message and is what a managed device will send to the NMS as an acknowledgement to other messages. The major difference between these two message types is that Inform Request messages are acknowledged by the receiver, unlike the Trap messages, which are not.

> **NOTE:** SNMPv3 is defined by the following RFCs: RFC 2571, RFC 2572, RFC 2573, RFC 2574, and RFC 2575.

SNMPv3 provides three security levels:

- **NoAuthNoPriv**: No authentication and no privacy mechanisms.
- **AuthNoPriv**: Authentication (e.g., MD5, SHA) but no privacy mechanisms.
- **AuthPriv**: The highest level; uses authentication (e.g., MD5, SHA) and privacy (e.g., DES).

Remote Network Monitoring

Remote Network Monitoring (RMON) is an MIB that allows proactive monitoring of LAN traffic in the network environment. RMON tracks individual data packets, the number and size of those packets, broadcast packet tracking, network utilization, errors, and statistics.

RMON agents run on various network devices, such as routers, switches, or servers. To save overhead on those specific devices, RMON can be configured on special workstations that operate as probes on specific network segments. RMON can diagnose faults within the LAN, and allows for network tuning and planning for growth and utilization.

RMON is implemented in two versions: RMON1 and RMON2. RMON1 operates only at the Physical and Data-link Layers, so it must be used only to probe, tune, plan, and look for faults on hubs (at the Physical Layer) and switches (at Layer 2). RMON2 provides much more functionality and can be used for Network Layer applications (Layer 3) and Layer 4 through Layer 7, so it can monitor database servers, exchange servers, e-mail, and Web traffic.

NOTE: RMON is documented in RFC 1757.

NetFlow

NetFlow is a monitoring and measurement technology that is superior to a simple SNMP/RMON solution because it offers enhanced functionality and provides much more detail on the data that passes through a specific interface. NetFlow scales to a large number of interfaces and this makes it a great Enterprise and ISP solution because it supports customer service programs by using popular data warehousing and data mining solutions that are critical for competitive vendor offerings (e.g., flexible accounting and billing that considers application usage, the time of day, bandwidth utilization, and QoS elements). NetFlow is also a great tool for network scalability planning and overall analysis, and it can help lower the organization's TCO. The NetFlow management architecture consists of three components:

- NetFlow data export service
- NetFlow flow collector service
- NetFlow data analysis

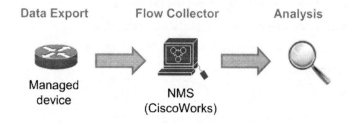

Figure 2.27 – NetFlow Management Architecture

As shown in Figure 2.27 above, the NetFlow data export service is the first layer of the three-tier NetFlow architecture. This is where the data warehousing and data mining solutions occur and where accounting statistics for traffic on the networking devices are captured, and it uses UDP to export data in a three-part process:

- Data switching
- Data export
- Data aggregation

The data is exported to the second tier, the NetFlow flow collector service, where servers and workstations accomplish data collection, data filtering, aggregation, data storage, and file system management using existing or third-party file systems. Network data analysis takes place at the lowest tier, which is at the Access Layer. At this level, network planning tools, overall network analysis tools, and accounting and billing tools can be used and data can be exported to various database systems or Excel spreadsheets.

Cisco Discovery Protocol

Cisco Discovery Protocol (CDP) is a proprietary Cisco protocol that operates at Layer 2 (Data-link Layer) between Cisco devices. Its main job is to summarize information discovered about directly connected routers, switches, or other Cisco devices. The Cisco devices themselves do not forward any CDP frames to their neighbors because its role is to share device information only between directly connected devices.

CDP is media and protocol independent, and it operates with TCP/IP, IPX, or AppleTalk. It can also run across different media types, such as LANs and ATM and Frame Relay networks. CDP should not be used on external Internet connections for security reasons, as it could expose information about the network's devices to outside users. It also should not be configured on links going to non-Cisco devices because it is unnecessary to do so.

Running the "show cdp neighbor" command on a device will give CDP-related information, such as:

- The MAC address of the directly connected neighbor
- The local interface connecting to that particular neighbor
- Information about the device type (router, switch, or other)
- Device platform/mode
- Port numbers

NOTE: Link Layer Discovery Protocol (LLDP) is an open-standard version of CDP, with similar functionality. LLDP can be used when interconnecting non-Cisco devices.

Network-Based Application Recognition

Network-Based Application Recognition (NBAR) is a Cisco IOS-embedded technology that helps identify well-known applications, protocols, and services. It offers an application-level intelligent classification engine that recognizes many protocols and applications for the delivery of Quality of Services. Some of the protocols that are automatically recognized by NBAR include the following:

- Enterprise applications: Citrix, Oracle, PCAnywhere, SAP, Exchange
- Routing protocols: BGP, EIGRP, OSPF, RIP
- Database: SQL
- Financial: FIX
- Security and tunneling: GRE, IPsec, L2TP, PPTP, SFTP, SHTTP, SOCKS, SSH
- Network management: ICMP, SNMP, Syslog
- Network mail services: IMAP, POP3, SMTP
- Directory: DHCP, DNS, Kerberos, LDAP
- Internet: FTP, HTTP, IRC, Telnet, TFTP
- Signaling: IPX, ISAKMP, RSVP
- Remote Procedure Call (RPC): NFS, Sunrpc
- Voice: H.323, SIP, Skype, RTP
- Peer-to-peer file-sharing applications: BitTorrent, DirrectConnect, eDonkey, FastTrack, Gnutella, KaZaA

These protocols use statically or dynamically assigned TCP or UDP port numbers, and as new iterations of an operating system are introduced, Cisco adds new protocols via Packet Description Language Modules (PDLMs). One of the great features of NBAR is its ability to go beyond the TCP and UDP port numbers of a packet and look into the packet payload.

NBAR is configured in the CLI MQC configuration mode, using the "match protocol" command structure. The network management of the traffic can be improved by classifying a wide variety of elements and functions, beyond the statically assigned TCP or UDP port numbers. For example, non-TCP/UDP IP protocols like OSPF and EIGRP use their own transport mechanisms. NBAR can also inspect and classify dynamically assigned port numbers and achieve deep packet inspection.

NBAR is easy to configure because of its modularity and is preferred over using elaborate and complex Access Control Lists to classify static port protocols. Identifying and classifying the traffic is the first major step in implementing QoS. Once the amount of application traffic and the variety of applications and protocols in the network is identified, QoS solutions can be created.

A special feature of NBAR called Protocol Discovery can be applied to interfaces using the "ip nbar protocol-discovery" command to automatically discover the application protocols over that interface, at any point in time. This command monitors all ingress and egress traffic on the specific interface and it builds statistics on a protocol-by-protocol basis.

These statistics help to deliver the traffic classes and policies, and they contain the following:

- The number of input packets
- The number of output packets
- The number of bytes
- Input and output bit rates

An external PDLM can also be manually loaded from the global configuration mode to extend and improve the classification engine for many of the existing and emerging application protocols in the NBAR list of protocols.

NBAR and NetFlow are complimentary embedded technologies that have some overlap functionalities. For example, both can function on the IP header, the source and destination IP address, and the source and destination port. The most important difference between the two mechanisms is that NBAR offers deep packet inspection features and NetFlow traditionally works based on the Type of Service (ToS) and the interface. Another important difference between the two mechanisms is that NetFlow monitors data from Layer 2 to Layer 4 and NBAR monitors data from Layer 3 to Layer 7. One of the most powerful features of NBAR is its ability to classify HTTP and its various packet options.

NOTE: NetFlow version 9 offers some of the flexibility available in the NBAR PDLMs and Protocol Discovery features.

NBAR can work with Cisco AutoQoS, which is a feature in the Cisco IOS that generates pre-defined policy maps for voice. This helps to simplify the deployment and provisioning of QoS by leveraging the existing NBAR traffic classification, which can be done with NBAR discovery. AutoQoS works by creating a trust zone that allows Differentiated Services Code Point (DSCP) markings to be used for classification. If the optional "trust" keyword is used, the existing DSCP marking can be used, but if the keyword is not specified, NBAR will be used to mark the DSCP values.

Another feature that can be used with NBAR is QoS for the Enterprise Network, which uses NBAR discovery to collect traffic statistics. Based on that discovery, NBAR will generate policy maps (as opposed to AutoQoS, which has predefined policy maps) and make its bandwidth settings via Cisco suggestions on a class-by-class basis. This is an appropriate solution for medium-sized companies and Enterprise organizations' branch offices, and it is based on the Cisco best practice recommendations that come from the NBAR discovery process. This is a two-phase process: the first phase involves an auto discovery QoS command on the appropriate link, and the second phase involves automatically configuring the link with the "auto qos" command.

IP Service Level Agreement

Network redundancy involves the existence of multiple paths between different points in the topology. Path control manipulates the way a packet is forwarded by default across the network. This can be accomplished in different ways, including policy-based routing or filtering (e.g., prefix lists, distribute lists, or offset lists).

An IP Service Level Agreement (SLA) executes network performance measurements within Cisco devices. This will leverage active traffic monitoring; in other words, traffic is generated in a predictable, measurable, and continuous way with the goal of achieving optimized network performance. End-to-end network performance tests are conducted based on clear measurement metrics.

Different types of data (synthetic traffic) will be sent across the network to measure performance between different locations. Timestamp data generate the metrics used to calculate issues such as jitter, latency, response time, or packet loss. The process of configuring IP SLA involves the following steps:

1. Define one or more probes.
2. Define one or more tracking objects.
3. Define the action that will be taken for each tracking object.

Response times are of great importance in terms of the WAN, as they relate to the supported applications. Many modern applications will give an indication of the necessary response times. VoIP is an excellent example of this. When a VoIP call is made over many network devices, the necessary response time must be met for proper voice communications (one-way latency should not exceed 120 ms), and response time testing can be carried out using IP SLA on Cisco devices.

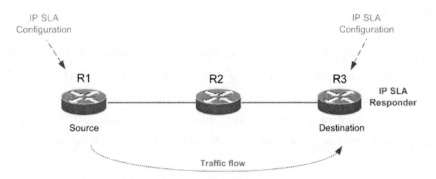

Figure 2.28 – Example of an IP SLA

Figure 2.28 above illustrates an example of IP SLA in action. R1 is the first hop in the traffic path and R3 is the last hop. Configuring IP SLA in an active configuration will generate synthetic traffic that flows over the intermediary devices so that the necessary parameters can be measured. R1 is considered the IP SLA sender and R3 is considered the responder. The responder functionality on R3 ensures that there are no false measurements, and this is a much more accurate test.

NOTE: IP SLA used to be called the Service Assurance Agent (SAA) or the Real Time Responder (RTR).

The most important parameters measured with the IP SLA feature are delay and jitter. Delay represents the amount of time required for a packet to reach its destination and jitter is the variation in delay. These parameters are of great importance, especially in highly congested WAN environments. Another important key design parameter is the overall available bandwidth (i.e., throughput). This measures the amount of data that can be sent in a particular timeframe through a specific WAN area.

SUMMARY

The process of Core Layer collapsing implies combining it with the Distribution Layer, and this is one of the first decisions small- and medium-sized companies make when analyzing the Enterprise Campus design. The Core Layer is the aggregation point for all of the other layers and submodules in the Enterprise Campus architecture. The main technology features required inside the Core Layer include a high level of redundancy, high-speed switching, and high reliability. Some of the advantages of implementing a dedicated Core Layer include the following:

- Distribution Layer switches can be connected hierarchically to the backbone switches
- Less physical cabling
- Less complex routing environment
- Improved scalability
- Easier data and voice integration
- Easier to converge LAN and WAN

Cisco Nonstop Forwarding (NSF) allows the standby route processor (RP) to take control of the router after a hardware or software fault on the active route processor. Cisco NSF will continue to forward packets until route convergence is complete. Stateful Switchover (SSO) allows the standby RP to take immediate control and keep connectivity protocols (e.g., BGP sessions). The most important advantages of Cisco IOS software modularity include the following:

- Minimizes unplanned downtime
- Makes software modifications much easier to accomplish
- Can be integrated with the change control policy
- Allows for process-level policy control

Implementing the Spanning Tree Protocol (STP) is another key issue when considering Layer 2 Enterprise Campus infrastructure best practices. Although many designers disable STP at the network edge, Cisco does not recommend this because the loss of connectivity without STP will be a much bigger issue than any information that might be revealed through STP to the outside world. The Cisco STP toolkit includes the following technologies:

- PortFast
- UplinkFast
- BackboneFast
- Loop Guard
- Root Guard
- BPDU Guard
- UDLD

EtherChannels are important when using STP because when all of the links look like one link, STP will not consider them a possible loop threat and will not shut down any link from that specific bundle. The links in an EtherChannel can be dynamically load balanced without STP interfering in this situation.

In any network environment, there are seldom situations in which all of the users will access the same servers at the same time. The concept of data oversubscription is usually applied at the Access and Distribution Layers and implies understanding that not everyone will be accessing the bandwidth at the same time.

Routing protocols are usually used, especially in the Distribution Layer to Core Layer and the Core Layer to Core Layer connections. In addition, a Layer 3 routing implementation can move to the Access Layer, which is becoming more and more popular due to STP problems. There are primarily three methods to quickly re-route around failed links and failed multilayer switches to provide load balancing with redundant paths:

- Building redundant triangle topologies for deterministic convergence (avoid using squares)
- Controlling unnecessary peering across the Access Layer by peering only on transit links
- Summarizing at the Distribution Layer to Core Layer for optimal results (limit the EIGRP query diameter and propagation of OSPF LSAs)

A critical aspect of convergence and high availability in the network design is the ability to have redundancy on behalf of the end-user in the Access Layer to the first hop (or the default gateway). Since Layer 2 switches are typically dealt with at the Access Layer with Layer 3 switches at the

Distribution Layer, the default gateway is usually the interface on the Distribution Layer switch that connects to the Access Layer.

The three First Hop Redundancy Protocols (FHRPs) are as follows:

- **Hot Standby Router Protocol (HSRP):** A Cisco proprietary protocol, the most common and preferred option when using Cisco equipment.
- **Virtual Router Redundancy Protocol (VRRP):** An IETF standard.
- **Gateway Load Balancing Protocol (GLBP):** The most recent protocol (again, a Cisco invention) and the most sophisticated FHRP.

Network virtualization refers to one physical network supporting a wide number of logical topologies. This allows actions such as outsourcing in the IT department by creating a logical topology that an external IT professional can access. Another example is creating a dedicated logical topology for quality assurance or various tests. In the network security world, virtualization is present in firewall devices, under the form of virtual contexts. Network virtualization with Cisco products is typically classified into four different areas:

- Control plane virtualization
- Data plane virtualization
- Management plane virtualization
- Pooling and clustering

Wireless networks are experiencing widespread growth because of their availability, flexibility, and service offerings. WLANs offer network access via radio waves. Wireless clients (such as a PC or a PDA) access a wireless access point (AP) using half-duplex communication. The wireless AP allows a wireless client to reach the rest of the network. The major components of the Cisco Unified Wireless Network (CUWN) architecture are as follows:

- Wireless clients
- Access points
- Network management
- Network unification
- Network services

Aside from autonomous mode, CUWN can alternatively operate in split-MAC mode. With split-MAC operation, an AP is considered to be a "lightweight" access point (LWAP), which cannot function without a wireless LAN controller (WLC).

The LWAP performs functions such as beaconing, packet transmission, and frame queuing, while the WLC assumes roles such as authentication, key management, and resource reservation. The operation of the wireless AP discussed thus far is referred to as local mode. However, several other AP modes exist:

- REAP (Remote Edge Access Point) mode
- Monitor mode
- Rogue Detector (RD) mode
- Sniffer mode
- Bridge mode

After a wireless client such as a PC associates with its AP, the AP allows the client to communicate only with the authentication server until the client successfully logs in and is authenticated.

The WLC uses the Extensible Authentication Protocol (EAP) to communicate with the authentication server. The Cisco Secure Access Control Server (ACS) could, for example, act as the authentication server. Supported EAP types include the following:

- EAP-Transport Layer Security (EAP-TLS)
- EAP-Protected EAP (EAP-PEAP)
- EAP Tunneled Transport Layer Security (EAP-TTLS)
- Cisco Lightweight Extensible Authentication Protocol (LEAP)
- Cisco EAP-Flexible Authentication via Secure Tunneling (EAP-FAST)

WLCs consist of the following components:

- Ports
- Interfaces
- WLANs

Wireless networks offer users mobility, where the users can physically move throughout a campus. As the users move, their wireless clients update their AP association to the most appropriate AP, based on location. With Layer 2 roaming, the WLCs with which the APs associate are in the same subnet. However, with Layer 3 roaming, the APs associate with WLCs on different subnets.

When designing a wireless network, one of the first steps in the design process is to conduct a Radio Frequency (RF) site survey, which will provide the network designer with a better understanding of an environment's RF characteristics (e.g., coverage areas and RF interference). Based on the results of the RF site survey, the network designer can strategically position the wireless infrastructure devices.

When designing a wireless network for an Enterprise Campus, a network designer should determine the following:

- The number of APs
- The placement of APs
- Power options for APs
- The number of WLCs
- The placement of WLCs

When designing networks to traverse the WAN, a primary design consideration is making the most efficient use of the relatively limited WAN bandwidth. Cisco and other vendors provide a variety of QoS mechanisms that can help in this regard:

- **Compression:** Making the packet smaller requires less bandwidth for transmission across a WAN. Therefore, compressing traffic is akin to adding WAN bandwidth.
- **Link aggregation:** Cisco routers support the bonding together of physical links into a virtual link.
- **Window size:** Network delay can be reduced by increasing the window size (i.e., sending more TCP segments before expecting an acknowledgment).
- **Queuing:** When a router is receiving traffic (e.g., from a LAN interface) faster than it can transmit that traffic (e.g., out of a WAN interface), the router delays the excess traffic in a buffer called a queue. To prevent bandwidth-intense applications from consuming too much of the limited WAN bandwidth, various queuing technologies can place different types of traffic into different queues, based on traffic priority. Then, different amounts of bandwidth can be given to the different queues.
- **Traffic shaping and policing:** To prevent some types of traffic (e.g., music downloads from the Internet) from consuming too much WAN bandwidth, a traffic conditioner called policing can be used to set a "speed limit" on those specific traffic types and drop any traffic exceeding that limit. Similarly, to prevent a WAN link from becoming oversubscribed (e.g., oversubscribing a remote office's 128 kbps link when receiving traffic from the headquarters that is transmitting at a speed of 768 kbps), another traffic conditioner called shaping can be used to prevent traffic from exceeding a specified bandwidth. With shaping, excessive traffic is delayed and transmitted when bandwidth becomes available, instead of being dropped as happens with policing. Unlike shaping, policing mechanisms can also re-mark traffic, giving lower-priority QoS markings to traffic exceeding a bandwidth limit.

The most important network management mechanisms available in Cisco IOS are as follows:

- Simple Network Management Protocol (SNMP)
- Remote Monitoring (RMON)
- NetFlow
- Cisco Discovery Protocol (CDP)
- Network-Based Application Recognition (NBAR)
- IP Service Level Agreement (IP SLA)

END OF CHAPTER QUIZ

1. Which of the following terms defines the process of combining the Distribution Layer with the Core Layer?
   a. Extended distribution
   b. OSI model
   c. Redundant Core Layer
   d. Collapsed Core Layer
   e. Access Layer

2. Which of the following are advantages of implementing a dedicated network Core Layer (choose all that apply)?
   a. Limited scalability
   b. Less physical cabling
   c. Easier data and voice integration
   d. No convergence possibility
   e. Less complex routing environment
   f. More network devices to manage

3. Cisco NSF with SSO technology is not usually implemented in Cisco Catalyst 6500 switches.
   a. True
   b. False

4. Which of the following Cisco IOS features allows minimizing unplanned downtime by allowing image upgrading, without the need for device reloading?
   a. Cisco IOS software modularity
   b. Cisco NetFlow
   c. Cisco collapsed Core Layer
   d. CEF polarization

5. Which of the following STP features allows securing the Root device by stopping external switches from becoming Roots?
   a. PortFast
   b. UplinkFast
   c. Loop Guard
   d. BPDU Guard
   e. Root Guard

6. Which of the following STP features forces a port to shut down when receiving a BPDU?
    a. PortFast
    b. UplinkFast
    c. Loop Guard
    d. BPDU Guard
    e. Root Guard

7. Which of the following is NOT recommended when using trunking?
    a. Setting the native VLAN to an unused VLAN
    b. Using ISL instead of 802.1Q as the encapsulation technique
    c. Hard coding all of the access ports
    d. Using VTP "transparent" mode

8. Which EtherChannel technologies are supported on Cisco devices (choose two)?
    a. PagP
    b. LLDP
    c. LACP
    d. STP

9. Which of the following techniques aims to avoid the negative effect of not utilizing some of the redundant links in a network topology?
    a. LACP
    b. Trunking
    c. STP
    d. CEF polarization

10. Which of the following is an IETF-defined First Hop Redundancy Protocol?
    a. HSRP
    b. VRRP
    c. GLBP

11. Which of the following FHRPs offers load balancing capabilities?
    a. HSRP
    b. VRRP
    c. GLBP

12. Which of the following terms defines the process of allowing a primary HSRP to maintain its primary role, even if it goes down and back up again?

    a. Preemption

    b. IP SLA

    c. Prevention

    d. CEF polarization

13. VRF technology allows an interface to have multiple routing tables associated with it.

    a. True

    b. False

14. In which spectrum does the 802.11g standard operate?

    a. 1 GHz

    b. 2 GHz

    c. 2.4 GHz

    d. 3.6 GHz

    e. 5 GHz

15. Which of the following authentication mechanisms provides the strongest level of security?

    a. WEP

    b. WPA

    c. WPA2

    d. Extended WPA

16. Which of the following are Extensible Authentication Protocol types (choose all that apply)?

    a. EAP-TLS

    b. LEAP

    c. EAP-FAST

    d. DEAP

    e. EAP-DDS

    f. PEAP

17. Which Cisco technology can be used to test response times and other parameters between two devices by generating synthetic traffic?

    a. IP SLA

    b. CDP

    c. OSPF

    d. LACP

18. Which queuing technique does the interface hardware queue (TX Ring) use?

    a. FIFO

    b. PQ

    c. CQ

    d. CBWFQ

19. Which of the following queuing mechanisms can cause non-VoIP packet starvation?

    a. WFQ

    b. LLQ

    c. PQ

    d. CQ

20. The LLQ congestion management technique does not work well with VoIP traffic.

    a. True

    b. False

CHAPTER 3

Designing Advanced IP Addressing

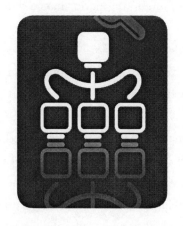

This chapter covers the following topics:

- Summarizable and structured addressing designs
- IPv6 for Enterprise Campus design considerations

When designing IP addressing at a professional level, several issues must be taken into consideration. This chapter will cover generic IP addressing designs, including subnets and summarizable blocks design recommendations, address planning, and advanced addressing concepts, in addition to IPv6 design considerations, which will be covered in the last section of the chapter.

IMPORTANCE OF IP ADDRESSING

One of the major concerns in the network design phase is ensuring that the IP addressing scheme is properly designed. This aspect should be carefully planned and an implementation strategy should exist for the structural, hierarchical, and contiguous allocation of IP address blocks. A solid addressing scheme should be hierarchical, structural, and modular.

These features will add value to the continually improving concept of the Enterprise Campus design. This is also important in scaling any of the dynamic routing protocols. A solid IP addressing scheme helps routing protocols function in an optimal manner, using RIPv2, EIGRP, OSPF, or BGP. Facilitating summarization and the ability to summarize addresses provides several advantages for the network:

- Shorter Access Control Lists (ACLs)
- Reduces the overhead on routers (the performance difference is noticeable, especially on older routers)
- Faster convergence of routing protocols
- Addresses can be summarized to help isolate trouble domains
- Overall improvement of network stability

Address summarization is also important when there is a need to distribute addresses from one routing domain into another, as it impacts both the configuration effort and the overhead in the routing processing. In addition, having a solid IP addressing scheme not only makes ACLs easier to implement and more efficient for security, policy, and QoS purposes, but also it facilitates advanced routing policies and techniques (such as zone-based policy firewalls), where modular components and object groupings that are based on the defined IP addressing schemes can be created.

Solid IP address planning supports several features in an organization:

- Route summarization
- A more scalable network
- A more stable network
- Faster convergence

SUBNET DESIGN RECOMMENDATIONS

The importance of IP addressing is reflected in the new requirements that demand greater consideration of IP addressing, as the following examples illustrate:

- The transition to VoIP Telephony and the additional subnet ranges required to support voice services. Data and voice VLANs are usually segregated, and in some scenarios, twice as many subnets may be needed when implementing Telephony in the network.

- Layer 3 switching at the edge, replacing the Layer 2 switching with multi-layer switches. This involves more subnets needed at the Enterprise Edge, so the number of smaller subnets will increase. There should be as little re-addressing as necessary, and making efficient use of the address space should be a priority. Sometimes, Layer 3 switching moved to the edge will involve a redesign of the IP addressing hierarchy.

- The company's needs are changing and sometimes servers will be isolated by functions or roles (also called segmentation). For example, the accounting server, the development subnets, and the call-center subnets can be separated from an addressing standpoint. Identifying the subnets and ACLs based on corporate requirements can also add complexity to the environment.

- Many organizations use technologies like Network Admission Control (NAC), Cisco 802.1x (IBNS), or Microsoft NAP. These types of deployments will be dynamically assigning VLANs based on the user login or port-based authentication. In this situation, an ACL can actually manage connectivity to different servers and network resources based on the source subnet (which is based on the user role). Using NAC over a wired or wireless network will add more complexity to the IP addressing scheme.

- Many network topologies involve having separated VLANs (i.e., data, voice, and wireless). Using 802.1x may also involve a guest VLAN or a restricted VLAN, and authorization policies can be assigned based on VLAN membership from an Authentication, Authorization, and Accounting (AAA) server.

- Using role-based security techniques might require different sets of VPN clients, such as administrators, customers, vendors, guests, or extranets, so different groups can be implemented for different VPN client pools. This role-based access can be managed through a group password technique for each Cisco VPN client; every group can be assigned a VPN endpoint address from a different pool of addresses. If the pools are subnets of a summarizable block, then routing traffic back to the client can also be accomplished in a simplified fashion.

- Network designers should also consider that Network Address Translation (NAT) and Port Address Translation (PAT) can be applied on customer edge routers (often on the PIX firewall or on the ASA devices). NAT and PAT should not be used internally on the LAN or within the Enterprise Network to simplify the troubleshooting process. NAT can be used in a data center to support the Out-of-Band (OOB) management of the VLAN (i.e., on devices that cannot route or cannot find a default gateway for the OOB management of the VLAN).

SUMMARIZATION

After planning the IPv4 addressing scheme and determining the number and types of necessary addresses, a hierarchical design might be necessary. This design is useful when finding a scalable solution for a large organization and this involves address summarization. Summarization reduces the number of routes in the routing table and involves taking a series of network prefixes and representing them as a single summary address. It also involves reducing the CPU load and the memory utilization on network devices. In addition, this technique reduces processing overhead because routers advertise a single prefix instead of many smaller ones.

A summarizable address is one that contains blocks with sequential numbers in one of the octets. The sequential patterns must fit a binary bit pattern, with X numbers in a row, where X is a power of 2. The first number in this sequence must be a multiple of X. For example, 128 numbers in a row could be summarized with multiples starting at 0 or 128. If there are 64 numbers in a row (2^6), these will be represented in multiples of 64, such as 0, 64, 128, or 192, and 32 numbers in a row can be summarized with the multiples 0, 32, 64, and so on. This process can be easily accomplished using software subnet calculators.

Another planning aspect of summarizable blocks involves medium or large blocks of server farms or data centers. Servers can be grouped based on their functions and on their level of mission criticality, and they can all be in different subnets. In addition, with servers that are attached to different Access Layer switches, it is easier to assign subnets that will provide a perfect pattern for wildcarding in the ACLs. Simple wildcard rules and efficient ACLs are desired, as complex ACLs are very difficult to deal with, especially for new engineers who must take over an existing project.

When implementing the hierarchical addressing scheme, it is important to have a good understanding of the math behind it and how route summarization works. Below is an example of combining a group of Class C addresses into an aggregate address. Summarization is a way to represent several networks in a single summarized route. In a real-world scenario, a subnet calculator can be used to automatically generate the most appropriate aggregate route from a group of addresses.

In this example, the Enterprise Campus backbone (Core Layer) submodule is connected to several other buildings. In a single building, there are several networks in use:

- A network for the server farm
- A network for the management area
- A few networks for the Access Layer submodule (that serve several departments)

The goal is to take all of these networks and aggregate them into one single address that can be stored at the edge distribution submodule or at the Core Layer of the network. The first thing to understand when implementing a hierarchical addressing structure is the use of continuous blocks of IP addresses. In this example, the addresses 192.100.168.0 through 192.100.175.0 are used:

192.100.168.0	11000000.01100100.10101	000.	00000000
192.100.169.0	11000000.01100100.10101	001.	00000000
192.100.170.0	11000000.01100100.10101	010.	00000000
192.100.171.0	11000000.01100100.10101	011.	00000000
192.100.172.0	11000000.01100100.10101	100.	00000000
192.100.173.0	11000000.01100100.10101	101.	00000000
192.100.174.0	11000000.01100100.10101	110.	00000000
192.100.175.0	11000000.01100100.10101	111.	00000000

In this scenario, summarization will be based on a location where all of the uppermost bits are identical. Looking at the first address above, the first 8 bits equal the decimal 192, the next 8 bits equal the decimal 100, and the last 8 bits are represented by 0. The only octet that changes is the third one; to be more specific, only the last 3 bits in that octet change when going through the address range.

The summarization process requires writing the third octet in binary format and then looking for the common bits on the left side. In the example above, all of the bits are identical up to the last three bits in the third octet. With 21 identical bits, all of the addresses will be summarized to 192.100.168.0/21.

After deciding on a hierarchical addressing design and understanding the math involved in this process, the next approach will be a modular and scalable design, which will involve deciding how to divide the organization (i.e., Enterprise Network modules, submodules, and remote locations) in terms of addressing. This includes deciding whether to apply a hierarchical address to each module/ submodule or to the entire Enterprise Network.

Another aspect to consider is the way summarization may affect the routing protocols used. Summarization usually affects routing because it reduces the size of the routing tables, the processor, and memory utilization, and it offers a much faster convergence of the routed network. The following are the most important advantages of using route aggregation:

- Lower device processing overhead
- Improved network stability
- Ease of future growth

Figure 3.1 below offers another example of a large organization using a campus with multiple buildings:

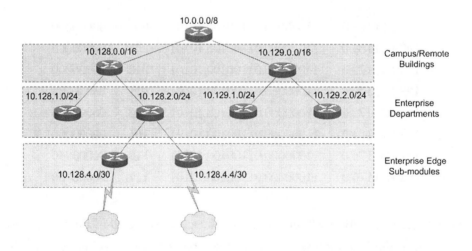

Figure 3.1 – Addressing for a Large Organization with Multiple Buildings

The internal private addressing will use the popular 10.0.0.0/8 range. Within the organization's domain, two separate building infrastructures (on the same campus or in remote buildings) will be aggregated using the 10.128.0.0/16 and 10.129.0.0/16 ranges.

NOTE: The 10.128.0.0 and 10.129.0.0 ranges are used instead of 10.1.0.0 or another lower second octet because many organizations already use those lower octet ranges, and there would be problems if the company decided to buy another company that uses one of those ranges. This minimizes the changes in overlap when merging other infrastructures with the network.

Going deeper within each building, the addressing scheme can be broken down within different departments, using the 10.128.1.0, 10.128.2.0 or the 10.129.1.0, 10.128.2.0 networks with a 24-bit mask. Because of the scalable design, another tier could be included above the departmental addresses that would be within the 10.129.0.0/21 range, for example. Moving beyond that point leads to the Enterprise Edge module and its various submodules (e.g., e-commerce, Internet connectivity, etc.) that can have point-to-point connections to different ISPs. Variable Length Subnet Masking (VLSM) can be used to break down the addressing scheme further.

To summarize, from a network designer standpoint, it is very important to tie the addressing scheme to the modular Enterprise Network design. The advantages of using route summarization and aggregation are numerous but the most important ones are as follows:

- Isolates changes to the topology to a particular module
- Isolates routing updates to a particular module
- Fewer updates need to be sent up the hierarchy (preventing all of the updates from going through the entire network infrastructure)
- Lower overall recalculation of the entire network when links fail (e.g., a change in a routing table does not converge to the entire network); for example, route flapping in a particular department is constrained within the specific department and does not have a cascading effect on other modules (considering the example above)
- Narrow scope of route advertisement propagation
- Summarized module is easier to troubleshoot

NOTE: The ultimate route summary is the default route, which summarizes everything. This can be created automatically using routing protocols or manually using the "ip route 0.0.0.0 0.0.0.0 <interface>" command.

Routing Protocols and Summarization

Different routing protocols handle summarization in different manners. Routing Information Protocol (RIP) version 2 (RIPv2) has classful origins (it summarizes by default), although it can act in a classless manner because it sends subnet mask information in the routing updates.

Because of its classful origins, RIPv2 performs automatic summarization on classful boundaries, so any time RIPv2 is advertising a network across a different major network boundary, it summarizes to the classful mask without asking for permission. This can lead to big problems in the routing infrastructure of discontiguous networks. RIPv2's automatic summarization behavior should be disabled in many situations to gain full control of the network routing operations.

In addition to the automatic summarization feature, RIPv2 allows for manual route summarization to be performed at the interface level. The recommendation is to disable automatic summarization and configure manual summarization where necessary. RIPv2 does not allow for summarization below the classful address. The next example involves the following prefixes:

210.22.10.0/24
210.22.9.0/24
210.22.8.0/24

RIPv2 will not allow the summarization of addresses above a /22 address because these are Class C addresses, and this would involve trying to summarize beneath this class. This is a limitation due to the classful origin of RIP.

EIGRP functions similar to RIPv2 regarding summarization, as EIGRP also has classful origins because it is an enhanced version of the Interior Gateway Routing Protocol (IGRP). EIGRP automatically summarizes on classful boundaries and, just like with RIPv2, this feature can be disabled and manual summarization can be configured on specific interfaces. The biggest issue with this behavior is that there might be discontiguous networks and this could cause problems with any of the automatic summarization mechanisms described.

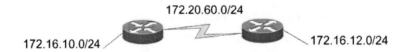

172.20.60.0/24

172.16.10.0/24   172.16.12.0/24

Figure 3.2 – Discontiguous Network Issue

An example of a discontiguous network issue is illustrated in Figure 3.2 above. The 172.16.10.0/24 subnet is on the left side and the 172.16.12.0/24 subnet is on the right side. These networks are divided by a different major network in the middle (172.20.60.0/24), which causes a problem. Applying EIGRP in this scenario, automatic summarization will be enabled by default, with summarization toward the middle of the topology (172.16.0.0) from both sides, and this will cause great confusion to that device. As a result of this confusion, the device might send one packet to the left side and one packet to the right side, so there will be packets going in the wrong direction to get to a particular destination. To solve this issue, the automatic summarization feature should be disabled in discontiguous networks. Another possible fix to this problem is designing the addressing infrastructure better so that no discontiguous subnets are present.

NOTE: RIPv1 and IGRP cannot be replaced with modern routing protocols, but discontiguous network issues can be solved using static routes.

OSPF does not have an automatic summarization feature but two different forms of summarization can be designed:

- Summarization between the internal areas
- Summarization from another separate domain

Two separate commands are used to handle these different summarization types. Summarizing from one area to another involves a Type 3 Link-State Advertisement (LSA). Summarizing from another domain involves two types of LSAs in the summarization process: a Type 4 LSA, which advertises the existence of the summarizing device (e.g. the OSPF Autonomous System Border Router – ASBR), and the actual summary of information, carried in a Type 5 LSA.

Border Gateway Protocol (BGP) uses a single type of summarization called aggregation, and this is accomplished during the routing process. BGP is used to summarize automatically, just like RIPv2 and EIGRP, but this behavior has been automatically disabled by the 12.2(8)T IOS code.

VARIABLE LENGTH SUBNET MASKING AND STRUCTURED ADDRESSING

A structured addressing plan involves the concept of Variable Length Subnet Masking (VLSM), a technology that all of the modern routing protocols can easily handle. VLSM provides efficiency, as it disseminates an addressing plan that does not waste address space (i.e., it assigns only the number of addresses needed for a certain subnetwork). VLSM also accommodates efficient summarization. The most important benefits of VLSM and summarization include the following:

- Less CPU utilization on network devices
- Less memory utilization on network devices
- Smaller convergence domains

172.16.1.0/24 ⎯⎯ Fa0/0 ⎯⎯ Fa0/1 ⎯⎯ 172.16.2.0/24

Figure 3.3 – VLSM Example (Part 1)

VLSM functions by taking unused subnets from the address space used and further subnets them. Figure 3.3 above starts with the major network of 172.16.0.0/16 (not shown in the example), which is initially subnetted using a 24-bit mask, resulting in two large subnets on the two router interfaces (Fa0/0 and Fa0/1), 172.16.1.0/24 and 172.16.2.0/24, respectively. Two key formulas can be used when calculating the number of subnets and hosts using VLSM. An example of the subnet and host split in the address is shown below in Figure 3.4:

$$172.16.1.0/24$$

$$172.16.\text{ssssssss}.\text{hhhhhhhh}$$

subnet bits   host bits

Figure 3.4 – VLSM Subnet and Host Split

The formula for calculating the number of subnets is 2^s, where "s" is the number of borrowed subnet bits. In Figure 3.3 above, the network expanded from a /16 network to a /24 network by borrowing 8 bits. This means $2^8 = 256$ subnets can be created with this scheme.

The formula for calculating the number of hosts that can exist in a particular subnet is 2^h-2, where "h" is the number of host bits. Two hosts are subtracted from the 2^h formula because the all-zeros host portion of the address represents the major network itself and the all-ones host portion of the address represents the broadcast address for the specific segment, as illustrated below:

- Major networks (all zeros in the host portion): 172.16.1.0 and 172.16.2.0
- Broadcast networks (all ones in the host portion): 172.16.1.255 and 172.16.2.255

After summarizing the 172.16.0.0/16 address space into 172.16.1.0/24 and 172.16.2.0/24, further subnetting might be needed to accommodate smaller networks, which can be achieved by taking one of the next available subnets (after the subnetting process), for example, 172.16.3.0/24. This will create additional subnets such as those below:

- 172.16.3.32/27
- 172.16.3.64/27

The /27 subnets are suitable for smaller networks and can accommodate the number of machines in those areas. The number of hosts that can be accommodated is $2^5-2=30$.

172.16.1.0/24   172.16.3.100/30   172.16.3.32/27

172.16.2.0/24   172.16.3.64/27

Figure 3.5 – VLSM Example (Part 2)

A subnet might be needed for the point-to-point link that will connect two network areas, and this can be accomplished by further subnetting one of the available subnets in the /27 scheme, for example 172.16.3.96/27. This can be subnetted with a /30 to obtain 172.16.3.100/30, which offers just two host addresses: 172.16.3.101 and 172.16.3.102. This scheme perfectly suits the needs for the point-to-point connections (one address for each end of the link). By performing VLSM calculations, subnets that can accommodate just the right number of hosts in a particular area can be obtained.

PRIVATE VERSUS PUBLIC ADDRESSING

As a network designer, after determining the number of necessary IP addresses, the next big decision is to find out whether private, public, or a combination of private and public addresses will be used. Private internetwork addresses are defined in RFC 1918 and are used internally within the network. From a real-world standpoint, because of the limitation of the number of public IP addresses, NAT techniques are usually used to translate the private internal numbers to external public addresses. Internally, one of the following three ranges of addresses can be used:

- 10.0.0.0/8 (10.0.0.0 to 10.255.255.255), usually used in large organizations
- 172.16.0.0/12 (172.16.0.0 to 172.31.255.255), usually used in medium organizations
- 192.168.0.0/16 (192.168.0.0 to 192.168.255.255), usually used in small organizations

Any address that falls within the three private address ranges cannot be routed on the Internet. Service Provider Edge devices usually have policies and ACLs configured to ensure that any packet containing a private address that arrives at an inbound interface will be dropped.

All of the other addresses are public addresses that are allocated to ISPs or other point of presence nodes on the Internet. ISPs can then assign Class A, B, or C addresses to customers to use on devices that are exposed to the Internet, such as:

- Web servers
- DNS servers
- FTP servers
- Other servers that run public-accessible services

NOTE: Customers can also be assigned IP addresses by one of the following five Regional Internet Registries (RIRs) that are controlled by the Internet Assigned Numbers Authority (IANA):

- AfriNIC (for Africa)
- ARIN (for USA and Canada)
- APNIC (for Asia, Australia, and New Zealand)
- LACNIC (for Latin America)
- RIPE NCC (for Europe, Russia, the Middle East, and Central Asia)

When deciding to use private, public, or a combination of private and public addresses, one of the following four types of connections will be used:

- No Internet connectivity
- Only one public address (or a few) for users to access the Web
- Web access for users and public-accessible servers
- Every end-system has a public IP address

No Internet connectivity would imply that all of the connections between the locations are private links and the organization would not be connected to the Internet in any of its nodes. In this case, there is no need for any public IP addresses because the entire address scheme can be from the private address ranges.

Another situation would be the one in which there is Internet connectivity from all of the organization's locations but there are no servers to run public-accessible services (e.g., Web, FTP, or others). In this case, a public IP address is needed that will allow users to access the Web. NAT can be used to translate traffic from the internal network to the outside network, so the internal networks contain only private IP addresses and the external link can use just one public address.

The third scenario is one of the most common, especially when considering the growth of enterprise networking. This involves having user Internet connectivity (just like in the previous scenario) but also having public-accessible servers. Public IP addresses must be used to connect to the Internet and access specific servers (e.g., Web, FTP, DNS, and others). The internal network should use private IP addresses and NAT to translate them into public addresses.

The most highly unlikely scenario would be the one in which every end-system is publicly accessible from the global Internet. This is a dangerous situation because the entire network is exposed to Internet access and this implies high security risks. To mitigate these risks, strong firewall protection policies must be implemented in every location. In addition to the security issues, this scenario is also not very effective because many IP addresses are wasted and this is very expensive. All of these factors make this scenario one not to be used in modern networks.

The two most common solutions from the scenarios presented above are as follows:

- One or a few public addresses for users to access the Web
- A few public addresses that provide Web access for users and public-accessible servers

Both scenarios imply using private internal addresses and NAT to reach outside networks.

For a deeper analysis of these aspects, it is useful to focus on how they map to the Cisco Enterprise Architecture model and where private and public addresses should be used, which is illustrated in Figure 3.6 below:

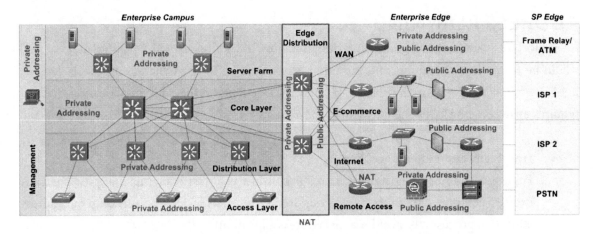

Figure 3.6 – Cisco Enterprise Architecture Model Addressing Scheme

First, in the figure above, assume that there is some kind of Internet presence in the organization that offers services either to internal users in the Access Layer submodule or to different public-accessible servers (e.g., Web, FTP, or others) in the Enterprise Edge module. Regardless of what modules receive Internet access, NAT is run in the edge distribution submodule to translate between the internal addressing structure used in the Enterprise Campus and the external public IP addressing structure. NAT mechanisms can also be used in the Enterprise Edge module.

Using the 10.0.0.0/8 range internally, both in the Enterprise Campus module and in the network management submodule, Enterprise Campus devices that use private IP addresses include all of its component submodules:

- Access Layer
- Distribution Layer
- Core Layer
- Server farm

The edge distribution submodule will use a combination of private and public IP addresses. The Enterprise Edge module will use a combination of private and public addresses, depending on each submodule. The remote access submodule can use a combination of private and public addresses but it will need to support some kind of NAT techniques. The WAN submodule can use either private addresses (when connecting to other remote sites) or public addresses (when connected to outside locations for a backup solution).

NOTE: When connecting to the outside world using public addresses, consider implementing efficient security features.

ADDRESS PLANNING

An important issue in the IP addressing design is how the addresses will be assigned. One way would be to use static assigning and the other way would be to use dynamic protocols such as the Dynamic Host Configuration Protocol (DHCP). Deciding on the address allocation method requires answering the following questions:

- **How many end-systems are there?**
  For a small number of hosts (less than 50), consider using statically/manually assigned addresses; however, if there are several hundred systems, use DHCP to speed up the address allocation process (i.e., avoid manual address allocation).

- **What does the security policy demand?**
  Some organizations demand the use of static IP addressing for every host or for every node to create a more secure environment. For example, an outsider cannot plug in a station to the network, automatically get an IP address, and have access to internal resources. The organization's security policy might demand static addressing, regardless of the network size.

- **What is the likelihood of renumbering?**
  This includes the possibility of acquisitions and mergers in the near future. If the likelihood of renumbering is high, DHCP should be used.

- **Are there any high availability demands?**
  If the organization has high availability demands, DHCP should be used in a redundant server architecture.

In addition, static addressing should always be used on certain modules in certain devices:

- Corporate servers
- Network management workstations
- Standalone servers in the Access Layer submodule
- Printers and other peripheral devices in the Access Layer submodule
- Public-accessible servers in the Enterprise Edge module
- Remote Access Layer submodule devices
- WAN submodule devices

ROLE-BASED ADDRESSING

From a Cisco standpoint, the best way to implement role-based addressing is to have it mapped to the corporate structure or to the roles of the servers or end-user stations. Using an example based on the 10.0.0.0/8 network, consider the first octet to be the major network number, the second octet to be the number assigned to the closet (i.e., the server room or wiring closets throughout the organization), the third octet to be the VLAN numbers, and the last octet to be the number of hosts. An address of 10.X.Y.Z would imply the following octet definitions:

- X = closet numbers
- Y = VLAN numbers
- Z = host numbers

This is an easy mechanism that can be used with Layer 3 closets. Role-based addressing avoids binary arithmetic, so if there are more than 256 closets, for example (more than can be identified in the second octet), some bits can be borrowed from the beginning of the third octet because there will not be 256 VLANs for every switch. Thereafter, advanced binary arithmetic or bit splitting can be used to adapt the addressing structure to specific needs. Bit splitting can be used with routing protocols, as well as route summarization, to help number the necessary summarizable blocks. In this case, addresses will be split into a network part, an area part, a subnet part, and a host part.

Network designers might not always have the luxury of using the summarizable blocks around simple octet boundaries and sometimes this is not even necessary, especially when some bit splitting techniques would better accommodate the organization and the role-based addressing scheme. This usually involves some binary math, such as the example below:

172.16.aaaassss.sshhhhhh

The first octet is 172 and the second octet is 16. The "a" bits in the third octet identify the area and the "s" bits identify the network subnet or VLAN. Six bits are reserved for the hosts in the forth octet. This offers 62 hosts per VLAN or subnet, or 2^{16}-2 (two host addresses will be reserved for the network address – all zeros in the last bits and the broadcast address and all ones in the last bits).

This logical scheme will result in the following address ranges, based on the network areas:

- Area 0: 172.16.0.0 to 172.16.15.255
- Area 1: 172.16.16.0 to 172.16.31.255
- Area 2: 172.16.32.0 to 172.16.47.255

Subnet calculations should be made to ensure that the right type of bit splitting is used to represent the subnet and VLANs. Remember that a good summarization technique is to take the last subnet in every area and divide it so that the /30 subnet can be used for any WAN or point-to-point links. This will maximize the address space so for each WAN link there will be only two addresses with a /30 or .252 subnet mask.

NOTE: Binary and subnet calculations can be also achieved using subnet calculator software that can be found on a variety of Internet sites.

Most organizations have their addressing schemes mapped out onto spreadsheets or included in different reports and stored as part of their documentation for the network topology. This should be done very systematically and hierarchically, regardless of the addressing scheme used. Always take into consideration the possible growth of the company through mergers or acquisitions.

NETWORK ADDRESS TRANSLATION APPLICATIONS

Although the goal with IPv6 is to avoid the need for NAT, NAT for IPv4 will still be used for a while. NAT is one of the mechanisms used in the transition from IPv4 to IPv6, so it will not disappear any time soon. In addition, it is a very functional tool for working with IPv4 addressing. NAT and PAT (or NAT Overload) are usually carried out on ASA devices, which have powerful tools to accomplish these tasks in many forms:

- Static NAT
- Dynamic NAT
- Identity NAT
- Policy NAT

A recommended best practice is to try to avoid using NAT on internal networks, except for situations in which NAT is required as a stop-gap measure during mergers or migrations. NAT should not be performed between the Access Layer and the Distribution Layer or between the Distribution Layer and the Core Layer. Following this recommendation will prevent address translation between OSPF areas, for example.

Organizations with a merger in progress usually use the same internal network addressing schemes and these can be managed with NAT overlapping techniques (also referred to as bidirectional NAT), which translates between the two organizations when they have an overlapping internal IP addressing space that uses RFC 1918 addressing.

If there are internal servers or servers in the DMZ that are reached using translated addresses, it is a good practice to isolate these servers into their own address space and VLAN, possibly using private VLANs. NAT is often used to support content load balancing servers, which usually must be isolated by implementing address translation.

NAT can also be used in the data center submodule to support a management VLAN that is Out-of-Band from production traffic. It should also be implemented on devices that cannot route or cannot define a gateway for the management VLAN. This results in smaller management VLANs, not a single large management VLAN that covers the entire data center. In addition, large companies or Internet entities can exchange their summary routes, and then they can translate with NAT blocks into the network. This will offer faster convergence but the downside is an increased troubleshooting process because of the use of NAT or PAT.

PAT is harder to troubleshoot because one or a few IP addresses are used to represent hundreds or even thousands of internal hosts, all using TCP and UDP ports to create logical sockets. This increases the complexity of the troubleshooting process because it is difficult to know what IP address is assigned to a particular host. Each host uses a shared IP address and a port number. If the organization is connected to several different partners or vendors, each partner can be represented by a different NAT block, which can be translated in the organization.

DESIGNING IPV6 ADDRESSING

CCDP certification requires a solid understanding of the IP version 6 specifications, addressing, and some of the design issues. The IPv6 protocol is based on RFC 2460. From a network designer standpoint, the most important features offered by IPv6 include the following:

- A 128-bit address space
- Supports hierarchical addressing and auto-configuration
- Every host can have a globally unique IPv6 address; no need for NAT
- Hosts can have multiple addresses
- Efficient fixed header size for IPv6 packets
- Enhanced security and privacy headers
- Improved multicasting and QoS
- Dedicated IPv6 routing protocols: RIPng, OSPFv3, Integrated IS-ISv6, BGP4+
- Every major vendor supports IPv6

IPv6 is a mechanism that was created to overcome the limitations of the current IPv4 standard. One of the major shortcomings of IPv4 is that it uses a 32-bit address space. Because of the classful system and the growth of the Internet, the 32-bit address space has proven to be insufficient. The key factors that led to the evolution of IPv6 were large institutions, Enterprise Networks, and ISPs that demanded a larger pool of IP addresses for different applications and services.

Address Representation

IPv4 uses a 32-bit address space, so it offers around 4.2 billion possible addresses, including the multicast, experimental, and private ones. The IPv6 address space is 128 bits, so it offers around 3.4×10^{38} possible addressable nodes. The address space is so large that there are about 5×10^{28} addresses per person in the world. IPv6 also gives every user multiple global addresses that can be used for a wide variety of devices (e.g., PDAs, cell phones, and IP-enabled devices). IPv6 addresses will last a very long time. An IPv6 packet contains the following fields, as depicted in Figure 3.7 below:

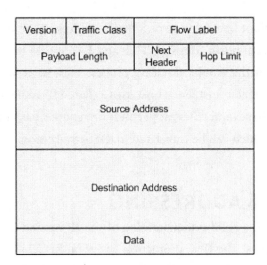

Figure 3.7 - IPv6 Packet Fields

Field	Size	Description
Version	4 bits	Identifies the IP version (which is 6 in this case).
Traffic Class	8 bits	Similar to the ToS byte in the IPv4 header; QoS marking functionality.
Flow Label	20 bits	Used to identify and classify packet flows.
Payload Length	16 bits	The size of the packet payload.
Next Header	8 bits	Similar to the Protocol field in the IPv4 header; defines the type of traffic contained within the payload and which header to expect.
Hop Limit	8 bits	Similar to the TTL field in the IPv4 header; prevents endless loops.
Source IP Address	128 bits	Source logical IPv6 address.
Destination IP Address	128 bits	Destination logical IPv6 address.
Data	Variable	Transport Layer data.

Knowing what is in the IPv4 header is important from a network designer standpoint because many of the fields in the header are used for features such as QoS or protocol type. The IPv6 header offers additional functionality, even though some fields from the IPv4 header have been eliminated, such as the Fragment Offset field and the Flags field.

The Version field, as in the IPv4 header, offers information about the IP protocol version. The Traffic Class field is used to tag the packet with the class of traffic it uses in its DiffServ mechanisms. IPv6 also adds a Flow Label field, which can be used for QoS mechanisms, by tagging a flow. This can be used for multilayer switching techniques and will offer faster packet switching on the network devices. The Payload Length field is the same as the Total Length field in IPv4.

The Next Header is an important IPv6 field. The value of this field determines the type of information that follows the basic IPv6 header. It can be a Transport Layer packet like TCP or UDP or it can designate an extension header. The Next Header field is the equivalent of the Protocol field in IPv4. The next field is Hop Limit, which designates the maximum number of hops an IP packet can traverse. Each hop/router decrements this field by one, so this is similar to the TTL field in IPv4. There is no Checksum field in the IPv6 header, so the router can decrement the Hop Limit field without recalculating the checksum. Finally, there is the 128-bit source address and the 128-bit destination address.

In addition to these fields there are a number of extension headers. The extension headers and the data portion of the packet will follow the eight fields covered thus far. The total length of an extension header's chain can be variable because the number of extension headers is not fixed. There are different types of extension headers, such as the following:

- Routing header
- Fragmentation header
- Authentication header
- IPsec ESP header
- Hop-by-Hop Options header

The IPv4 address is comprised of a string of 32 bits represented in four octets using a dotted decimal format. IPv6, on the other hand, is comprised of 128 bits represented in eight groups of 16 bits using a hexadecimal format (i.e., 16 bits separated by colons), for example:

2001:43aa:0000:0000:11b4:0031:0000:c110.

Considering the complex format of IPv6 addresses, some rules were developed to shorten them:

- One or more successive 16-bit groups that consist of all zeros can be omitted and represented by two colons (::).
- If a 16-bit group begins with one or more zeros, the leading zeros can be omitted.

Considering the IPv6 example above, here are its shortened representations:

2001:43aa::11b4:0031:0000:c110
2001:43aa::11b4:0031:0:c110
2001:43aa::11b4:31:0:c110

NOTE: The double colon (::) notation can appear only one time in an IPv6 address.

In a mixed IPv4 and IPv6 environment, the IPv4 address can be embedded in the IPv6 address, specifically in the last 32 bits.

The prefix portion in IPv6 is the number of contiguous bits that represent the network host. For example, the address 2001:0000:0000:0AABC:0000:0000:0000:0000/60 can be represented as 2001:0:0:ABC::/60.

Several types of IPv6 addresses are required for various applications. When compared to IPv4 address types (i.e., unicast, multicast, and broadcast), IPv6 presents some differences: special multicast addresses are used instead of broadcast addressing, and a new address type was defined called anycast.

Address Type	Range	Description
Aggregatable Global Unicast	2000::/3	Public addresses, host-to-host communications; equivalent to IPv4 unicast.
Multicast	FF00::/8	One-to-many and many-to-many communications; equivalent to IPv4 multicast.
Anycast	Same as Unicast	Interfaces from a group of devices can be assigned the same anycast address; the device closest to the source will respond; application-based, including load balancing, optimization traffic for a particular service, and redundancy.
Link-local Unicast	FE80::/10	Connected-link communications; assigned to all device interfaces and used only for local link traffic.
Solicited-node Multicast	FF02::1:FF00:0/104	Neighbor solicitation.

Anycast addresses are generally assigned to servers located in different geographical locations. By connecting to the anycast address, users will reach the closest server. Anycast addresses are also called one-to-nearest addresses. The IPv6 multicast address is a one-to-many address that identifies a set of hosts that will receive the packet. This is similar to an IPv4 Class D multicast address. IPv6 multicast addresses also supersede the broadcast function of IPv4 broadcast. IPv6 broadcast functionality is an all-nodes multicast behavior. The following are well-known multicast addresses that should be remembered:

- FF01::1 = all-nodes multicast address (broadcast)
- FF02::2 = all-routers multicast address (used for link-local address mechanisms)

Another important multicast address is the solicited node multicast address, which is created automatically and placed on the interface. This is used by the IPv6 Neighbor Discovery process to improve upon IPv4 ARP. A special IPv6 address is 0:0:0:0:0:0:0:1, which is the IPv6 loopback address, equivalent to the 127.0.0.1 IPv4 loopback address. This can also be represented as ::1/128.

The link-local addresses are significant only to individual nodes on a single link. Routers forward packets with a link-local source or destination address beyond the local link. Link-local addresses can be configured automatically or manually. Global unicast addresses are globally unique and routable and are defined in RFC 2374 and RFC 3587.

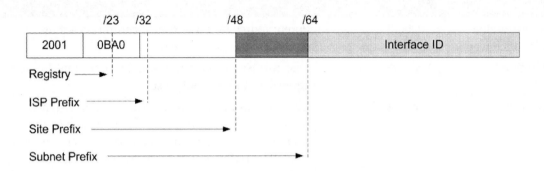

Figure 3.8 – IPv6 Global Unicast Address Format

Based on the IPv6 global unicast address format shown in Figure 3.8 above, the first 23 bits represent the registry, the first 32 bits represent the ISP prefix, the first 48 bits are the site prefix, and /64 represents the subnet prefix. The remaining bits are allocated to the interface ID.

The global unicast address and the anycast address share the same format. The unicast address space actually allocates the anycast address. To devices that are not configured for anycast, these addresses will appear as unicast addresses.

IPv6 global unicast addressing allows aggregation upward to the ISP. A single interface may be assigned multiple addresses of any type (i.e., unicast, anycast, and multicast). However, every IPv6-enabled interface must have a loopback address and a link-local address.

The IPv6 global unicast address is structured as presented above in Figure 3.8 to facilitate aggregation and reduce its number in the global routing tables, just like with IPv4. Global unicast addresses are defined by a global routing prefix, a subnet ID, and an interface ID. Typically, a global unicast address is made up of a 48-bit global routing prefix and a 16-bit subnet identifier.

IPv6 Mechanisms

As with IPv4, there are different mechanisms available for IPv6 and the most important of these includes the following:

- ICMPv6
- IPv6 Neighbor Discovery (ND)
- Name resolution
- Path Maximum Transmission Unit (MTU) Discovery
- DHCPv6
- IPv6 security
- IPv6 routing protocols

The Internet Control Message Protocol (ICMP) was modified to support IPv6 and is one of the most important mechanisms that support IPv6 functionality. ICMPv6 uses a Next Header number of 58. ICMP provides informational messages (e.g., Echo Request and Echo Reply) and error messages (e.g., Destination Unreachable, Packet Too Big, and Time Exceeded). IPv6 also uses ICMPv6 to determine important parameters, such as neighbor availability, Path MTU Discovery, destination addresses, or port reachability.

IPv6 uses a Neighbor Discovery protocol (RFC 2461), unlike IPv4, which uses the Address Resolution Protocol (ARP). IPv6 hosts use ND to implement "plug and play" functionality and to discover all other nodes on the same link. ND is also used in checking for duplicate addresses and finding the routers on a specific link. ND uses the ICMPv6 message structure in its operations and its type codes are 133 through 137:

- Router Solicitation
- Router Advertisement
- Neighbor Solicitation
- Neighbor Advertisement
- Redirect

Neighbor Discovery goes beyond the capabilities of ARP, as it performs many functions:

- Address Auto-Configuration (a host can find its full address without using DHCP)
- Duplicate Address Detection (DAD)
- Prefix Discovery (learns prefixes on local links)
- Link MTU Discovery
- Hop Count Discovery
- Next-Hop Determination
- Address Resolution
- Router Discovery (allows routers to find other local routers)
- Neighbor Reachability Detection
- Redirection
- Proxy Behavior
- Default Router Selection

Many of the features mentioned above have IPv4 equivalencies but some of them are unique to IPv6 and provide additional functionalities.

One of the important features made possible by the ND process is DAD, as defined in RFC 4862. This is accomplished through Neighbor Solicitation messages that are exchanged before the interface is allowed to use a global unicast address on the link, and this can determine whether the particular address is unique. The Target Address field in these specific packets is set to the IPv6 address for which duplication is being detected and the source address is set to unspecified (::).

The IPv6 stateless Auto-Configuration feature avoids using DHCP to maintain a mapping for the address assignment. This is a very low-overhead manner in which to disseminate addresses and it accommodates low-overhead re-addressing. In this process, the router sends a Router Advertisement message to advertise the prefix and its ability to act as a default gateway. The host receives this information and uses the EUI-64 format to generate the host portion of the address. After the host generates the address, it starts the DAD process to ensure that the address is unique on the network.

IPv4 performs Name Resolution by using A records in the DNS. RFC 3596 offers a new DNS record type to support the transition to IPv6 Name Resolution, which is AAAA (Quad A). The Quad A record will return an IPv6 address based on a given domain name.

IPv6 does not allow packet fragmentation through the network (except for the source of the packet), so the MTU of every link in an IPv6 implementation must be 1280 bytes or greater. The ICMPv6 Packet Too Big error message determines the path MTU because nodes along the path will send this message to the sending hosts if the packet is larger than the outgoing interface MTU.

DHCPv6 is an updated version of DHCP that offers dynamic address assignment for version 6 hosts. DHCPv6 is described in RD 3315 and provides the same functionality as DHCP but it offers more control, as it supports renumbering without numbers.

IPv6 also has some security mechanisms. Unlike IPv4, IPv6 natively supports IPsec (an open security framework) with two mechanisms: the Authentication Header (AH) and the Encapsulating Security Payload (ESP).

The support for IPsec in IPv6 is mandatory, unlike with IPv4. By making it mandatory in all the IPv6 nodes, secure communication can be created with any node in the network. An example of mandatory and leveraged IPsec in IPv6 is OSPF, which carries out its authentication using only IPsec. Another example of the IPsec IPv6 mechanism is the IPsec Site-to-Site Virtual Tunnel Interface, which allows easy creation of virtual tunnels between two IPv6 routers to very quickly form a site-to-site secured Virtual Private Network (VPN).

The following new routing protocols were developed for IPv6:

- RIPng (RIP new generation)
- Integrated Intermediate System-to-Intermediate System Protocol (IS-IS)
- EIGRP for IPv6
- OSPFv3
- BGP4 multiprotocol extensions for IPv6

Transitioning from IPv4 to IPv6

Because IPv6 almost always comes as an upgrade to the existing IPv4 infrastructure, IPv6 design and implementation considerations must include different transition mechanisms between these two protocol suites. The IPv4 to IPv6 transition can be very challenging, and during the transition period it is very likely that both protocols will coexist on the network.

The designers of the IPv6 protocol suite have suggested that IPv4 will not go away anytime soon, and it will strongly coexist with IPv6 in combined addressing schemes. The key to all IPv4 to IPv6 transition mechanisms is dual-stack functionality, which allows a device to operate both in IPv4 mode and in IPv6 mode.

One of the most important IPv4 to IPv6 transition mechanisms involves tunneling between dual-stack devices and this can be implemented in different flavors:

- **Static tunnels:**
  - Generic Routing Encapsulation (GRE) – default tunnel mode
  - IPv6IP (less overhead, no CLNS transport)

- **Automatic tunnels:**
  - 6to4 (embeds IPv4 address into IPv6 prefix to provide automatic tunnel endpoint determination); automatically generates tunnels based on the utilized addressing scheme
  - Intra-Site Automatic Tunnel Addressing Protocol (ISATAP) – automatic host-to-router and host-to-host tunneling

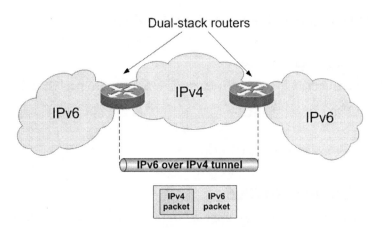

Figure 3.9 – IPv6 over IPv4 Tunneling

Analyzing Figure 3.9 above, the IPv4 island contains two dual-stack routers that run both the IPv4 and the IPv6 protocol stacks. These two routers will be able to support the transition mechanisms by tunneling IPv6 inside IPv4, and the two routers each connect to an IPv6 island. To carry IPv6 traffic between the two edge islands, a tunnel is created between the two routers that encapsulate IPv6 packets inside IPv4 packets. These packets are sent through the IPv4 cloud as regular IPv4 packets and they get de-encapsulated when they reach the other end. An IPv6 packet generated in the left-side network reaches a destination in the right-side network, so it is very easy to tunnel IPv6 inside IPv4 because of the dual-stack routers at the edge of the IPv4 infrastructure. Static tunneling methods are generally used when dealing with point-to-point links, while dynamic tunneling methods work best when using point-to-multipoint connections.

Network Address Translation Protocol Translation (NAT-PT) is another technology that can be utilized to carry out the transition to an IPv6 network. NAT-PT is often confused with NAT but it is a completely different technology. Simple NAT can also be used in IPv6 but this is very rare because IPv6 offers a very large address space and private addresses are not necessary. NAT-PT is another translation mechanism that will dynamically convert IPv4 addresses to IPv6 addresses, and vice-versa.

Another static tunneling technology is IPv6IP, which encapsulates IPv4 packets directly into IPv6. This is also called manual tunneling. Another type of static tunnel that can be created is a GRE tunnel that encapsulates the IPv6 packets within a GRE packet. GRE tunneling might be necessary when using special applications and services, like the IS-IS routing protocol for IPv6.

The dynamic tunnel types include the 6to4 tunnel, which is appropriate when a group of destinations needs to be connected dynamically utilizing IPv6. ISATAP is a unique type of host-to-router dynamic tunnel, unlike the previously mentioned tunneling techniques, which are router-to-router. ISATAP allows hosts to dynamically get to their IPv6 default gateway.

NOTE: ISATAP is a protocol that will soon fade away because almost all modern hosts and routers have native IPv6 support.

IPv6 Compared to IPv4

A network designer should have a very clear picture of the advantages IPv6 has over IPv4. The enhancements of IPv6 can be summarized as follows:

- IPv6 uses hexadecimal notation instead of dotted-decimal notation (IPv4).
- IPv6 has an expanded address space, from 32 bits to 128 bits.
- IPv6 addresses are globally unique due to the extended address space, eliminating the need for NAT.
- IPv6 has a fixed header length (40 bytes), allowing vendors to improve switching efficiency.
- IPv6 supports enhanced options (that offer new features) by placing extension headers between the IPv6 header and the Transport Layer header.
- IPv6 offers Address Auto-Configuration, providing for the dynamic assignment of IP addresses even without a DHCP server.
- IPv6 offers support for labeling traffic flows.
- IPv6 has security capabilities built-in, including authentication and privacy via IPsec
- IPv6 offers Path MTU Discovery before sending packets to a destination, eliminating the need for fragmentation.
- IPv6 supports site multi-homing.
- IPv6 uses the ND protocol instead of ARP.
- IPv6 uses AAAA DNS records instead of A records (IPv4).
- IPv6 uses site-local addressing instead of RFC 1918 (IPv4).
- IPv4 and IPv6 use different routing protocols.
- IPv6 provides for anycast addressing.

SUMMARY

Good IP addressing design uses summarizable blocks of addresses that enable route summarization and provide a number of benefits:

- Reduced router workload and routing traffic
- Increased network stability
- Faster convergence
- Significantly simplified troubleshooting

Creating and using summary routes depends on the use of summarizable blocks of addresses. Sequential numbers in an octet may denote a block of IP addresses as summarizable. For sequential numbers to be summarizable, the block must be X numbers in a row, where X is a power of 2, and the first number in the sequence must be a multiple of X. The created sequence will then end one before the next multiple of X in all cases.

Efficiently assigning IP addresses to the network is a critical design decision, impacting the scalability of the network and the routing protocols that can be used. IPv4 addressing has the following characteristics:

- IPv4 addresses are 32 bits in length.

- IPv4 addresses are divided into various classes (e.g., Class A networks accommodate more than 16 million unique IP addresses, Class B networks support more than 65 thousand IP addresses, and Class C networks permit 254 usable IP addresses). Originally, organizations applied for an entire network in one of these classes. Today, however, subnetting allows an ISP to give a customer just a portion of a network's address space, in an attempt to conserve the depleting pool of IP addresses. Conversely, ISPs can use supernetting (also known as Classless Inter-Domain Routing – CIDR) to aggregate the multiple network address spaces that they have. Aggregating multiple network address spaces into one address reduces the amount of route entries a router must maintain.

- Devices such as PCs can be assigned a static IP address, by hard coding the IP address in the device's configuration. Alternatively, devices can dynamically obtain an address from a DHCP server, for example.

- Because names are easier to remember than IP addresses are, most publicly accessible Web resources are reachable by their name. However, routers must determine the IP address with which the name is associated to route traffic to that destination. Therefore, a DNS server can perform the translation between domain names and their corresponding IP addresses.

- Some IP addresses are routable through the public Internet, whereas other IP addresses are considered private and are intended for use within an organization. Because these private IP addresses might need to communicate outside the LAN, NAT can translate a private IP address into a public IP address. In fact, multiple private IP addresses can be represented by a single public IP address using NAT. This type of NAT is called Port Address Translation (PAT) because the various communication flows are identified by the port numbers they use to communicate with outside resources.

When beginning to design IP addressing for a network, the following aspects must be determined:

- The number of network locations that need IP addressing
- The number of devices requiring an IP address at each location
- Customer-specific IP addressing requirements (e.g., static IP addressing versus dynamic IP addressing)
- The number of IP addresses that need to be contained in each subnet (e.g., a 48-port switch in a wiring closet might belong to a subnet that supports 64 IP addresses)

A major challenge with IPv4 is the limited number of available addresses. A newer version of IP, specifically IPv6, addresses this concern. An IPv6 address is 128 bits long, compared to the 32-bit length of an IPv4 address.

To make such a large address more readable, an IPv6 address uses hexadecimal numbers and the 128-bit address is divided into eight fields. Each field is separated by a colon, as opposed to the four fields in an IPv4 address, which are each separated by a period. To further reduce the complexity of the IPv6 address, leading 0s in a field are optional and if one or more consecutive fields contain all 0s, those fields can be represented by a double colon (::). A double colon can be used only once in an address; otherwise, it would be impossible to know how many 0s are present between each pair of colons.

Consider some of the benefits offered by IPv6:

- IPv6 dramatically increases the number of available addresses.
- Hosts can have multiple IPv6 addresses, allowing those hosts to multi-home to multiple ISPs.
- Other benefits include enhancements relating to QoS, security, mobility, and multicast technologies.

Unlike IPv4, IPv6 does not use broadcasts. Instead, IPv6 uses the following methods for sending traffic from a source to one or more destinations:

- **Unicast (one-to-one):** Unicast support in IPv6 allows a single source to send traffic to a single destination, just as unicast functions in IPv4.
- **Anycast (one-to-nearest):** A group of interfaces belonging to nodes with similar characteristics (e.g., interfaces in replicated FTP servers) can be assigned an anycast address. When a host wants to reach one of those nodes, the host can send traffic to the anycast address and the node belonging to the anycast group that is closest to the sender will respond.

- **Multicast (one-to-many):** Like IPv4, IPv6 supports multicast addressing, where multiple nodes can join a multicast group. The sender sends traffic to the multicast IP address and all members of the multicast group receive the traffic.

The migration of an IPv4 network to an IPv6 network can take years because of the expenditures of upgrading equipment. Therefore, during the transition, IPv4-speaking devices and IPv6-speaking devices need to coexist on the same network. Consider the following solutions for maintaining both IPv4 and IPv6 devices in the network:

- **Dual stack:** Some systems (including Cisco routers) can simultaneously run both IPv4 and IPv6, allowing communication to both IPv4 and IPv6 devices.
- **Tunneling:** To send an IPv6 packet across a network that uses only IPv4, the IPv6 packet can be encapsulated and tunneled through the IPv4 network.
- **Translation:** A device, such as a Cisco router, could sit between an IPv4 network and an IPv6 network and translate between the two addressing formats.

IPv6 allows the use of static routing and supports specific dynamic routing protocols that are variations of the IPv4 routing protocols modified or redesigned to support IPv6:

- RIPng
- OSPFv3
- EIGRPv6
- IS-IS
- BGP

END OF CHAPTER QUIZ

1. Which of the following is NOT an advantage of using address summarization?
   a. Reduced overhead on network devices
   b. Faster convergence of router protocols
   c. Decreased network stability
   d. Increased network scalability

2. What is the name of the most general summary route that summarizes everything using the "ip route 0.0.0.0 0.0.0.0 <interface>" command?
   a. Null route
   b. Aggregate route
   c. Binary route
   d. Default route
   e. Ultimate route

3. The process of address summarization has the benefit of reducing the size of the ACLs.
   a. True
   b. False

4. What does RFC 1918 describe?
   a. Address allocation for public IP addresses
   b. Address allocation for private IP addresses
   c. Multicast address allocation
   d. External IP address allocation

5. Which of the following summarization mechanisms are available in OSPF (choose all that apply)?
   a. Summarization between internal areas
   b. Summarization on every interface
   c. Summarization from another separate (external) domain
   d. Summarization only on Area 0 devices
   e. Summarization only on stub area devices

6. Which type of summarization is available in BGP?
   a. Automatic summarization only
   b. Summarization under the routing process
   c. Summarization on the interface level
   d. BGP does not offer summarization capabilities

7. RIPv2 does not allow manual route summarization.
   a. True
   b. False

8. What are the most important benefits of using VLSM (choose all that apply)?
   a. Smaller convergence domains
   b. Increased bandwidth utilization
   c. Lower memory utilization
   d. Increased security
   e. Lower CPU utilization

9. What does the subnet broadcast address represent in terms of the binary form of an address?
   a. The address that contains all zeros in the host portion
   b. The address that contains all zeros in the network portion
   c. The address that contains all ones in the network portion
   d. The address that contains all ones in the host portion

10. By using route summarization, changes in a topology are isolated to a particular module.
    a. True
    b. False

11. How large is the IPv6 address space?
    a. 32 bits
    b. 64 bits
    c. 128 bits
    d. 256 bits

12. With IPv6, every host in the world can have a unique address.
    a. True
    b. False

13. Which of the following are major differences between IPv4 and IPv6 (choose two)?
    a. IPv6 uses a larger address space
    b. IPv6 allows for hierarchical addressing
    c. IPv6 natively supports efficient security features
    d. IPv6 supports dynamic routing protocols

14. IPv6 implementations very often include address translation technologies.
    a. True
    b. False

15. Which of the following are advantages of using route aggregation (choose all that apply)?
    a. Lowered overhead
    b. Ease of future growth
    c. Increased bandwidth
    d. Improved network stability

16. IPv6 implementations allow hosts to have multiple addresses assigned.
    a. True
    b. False

17. Which IPv6 header field is similar to the ToS field used in IPv4?
    a. Traffic Group
    b. Traffic Class
    c. Class Map
    d. Traffic Type

18. The network management submodule generally uses private IP addressing.
    a. True
    b. False

19. How many times can the double colon (::) notation appear in an IPv6 address?
    a. One time
    b. Two times
    c. Three times
    d. An unlimited number of times

20. How can broadcast functionality be simulated in an IPv6 environment?
    a. IPv6 does not support any kind of broadcast behavior
    b. IPv6 supports broadcast functionality, just like IPv4 does
    c. Anycast
    d. All-nodes multicast

CHAPTER 4

Designing Advanced IP Multicast

This chapter covers the following topics:

- IPv4 multicast routing
- IPv4 multicast services and security designs

IP multicast is a complex technology and students should have a basic understanding of multicasting before reviewing the advanced topics presented in this chapter, which presents the Cisco multicast architecture and includes best practices for implementing PIM and securing IP multicast solutions.

DEFINING THE CONCEPT OF IP MULTICAST

Enterprise network architectures should support the transfer of all kinds of content and data (voice or video), but a traditional IP backbone is not efficient when sending the same data to many locations. This is because the specific data stream must be replicated to all of the different destinations and this involves utilizing many resources, especially bandwidth.

With the incredible advances in collaboration tools using the World Wide Web and the Internet, it is very likely that organizations will have to support multicast traffic. Multicasting implies taking a single data packet and sending it to a group of destinations simultaneously. This behavior can be considered a one-to-many transmission, as opposed to other types of communication:

- **Unicast:** One-to-one transmission.
- **Broadcast:** One-to-all transmission.
- **Anycast:** One-to-any transmission.

With the unicast one-to-one transmission process, network resources could suffer because a packet would be generated for each destination and this would result in a heavy network load and device CPU utilization, as illustrated in Figure 4.1 below:

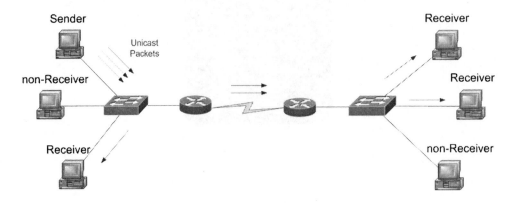

Figure 4.1 – Unicast One-to-One Transmission

Senders in unicast transmissions must know the addresses of all the receivers. When using multicast, traffic can be sent to the multicast address, so there is no need to know specific address information for the receivers. In addition, the router processing of the packets is dramatically reduced in multicast environments.

Broadcast transmissions could also create issues because devices that do not need the packets still receive them, as illustrated in Figure 4.2 below. When a device receives an unwanted packet, that specific device must stop running its processes and analyze the packet received, even if it was not destined to the device. This behavior affects device functionality, so sending unnecessary broadcast packets should be avoided, as they interrupt normal device functionality.

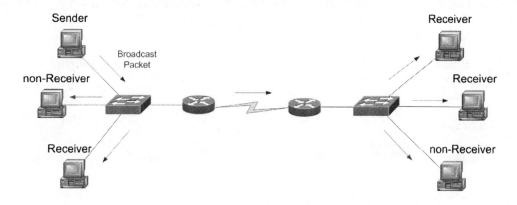

Figure 4.2 – Broadcast One-to-All Transmission

This behavior can be avoided by using multicast transmissions because devices that do not subscribe to a particular group do not receive packets in the specific stream.

The process of multicasting, as opposed to the process of broadcasting or unicasting, has the advantage of saving bandwidth because it sends a single stream of data to multiple nodes. The multicasting concept is exercised by most modern corporations worldwide to deliver data to groups in the following ways:

- Corporate meetings
- Video conferencing
- E-learning solutions
- Webcasting information
- Distributing applications
- Streaming news feeds
- Streaming stock quotes

The main goals of using multicasting are as follows:

- Reduce processing on network devices.
- Reduce bandwidth consumption.
- Reduce processing for the receiving host if it is not interested in the transmission.

Multicast generates a single feed for all the devices interested in receiving it and the source sends out the data, as illustrated in Figure 4.3 below. The routers along the multicast tree make the forwarding decisions. This behavior of radiating information away from a source is completely different from the behavior in unicast transmissions, where information is sent to a specific destination. Multicast behavior is actually called Reverse Path Forwarding (RPF), as packets are forwarded along a reverse path.

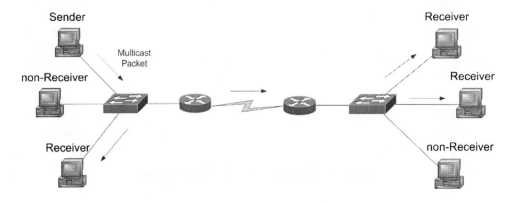

Figure 4.3 – Multicast One-to-Many Transmission

IP multicast does utilize UDP in its operations, as UDP has a connectionless behavior. This results in several disadvantages to using multicast technology:

- Best effort behavior
- Lack of an acknowledgement process
- Lack of a congestion avoidance process (such as the slow-start process in TCP)
- Possibility of duplicate packets existing that arrive at a particular destination (usually only during network reconvergence)
- Possibility of out-of-order packets (no resequencing in UDP applications)

These disadvantages can be easily managed using the multicast software that is running on the hosts. The actual multicast applications can sort out these unreliable communication issues that can occur when using the multicast approach.

IP MULTICAST FUNCTIONALITY

In multicasting, a source application sends multicast traffic to a group destination address. The hosts interested in receiving this traffic join the specific group address by signaling their upstream devices. The routers then build a tree from the senders to the receivers and portions of the network that do not have receivers do not receive this potentially bandwidth-intense traffic. Examples of multicast applications include:

- IPTV
- Videoconferencing applications
- Data center replication
- Stock tickers
- Routing protocols

NOTE: The first RIP version used broadcasting to send updates. RIPv2 and RIPng use multicasting to accomplish this process.

The major IPv4 multicast components include the following:

- **Group addressing:** Layer 3 addresses and the underlying Layer 2 multicast MAC addresses.
- **Multicast routing (control plane):** Internet Group Management Protocol (IGMP) and Protocol Independent Multicast (PIM).
- **Forwarding mechanisms (data plane):** Reverse Path Forwarding (RPF).

A critical concept in multicasting is the multicast group address, which is an address that is agreed upon between the sender and the receivers for particular multicast transmissions. The source sends traffic to this destination group address and the receiver listens for traffic that is destined for this group address. Traffic is always sent to a group but the group never sends traffic back to the source; however, there may be situations in which a multicast receiver in a group is a source for other groups.

IPv4 multicasting uses the Class D address space, meaning the 224.0.0.0/4 range (224.0.0.0 to 239.255.255.255). This address space is not fully available to multicast designers due to some address range reservations, which include:

- **Link-local addresses:** 224.0.0.0/24 (224.0.0.0 to 224.0.0.255); link-local addressing is very common with routing protocols. For example, OSPF utilizes 224.0.0.5 and 224.0.0.6 in its operation.
- **Source-specific multicast:** 232.0.0.0/8 (232.0.0.0 to 232.255.255.255).

- **Administratively scoped:** 239.0.0.0/8 (239.0.0.0 to 239.255.255.255). The administratively scoped address range can be used for multicast applications inside corporate boundaries.

The control plane is one of the most complex components of multicast. Multicast control plane is used to determine the following:

- Who is sending traffic and to what groups
- Who is receiving traffic and for what groups
- How traffic should be forwarded when it is received

The control plane is built with host-to-router and router-to-router communication protocols. Host-to-router communication is accomplished with the Internet Group Management Protocol (IGMP) and router-to-router communication is achieved with Protocol Independent Multicast (PIM).

IP multicast technology allows information to be sent over networks to a group of destinations in a very efficient way. The multicast data is sent to a multicast group and the users receive the information by joining the specific multicast group using IGMP, as shown in Figure 4.4 below:

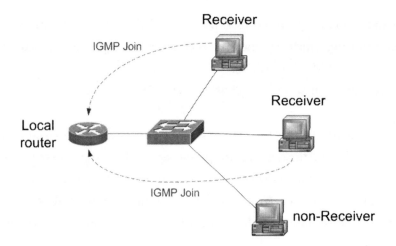

Figure 4.4 – Multicast IGMP

IGMP is used for receiver devices to signal routers on the LAN that they want traffic for a specific group. IGMP comes in the following versions:

- IGMPv1, defined in RFC 1112 (Host Extensions for IP Multicasting)
- IGMPv2, defined in RFC 2236 (Internet Group Management Protocol, Version 2)
- IGMPv3, defined in RFC 3337 (Internet Group Management Protocol, Version 3)

The most common IGMP version used in modern infrastructures is version 2, as IGMPv1 has major issues. One big issue with IGMPv1 was that it defined a Membership Query and a Membership Report, so host machines would express their interest in joining a group by sending a Host Membership Request to the local router. The Host Membership Query would be used to find out whether members of the group were still present on the local network. This caused "leave latency," which presented the problem in which all of the receivers would disappear (e.g., power off) and multicast traffic would unnecessarily still be sent to that segment. This timeout (idle timer for the group) would have to occur before the multicast traffic stopped flowing into that area. In other words, the router would send a query on a timed interval, and then it would eventually find out that every receiver had left.

This behavior was very inefficient and could be improved by having the devices send a Leave message to signal that they wanted to leave the specific multicast group. This was the major enhancement that generated the development of IGMPv2, which is backward compatible with IGMPv1. IGMPv2's major enhancements include the following:

- **Querier election:** Deals with the situation in which there are multiple routers on a segment.
- **Tunable timers:** They can speed up query response timeouts.
- **Group-specific queries:** Queries are sent to the group address instead of all multicast hosts.
- **Explicit leave:** Speeds up convergence if no other hosts are joined to that group.

IGMPv3 is used to support Source Specific Multicasting (SSM). IGMPv3 allows a device to request a particular multicast feed from a particular source or sources.

In most networks, the hosts are connected to Layer 2 or multilayer switches that are connected to upstream routers. IGMP is a protocol that operates at Layer 3, so the Layer 2 switches are not aware of the hosts that want to join the multicast groups. By default, Layer 2 switches flood the received multicast frames to all of the ports in the VLAN, even if only one device on one port needs the specific information. This issue is solved by using specific multicast protocols available for switched environments, namely Cisco Group Management Protocol (CGMP) and IGMP snooping. These protocols will be presented later in this chapter.

PIM is used by multicast-enabled routers to forward incoming multicast streams to a particular switch port. PIM uses the typical routing tables that are populated by regular unicast routing protocols (like EIGRP and OSPF) and exchanges multicast messages between PIM routers, as illustrated in Figure 4.5 below:

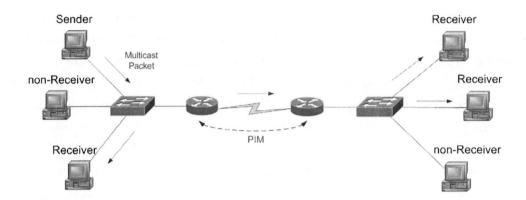

Figure 4.5 – Protocol Independent Multicast

PIM operates in multiple modes:

- PIM Sparse Mode (PIM-SM)
- PIM Dense Mode (PIM-DM)
- Bidirectional PIM
- PIM Source-Specific Multicast (PIM-SSM)

NOTE: PIM-DM is not used very often in large modern networks.

Other advanced multicast protocols are used mainly in the following inter-domain scenarios:

- **Multiprotocol BGP (MBGP):** Used for multicast routing between domains.
- **Multicast Source Discovery Protocol (MSDP):** Used with PIM-SM for multicast source discovery.
- **Multicast VPN (MVPN):** Used for secure connectivity.

Understanding whether the organization will use multicast traffic and the way this will be accomplished is an important issue when designing Enterprise Campus switching. Multicast deployments involve three components:

- The multicast application (like WebEx)
- The network infrastructure
- Multicast client devices

PROTOCOL INDEPENDENT MULTICAST DEPLOYMENT METHODS

IGMP helps the router know who wants to receive specific multicast traffic, but that router needs to communicate this information with the rest of the network. In other words, it needs to tell the rest of the network how to deliver traffic for that group. This process is accomplished using multicast routing protocols and one that is used in modern networks is PIM. Some legacy multicast protocols include:

- **Multicast OSPF (MOSPF):** Not supported on Cisco equipment.
- **Distance Vector Multicast Routing Protocol (DVMRP):** Supported on Cisco equipment, but not commonly used.

From a design standpoint, a network designer must understand three major PIM deployment methods that are used in modern networks: PIM-SM, PIM-SSM, and Bidirectional PIM. PIM is a router-to-router control protocol that builds a loop-free tree from the sender to the receivers. It is called "protocol independent" because it relies on the underlying unicast routing protocol used and it does not care what that routing protocol is. PIM will rely on whatever IGMP is used (e.g., RIP, EIGRP, OSPF, IS-IS, etc.) and will base its operation on the information received from the IGMP.

PIM comes in two versions (PIMv1 and PIMv2) and it comes in two important modes, Dense Mode and Sparse Mode. Dense Mode, which is now becoming a legacy mode, uses an implicit join approach and sends the multicast traffic everywhere, unless a specific host says it does not want it. This is also known as "flood and prune" behavior. PIM-DM is suitable for multicast environments with a dense distribution of receivers.

PIM-SM is also known as Any Source Multicast (ASM) and is described in RFC 4601. It uses a combination of Shared Trees, Source-based Trees, and Rendezvous Points (RPs) and is used by the majority of modern multicast deployments.

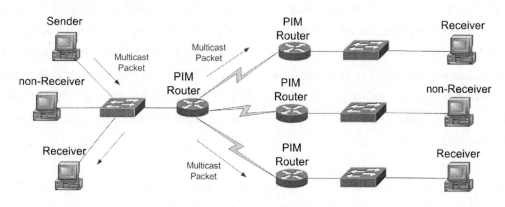

Figure 4.6 – PIM Sparse Mode

As shown in Figure 4.6 above, Sparse Mode utilizes an explicit join-type behavior, so the receiver does not get the multicast traffic unless it asks for it. This can be considered a "pull" mechanism, as opposed to the "push" mechanisms used in PIM-DM. The "pull" mechanism allows PIM-SM to forward multicast traffic only to the network segments with active receivers that have actually requested the data. PIM-SM distributes the data about active sources by forwarding data packets on Shared Trees. PIM-SM utilizes the concept of an RP to process the Join requests. Sparse Mode turned out to be the optimal solution for environments with both dense and sparse receiver distribution.

The control plane helps build the multicast tree from the senders to the receivers, and traffic can then start to flow over the multicast data plane. When routers receive multicast packets, they perform two actions:

- In the CEF architecture, they do an RPF check. This is a loop prevention mechanism.
- They check their multicast routing table. Similar to the unicast routing table, this will tell the router which interfaces it should use to forward packets.

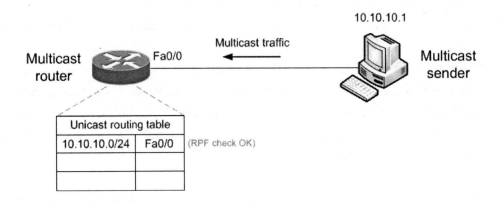

Figure 4.7 – Reverse Path Forwarding Verification

The RPF check uses the underlying IGMP information (routing table). In Figure 4.7 above, the R1 router received multicast traffic on its Fa0/0 interface from a device with the source address 10.10.10.1. The multicast RPF check verifies the unicast routing table to see which interface traffic should be coming in from for that particular source. If unicast traffic reaches that particular destination through the Fa0/0 interface (according to the unicast routing table), then RPF verification passes. If the source is not associated with the Fa0/0 interface, the multicast device will drop the multicast traffic.

PIM-DM would be suitable only for small multicast implementations because of the flooding behavior of the multicast traffic to all potential segments, and then for pruning the segments that do not want the traffic. With Dense Mode flooding, there is a collection of Shortest Path Tree (SPT) entries for multicast, as all of the sources are building their independent trees to flood out the multicast traffic. This flooding and pruning behavior, on top of this SPT-type of approach, is not very efficient. The major problem with this process is that even after the pruning phase, traffic is periodically re-flooded at a defined interval. To avoid waiting for the periodic re-flood, PIM-DM uses a Graft message to un-prune a particular segment, similar to a Join message. This is useful in situations where multicast receivers come up after the initial Dense Mode flooding phase.

Another PIM-specific concept is called the "assert." This is what happens when multiple multicast speakers are on the same LAN (broadcast) segment. In this situation, the assert process will start and someone will take over as the assert winner. This is based on the lowest metric or the highest IP address when the metrics are equal.

One of the biggest issues when designing Dense Mode multicast implementations is Dense Mode State Refresh; this happens because after three minutes the traffic re-floods the previously pruned areas. This behavior can be overwritten with certain mechanisms designed by Cisco, but the recommendation is to use PIM-SM to avoid this process.

PIM-SM also supports SPT switchover, so the last-hop router (the router that is directly connected to the active receiver group) can switch to a Source Tree to bypass the RP if the traffic rate goes over a certain threshold (i.e., the SPT threshold). SPT switchover allows PIM-SM to be more effective in supporting multicast traffic. This is configured with the "ip pim spt-threshold [value]" command in global configuration mode on the multicast router.

Bidirectional PIM is an enhancement that was designed for the effective many-to-many communication in an individual PIM domain. Many multicast applications use the many-to-many model, where every host is both a receiver and a sender. Bidirectional PIM allows packets to be forwarded from a source to the RP using only the Shared Tree state, so the traffic is routed through a bidirectional Shared Tree that is rooted at the RP for the specific group.

Bidirectional PIM represents a Sparse Mode implementation with no Source-based Trees. This is used in particular environments, such as where Source-based Trees are not wanted. Examples of such environments include many-to-many applications, where there are many different sources available that send traffic to many different receivers, and the use of an SPT does not scale well. Bidirectional PIM simply forces Shared Tree usage. In Bidirectional Mode, multicast groups can scale to include an arbitrarily large number of sources, with only a little extra overhead. Bidirectional PIM uses a Designated Forwarder (DF) on each link.

Another extension to the PIM protocol is SSM, which utilizes Source Trees exclusively, and Cisco recommends using it to support one-to-many applications. SSM makes the network much simpler to manage and eliminates the need for RP engineering. In other words, SSM uses only Source Trees; there are no Shared Trees and therefore no RPs are required.

SSM is a method for delivering multicast packets from a specific source address that is requested by the receiver. SSM is easy to install and is easy to provision in the network, as it does not require the network to maintain records of which active sources are sending what to multicast groups. SSM is the recommended practice for Internet broadcast-style or one-to-many applications, for example online training sessions.

PIM SPARSE MODE AND RP DESIGN CONSIDERATIONS

PIM-SM uses a pull model (or "explicit join" model) that does not rely on flooding traffic. While PIM-DM uses only Source-based Trees, PIM-SM uses a combination of Shared Trees and Source-based Trees. This makes Sparse Mode much more scalable compared to Dense Mode. Sparse Mode will choose to use a Shared Tree approach if it is more efficient to use the RP concept and will use a Source-based Tree approach if it is more efficient. Overall, Sparse Mode is more efficient, even when there is a dense distribution of multicast receivers.

In Sparse Mode, the PIM neighbors are discovered and a designated router is selected; then, the RP is discovered. The RP learns information about sources and receivers, and a Shared Tree from the senders to receivers is built through the RP. For more efficient dissemination of multicast traffic, SPT joins and Shared Trees leave. This is a much more scalable approach, as the Shared Tree can be used through the RP where it is more appropriate and the SPTs can be built where they are more appropriate.

The RP is the reference and aggregation point for the Shared Tree. It learns source information with unicast PIM Register messages and it learns about receivers through PIM Join messages. In multicast environments, routers must have knowledge of the RP because without this information, sources cannot register and clients cannot join multicast groups. The routers must agree on the RP information on a per group basis. An RP is required in networks that have a Shared Tree, such as those that use PIM-SM or Bidirectional PIM. RPs can be configured using many methods:

- Static RP addressing
- Anycast RP
- Auto-RP
- Bootstrap Router (BSR)

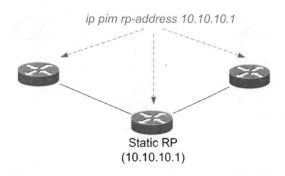

ip pim rp-address 10.10.10.1

Static RP
(10.10.10.1)

Figure 4.8 – Static RP Configuration

The first consideration regards static addressing on the RP, which is shown in Figure 4.8 above. With static RP, every router in the network must be configured manually with the IP address of a single RP, using the "ip pim rp-address <rp_address>" command. If the RP fails, the routers will not be able to failover to a standby RP. The only way a static RP can failover involves using anycast RPs. In this situation, the Multicast Source Discovery Protocol (MSDP) must be running between each RP in the network to share information about active sources.

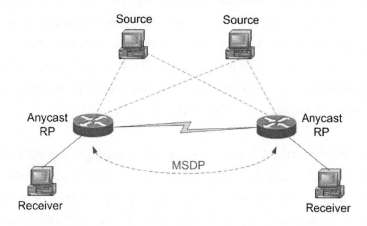

Source   Source

Anycast   Anycast
RP   RP

MSDP

Receiver   Receiver

Figure 4.9 – Anycast RP with MSDP

Anycast uses an address shared by devices, such as RPs, DNS servers, or Web servers, which are performing the same function. Analyzing Figure 4.9 above, a packet addressed to an anycast address is actually sent to the geographically closest device, so anycast provides load-sharing capabilities. Anycast RP is a technique that allows the configuration of a PIM-SM network to allow fault-tolerant and load-sharing capabilities in a single multicast domain.

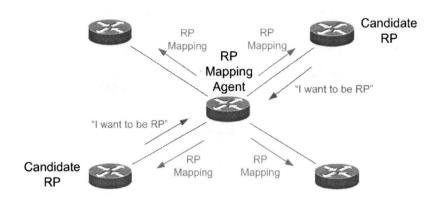

Figure 4.10 – Multicast Auto-RP

Auto-RP is a mechanism that permits all of the routers in the network to learn the RP data dynamically, as shown in Figure 4.10 above. Auto-RP has two IANA-assigned group addresses: 224.0.1.39 and 224.0.1.40. Auto-RP advertises the RP information dynamically and uses the concept of a "candidate RP" to define a router on the network that can assume the RP role. The second role defined by Auto-RP technology is the "mapping agent," which listens for a potential candidate RP, chooses one, and then relays this information to the rest of the PIM environment. This allows for redundancy of RPs to be designed. The candidate RPs generate an advertisement to multicast group 224.0.1.39. Mapping agents listen automatically on 224.0.1.39 to learn about the candidates, and then generate an advertisement using group 224.0.1.40 to distribute this information. This behavior presents an issue, as Auto-RP is using multicast groups in its operation, and multicast communication might not be available before using Auto-RP.

Another important issue is that the dynamically learned RP mappings are preferred over the statically configured ones, so Auto-RP cannot be used as a backup mechanism for the static RP configuration process. In addition, because Auto-RP relies on multicast groups, Auto-RP control plane messages are subject to an RPF check, which can result in failure in the Auto-RP communication process.

The major issue with Auto-RP is that in a Sparse Mode environment, RPs do not exist for the 224.0.1.39 and 224.0.1.40 groups. Sparse mode devices cannot really function with these groups because they do not know where the RP is. This Auto-RP paradox occurs because clients cannot join the Auto-RP groups, as they do not have the RP and the RP is not known because the Auto-RP groups cannot be joined.

The solution to this issue is statically assigning an RP for just the two Auto-RP groups, 224.0.1.39 and 224.0.1.40. This defeats the purpose of automatic assignment, so Cisco invented PIM Sparse-Dense Mode as a solution to this problem. Cisco Sparse-Dense Mode is not a perfect solution because if there is an RP failure, Dense Mode flooding of the other multicast traffic that is involved with these groups will occur.

These downsides led to the development of a more efficient solution of using Auto-RP in a Sparse-Mode-only environment, which is called the Auto-RP Listener feature. This is a simple command placed on every multicast speaker and it allows just the 224.0.1.39 and 224.0.1.40 groups to operate in Dense Mode. Everything else is guaranteed to work in a Sparse Mode fashion, so there are no potential issues.

> **NOTE:** Auto-RP is a Cisco proprietary protocol that can be implemented only on Cisco devices. This technology will soon become legacy, as the newer Bootstrap Router (BSR) method is preferred in modern multicast implementations.

Because of all of the issues presented above, BSR is a much preferred solution to the problems presented by Auto-RP. BSR is similar to Auto-RP but it lacks the issues Auto-RP presents. BSR allows for better interoperability between vendors. Similar to Auto-RP, BSR works by implementing a candidate router for the RP function and for relaying RP data in a group. The network administrator can configure one or more routers in a network to serve as a candidate BSR. The most important improvement offered by BSR is that it does not use multicast in its operation. BSR defines two roles in the multicast domain:

- **RP candidate:** Similar to the candidate RP from Auto-RP.
- **BSR:** Similar to the mapping agent from Auto-RP.

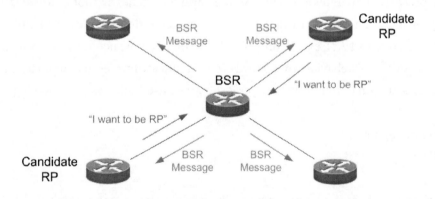

Figure 4.11 – Multicast BSR

When the network is initialized, all of the candidate BSR (C-BSR) routers will participate in an election process by sending a PIM BSR message, as illustrated in Figure 4.11 above. This process is similar to the STP Root-election or OSPF DR-election process. This information is distributed through the local-link multicast messages that travel from one PIM router to another PIM router, and the BSR messages are flooded hop-by-hop through the entire domain. At the end of the election process, the BSR with the highest BSR priority is elected and becomes the active BSR.

NOTE: BSR is a standardized implementation and is defined as PIMv2.

ETHERNET MULTICASTING

In Ethernet environments, the Layer 2 multicast process is seamlessly supported. A 48-bit multicast address is utilized and the stations listen for the address at Layer 2. These addresses are used for various purposes beyond traditional multicast implementations, for example, Cisco Discovery Protocol (CDP) and Layer 2 protocol tunneling techniques.

When multicast applications are created, developers must be aware that there is some overlap in the addressing when mapping IPv4 to MAC addresses. The IPv4 multicast group range is 224.0.0.0 to 239.255.255.255 (a total of 2^{28} groups) and the MAC address range allocated by IEEE is 01-00-5E-00-00-00 to 01-00-5E-7E-FF-FF, with the first 25 bits being fixed and the last 23 bits mapped to the group address. This means that there are 2^{28} possible groups but only 2^{23} possible groups can be mapped. As a result, each MAC address maps 32 IPv4 groups so it is possible to create overlapping groups accidentally.

MULTICAST IN SWITCHED ENVIRONMENTS

IGMP is a protocol that operates at Layer 3, so the Layer 2 switches are not aware of the hosts that want to join the multicast groups. By default, Layer 2 switches flood the received multicast frames to all of the ports in the VLAN, even if only one device on one port needs the specific information. To improve the switches' behavior when they receive multicast frames, technologies that facilitate effective implementation of multicast at Layer 2 should be used, such as the following:

- IGMP snooping
- CGMP

Most of the time, switches treat multicast traffic like traditional broadcast traffic, flooding multicast packets out to all ports in the VLAN. This is not an efficient approach, so solutions had to be found. An initial solution to this issue was a protocol invented by Cisco called Cisco Group Management Protocol (CGMP). This Cisco proprietary protocol is implemented between multicast routers and switches so that the switches know where to send the multicast traffic.

CGMP works based on a client-server model, where the router is a CGMP server and the switch is a CGMP client. CGMP allows switches to communicate with multicast-enabled routers to figure out whether any users attached to the switches are part of any particular multicasting groups and whether they qualify for receiving the specific stream of data.

CGMP eventually became a legacy protocol and Cisco has since adopted a protocol called IGMP snooping. This applies overhead to the switch because it now has to eavesdrop on IGMP reports and Leave messages. Cisco handled this issue by building particular Application Specific Integrated Circuits (ASICs) in the switches that would speed up this process by running it in hardware. IGMP is the ideal solution in modern networks, as the switches constrain the multicast traffic.

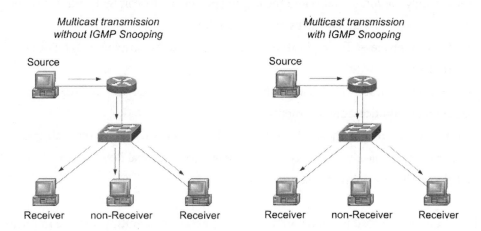

Figure 4.12 – IGMP Snooping

When using IGMP snooping, switches listen in on the IGMP messages between the router and the hosts and automatically update their MAC address tables, as shown in Figure 4.12 above. In other words, IGMP snooping allows the switch to intercept the multicast receiver's Registration message, and based on the gathered information it makes changes to its forwarding table.

NOTE: CGMP is a Cisco-specific protocol which is becoming deprecated. As a result, IGMP snooping is now used more in both Cisco and non-Cisco devices.

In addition to IGMP snooping, Catalyst 6500 series switches and Catalyst 4500 series switches support multicast packet replication in hardware, which makes it more efficient to copy multicast packets to network interfaces where the multicast paths flow.

IP MULTICAST SECURITY AND OPTIMIZATION

Multicast deployments have additional security considerations that go beyond just a unicast routing environment. Additional security considerations can be requested by several components and processes of multicast systems, which can add complexity to the existing network infrastructure.

When designing IP multicast solutions, the security goals should be defined because multicast traffic has a different nature compared to unicast traffic. The security goals must focus on the differences between unicast and multicast and they include the following aspects:

- **State information**: Multicast state information is different from unicast state information. In unicast, only the routing table and the routing protocol are dealt with, but this is not the case with multicasting, which involves other constraints.
- **Replication process**: The replication process can create security vulnerabilities in multicast environments.
- **Join process**: The security threats in this area include rogue devices and rogue RPs that might be present in multicast environments.
- **Unidirectional flows**: These add complexity to the network due to the lack of chosen path predictability. Typically, in unicast environments, bidirectional flows are involved, but this is not always the case in multicast networks.

In a multicast environment, it is important to keep the network operating and the multicast traffic flowing, even when experiencing the following:

- DoS (Denial of Service) attacks
- Malfunctioning RPs
- Configuration errors

Many of the multicast security features are related to ensuring that the network resources, as well as the access control mechanisms for the different senders and receivers, are managed properly. Regarding the types of multicast traffic that are allowed on the network, a well-defined solution should be in place because there are many different types of multicast applications, and some of these may not be allowed in the organization. An important consideration regarding IP multicast security is the potential for various types of attack traffic (e.g., from rogue sources to multicast hosts and to networks that do not have receivers, and from rogue receivers).

With unicast traffic, any node can send a packet to another node on the unicast network, and there is no implicit protection of the receivers from the source, which is the reason firewalls and ACLs are used. However, in multicast routing, the source devices send traffic to a multicast group, not to specific devices, and a receiver on a branch in the network must explicitly join the multicast group before traffic is forwarded to that branch. In other words, multicast has built-in protection mechanisms to implicitly protect receivers against packets from unknown sources or potential attackers, such as Reverse Path Forwarding.

With SSM, unknown attacks will not happen because the receivers must join a specific host in a specific multicast group. Any unwanted traffic will reach only the first-hop router closest to the source and then it will be discarded. The attack traffic will not even generate state information on the first-hop router.

With Any Source Multicast (ASM), or PIM-SM and Bidirectional PIM, an end-device will receive traffic only when it joins a group, and an attacker cannot attack a particular host explicitly but it can send attacks against a multicast group, as well as a network. With multicasting, DoS attacks, also referred to as state attacks or control plane attacks, are always a threat. The goal is to increase the amount of multicast state information on the routers above some manageable threshold. However, this can lead to non-responsive services or even crashed devices.

SSM will drop traffic from unknown sources at the first-hop router closest to the source. When considering DoS attacks, the main areas of concern regarding the impact on the multicast state include ASM or Bidirectional PIM implementations.

A multicast network can also be subject to receiver attacks, which come in three categories based on the target of the attacks:

- **Content attacks:** In this type of attack, the unauthorized rogue receiver tries to gain access to the application content.
- **Bandwidth attacks:** This attack against other receivers involves the receiver trying to over-load the network bandwidth.
- **Attacks against routers and switches:** In this type of attack, the attacker tries to create more state information than a switch or a router can deal with. For example, a router trying to process multiple Join requests can affect convergence time or other states. This attack can cause the network device to reboot or to reload.

Unicast has two scoped addresses (public and private spaces) that provide a layer of security by hiding internal hosts using NAT and PAT technologies. There can also be overlapping scoped addresses between different companies. On the other hand, multicast has its own scoped addresses as defined by IANA. IPv4 multicast supports the ability to administratively scope definitions within the 239.0.0.0/8 range. One of the most common actions is to configure a router with ACLs that can allow or prevent multicast traffic in an address range from flowing outside of an autonomous system or any user-defined domain.

Using a configuration of Group Encrypted Transport (GET) VPN as an example, it will replicate its keys using multicast technology, so the ACLs should be configured to allow traffic to go from the key server to all of the participants. This should include the networks that are being secured across the cloud, as well as the multicast range, either globally or the specific range that GET VPN uses for its key exchange, replication, and refreshing.

Within an autonomous system or domain, there is a limited scope address range that should be further subdivided so that local multicast boundaries can be defined. This subdivision process is called address scoping and it allows for address reuse between smaller domains.

Multicast access control is the process of using packet-based filtering (with the "ip access-group in/out" command in interface configuration mode) to permit and deny multicast packets. When using ACLs, the appropriate unicast and routing traffic with the multicast destinations must be allowed. This type of filtering should be implemented on different places in the network, including the source and receiver hosts.

The state requirements between unicast and multicast will influence the multicast design scenarios in terms of security and optimization. When designing multicast, it is important to understand the differences between the unicast state and the multicast state.

The unicast state is derived from the IP routing table and this can be populated differently based on the routing protocol used (e.g., EIGRP and OSPF use topology/link-state databases that ultimately lead to the routing table). Most routers run Cisco Express Forwarding (CEF), so the routing table is a representation in real time of the Forwarding Information Base (FIB) of CEF. The state changes only when there is a change in the topology, and this is the only factor that affects the CPU on the router because of CEF and the FIB. In other words, end-user functions will not impact the state of the router or the activity on the router, other than the traffic that moves through the links. One of the benefits of the FIB is that this activity is accomplished very preemptively and without having to use the route processor.

However, with multicast, the state also includes additional sources and receivers for new applications that are being used in the multicast design. Application state change and user activity can affect the CPU because both of these aspects can affect multicast traffic and state information. In a multicast environment, the multicast sources and the applications are additional network design constraints that go beyond routing topology changes. This is a key consideration when designing multicast.

Figure 4.13 – Multicast Router Traffic Flow

Considering Figure 4.13 above, as traffic comes into a multicast router (ingress direction), state information will be linked to ingress lookups on a per-application basis on the multicast server. This causes scalability issues of memory, especially as the number of applications grows. According to the way multicast works, the outbound (egress) state information will deal with the replication of packets to multiple interfaces that support receiver branches and the distribution tree. The state information on the outgoing interfaces will scale up as the number of applications span across the receiver branches. Hardware acceleration can be used to deal with this issue, as it is a key optimization factor for multicast routers.

Another design consideration for unicast and multicast routing is throughput parameters. Unicast routing generally deals with the amount of traffic that is received (ingress packet rate), while multicast routing is much more concerned with the egress packet rate, as well as the ability to replicate the outgoing packets. The egress throughput will be a key factor on both routers and Layer 3 switches that support IGMP snooping.

IPV6 MULTICAST

The IPv6 multicast address space covers the FF00::/8 range, and more specific addresses include the following:

- All nodes multicast – FF02::1
- All routers multicast – FF02::2
- OSPF DR routers – FF02::6
- EIGRP routers – FF02::A
- PIM routers – FF02::D

NOTE: All of the addresses above have a link-local scope.

In IPv6, IGMP is replaced by the Multicast Listener Discovery (MLD) protocol, which is based on ICMPv6 behavior. MLDv1 is equivalent to IGMPv2, and MLDv2 is roughly equivalent to IGMPv3. MLD is the optional version to implement if using a source-specific multicast approach, which is shown in Figure 4.14 below:

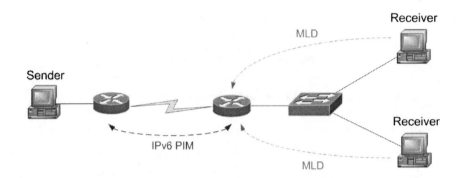

Figure 4.14 – IPv6 Multicast

PIMv2 for IPv6 supports only PIM-SM behavior, not Dense Mode or Sparse-Dense Mode behavior (Bidirectional PIM is supported only for static configuration). Just as in IPv4, the IPv6 unicast Routing Information Base (RIB) is used for the RPF checks. When configuring PIMv2, it uses tunnels that are dynamically created and those tunnels are used as an efficient way to carry out the multicast source registration process.

IPv6 PIM configuration commands are almost identical to IPv4 PIM configuration commands, so there should not be a big learning curve for the implementing engineers of IPv4 multicast. The following are some equivalent commands:

IPv4 Multicast Commands	IPv6 Multicast Commands
ip multicast-routing	ipv6 multicast-routing
show ip pim interface	show ipv6 pim interface
show ip pim neighbor	show ipv6 pim neighbor

Considering that IPv6 multicast uses only sparse mode, RPs will be present in every implementation. The IPv6 RPs are assigned using the following methods:

- Statically assigned RPs
- BSR for IPv6
- Embedded RPs

The embedded RP is a new way of assigning the RP by taking advantage of the fact that IPv6 addresses are 128 bits long. A flag is set in the IPv6 multicast address to signal that the RP address is in the multicast group address. Every device identifies the RP address just by examining the multicast address, which embeds the RP information.

SUMMARY

Multicasting implies taking a single data packet and sending it to a group of destinations simultaneously. This behavior is a many-to-many transmission, as opposed to other types of communication such as unicast, broadcast, or anycast.

Senders in unicast transmissions must know the addresses of all of the receivers. When using multicast, traffic can be sent to the multicast address, without the need to know specific address information for the receivers. In addition, the router processing of packets is dramatically reduced in multicast environments. The main goals of using multicasting are as follows:

- Reduce processing on the sending devices
- Reduce bandwidth consumption
- Reduce forwarding processing on routers
- Reduce processing on the receiving host, especially if they are not interested in the transmission

The major IPv4 multicast components include the following:

- **Group addressing:** Layer 3 addresses and the underlying Layer 2 multicast MAC addresses.
- **Multicast routing (control plane):** IGMP and PIM.
- **Forwarding mechanisms (data plane):** Reverse Path Forwarding (RPF).

IPv4 multicast uses the Class D address space, meaning the 224.0.0.0/4 range (224.0.0.0 to 239.255.255.255). This address space is not fully available to multicast designers due to some address range reservations, which include:

- **Link-local addresses:** 224.0.0.0/24 (224.0.0.0 to 224.0.0.255); link-local addressing is very common with routing protocols. For example, OSPF utilizes 224.0.0.5 and 224.0.0.6 in its operation.
- **Source-specific multicast:** 232.0.0.0/8 (232.0.0.0 to 232.255.255.255).
- **Administratively scoped:** 239.0.0.0/8 (239.0.0.0 to 239.255.255.255); the administratively scoped address range can be used for multicast applications inside corporate boundaries.

The control plane is built with host-to-router and router-to-router communication protocols. Host-to-router communication is accomplished with the Internet Group Management Protocol (IGMP), and router-to-router communication is achieved with Protocol Independent Multicast (PIM).

IP multicast technology allows information to be sent over networks to a group of destinations in a very efficient way. In campus networks, the most important protocol used for implementing multicast is IGMP. The multicast data is sent to a multicast group and the users receive the information by joining the specific multicast group using IGMP.

PIM is used by multicast-enabled routers to forward incoming multicast streams to a particular switch port. PIM uses typical routing tables that are populated by regular unicast routing protocols (like EIGRP and OSPG) and exchanges multicast routing updates between PIM routers. PIM operates in multiple modes:

- PIM Sparse Mode (PIM-SM)
- PIM Dense Mode (PIM-DM)
- Bidirectional PIM
- PIM Source-Specific Multicast (PIM-SSM)

The PIM operation mode used most often is Sparse Mode, which utilizes an explicit join-type behavior, so the receiver does not get the multicast traffic unless it asks for it. This can be considered a "pull" mechanism, as opposed to the "push" mechanisms used in PIM-DM. The "pull" mechanism allows PIM-SM to forward multicast traffic only to the network segments with active receivers that have actually requested the data. PIM-SM distributes the data about active sources by forwarding data packets on Shared Trees.

Bidirectional PIM is an enhancement that was designed for the effective many-to-many communication in an individual PIM domain. Many multicast applications use the many-to-many model, where every host is both a receiver and a sender. Bidirectional PIM allows packets to be forwarded from a source to the RP using only the Shared Tree state, so the traffic is routed through a bidirectional Shared Tree that is rooted at the RP for the specific group.

In multicast environments, hosts must have knowledge of the RPs because without this information, sources cannot register and clients cannot join multicast groups. Routers must agree on the RP information on a per-group basis. An RP is required in networks that have a Shared Tree, meaning networks that use PIM-SM or Bidirectional PIM. RPs can be configured using many methods, such as the following:

- Static RP addressing
- Anycast RP
- Auto-RP
- Bootstrap Router (BSR) – the most preferred method

IGMP is a protocol that operates at Layer 3, so the Layer 2 switches are not aware of the hosts that want to join the multicast groups. By default, Layer 2 switches flood the received multicast frames to all of the ports in the VLAN, even if only one device on one port needs the specific information. To improve the switches' behavior when they receive multicast frames, technologies that allow for effective implementation of multicast at Layer 2 can utilize the following:

- IGMP snooping
- Cisco Group Management Protocol (CGMP)

CGMP is a Cisco proprietary protocol that runs between the multicast router and the switch. It works as a client-server model, where the router is a CGMP server and the switch is a CGMP client. CGMP allows switches to communicate with multicast-enabled routers to figure out whether any users attached to the switches are part of any particular multicasting groups and whether they qualify for receiving the specific stream of data.

When using IGMP snooping, switches listen in on the IGMP messages between the router and the hosts and automatically update their MAC address tables. In other words, IGMP snooping allows the switch to intercept the multicast receiver registration message, and based on the information gathered it makes changes to its forwarding table.

When designing IP multicast solutions, the security goals should be defined because multicast traffic has a different nature than unicast traffic does. The security goals must focus on the differences between unicast and multicast and they include the following aspects:

- State information
- Replication process
- The join process
- Unidirectional flows

In a multicast environment, it is important to keep the network operating and the multicast traffic flowing, even when experiencing the following:

- DoS (Denial of Service) attacks
- Malfunctioning RPs
- Configuration errors

An important consideration regarding IP multicast security is the potential for various types of attack traffic (e.g., from rogue sources to multicast hosts and to networks that do not have receivers, and from rogue receivers).

A multicast network can also suffer from receiver attacks, which come in three categories based on the target of the attacks:

- Content attacks
- Bandwidth attacks
- Attacks against routers and switches

In IPv6, IGMP is replaced by the Multicast Listener Discovery (MLD) protocol, which is based on ICMPv6 behavior. PIMv2 for IPv6 supports only PIM-SM behavior, not Dense Mode or Sparse-Dense Mode (Bidirectional PIM is supported only in static configurations). Just as in IPv4, the IPv6 unicast Routing Information Base (RIB) is used for the RPF checks. When configuring PIMv2, it uses tunnels that are dynamically created and those tunnels are used as an efficient way to carry out the multicast source registration process.

END OF CHAPTER QUIZ

1. Which of the following is NOT a main goal of utilizing multicasting?

    a. Reducing the processing on sending devices

    b. Increasing bandwidth consumption

    c. Reducing the forwarding processing on routers

    d. Reducing the processing on receiving hosts, especially if they are not interested in the transmission

2. Which underlying protocol does multicast use in its operations?

    a. TCP

    b. ICMP

    c. UDP

    d. RIP

    e. CDP

3. Because of its underlying Transport Layer protocol, multicast has a connectionless behavior and offers best effort packet transport.

    a. True

    b. False

4. Which of the following are multicast-specific protocols (choose all that apply)?

    a. PIM

    b. ICMP

    c. CDP

    d. IGMP

    e. RIP

5. Which of the following concepts describe the 239.0.0.0/8 multicast range?

    a. The Class D multicast range

    b. The link-local multicast range

    c. The source-specific multicast range

    d. The administratively scoped multicast range

6. Which of the following protocols is used for receiver devices to signal routers on the LAN that they want traffic for a specific group?
   a. PIM
   b. ICMP
   c. CDP
   d. IGMP
   e. RIP

7. IGMPv1 is used to support Source-Specific Multicasting (SSM).
   a. True
   b. False

8. Which of the following protocols is used by multicast-enabled routers to forward incoming multicast streams to a particular switch port?
   a. PIM
   b. ICMP
   c. CDP
   d. IGMP
   e. RIP

9. Which of the following are valid PIM modes of operation (choose all that apply)?
   a. PIM-AM
   b. PIM-DM
   c. PIM-SSM
   d. PIM MSDP
   e. PIM-SM

10. MOSPF and DVMRP are modern multicast protocols based on the PIM framework.
    a. True
    b. False

11. Which of the following PIM modes of operation uses an explicit join-type behavior (or a "pull" mechanism)?
    a. PIM-AM
    b. PIM-DM
    c. PIM-SSM
    d. PIM MSDP
    e. PIM-SM

12. PIM-DM was design to be used in environments with a dense distribution of receivers.
    a. True
    b. False

13. Which of the following describes the concept used by PIM-SM to process Join requests?
    a. RP
    b. AP
    c. CDP
    d. MLD

14. One of the biggest issues with PIM-DM implementations is the State Refresh mechanisms that flood traffic every three minutes by default.
    a. True
    b. False

15. Which of the following is a mechanism that allows PIM-SM to switch to a Source Tree mode of operation if the traffic rate goes over a certain threshold?
    a. Anycast RP
    b. SPT switchover
    c. SSM switchover
    d. Auto-RP

16. Static addressing is the most preferred method of RP configuration, especially in large multicast deployments.
    a. True
    b. False

17. Which of the following is NOT a method of RP configuration?
    a. Static addressing
    b. Auto-RP
    c. DHCP
    d. BSR

18. Auto-RP is a Cisco proprietary protocol.
    a. True
    b. False

19. Which of the following is the recommended protocol to be used in switched environments to improve the switches' behavior when they receive multicast frames?

    a. PIM

    b. CGMP

    c. IGMP

    d. IGMP snooping

20. Which of the following protocols replaces IGMP in IPv6 multicast environments?

    a. BSR

    b. ICMP

    c. MLD

    d. PIM

CHAPTER 5

Designing Advanced Routing Solutions

This chapter covers the following topics:

- Stable and scalable routing designs for EIGRP for IPv4
- Stable and scalable routing designs for OSPF for IPv4
- Stable and scalable routing designs for BGP for IPv4

This chapter is essential for ARCH certification and it will begin by reviewing some general routing concepts and aspects regarding route summarization. Next, it will analyze other routing topics, such as route filtering and redistribution. Finally, it will explore details and best practices that are essential for scalable routing designs when using EIGRP, OSPF, and BGP.

CONCEPTS OF ROUTING PROTOCOLS

Before analyzing details about each individual routing protocol, some general information about IP routing will be presented first. Network designers should know the key characteristics that different routing protocols have because they will be in a position to recommend specific routing protocols for different projects. The first key decision criteria is figuring out whether static or dynamic routing should be used. Static routing implies manually defining routes on devices and dynamic routing implies using a dedicated routing protocol that will build the routing table.

Static Routing

Even though static routes may not seem necessary in modern networks, there are situations in which they can offer granular control and optimization of the information learned by the routing protocols. Static routes can be used in conjunction with dynamic routing protocols to reach specific networks or to provide the default gateway (e.g., pointing to the ISP), which is useful in situations where the destination network is not part of the routing protocol database.

Another scenario in which static routes are used is to override some dynamically learned routing information. Static routing can also be used in the form of floating static routes, for example, setting the Administrative Distance (AD) of a particular static route to a higher (worse) value than the AD value of the same route learned via a routing protocol for failover reasons.

Dynamic Routing

An important decision to be made when choosing the routing protocol is whether an Interior Gateway Routing Protocol (IGRP) or an Exterior Gateway Routing Protocol (EGRP) will be needed. When routing between devices within an organization (Autonomous System – AS), there are many IPv4-based IGRPs to choose from, such as the following:

- RIPv1
- RIPv2
- OSPF
- IS-IS
- IGRP
- EIGRP
- ODR

NOTE: RIPv1 and IGRP are considered legacy protocols and some modern network devices do not support them.

On Demand Routing (ODR) is a Cisco proprietary protocol designed for hub-and-spoke topologies. It offers basic routing functionality and works over Cisco Discovery Protocol (CDP). The most common interior protocols used in non-hub-and-spoke environments are RIPv2, OSPF, IS-IS, and EIGRP. IPv6 uses specially developed versions of routing protocols, such as the following:

- IS-IS
- RIPng
- OSPFv3
- EIGRP for IPv6

Routing between ASs (from large corporations to the Internet, or between ISPs) is accomplished using special routing protocols called EGRPs. The most common EGRP for both IPv4 and IPv6 is the Border Gateway Protocol (BGP). Some companies have a very complex and large network infrastructure that spans worldwide, so they use BGP inside their network as their IGRP.

Large networks, including the Internet, are based on the AS concept. An AS defines a group of network devices under a common administration, and most often this defines a large organization or an ISP. Routing protocols can be classified based on different criteria. Depending on the zone in which they operate, they can be considered interior (inter-AS) routing protocols or exterior (intra-AS) routing protocols. Interior routing protocols can be further classified as distance vector routing protocols and link-state routing protocols, based on their behavior regarding the router update exchange process. Each routing protocol type will be covered in detail in the following sections, along with their respective design considerations.

Interior Routing Protocols

Interior routing protocols are configured on groups of routers from the same AS; thus, the routing activity never leaves the organization's premises.

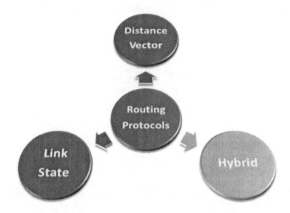

Figure 5.1 – Routing Protocols

Figure 5.1 above illustrates the different routing protocols available. An important aspect that must be considered when selecting the routing protocol is the difference between distance vector and link-state routing protocols. Link-state routing protocols were developed after distance vector routing protocols and they are much more sophisticated. A special category involves the hybrid routing protocols that feature the best attributes of distance vector and link-state technologies. The only hybrid routing protocol used in modern networks is EIGRP.

Distance vector routing protocols include:

- RIPv1
- RIPv2
- IGRP
- RIPng

Link-state routing protocols include:

- OSPF
- IS-IS
- OSPFv3

Distance Vector Routing Protocols

Distance vector routing is a property of certain routing protocols that build an internal picture of the topology by periodically exchanging full routing tables between the neighbor devices. The main difference between distance vector routing protocols and link-state routing protocols is the way they exchange routing updates. Distance vector routing protocols function using the "routing by rumor" technique, as every router relies on its neighbors to maintain correct routing information.

This means the entire routing table is sent periodically to the neighbors, as illustrated in Figure 5.2 below:

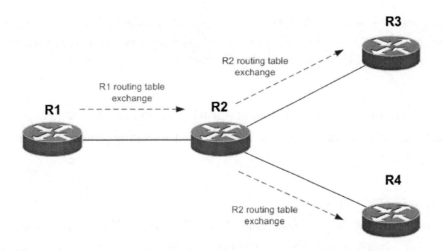

Figure 5.2 – Distance Vector Routing Protocol Behavior

The most important advantage of distance vector routing protocols is that they are easy to implement and maintain. The downside is the convergence time. A converged network is a network in which every router has the same perspective of the topology. When a topology change occurs, the routers in the respective area propagate the new information to the rest of the network. Because this is done on a hop-by-hop basis (i.e., every router passes its fully updated routing information to each neighbor), network convergence is finally established after a significant amount of time has passed.

In addition to the downside of slow convergence, because full routing table exchanges occur between the routers, distance vector routing protocols are more bandwidth intensive than link-state routing protocols are. This happens especially in large networks, where routing tables can be of considerable size. Based on these aspects, distance vector routing protocols are recommended only in small Enterprise Network implementations.

An example of a distance vector routing protocol still used in modern networks is RIPv2 (described in RFC 2453). RIPv2 uses a hop count as the metric for path selection, with a maximum hop count of 15. RIPv2 updates are sent using multicast by default, although they can be configured as unicast or broadcast, and, unlike its predecessor (RIPv1), RIPv2 permits Variable Length Subnet Masking (VLSM) on the network.

Devices receive routing information from their neighbors and pass it on to other neighbors. RIP repeats this process every 30 seconds. The downside in this scenario is that when the network is stable and there are no changes in the topology, RIP still sends its routing table every 30 seconds, which is not very effective because it wastes bandwidth.

NOTE: Although it is widely believed that all of the routing table information is exchanged between neighbors, actually only the best routes are exchanged through the routing updates. Alternate routes are not included in the routing update packets.

If a router that uses a distance vector routing protocol has inaccurate information, that information will propagate through the entire network. Distance vector routing protocols are prone to major problems, including routing loops.

Link-State Routing Protocols

Link-state routing protocols do not generally "route by rumor." The routing devices exchange information about their link-states between them. Devices build a map of the network (i.e., they do not rely on a map of a particular node) independently and loop-free based on the link-state information each router generates and propagates to the other routers.

Unlike distance vector routing protocols, link-state routing protocols flood information about its links to a specific area or to all of the routers in a specific area. This way, every router in the topology has detailed knowledge of a specific area, unlike the routers using distance vector routing protocols, where only the best routes are exchanged between neighbors. The routing decisions are made by applying the Shortest Path First (SPF) or Dijkstra's algorithm to the information received from various sources. The result of this calculation consists of the shortest path to each destination in the network.

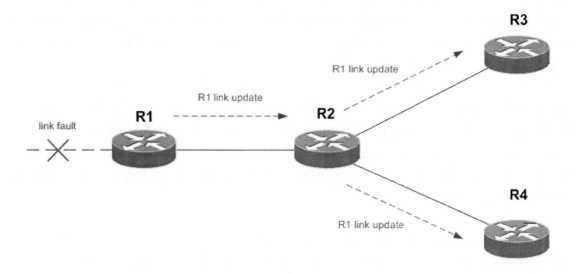

Figure 5.3 – Link-State Routing Protocol Behavior

Figure 5.3 above illustrates link-state routing protocol behavior. This is a much more efficient approach to building routing databases, and there is no fixed updated timer like in the distance vector technologies case. Link-state protocols re-flood their entire routing information periodically to ensure that the network is properly converged.

Link-state routing protocols offer a series of important advantages compared to distance vector routing protocols. The most important advantage relates to the convergence factor. Convergence occurs much faster because as soon as a network topology changes, only that specific information is sent to the routers in a given area. The routing updates stop after all of the routers learn about the specific change, thus decreasing the need for bandwidth, unlike with distance vector routing protocols that periodically exchange routing tables, even if no topology change occurs. In link-state routing, updates are triggered only when a link-state changes somewhere in the network. Depending on the routing protocol used, this can mean a link going up or down or changing some of its parameters (e.g., bandwidth).

Examples of link-state routing protocols are OSPF (Open Shortest Path First), described in RFC 2328, and IS-IS (Intermediate System-to-Intermediate System), described in RFC 1142.

> **NOTE:** An interesting and special routing protocol is EIGRP (Enhanced Interior Gateway Routing Protocol), a Cisco proprietary protocol. It has both distance vector and link-state characteristics. It is also called a hybrid or an advanced distance vector routing protocol.

Exterior Routing Protocols

Exterior routing protocols run between ASs and the most common example is BGPv4. The main reason to use different types of routing protocols to carry routes outside of the AS boundaries is to exchange a large amount of route entries. In this regard, exterior routing protocols support special options and features that are used to implement various policies. The routing metrics for these kinds of protocols include more parameters than for interior routing protocols because of the need for flexible routing policies and choosing the best possible path.

While interior routing protocols are used within Enterprise Networks, BGP is typically used in ISP-to-ISP or ISP-to-Enterprise connections. Unlike intra-AS protocols that make routing decisions based exclusively on the metric value, the policies for inter-AS protocols can also include other factors, such as business decisions or possible AS vulnerabilities (e.g., monetary costs, preferred provider, non-secure provider, geographical traffic path, and others). These are technically implemented by configuring different BGP parameters.

A typical scenario in which the use of BGP is beneficial because of its flexible policy implementation is an organization that is connected to multiple ISPs (multi-homing). BGP can interconnect with any interior routing protocol used inside the Enterprise Network, so administrators have maximum flexibility when it comes to choosing a suitable interior routing protocol. A simple example of this scenario is presented in Figure 5.4 below:

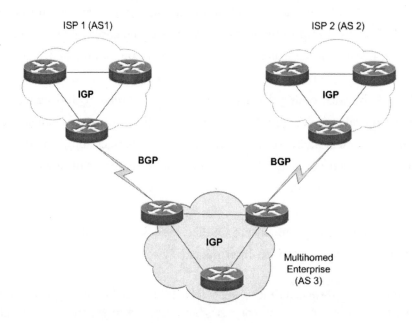

Figure 5.4 – Enterprise Multi-Homing Scenario

Other Considerations for Routing Protocols

Another key parameter of routing protocols and a measure of their sophistication is whether they have a hierarchical or a flat behavior. IS-IS and OSPF and can be configured in a hierarchical manner and they offer improved scalability. For example, OSPF splits the topology into multiple areas and uses the Area 0 (backbone) concept, which connects to every other area in the topology. Routes can be summarized as they enter or leave the backbone, which leads to increased efficiency and bandwidth optimization. IGRP and RIP are examples of routing protocols that are based on a flat behavior because they are not optimized and they use a single structure, no matter how large the network is.

One task for the router is choosing the best way to get to a destination. If a router learns different paths to a destination from different protocols, the router must decide which prefix it should listen to. To make this decision it uses Administrative Distance (AD). Lower AD values are preferred over higher AD values, so, for example, OSPF routes (AD=110) will be preferred over RIP routes (AD=120). The AD value represents how trustworthy a particular routing protocol is. The most common AD values are summarized below:

Routing Protocol	AD Value
Connected	0
Static Pointing at IP Address	1
EIGRP Summary	5
External BGP	20
EIGRP	90
OSPF	110
RIP	120
External EIGRP	170
Internal BGP	200

The AD is the way a router selects a route based on one protocol over another, but something else that must be decided is the way in which the device will select a routing table entry over another entry from the same protocol. Routing protocol metrics are used to make this decision.

Different routing protocols use different metrics. RIP uses the hop count as a metric, selecting the best route based on the lowest number of routers it passed through. This is not very efficient because the shortest path can have a lower bandwidth than other paths. OSPF is more evolved and takes bandwidth into consideration, creating a metric called cost. Cost is directly generated from the bandwidth value, so a low bandwidth has a high cost and a high bandwidth has a low cost.

EIGRP is even more sophisticated and uses a composite metric, considering both bandwidth and delay values to create the metric value. BGP, the most sophisticated of all, uses many different attributes grouped in path vectors that can be used to calculate the best path.

NOTE: One of the reasons RIP has a high AD value is that it uses the hop count metric, which is not very efficient in complex environments. The more sophisticated the metric calculation is, the lower the AD value assigned to different routing protocols.

Routing Problems and Avoidance Mechanisms

As mentioned, distance vector routing protocols are prone to major problems as a result of their simplistic "routing by rumor" approach. Distance vector and link-state routing protocols use different techniques to prevent routing problems. The most important mechanisms are as follows:

- **Invalid timers:** These are used to mark routes as unreachable when updates for those routes are not received for a long time.
- **Hop-count limit:** This parameter marks routes as unreachable when they are more than a predefined number of hops away. The hop-count limit for RIP is 15, as it is not usually used in

large networks. Unreachable routes are not installed in the routing table as best routes. The hop-count limit prevents updates from looping in the network, just like the TTL field in the IP header.

- **Triggered updates:** This feature allows the update timer to be bypassed in the case of important updates. For example, the RIP 30-second timer can be ignored if a critical routing update must be propagated through the network.
- **Hold down timers:** If a metric for a particular route keeps getting worse, updates for that route will not be accepted for a delayed period.
- **Asynchronous updates:** These offer another safety mechanism that prevents the routers from flooding the entire routing information at the same time. As mentioned, OSPF does this every 30 minutes. The asynchronous updates mechanism generates a small delay for every device so they do not flood the information exactly at the same time. This improves bandwidth utilization and processing capabilities.
- **Route poisoning:** This prevents routers from sending packets through a route that has become invalid. Distance vector routing protocols use this to indicate that a route is no longer reachable. This is accomplished by setting the route metric to a maximum value.
- **Split horizon:** Split horizon prevents updates from being sent out of the same interface they came from because routers in that area should already know about that specific update.
- **Poison reverse:** This is an exception to the split horizon rule for the poisoned routes.

ROUTE SUMMARIZATION AND FILTERING

Route summarization results in routing designs that are more scalable, regardless of the routing protocol used (e.g., RIPv2, EIGRP, or OSPF), as it places network addresses into usable blocks, which can be used for multiple purposes; for example:

- NAT blocks
- Blocks used in redistribution
- Blocks for management VLANs
- Blocks for content services

Route summarization can be used in medium-sized to large networks for faster convergence and to better support sensitive traffic and services, such as VoIP and storage. Convergence time is measured based on the time the SPF recalculations take place in OSPF or the diffusing algorithm runs in EIGRP. An example of route summarization is aggregating a number of Access Layer addresses (172.30.16.0/24 through 172.30.23.0/24) into a single prefix (172.30.16.0/21).

Default Routing

A special form of route summarization can be implemented in the form of default routing. Every modern network usually uses some type of default routing. A best practice is to dynamically advertise the default route 0.0.0.0/0 in an organization from the edge routers, as they connect to the ISPs, as opposed to performing a static route configuration on every router in the organization. This way, all of the external traffic can be routed to the ISP.

When configuring a static default route on every router in the organization to the ISP router, the next hop is the ISP-connected router instead of the directly connected peer router. This could be a problem as it can cause black holes in the network if the path to the ISP router is not available. In addition, this creates a great deal of configuration overhead, as every router must be reconfigured as the exit point changes or another ISP connection is added for redundancy or high availability. Since this implies using manual configuration, this process will involve much more overhead.

A more efficient scenario would be to configure a static route on the organization's edge devices, and then redistribute that route into the dynamic routing protocol. The egress traffic will leverage whatever metric the routing protocol uses and will find the best path to the ISP.

With any interior routing protocol (except for EIGRP), the "default-information originate" command can be used to generate a default route. However, with EIGRP, the "ip default-network <prefix>" command must be used to configure the last-resort gateway or the default route. This network must be in the route, either as a static route or as an IGRP route, before the EIGRP router will announce the network as a candidate default route to other EIGRP routers.

With a site-to-site VPN connection, it might be a good idea to advertise the corporate summary route or a default route to the company's headquarters. For example, if the goal is to advertise the 10.0.0.0/8 route to remote sites using Easy VPN Server and Easy VPN Remote, Reverse Route Injection (RRI) can be used to make that possible.

Default Routes and OSPF Stub Areas

OSPF can define different types of stub areas. This method allows for automatic route filtering between areas on the Area Border Routers (ABRs). OSPF supports the following area types:

- Normal area
- Stub area
- Totally stubby area
- Not so stubby area (NSSA)
- Totally not so stubby area (totally NSSA)

Whatever information is filtered or suppressed will be replaced by a default route (0.0.0.0/0). OSPF filters routes between areas only on ABRs; it does not filter prefixes within a single area (intra-area).

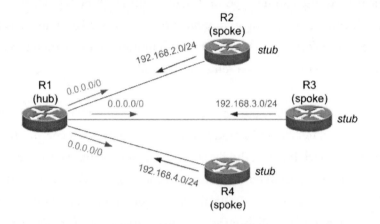

Figure 5.5 – Default Route in a Hub-and-Spoke Scenario

In Figure 5.5 above, R1 is the hub (headquarters) in the hub-and-spoke topology and the default route to R1 is advertised to the spokes (branches). The branches are defined as stub areas and they cover different networks: 192.168.2.0/24, 192.168.3.0/24, and 192.168.4.0/24. When the spoke routers (R2, R3, or R4) need to communicate with another spoke router, they send traffic to the hub because of the default route and the default route forwards it to the specific spoke. This way, spokes do not have knowledge of the entire network topology and they learn to send all external traffic to the hub router. Something similar can be achieved with EIGRP by originating the default route to a remote location and filtering other prefixes to the stub routers.

Route Filtering

Route filtering allows the control of network traffic flow and it prevents unwanted transit traffic, especially in situations that feature redundancy or multiple paths. Route filtering protects against erroneous routing updates and there are several techniques that can be used in this regard. For example, if OSPF Core Layer connectivity is lost, traffic should not be rerouted through a remote site.

OSPF inter-area transit traffic is achieved only by transiting Area 0 or by creating a virtual link as a temporary workaround for possible design issues that prevent having a continuous backbone area. With EIGRP, stub routers can be configured or routes other than the default route can be filtered. With BGP, route filtering can be used to stop a router from becoming a transit between two ISPs to prevent a large amount of traffic from going through the network.

"Defensive filtering," in which route filtering protects against illegal or unwanted routing traffic, can also be implemented. It is very common for organizations to have extranets, partner networks, or connections to other business or strategic partners. Defensive filtering offers protection in situations where unauthorized routing information is received from an external partner network (e.g., the network is advertising back to the campus prefix).

Without defensive route filtering, erroneous partner advertisements can cause many problems. For example, a strategic partner might have a static route to the Microsoft SharePoint server farm because they are using those services on port 80. If these routes start leaking into the EIGRP or OSPF routing process, then part of the original network might think the SharePoint server farm has actually been moved to an area behind the partner router. Defensive filtering will help prevent this type of scenario, as it prevents leakage and network disruption and enhances security. Defensive filtering is also known as route hiding or route starvation and it can be accomplished using a variety of techniques, for example, with route filters and prefix-lists.

Route redistribution is a very effective route manipulation and management tool, and some of the most important reasons for redistributing routes include the following:

- It is an excellent way to control, manipulate, and manage the routing updates.
- It is an essential mechanism when deploying two or more routing protocols.
- It is a beneficial tool after a merger/acquisition has been achieved.

Route redistribution should be carefully implemented because it can cause suboptimal routing and create black holes in the network. Cisco recommends having distinct regions of routing protocols and to carefully redistribute routing information, as opposed to following an ad-hoc approach to implementing routing protocols.

In addition, if there is more than one link between two network regions using different routing protocols (e.g., EIGRP and OSPF), mutual redistribution might be a consideration, with the redistribution of OSPF into EIGRP and EIGRP into OSPF. When implementing mutual redistribution, it is important to prevent the re-advertisement of information back into the routing area from which it originally came.

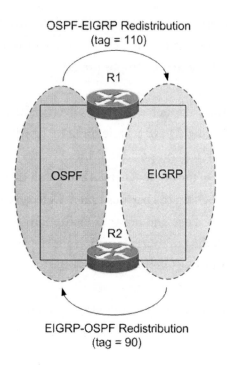

OSPF-EIGRP Redistribution
(tag = 110)

EIGRP-OSPF Redistribution
(tag = 90)

Figure 5.6 – EIGRP to/from OSPF Route Redistribution

Analyzing Figure 5.6 above, filters are used to prevent the OSPF information that was redistributed into EIGRP information from being re-advertised back into the OSPF part of the organization. This is often referred to as "manual split horizon." If filtering is not used and there is an outage, routing loops or a strange convergence behavior can appear and this leads to instability in the network design. Both OSPF and EIGRP support route tagging, which facilitates this process. Route maps can be used to add numeric tag-specific prefixes. The tag information is passed along in routing updates and other routers can filter routes that match or do not match specific tags. This can be accomplished using route maps in distribution lists.

> **NOTE:** The tag values of 110 and 90 used in Figure 5.6 above reflect the ADs of OSPF and EIGRP. While this is not mandatory, it is a recommended best practice when carrying out complex redistribution because this technique helps to easily identify the original protocol that generated each route.

ROUTING PROTOCOL MIGRATION

Some situations call for migrating between routing protocols, for example, where one company is purchased by a larger company that has a security policy that prevents the use of any proprietary protocols anywhere in the organization. If the purchased company previously used EIGRP, it would have to migrate quickly to OSPF to adhere to the new organization's policy. There are two ways to migrate between routing protocols:

- **Using AD:** This involves turning on the new protocol (OSPF in the example above) and then making certain that it has a higher AD than the existing EIGRP routing protocol. This procedure enables OSPF and allows adjacency and the routing databases to be referred to, but it will not actually rely on the OSPF routing protocol for routing decisions. When OSPF is fully deployed, the AD can be changed for one of the two protocols so that OSPF will not have the lower AD.

- **Performing redistribution by moving the boundary routers in small steps:** With migration by redistribution, in each step of the process a different part of the network will be converted from one routing protocol to another (EIGRP to OSPF in the example above).

To migrate between routing protocols in a large enterprise organization, the first approach (changing the AD) is often the best option. To achieve full connectivity using the second option (migration by redistribution), the boundary routers between the two parts of the networks will have to be bidirectionally redistributed between the two routing protocols. Then, filtering can be implemented using the tagging procedure mentioned previously. After this process, the boundary routers will "move" as more of the organization is migrated to the new routing protocol.

ADVANCED EIGRP

EIGRP is a unique protocol because it uses a hybrid approach, combining distance vector and link-state characteristics. Combining these features makes EIGRP very robust and allows for fast convergence, even in large topologies. The first thing a network designer should consider is that EIGRP is a Cisco proprietary protocol, so it can be used only in environments that contain Cisco devices. Like RIPv2, EIGRP is a classless protocol and it allows for VLSM. Another similarity between the two protocols is their automatic summarization behavior, but this can be disabled just as easily.

EIGRP Operations

The algorithm that EIGRP uses is called the Diffusing Update Algorithm (DUAL). DUAL is the engine that makes EIGRP such a powerful protocol. DUAL operates based on a topology table that contains all of the possible prefixes and information about how to reach those prefixes. The topology table is used to identify a best prefix, called the successor, and puts this route into the routing table. After determining the best route in the topology table, EIGRP identifies second-best routes called feasible successors. Feasible successors are not installed in the routing table until the best route is lost. At that moment, the next best successor in the topology table is installed in the routing table almost immediately because there is no need for other computations. This is the reason EIGRP provides such fast convergence times.

EIGRP is the only IGRP that can perform unequal cost load balancing across different paths. This is accomplished using the "variance" command, which defines a tolerance multiplier that can be applied to the best metric and that will result in the maximum allowed metric.

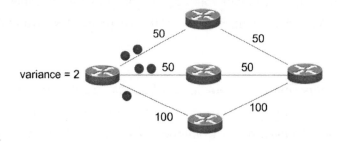

Figure 5.7 – EIGRP Unequal Cost Load Balancing

Figure 5.7 above is an example in which there are two routes with a cumulative metric of 100 to a destination and a route with a cumulative metric of 200 to the same destination. By default, EIGRP performs only equal cost load balancing, so it will send traffic across only the first two links, which have the best metric of 100. If traffic was sent over a third link, the variance should be set to 2, meaning the maximum allowed metric is two times the lowest metric, equaling 200. Traffic will be sent proportionally to the metric, meaning for each packet sent over the third link, two packets are sent over the first two links because their metric is better.

EIGRP creates neighbor relationships with adjacent routes and exchanges information with them using Reliable Transport Protocol (RTP). This protocol ensures that neighbors can exchange information in a reliable manner.

NOTE: Do not confuse the EIGRP-specific RTP (Reliable Transport Protocol) with the Real-time Transport Protocol used in VoIP environments.

By default, EIGRP calculates route metrics based on bandwidth and delay but it can use other parameters in the calculation, including load and reliability. Enabling the metric calculation based on load and reliability is not recommended by Cisco because the network might become unstable.

Scalable EIGRP

EIGRP offers more flexibility than OSPF, which is more rigid and is much more governed by operational and technical considerations. A small- to medium-sized business with an arbitrary network architecture can use EIGRP without many problems because the network does not have to be restructured until scaling up to a larger topology. However, if the topology reaches the point where there are hundreds of routers, then EIGRP might become instable and present long convergence times.

When scaling EIGRP, the structured IP hierarchy should include good route summarization. The most important issue with EIGRP as it relates to stability and convergence is trying to lower the propagation of EIGRP queries, especially when trying to find a feasible successor. One of the key aspects of a scalable EIGRP design (especially in large deployments) is to ensure that there are feasible successors. This can be achieved through an efficient equal cost routing design. In addition, summarization points and filtered routes can also limit EIGRP query propagation and lower the convergence times.

Adjusting the delay timers and tuning using variance, unlike one might think, are suboptimal solutions when trying to achieve low convergence times because this will become almost impossible to perform as the network scales to hundreds of routers. Another suboptimal way many organizations have tried to achieve low convergence times is implementing multiple EIGRP ASs or process numbers. Scaling two or three EIGRP ASs to limit EIGRP queries has proven to be an inefficient solution.

Having multiple EIGRP systems would be justified in a limited number of scenarios, the most common of which are as follows:

- After a merger/acquisition, as a migration strategy.
- Having different groups administering different EIGRP ASs, which is a suboptimal option because this will induce a larger degree of complexity in the network infrastructure; however, it might be necessary to have different trust domains or administrative control boundaries.
- Having an organization with an extremely large network that uses multiple EIGRP ASs to divide the network. This will involve using summary routes at the AS boundaries to advertise blocks of prefixes in the large network.

The most efficient methods for limiting EIGRP queries and achieving a scalable EIGRP design are as follows:

- Using a solid summarization design
- Using distribution lists
- Using stubs
- Ensuring there are feasible successors
- Implementing equal cost routing
- Avoiding having many EIGRP routers
- Avoiding scaling by multiple EIGRP ASs, if possible

ADVANCED OSPF

The OSPF protocol is one of the most complex routing protocols that can be deployed in modern networks. OSPF is an open-standard protocol, whereas EIGRP is not. OSPF is a classless routing protocol and this allows it to support VLSM. OSPF uses the Dijkstra SPF algorithm to select loop-free paths throughout the topology, while EIGRP uses DUAL. OSPF is designed to be very scalable because it is a hierarchical routing protocol, using the concept of "areas" to split the topology into smaller sections.

OSPF usually does not converge as fast as EIGRP but it does offer efficient updating and convergence, as it takes bandwidth into consideration when calculating route metrics (or costs). A higher bandwidth generates a lower cost and lower costs are preferred in OSPF. OSPF supports authentication, as does EIGRP and RIPv2, and it is very extensible, as are BGP and IS-IS, meaning the protocol can be modified in the future to handle other forms of traffic.

OSPF Functionality

OSPF discovers neighbors and exchanges topology information with them, acting much like EIGRP. Based on the information collected and the link costs, OSPF calculates the shortest paths to each destination using the SPF algorithm. The formula for calculating the interface cost is reference bandwidth/link bandwidth. The default reference bandwidth is 100 Mbps but this can be modified, as can the link bandwidth using the "bandwidth" command.

> **NOTE:** The reference bandwidth should be modified in networks that contain a combination of 100 Mbps and 1 Gbps links because, by default, all of these interfaces will be assigned the same OSPF cost.

Another aspect that adds to the design complexity of OSPF is that it can be configured to behave differently depending on the topology in which it is implemented. OSPF recognizes different network types and this will control issues such as:

- How updates are sent
- How many adjacencies are made between the OSPF speakers
- How the next hop is calculated

OSPF supports six network types:

- Broadcast
- Non-broadcast
- Point-to-point

- Point-to-multipoint
- Point-to-multipoint non-broadcast
- Loopback

OSPF does a good job of automatically selecting the network type that is most appropriate for a given technology. For example, configuring OSPF in a broadcast-based Ethernet environment will default to the broadcast type; configuring OSPF on a Frame Relay physical interface will default to the non-broadcast type; and configuring OSPF on a point-to-point serial link will default to the point-to-point network type.

Two network types that are never automatically assigned are point-to-multipoint and point-to-multipoint non-broadcast. These are most appropriate for partial mesh (hub-and-spoke) environments and must be manually configured.

The network types can influence the underlying OSPF protocol in many ways. The broadcast type will be the default on broadcast media, and once OSPF is configured on a broadcast environment, the systems will elect a Designated Router (DR) and, optionally, a Backup Designated Router (BDR) on each segment. To communicate with the DRs, OSPF will multicast updates to 224.0.0.6, and to communicate to every OSPF router, packets are multicasted to 224.0.0.5.

In a broadcast network, the DR is the device that all of the other routers will form their adjacency with and this is a protection mechanism to prevent the network from being overwhelmed with a full mesh of adjacencies. In addition to minimizing adjacencies, the DR also helps minimize the amount of OSPF traffic between OSPF nodes because it establishes a full OSPF adjacency only with the DR. The BDR is a node that will take the place of a DR if it fails.

On a broadcast OSPF segment, if every node had to form adjacencies for the information exchange with all of its neighbors, the number of total neighbor relationships would be $n*(n-1)/2$, where "n" is the number of routers. Using a DR helps reduce the total number of adjacencies and makes the process more efficient because nodes do not need a full mesh of relationships.

OSPF Router Types

The OSPF hierarchy uses the concept of areas to improve the scalability of the protocol. Link-state protocols operate by flooding information about the status of their links, but when the network is divided into areas, only the routers in a specific area have to agree on the topology map. Setting up areas reduces the convergence domain size because this can hide topology details between areas. This leads to the protocol becoming much more efficient.

Area 0 (backbone) is the critical area in an OSPF environment, and every OSPF design must start from this area. It is also called the transit area because all areas must connect to it and traffic between areas must go through Area 0. Another feature of the backbone area is that it must be contiguous, meaning it cannot be broken into multiple parts. Once the backbone area is designed, other areas, called non-transit areas, can be included and they can be assigned any number. This is illustrated in Figure 5.8 below:

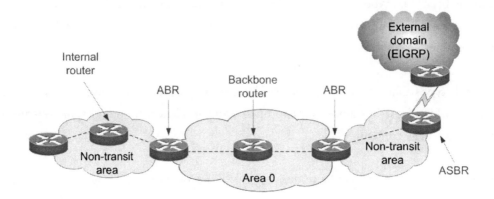

Figure 5.8 – OSPF Area Types and Router Roles

Network designers should also understand the different router roles that exist within OSPF:

- **Backbone router:** This is the terminology given to a router that has at least one link in Area 0.
- **Internal router:** This router has all links participating in one non-transit area.
- **Area Border Router (ABR):** The ABR is a router that is positioned between multiple areas. This means the router has at least one link to Area 0 and one link to a non-transit area. ABRs pass information between the backbone area and non-transit areas. They are also used to summarize information between the two areas, thus improving the efficiency and the scalability of the OSPF design.
- **Autonomous System Boundary Router (ASBR):** An ASBR has at least one link to the OSPF domain and at least one link outside of the OSPF domain touching another routing protocol (EIGRP, IS-IS, or BGP). ASBR is used to redistribute information to and from other routing domains and OSPF.

Virtual Links

If the backbone area is split into multiple pieces, virtual links can ensure its continuity. A virtual link is an Area 0 tunnel that connects the dispersed backbone areas. Virtual links are not considered a best design practice but they can be useful in particular situations, like company mergers, as depicted in Figure 5.9 below:

Figure 5.9 – OSPF Virtual Link (Example 1)

A virtual link is configured between ABRs as a temporary fix to the problem (split Area 0). The virtual link tunnels the backbone area between the devices so the topology is repaired until a network redesign is implemented.

Another classic case in which virtual links might be used is the situation in which there is an OSPF area not connected to the backbone. Looking at Figure 5.10 below, Area 100 is connected to Area 0 but Area 200 is connected only to Area 100. This poses a design problem because it goes against the principle stating that every area must be connected to Area 0. The solution in this case would be to configure a virtual link between Area 0 and Area 200 so the backbone is extended to reach Area 200.

Figure 5.10 – OSPF Virtual Link (Example 2)

NOTE: In the scenario depicted in Figure 5.10, the virtual link is often considered an extension of the non-transit area (Area 200 in this case) to reach Area 0. This is not true because the virtual link is part of Area 0, so in fact Area 0 is extended to reach the non-transit area (Area 200 in this case).

Link-State Advertisements

Another important OSPF aspect is represented by the different Link-State Advertisement (LSA) types. Each LSA type has a unique format that is defined by the type of information it contains (either internal or external prefixes). The LSA types are as follows:

- **Type 1 – Router LSA:** Used by routers in an area to advertise a link to another router in the same area.
- **Type 2 – Network LSA:** Generated by the DR to send updates about the attached routers.

- **Type 3 – Network Summary LSA:** Generated by the ABR to advertise information from one area to another.
- **Type 4 – ASBR Summary LSA:** Generated by the ABR to send information about the location of the ASBR.
- **Type 5 – External LSA:** Used by the ASBR to advertise external prefixes to the OSPF domain.
- **Type 6 – Multicast LSA:** Not implemented by Cisco.
- **Type 7 – NSSA External LSA:** Used in not so stubby areas to advertise external prefixes.
- **Types 8, 9, and 10 – Opaque LSA:** Used for extensibility.

The LSA types allow for a hierarchical structure:

- LSAs that only flow within an area (intra-area routes): Types 1 and 2 (O)
- LSAs that flow between areas (inter-area routes): Types 3 and 4 (O, IA)
- External routes: Type 5 (E1/E2) or Type 7 (N1/N2)

OSPF Area Types

OSPF offers the capability to create different area types that relate to the various LSA types presented above and the way they flow inside a specific area. The different area types are as follows:

- **Regular area:** This is the normal OSPF area, with no restrictions in the LSA flow.
- **Stub area:** This area prevents the external Type 5 LSAs from entering the area. It also stops Type 4 LSAs, as they are used only in conjunction with Type 5 LSAs.
- **Totally stubby area:** This area prevents Type 5, Type 4, and Type 3 LSAs from entering the area. A default route is automatically injected to reach the internal destinations.
- **Not so stubby area (NSSA):** The NSSA blocks Type 4 and Type 5 LSAs but it can connect to other domains and an ASBR can be in this area. The NSSA does not receive external routes injected in other areas but it can inject external routes into the OSPF domain. The external routes will be injected as Type 7 LSAs. These Type 7 LSAs convert to Type 5 LSAs using the NSSA ABR (the router that connects to the backbone), and they reach other OSPF areas as Type 5 LSAs.
- **Totally not so stubby area (totally NSSA):** This area has the same characteristics as the NSSA, except that it also blocks Type 3 LSAs from entering the area.

NOTE: All routers in an OSPF area must agree on the stub flag.

The various areas and LSA types are summarized in Figure 5.11 below:

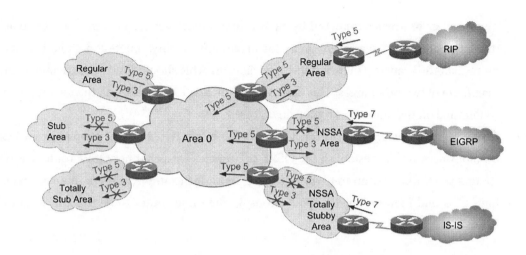

Figure 5.11 – OSPF Areas and LSA Types

All of these areas and LSA types make OSPF a very hierarchical and scalable routing protocol that can be tweaked and tuned for very large environments based on all of these design elements. OSPF allows for summarization, which can be carried out in two locations:

- Between areas (inter-area summarization), using Type 3 LSAs
- At the ASBR, summarizing external prefixes, using Type 5 and Type 7 LSAs

Scalable OSPF

When analyzing scalability on a router, there are three resource areas that should be taken into consideration:

- Memory
- CPU
- Interface bandwidth

The routing protocol places demands on the underlying router, and there are four factors that lead to the workload calculations:

- **The number of adjacent neighbors the router has (OSPF neighbors in this case).** OSPF will flood all of the link-state modifications to all of the routers in an area. Typically, one router should have no more than 60 neighbors.
- **The number of adjacent routers in an area.** Typically, there should be no more than 50 routers in an OSPF area. In situations where a larger number of areas might be needed, the topology can be split into multiple areas.

- **The number of areas supported by each router.** Since every ABR is in at least two areas (the backbone and one adjacent area), for maximum stability, one router should not be in more than three areas. Following this guideline, an ABR should touch the backbone and a maximum of two other areas. This design recommendation depends on the total number of routers and on the number of routers in one area.
- **Choosing the designated router.** DRs and BDRs are the "busiest" routers in an OSPF topology because they establish full OSPF adjacencies with all other OSPF routers. Proper routers should be chosen to carry out these tasks, for example, routers that can manage high CPU and memory loads. Avoid choosing the same router to be the DR in multiple LANs at the same time.

In situations where there are many branches or remote routers, the workload should be split across several peers. For example, IPsec VPN peers running OSPF over GRE tunnels form a less stable environment than a non-VPN peer environment. Proper lab testing should be done before implementing the production network.

EIGRP is more flexible and tolerant to an ad-hoc network topology, but OSPF needs a well-defined hierarchy with a clear backbone and area topology. Routing information can be reduced by having a good area design.

OSPF designers should use techniques to minimize the number of advertisements going into and out of an area. Anything in the LSA database must be sent to all of the routers in an area, so anytime a modification needs to be propagated, the CPU, memory, and bandwidth parameters will be affected. Network designers should be conservative in adding routers to Area 0. If possible, this area should contain only the necessary backbone routers and the ABRs to connect other OSPF areas.

If the OSPF design cannot be simplified, every non-backbone area should be configured to be some type of stub area or totally stubby area. Solid summarization techniques should also be used to build a scalable OSPF design.

An important issue network designers often face is deciding whether ABRs should be Core Layer or Distribution Layer routers. This depends on the network topology in the organization. The general guidelines recommend placing different functional network areas into different OSPF areas.

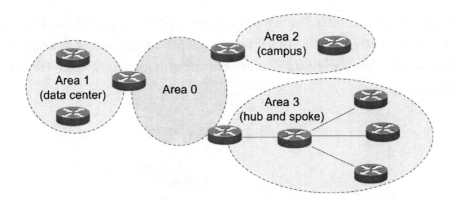

Figure 5.12 – OSPF Network Design

Analyzing Figure 5.12 above, different logical areas are separated into dedicated OSPF areas. An OSPF area exists for the following:

- The data center or server arm
- The Enterprise Campus area
- The hub-and-spoke topology to the regional offices

OSPF ABRs provide the ability to support route summarization or to create stubby or totally stubby areas whenever possible. The effectiveness of route summarization will depend entirely on how good the addressing scheme and hierarchy is. Some guidelines regarding summarization in and out of areas include the following:

- Configure the addressing scheme so the range of subnets assigned within an area is contiguous.
- Develop an address space scheme that will be easy to partition as the network grows.
- Assign subnets according to simple octet boundaries, where possible.
- Always plan ahead for new routers and new areas.
- Ensure that new routers are placed properly as ABRs, backbone routers, or other types of routers.

Routes can be summarized and the LSA database size and flooding can be reduced in OSPF by using the "area range" command (internal summarization) and the "summary-address" command (external summarization), by implementing filtering, or by originating default routes into certain areas. Different type of routes can also be filtered in stub and totally stubby areas.

OSPF Hub-and-Spoke Design Considerations

The hub-and-spoke topology in Figure 5.13 below should be carefully designed, as specific considerations relate to this type of topology. Network designers should take into consideration the fact that any change performed on any of the spokes will be propagated to the hub and then replicated to all of the other spokes. This behavior can put a great deal of overhead on the hub router and this is called "change flooding." To prevent this issue, use stub areas, totally stubby areas, or totally NSSAs.

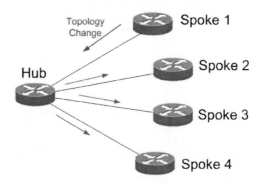

Figure 5.13 – OSPF Hub-and-Spoke Router

In hub-and-spoke scenarios, the number of spokes and the area selection criteria should be carefully controlled. If there are a few remote sites (spokes), the hub and the spokes can be placed within the same area. However, if there are many remote sites, the spokes might need to be split into more areas, which would result in implementing a multi-area design. To summarize in and out of the remote areas, the hub must be an ABR. Another good practice is to design the OSPF network so that it has a small and very stable Area 0 because the backbone area is critical in an OSPF topology.

NOTE: The most simplified backbone area design involves grouping the ABRs only in Area 0.

If the spokes have low-speed links, the link speeds should be increased to improve the design. Not having enough bandwidth to flood LSAs when there are topology changes is a major issue.

OSPF has several choices for the type of networks to use. Cisco recommends avoiding the use of broadcast or Non-Broadcast Multi-Access (NBMA) network types and instead using one of the following types:

- A single interface on the hub treated as a point-to-multipoint network
- Individual point-to-point interfaces on the hub for each spoke and a point-to-point designation

OSPF Full-Mesh Design Considerations

Some organizations need to deploy their OSPF speaker or their peer into a full-mesh topology, like in Figure 5.14 below. The problem with flooding in an OSPF full-mesh topology is that it is extremely difficult and it is not scalable. A full-mesh topology implies a number of total connections equal to n*(n-1)/2, where "n" equals the number of nodes. If there are eight OSPF neighbors, then 28 links between all the nodes will be needed. Adding one more router to the OSPF full-mesh topology would increase the amount of links, from 28 to 36, which is not scalable. To deploy this implementation, an OSPF "mesh group" can be used. This is a manual method to reduce flooding and it works by selecting two routers (DRs) to handle the flooding process and filter out all of the other routers.

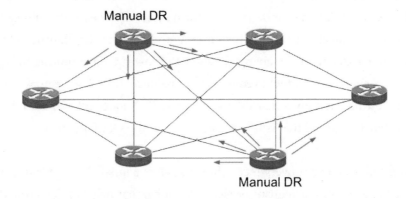

Figure 5.14 – OSPF Full-Mesh Topology

On broadcast, non-broadcast, and point-to-point networks, the "ip ospf database-filter all out" command in interface configuration mode can be issued on all of the routers that are not selected as DRs to manually prevent the flooding of OSPF LSAs. When using point-to-multipoint networks, the "neighbor <ip_address> database-filter all out" command in routing configuration mode can be used.

An additional feature called OSPF Flood Reduction can also be implemented if LSA flooding is creating too much overhead on the CPU or on bandwidth. This feature can be configured using the "ip ospf flood-reduction" command at the interface level. This feature eliminates the periodic refreshing of unmodified LSAs, which reduces the impact on router resources. An important thing to keep in mind is that OSPF flood reduction eliminates only the effect; it does not deal with the underlying issue of the unoptimized OSPF design. This command should be used in conjunction with some of the guidelines mentioned previously to fix the real OSPF issues that follow:

- Too many routers in an area or too many adjacencies
- An unstable OSPF design
- A heavy adjacency workload
- A large full-mesh topology that uses mesh groups, which does not always offer optimal results

OSPF Fast Convergence

One of the things that can be done to obtain fast convergence in OSPF includes using subsecond OSPF timers. This is implemented by setting the dead interval to one second and using a hello multiplier to designate how many hello packets will be sent in a one-second interval. Using fast hellos is recommended in small- to medium-sized networks but they should not be used in large networks. This can offer fast convergence but it is not a scalable solution.

Network designers should understand the SPF algorithm behavior in the OSPF environment to obtain fast convergence. This behavior depends on the number of nodes, links, and LSAs in the area. iSPF (Incremental SPF) can also be used, which uses a modified Dijkstra algorithm to compute the portion of the path tree that has been changed. Doing this instead of computing the entire tree will offer faster OSPF convergence and will reduce CPU overhead. iSPF has been available since IOS 12.3(2)T, and lab testing has shown that iSPF used on 10,000 nodes offered a 50 ms convergence time. iSPF is implemented using the "ispf" command under the OSPF process.

Another issue related to router convergence is how to detect a link failure. This is usually achieved using some type of keepalive mechanism or electrical signal that helps in detecting the loss of the link. A special technology used for this purpose is Bidirectional Forwarding Detection (BFD). BFD is a routing protocol technology that uses fast Layer 2 link hellos to notify an engineer of any failed links or one-way links. BFD is supported on multiple Cisco platforms, including 6500, 7600, 12000, and CRS routers. This is one method for configuring subsecond Layer 2 failure detection between adjacent network nodes. Routing protocols can also be configured to respond to BFD notifications and immediately begin the Layer 3 route convergence process.

ADVANCED BGP

Border Gateway Protocol is the only exterior gateway protocol in use today and its role is primarily to exchange routing information between organizations. BGP is a standard-based protocol defined in RFC 4271 and is the successor of EGP (Exterior Gateway Protocol).

Necessity of BGP

BGP is used to route between ASs and is considered to be a path vector routing protocol. Routing decisions are based on multiple attributes that can be tuned and controlled, resulting in the particular path the AS's data will take (i.e., this is the routing decision). This is more of a policy based routing approach and policy routing is very important for ISPs routing traffic between each other for different ASs.

BGP is a classless routing protocol and it supports VLSM and summarization (route aggregation). While IGRPs can scale to thousands of routes, BGP can scale to hundreds of thousands of routes, making it the most scalable routing protocol ever developed. Currently, the global BGP routing table has over 300,000 routes.

Another characteristic of BGP is its high rate of stability, as there is never a solid convergence of the Internet routing table (i.e., something is always changing in such a large routing table). In addition, it is stable enough to handle routing and decision making at the same time. Because BGP focuses on the enforcement of policies, it does not use a simple metric value that might be tied to a single parameter (like bandwidth). Instead, BGP has a group of attributes that can be manipulated to dictate a particular routing policy.

When used to exchange routing information between organizations, BGP can be configured in two particular scenarios (see Figure 5.15 below):

- **Transit networks:** ISPs that want to provide transit to other destinations on the public Internet.
- **Multi-homed networks:** Big Enterprise Networks that rely heavily on Internet traffic and have sophisticated connectivity requirements to two or more ISPs. BGP allows them to control inbound and outbound routing policies.

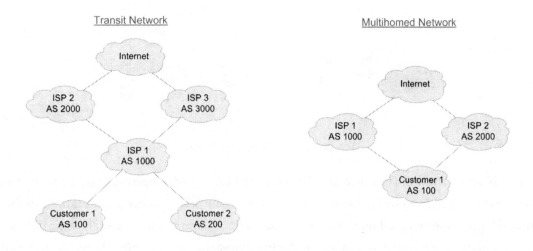

Figure 5.15 – BGP Deployment Scenarios

Most of the Enterprise Networks do not need BGP and this is for various reasons:

- The network requires single ISP connectivity and default routing configuration is sufficient. A default route will point to the ISP so all Internet traffic is routed to that single ISP.

- Memory and CPU resources are limited and do not support a BGP implementation. The global routing table needs more than 1 GB of memory just for storage.
- Not owning the IPv4 address space in use. This happens in situations where the organization's addresses are owned by the ISP, which is a frequent occurrence for small- and medium-sized organizations.

BGP Functionality

Similar to OSPF, IS-IS, and EIGRP, BGP uses a three-table data structure:

- **Neighbor table:** Contains information about adjacency with peers.
- **BGP table (topology table):** Contains all of the prefixes learned from peers.
- **IP routing table:** Contains the best routes from the BGP tables.

The devices running BGP will establish adjacencies to build the neighbor table and will then exchange updates to build the BGP table. After the BGP table is built, the best paths for routing information are chosen and are used to build the IP routing table. BGP allows for different peering types to be created:

- **External BGP (eBGP) peering:** BGP peering with a neighbor that is outside of the AS.
- **Internal BGP (iBGP) peering:** BGP peering with devices inside the AS.

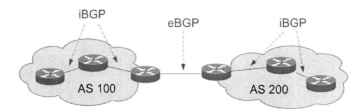

Figure 5.16 – BGP Peering Types

Figure 5.16 above shows an example of BGP peering types. The BGP peering types a route is being sent to and received from will influence the update and path selection rules. An example of this is that eBGP peers are assumed to be directly connected. If they are not, a special command called "ebgp multihop" must be entered to let the devices know they are not directly connected and to establish the BGP peering. This assumption has no equivalent when considering iBGP peering, where there is no requirement for direct connectivity.

Another example regarding the iBGP versus eBGP behavior is that an eBGP-learned route will not be advertised between iBGP peers because of a special loop prevention mechanism that prevents an update learned via iBGP to be sent to other iBGP peers. This happens because BGP assumes that all routers within an AS have complete information about each other. Multiple solutions exist to solve this issue, including the following:

- Configure a full mesh of iBGP peers
- Use BGP Route Reflectors
- Organize the AS into BGP Confederations

The solution that involves a full mesh of iBGP peers is the least preferred because of the increased number of connections. The total number of connections is n*(n-1)/2, where "n" equals the number of BGP routers, so for 1,000 routers there would be 499,500 peers. This is very hard to implement and maintain, so the Route Reflector and Confederations solutions are recommended instead. Details about BGP Route Reflectors and BGP Confederations will be covered later in this chapter.

BGP Path Vector Attributes

BGP can use multiple attributes to define a routing policy and the most important are as follows:

- **Next hop:** This attribute must be present in each BGP update; it indicates where the traffic should be sent to reach a particular destination.
- **AS-path:** This attribute lists all of the Autonomous Systems through which the prefix has passed. AS-path is similar to a hop count, except it uses AS numbers and provides more details about the path.
- **Origin:** This attribute provides information about how the prefix entered the BGP system, either directly advertised into BGP with the "network" command or redistributed from other routing protocols.
- **Local preference:** This attribute influences the way traffic enters the AS and the path that it takes; it can also influence the way packets exit the AS and the path that they take.
- **Community:** This attribute groups destinations in a certain community and applies routing decisions according to those communities.
- **Multi-Exist Discriminator (MED):** This attribute influences the way traffic enters the AS and the path that it takes.
- **Atomic aggregate:** This attribute is used when performing BGP summarization.
- **Aggregator:** This attribute is used when performing BGP summarization.

BGP attributes can be grouped into several categories, such as well-known and optional. The well-known attributes are supported by all BGP vendors and the optional attributes are supported only by certain BGP vendors. BGP attributes can also be mandatory and discretionary. The mandatory attributes are sent in every routing update, while the discretionary attributes may or may not be present in routing updates. Another category relies on the path attribute's transitivity, which can be either transitive (they pass between eBGP and iBGP neighbors) or non-transitive (they pass between iBGP neighbors only). Valid combinations of BGP attributes include the following:

- Well-known mandatory (next-hop, AS-path, origin)
- Well-known discretionary (local preference, atomic aggregate)
- Optional transitive (aggregator, community)
- Optional non-transitive (MED)

BGP systems will analyze all of these attributes and will determine the best path to get to a destination based on this very complex decision process. Only the best route is sent to the routing table and to the peers. Finding out whether the next hop is reachable must be determined first. If it is not, the prefixes will not have a best path available, but if it is, the decision process will analyze the following aspects:

- Weight (Cisco-specific attribute) – the highest weight is preferred.
- Local preference – the highest local preference is preferred.
- Locally originated routes – these are preferred.
- AS-path – the shortest AS-path is preferred.
- Origin – routes with the lowest origin type are preferred.
- MED – the lowest MED is preferred.
- Neighbor type – routes that came via eBGP over those that were learned via iBGP are preferred.
- IGP metric – if there is still a tie, the lowest IGP metric wins.
- If multiple paths exist in the routing table, the path that was received first is preferred.
- The route that comes from the BGP router with the lowest router ID is preferred.
- The path with the minimum cluster list length is preferred.
- The path that comes from the lowest neighbor address is preferred.

Scalable BGP

BGP typically has multi-homed links to ISPs and is found in MPLS VPN scenarios. When using BGP as an interior routing protocol, a full mesh of iBGP routers is necessary because they do not re-advertise routes that were learned from other iBGP peers, according to BGP behavior. Two methods for scaling iBGP and avoiding the need for a full-mesh topology are using Route Reflectors and Confederations.

BGP Route Reflectors

Route Reflectors (RRs) are nodes that reflect the iBGP updates to devices that are configured as RR clients. This solution is easy to design and implement and solves the iBGP split horizon rule. A full-mesh connection between RR nodes and normal nodes (non-RR clients) must be configured, but a full-mesh connection between the RR and its clients is not required. This concept is illustrated in Figure 5.17 below:

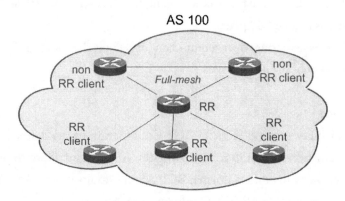

Figure 5.17 – BGP Route Reflectors

BGP RRs, defined in RF 2796, are iBGP speakers that reflect routes that were learned from iBGP peers to RR clients. They also reflect routes received from RR clients to other iBGP peers (non-RR clients). Route reflector client configuration is carried out only on the RR device, using the "neighbor <ip_address> route-reflector-client" command. This configuration process can be performed incrementally as more RRs or RR clients are added. The RR client will often establish peer sessions only with RR devices.

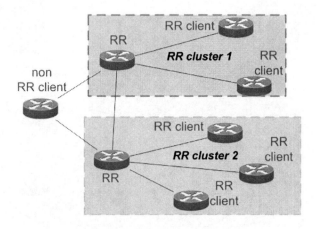

Figure 5.18 – BGP Route Reflector Redundancy

Often, redundant RRs are needed to avoid a single point of failure. An RR and its associated clients form an RR cluster, as depicted in Figure 5.18 above. In some situations there can be overlap in the RR clusters but this adds to the complexity of the design. RR functionality respects the following rules when propagating updates:

- When an RR receives a route from an eBGP peer, it sends the route to all clients and non-clients.
- When an RR receives a route from an RR client, it reflects the route to all RR clients and non-clients, as well as to all eBGP peers.
- When an RR receives a route from a non-client, it reflects the route to all RR clients and sends the route to all eBGP peers.

BGP Confederations

The second BGP scalability method is using BGP Confederations, as defined in RFC 3065. This implies injecting information into BGP routes using the AS-path attribute to prevent loops in the AS. This technique works by dividing a normal BGP AS into multiple sub-ASs. The only AS visible to the outside world is the outer AS (the Confederation AS). The BGP Confederation design is equivalent to having a VLAN and dividing it into private VLANs.

BGP Confederations are more complex than Route Reflectors and they function by creating sub-ASs within the main AS. The connections between sub-ASs behave like eBGP peer sessions and the connections inside sub-ASs are pure iBGP peer sessions. This means that only full-mesh configuration is needed inside the sub-ASs, where RRs can also be configured, so a combination of BGP design technologies is available.

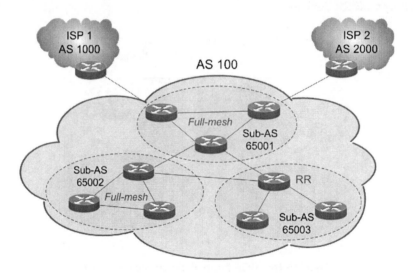

Figure 5.19 – BGP Confederations

Analyzing Figure 5.19 above, the Confederation AS 100 has been configured, and within this confederation AS, three sub-ASs (Confederation internal peers) have been configured: 65001, 65002, and 65003. The connections between the devices in the same sub-AS are BGP Confederation internal peers and the connections between the devices in different sub-AS areas are BGP Confederation external peers, and they have many similarities to eBGP connections.

As iBGP information is exchanged within a Confederation AS, the sub-AS numbers are put into the Confederation sequence, which functions similar to the AS-path attribute as a loop prevention mechanism. The route advertisement rules are similar to the RR distribution rules:

- A route that is learned from an eBGP peer is advertised to all the Confederation external and internal peers.
- A route that is learned from a Confederation internal peer is advertised to all Confederation external and eBGP peers.
- A route that is learned from a Confederation external peer is advertised to all Confederation internal and eBGP peers.

Private AS numbers are used within a Confederation AS and are then removed from updates sent out of the Confederation. This makes BGP more scalable and allows the number of connections to be reduced.

> **NOTE:** AS numbers are defined as 16-bit integers, so they range from 0 to 65535. Sub-ASs are usually assigned private AS numbers, ranging from 64512 to 65535. Because of the exhaustion of public AS numbers, IANA introduced 32-bit AS numbers and began allocating them over the last few years.

IPV6 ROUTING

Cisco routers do not route IPv6 by default and this capability should be activated with the "ipv6 unicast-routing" command. Cisco routers are dual-stack capable by default, meaning they are capable of running IPv4 and IPv6 simultaneously on the same interfaces.

IPv6 allows the use of static routing and it supports specific dynamic routing protocols that are variations of the IPv4 routing protocols modified or redesigned to support IPv6, such as the following:

- RIPng (RIP new generation)
- OSPFv3
- EIGRPv6
- IS-IS
- BGP

NOTE: IS-IS and BGP underwent the least amount of modifications to support IPv6 because they were built with extensibility in mind.

RIPng, OSPFv3, and EIGRPv6 are new routing protocols that work independently of the IPv4 versions and they run in a completely separate process on the device. BGP and IS-IS are exceptions to this rule, as they route IPv6 traffic using the same process used for IPv4 traffic, but they use the concept of address families that hold the entire IPv6 configuration.

Many of the issues with IPv4 (e.g., name resolution and NBMA environments) still exist with IPv6 routing. An important aspect is that IPv6 routing protocols communicate with the remote link-local addresses when establishing their adjacencies and exchanging routing information. In the routing table of an IPv6 router, the next hops are the link-local addresses of the neighbors.

As mentioned, static routing is one of the options that can be used in IPv6 and it has the same implications as in IPv4. The route can point to:

- The next hop (the next hop must be resolved)
- A multipoint interface (the final destination must be resolved)
- A point-to-point interface (no resolution is required)

RIPng, also called RIP for IPv6, was specified in RFC 2080 and is similar in operation to RIPv1 and RIPv2. While RIPv2 uses the multicast address 224.0.0.9 to exchange routing information with its neighbors, RIPng uses the similar FF02::9 address and UDP port 521. Another difference between the two versions is that IPv6 is configured at the interface level while RIPv1 and RIPv2 are configured at the global routing configuration level.

OSPFv3 is defined in RFC 2740 and is similar in operation to OSPFv2 (for IPv4). OSPFv3 even supports the same network types as OSPFv2:

- Broadcast
- Non-broadcast
- Point-to-point
- Point-to-multipoint
- Point-to-multipoint non-broadcast

EIGRPv6 is similar in operation to EIGRP for IPv4 and uses IP protocol 88 to multicast updates to FF02::A.

NOTE: An important aspect to consider when implementing EIGRPv6 is that, unlike EIGRP for IPv4, the process is shut down until it is manually enabled by issuing the "no shutdown" command under the routing process.

BGP for IPv6 is configured in the address family configuration mode but it is based on the same configuration principles used by BGP for IPv4:

- An underlying transport IGP is required.
- There is an implicit iBGP loop prevention mechanism that prevents iBGP-learned routes from being advertised to other iBGP neighbors (this can be solved by using Route Reflectors or Confederations).
- There is an implicit eBGP loop prevention mechanism that does not accept routes entering an AS that has the same AS in the path.
- It uses the same best-path selection process.

SUMMARY

When designing enterprise routing, network architects should first figure out whether they should use static or dynamic routing. Static routing implies manually defining routes on devices and dynamic routing implies using a dedicated routing protocol that will build the routing table. The dynamic routing protocols most often used in modern networks are EIGRP, OSPF, and BGP.

Large networks, including the Internet, are based on the Autonomous System (AS) concept. An AS defines a group of network devices under a common administration and most often this defines a large organization or an ISP. Routing protocols can be classified based on different criteria. Depending on the zone in which they operate, they can be interior (inter-AS) routing protocols or exterior (intra-AS) routing protocols.

Interior routing protocols can be further classified as distance vector routing protocols or link-state routing protocols, based on their behavior regarding the router update exchange process. Distance vector routing protocols include RIP, IGRP, and RIPng. Link-state routing protocols include OSPF, IS-IS, and OSPFv3.

The main difference between distance vector routing protocols and link-state routing protocols is the way they exchange routing updates. Distance vector routing protocols function using the "routing by rumor" technique, as every router relies on its neighbors to maintain correct routing information. This means the entire routing table is sent periodically to the neighbors.

Link-state routing protocols do not generally "route by rumor" like distance vector routing protocols do. The routing devices exchange information between them about their link-states. Devices build a map of the network independently and loop-free based on the link-state information each router generates and propagates to the other routers.

Link-state routing protocols offer a series of important advantages compared to distance vector routing protocols. The most important advantage relates to the convergence factor. Link-state routing protocols converge must faster because as soon as a network topology changes, only that specific information is sent to the routers in a given area.

Exterior routing protocols run between ASs (inter-AS) and the most common example is BGPv4. The main reason different types of routing protocols are used to carry routes outside of the AS boundaries is the need to exchange a large amount of route entries.

Routers use Administrative Distance (AD) to select the best route when multiple routing protocols advertise the same prefix. The AD value represents how trustworthy a particular routing protocol is.

Route summarization helps make the routing design more scalable, regardless of the routing protocol used (e.g., RIPv2, EIGRP, or OSPF). It also helps place network addresses into usable blocks (listed below), which can be used for multiple purposes:

- NAT blocks
- Blocks used in redistribution
- Blocks for management VLANs
- Blocks for content services

A special form of route summarization can be implemented in the form of default routing. Every modern network usually uses some type of default routing. The best practice is to dynamically advertise the default route 0.0.0.0/0 out of the Enterprise Network to the ISPs, as opposed to performing a static route configuration on every router in the organization.

Route filtering allows the control of network traffic flow and prevents unwanted transit traffic, especially in situations that feature redundancy or multiple paths. Route filtering protects against erroneous routing updates and there are several techniques that can be used in this regard. For example, with OSPF, if Core Layer connectivity is lost, traffic should not be rerouted through a remote site.

There are two ways to migrate between routing protocols:

- Using AD
- Performing redistribution by moving the boundary routers in small steps

Enhanced Interior Gateway Routing Protocol (EIGRP) is a unique protocol in that it uses a hybrid approach, combining distance vector and link-state characteristics. Combining these features makes EIGRP very robust and allows for fast convergence, even in large topologies. EIGRP functions by using DUAL and it is the only IGRP that can perform unequal cost load balancing.

When analyzing scalability on a router, there are three resource areas that should be taken into consideration: memory, CPU, and interface bandwidth.

The most efficient methods for limiting EIGRP queries and achieving a scalable EIGRP design are as follows:

- Using a solid summarization design
- Using distribute lists
- Using stub areas
- Ensuring there are feasible successors
- Implementing equal cost routing
- Avoiding scaling by multiple EIGRP ASs, if possible

Open Shortest Path First (OSPF) protocol is one of the most complex routing protocols that can be deployed in modern networks. OSPF is an open-standard protocol, while EIGRP is not. OSPF functions by using the Dijkstra SPF algorithm and by exchanging Link-State Advertisements (LSAs) between neighbors. LSA types are as follows:

- Type 1 – Router LSA
- Type 2 – Network LSA
- Type 3 – Network Summary LSA
- Type 4 – ASBR Summary LSA
- Type 5 – External LSA
- Type 6 – Multicast LSA
- Type 7 – NSSA External LSA
- Types 8, 9, and 10 – Opaque LSA

OSPF offers the capability to create different area types that relate to the various LSA types presented above and the way they flow inside a specific area. The different area types are as follows:

- Regular area
- Stub area
- Totally stubby area
- Not so stubby area (NSSA)
- Totally not so stubby area (totally NSSA)

The major points that should be taken into consideration when designing a scalable OSPF design are:

- The number of adjacent neighbors the router has (OSPF neighbors in this case)
- The number of adjacent routers in an area
- The number of areas supported by each router
- Choosing the designated router

BGP is a highly scalable path vector routing protocol. Its metric is based on multiple attributes that can be tuned and controlled to decide which path the AS's data will take.

BGP can be used in transit networks (ISPs that want to provide transit to other destinations on the public Internet) or in multi-homed networks (big organizations that connect to multiple ISPs).

When using BGP as an interior routing protocol, a full mesh of iBGP routers is necessary because they do not re-advertise routes that were learned from other iBGP peers, according to BGP protocol behavior.

Two methods for scaling iBGP and avoiding the need for a full-mesh topology are as follows:

- Route Reflectors
- Confederations

IPv6 allows the use of static routing and also supports specific dynamic routing protocols that are variations of the IPv4 routing protocols modified or redesigned to support IPv6:

- RIPng
- OSPFv3
- EIGRPv6
- IS-IS
- BGP

END OF CHAPTER QUIZ

1. What is the name of the 0.0.0.0/0 route?

    a. Broadcast route

    b. Static route

    c. Default route

    d. Subnet route

2. What is a floating static route?

    a. A static route that resides in flash memory

    b. A static route that has a lower AD than the same route learned via a routing protocol

    c. A static route that has a higher AD than the same route learned via a routing protocol

    d. A dynamic route

    e. A route to Null0

3. Which of the following processes happens when a route in the routing table does not have the next-hop IP address associated with a directly connected routing interface?

    a. Recursive routing

    b. Summary routing

    c. Default routing

    d. Dynamic routing

4. Which of the following concepts defines the process of route filtering implemented to protect against illegal or unwanted routing traffic?

    a. Route summarization

    b. Default route filtering

    c. Dynamic route filtering

    d. Defensive filtering

5. What is an Autonomous System?

    a. An ISP network

    b. The Internet

    c. A large Enterprise Network

    d. A group of devices under a common administration

6. The two ways to migrate between routing protocols include AD manipulation in the migration process and performing redistribution by moving the boundary routers in small steps.
   a. True
   b. False

7. Which of the following is the most efficient method for limiting the scope of EIGRP queries?
   a. Implementing a small backbone area
   b. Using a solid summarization design
   c. Avoiding stub areas
   d. There is no efficient way to limit EIGRP queries

8. Which of the following device resources should be taken into consideration when analyzing scalability on a router (choose three)?
   a. CPU
   b. Number of ports
   c. Memory
   d. Production date
   c. Router modules
   d. Interface bandwidth

9. Which of the following is considered to be a hybrid routing protocol?
   a. IS-IS
   b. IGRP
   c. OSPF
   d. EIGRP
   e. RIPv2

10. The most simplified OSPF backbone area design involves grouping the ABRs only in Area 0.
    a. True
    b. False

11. Which of the following concepts defines how trustworthy a particular routing protocol is when compared to another?
    a. Protocol version
    b. Cost value
    c. Administrative Distance value
    d. Metric value

12. BGP internal and external routes have the same AD value.
    a. True
    b. False

13. Which of the following is a mechanism used in conjunction with different routing protocols that uses fast Layer 2 link hellos to notify an engineer of any failed links or one-way links?
    a. BGP
    b. CDP
    c. BFD
    d. ODR

14. One of the tools that should NOT be used when trying to achieve OSPF fast convergence is implementing subsecond timers.
    a. True
    b. False

15. What makes EIGRP the fastest convergent routing protocol?
    a. It uses a metric calculated by using multiple parameters
    b. It uses DUAL and identifies feasible successors, even before a problem occurs
    c. It uses small update packets
    d. It is a distance vector routing protocol

16. OSPF uses only bandwidth to calculate its routing metric.
    a. True
    b. False

17. What is an OSPF ABR?
    a. A router that has all the links in Area 0
    b. A router that connects to an outside domain
    c. A router that aggregates routes
    d. A router positioned between multiple areas

18. Which OSPF mechanism is used to ensure continuity when the backbone area is split into multiple zones?
    a. Flex links
    b. Port channels
    c. Virtual links
    d. Backup links

19. Which of the following BGP mechanisms allow for protocol scalability and are used to avoid creating a full-mesh topology within the AS (choose two)?
    a. Route aggregation
    b. Confederations
    c. Virtual links
    d. Route reflectors

20. Which of the following is the only true affirmation of Route Reflector functionality regarding update propagation?
    a. When an RR receives a route from an eBGP peer, it sends the route to all clients and non-clients
    b. When an RR receives a route from an RR client, it reflects the route only to RR clients
    c. When an RR receives a route from a non-client, it reflects the route to all RR clients and other non-clients

CHAPTER 6

Designing Advanced WAN Services

This chapter covers the following topics:

- WAN connectivity options, including optical networking
- Metro Ethernet, including its various flavors
- VPLS technology options
  - VPN design considerations
  - IPsec VPN technology options
  - MPLS VPN technology options
  - WAN design methodologies, including SLAs

This chapter will first cover an overview of WAN design and will then discuss the various optical link technologies used in enterprise networking, including SONET, SDH, CWDM, DWDM, and RPR. It will then define the Metro Ethernet service and its various flavors. Next, it will cover Virtual Private LAN Service technologies and VPN design considerations, followed by IP security for VPNs and the popular MPLS VPN technology options. The chapter will finish with a discussion on WAN design methodologies and various SLA monitoring aspects related to WAN services.

WIDE AREA NETWORK DESIGN OVERVIEW

Wide Area Network technologies operate at the Enterprise Edge in the modular Cisco Enterprise Architecture model. WANs span across large geographical distances to provide connectivity for various parts of the network infrastructure. Unlike the Local Area Network environment, not all of the WAN components are usually owned by the specific organization they serve. Instead, WAN equipment or connectivity can be rented or leased from Internet Service Providers. Most ISPs are well trained to ensure they can properly support not just the traditional data traffic but also voice and video services (which are more delay sensitive) over large geographical distances.

With WANs, unlike with LANs, there is typically an initial fixed cost along with periodic recurring fees for services. Because the organization does not own everything and must pay recurring fees to ISPs, over-provisioning the network should be avoided. This leads to the need to implement effective Quality of Service mechanisms to avoid buying additional costly WAN bandwidth.

The design requirements for WAN technologies are typically derived from the following:

- Types of applications
- Availability of applications
- Reliability of applications

- Costs associated with a particular WAN technology
  - Usage levels for the applications

The Enterprise Edge represents a large block (or several blocks) of equipment. This large module is typically split into submodules that feature specialized functionality, including the following components:

- Internet submodule, which offers robust Internet access with some level of availability and redundancy
- DMZ submodule
- WAN submodule for branch offices/remote access connectivity
- E-commerce submodule, if this is a requirement for the organization
- Remote access VPN submodule, which provides secure connectivity for the large number of employees that work out of their home office

WAN Categories

An important topic when considering CCDP certification is the common categories within WAN. An essential concept in this regard is the circuit-switched technology, the most relevant example being the Public Switched Telephone Network (PSTN). One of the technologies that falls into this category is ISDN. Circuit-switched WAN connections function by getting established when needed and by terminating when they are no longer required. Another example of this circuit-switching behavior is the old-fashioned dial-up connection (dial-up modem analog access over the PSTN).

> NOTE: Not too long ago, dial-up technology was the only way to access Internet resources, offering an average usable bandwidth of around 40 kbps. Nowadays, this technology is almost obsolete.

The opposite of the circuit-switched option is leased-line technology. This is a fully dedicated connection that is permanently up and is owned by the company. An example of this is Time Division Multiplexing (TDM) based leased lines. These are usually very expensive because a single customer has full use of the connectivity offered.

Another popular category of WAN involves packet-switched concepts. In a packet-switched infrastructure, shared bandwidth utilizes virtual circuits. The customer can create a virtual path (similar to a leased line) through the ISP infrastructure cloud. This virtual circuit has a dedicated bandwidth, even though technically this is not a leased line. Frame Relay is an example of this type of technology.

> NOTE: Some legacy WAN technologies include X.25, which is a predecessor of Frame Relay. This technology is still present in some implementations but it is very rare.

Another WAN category relates to cell-switched technology. This is often included in packet-switched technologies, as they are very similar. One cell-switched technology example is Asynchronous Transfer Mode (ATM). This operates by using fixed-size cells, instead of using packets as in Frame Relay. Cell-switched technologies form a shared bandwidth environment from an ISP standpoint that can guarantee customers some level of bandwidth through their infrastructure.

Broadband is another growing category for WAN and this includes technologies such as the following:

- DSL
- Cable
- Wireless

Broadband has the capability of taking a connection, such as an old-fashioned coaxial cable that carries TV signals, and figuring out how to use different aspects of that bandwidth. For example, by using multiplexing, an additional data signal could be transmitted along with the original TV signal.

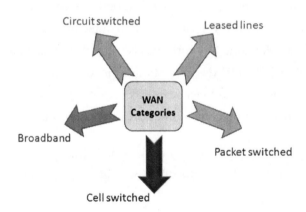

Figure 6.1 – WAN Categories

As detailed in Figure 6.1 above, there are many options when discussing WAN categories. All of these technologies can support the needs of modern networks that operate under the 20/80 rule, meaning 80% of the network traffic uses some kind of WAN technology to access remote resources.

WAN Topologies

WAN topologies are categorized as follows:

- Hub-and-spoke
- Full mesh
- Partial mesh

As presented in the previous chapter, full-mesh topologies require a large number of nodes and they add extra overhead. If there are "n" nodes, then n*(n-1)/2 connections will be needed. For example, connecting four nodes in a full-mesh topology will require six different connections. Full mesh is the best option when considering availability and reliability because if there is any kind of failure, failover will occur on the other links and devices. The downside of the full-mesh topology is the extra overhead associated with building and maintaining all of the connections, as well as the high costs required to install all of the links.

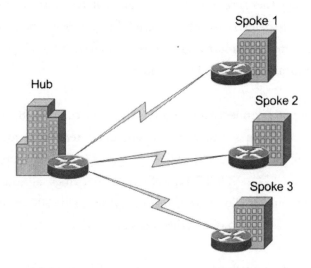

Figure 6.2 – WAN Hub-and-Spoke Topology

Hub-and-spoke is one of the most popular WAN topologies. Referring to Figure 6.2 above, the hub router is usually located at the headquarters location and connects to branch office routers. These various branch offices connect in a hub-and-spoke fashion. The downside to the hub-and-spoke topology is redundancy and availability. The location of the point of failure most often is the hub device. To achieve some form of high availability, the hub device and/or the connections between the hub and the spokes should be duplicated. Hub-and-spoke topologies are less complex and less expensive than full-mesh topologies.

NOTE: In a hub-and-spoke topology, the minimum number of required connections equals the number of spokes.

Another possible WAN topology is partial mesh and this involves a combination of full mesh and hub-and-spoke areas within a larger area. The partial-mesh topology is between the full-mesh and the hub-and-spoke topologies in terms of availability and costs. This is useful when a high level of availability and redundancy is required only in some areas (i.e., for certain nodes).

OPTICAL NETWORKING

Various optical link technologies are used in large enterprise infrastructures to assure some kind of connectivity. Some of the optical networking techniques include SONET/SDH, CWDM, DWDM, and RPR.

Synchronous Optical Network and Synchronous Digital Hierarchy

Synchronous Optical Network (SONET) and Synchronous Digital Hierarchy (SDH) are usually considered similar, although there are some key differences between the two technologies. SONET is the North American high-speed transport standard for digital-based bandwidth and it is an ANSI standard. It provides incrementally increased rates that can be used on digital optical links. On the other hand, SDH is European and it is an ITU standard.

SONET and SDH are popular connectivity solutions that ISPs can offer based on customer needs. SONET/SDH uses Time Division Multiplexing (TDM) as the technique for framing the data and voice on a single wavelink through the optical fiber. Single digital streams are multiplexed over the optical fiber using lasers or LEDs. SONET typically uses fiber rings, although it is not exclusively based on a ring topology, and it allows transmission distances of 80 km, without having to use repeaters. Single-mode fiber can also obtain distances up to 80 km without a repeater.

Much of the long-haul fiber connections are actually SONET because it can use repeater technology across a number of ISP networks to boost the signals over long distances. Although not all of the SONET topologies will be ring-based, customers who need a reliable link should agree on a strict SLA with the ISP to ensure high reliability through a ring topology.

Some common Optical Carrier (OC) rates and the mapped bandwidth for each standard are shown below. Various OC standards correspond to various SONET and SDH standards. Synchronous Transport Signal (STS) is a SONET standard and Synchronous Transport Module (STM) is an SDH standard.

OC Standard	SONET Standard	SDH Standard	Capacity
OC-1	STS-1	STM-0	50 Mbps
OC-3	STS-3	STM-1	150 Mbps
OC-12	STS-12	STM-4	600 Mbps
OC-24	STS-24	-	1.2 Gbps
OC-48	STS-48	STM-16	2.4 Gbps
OC-192	STS-192	STM-64	9.6 Gbps
OC-768	STS-768	STM-256	38 Gbps
OC-3072	STS-3072	STM-1024	153 Gbps

Some of the considerations that must be taken into account when new SONET connections are being purchased include the following:

- Details about the transport usage (whether the link will be used for data or voice transport)
- Details about the topology (linear or ring-based)
- Details about single points of failure in the transport
- Customer needs
- Costs
- Implementation scenarios (e.g., multiple providers, multiple paths, etc.)
- The type of oversubscription offered by the ISP

Also useful to know is whether the bandwidth will be dedicated or shared with other users. If the services are from two ISPs, to achieve high availability and redundancy they may have different SONET implementations and may follow different paths.

ISPs usually have the same physical fiber paths (i.e., along gas pipes or public electrical paths). Even if dual ISPs are used, the physical fiber path is often the same and the failure risk does not decrease. If something happens to the pipes that have the fiber links attached, all of the ISPs that follow that specific path will suffer. The recommended scenario is having two ISPs with different physical cabling paths.

Coarse Wave Division Multiplexing and Dense Wave Division Multiplexing

Coarse Wave Division Multiplexing (CWDM) and Dense Wave Division Multiplexing (DWDM) are two different types of Wavelength Division Multiplexing (WDM). Both of these use a multiplexor (MUX) at the transmitter to put several optical signals on the fiber. A de-multiplexer (DEMUX) is installed at the receiver and will achieve the inverse operation. This concept is similar to a modem (modulator-demodulator).

CWDM transmits up to 16 channels, with each channel operating in a different wavelength. CWDM boosts the bandwidth of the existing GigabitEthernet optical infrastructure, without having to add new fibre-optic strands. CWDM has a wider spacing between the channels compared to the DWDM technology, so it is a much cheaper technology for transmitting multiple gigabit signals on a single fibre-optic strand. There is a great amount of support for this equipment from Cisco, which offers many Small Form-factor Pluggable (SFP) transceivers that can be used with CWDM links.

CWDM is often used by organizations on leased dark fiber topologies to boost the capacity from 1 to 8 or 16 Gbps over metropolitan area distances. The downside to CWDM is that it is not compatible with modern fiber amplifier technologies, such as Erbium Doped Fiber Amplifier (EDFA). EDFA is a method for amplifying light signals and it is making repeaters obsolete. CWDM is also used in cable television implementations.

DWDM is a core technology for optical transport networks that is similar to CWDM in many ways. However, with DWDM, the wavelengths are much tighter, so there are up to 160 channels as opposed to 16 channels with CWDM. This makes the transceivers and equipment much more expensive. Even though there are 160 channels, Cisco DWDM cards can support 32 different wavelengths. In addition, DWDM is compatible with EDFA, so it can reach longer distances when using this technology, which better supports Metropolitan Area Networks (MANs) and WAN applications. Using EDFA with DWDM technology can achieve distances of up to 120 km between amplifiers. DWDM is a high-speed Enterprise WAN and MAN connectivity service.

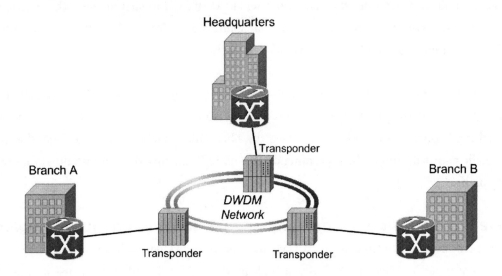

Figure 6.3 – DWDM Topology

Figure 6.3 above shows a sample topology of a DWDM optical network that connects three locations. This type of solution typically includes three components:

- **Transponders:** They receive the optical signal from a client, convert it into the electrical domain, and retransmit it using a laser.
- **Multiplexers:** They take the various signals and put them into a single-mode fiber. The multiplexer may support EDFA technology.
- **Amplifiers:** They provide powered amplification of the multi-wavelength optical signal.

Resilient Packet Ring

Resilient Packet Ring (RPR) is a Layer 2 transport architecture that offers packet transmission based on a dual-counter rotating ring topology.

RPR was standardized in 2004 under IEEE 802.17 and is a Layer 2 packet-based transport mechanism that can be offered by various ISPs. It is based on counter-rotating ring structures and using dual fibre-optic rings allows for a much higher level of packet survivability and availability. If one of the stations fails or the fiber is damaged, then data is transmitted over the other ring. RPR is a Layer 2 technology, so it can be used with either SONET/SDH or GigabitEthernet/10-GigabitEthernet at the Physical Layer. This supports Enterprise Network solutions, MANs, and transmission over long distances.

RPR is a proper solution for MANs with large organizations. A typical RPR topology contains the following components:

- The IP backbone network
- RPR supporting routers
- RPR ring, which is at the MAN Core and Distribution Layers

RPR can provide connectivity to campuses with different buildings or even different locations, where there are different business offices across multiple floors. RPR can also support VoIP gateways and provide data, multicasting, and video services.

RPR is a better solution than SONET or SDH when it comes to data traffic. SONET and SDH are capable of handling voice traffic because this type of traffic is consistent in terms of usage. However, data traffic is more bursty, especially when transferring large files, and RPR works better with this type of traffic behavior. RPR also works well in point-to-multipoint or multipoint-to-multipoint environments. It is good at leveraging QoS technologies to help various types of traffic.

RPR is excellent at providing oversubscription because of its bandwidth guarantees and it functions much like Ethernet in that it uses statistic multiplexing as opposed to TDM. RPR provides another valid solution in addition to some of the other mechanisms that operate over SONET and SDH.

METRO ETHERNET

Metro Ethernet is a rapidly emerging solution that defines a network infrastructure based on the Ethernet standard, as opposed to Frame Relay or ATM, which is supported over a MAN. Metro Ethernet extends MAN technology over to the Enterprise WAN at Layer 2 or Layer 3.

General Considerations for Metro Ethernet

This flexible transport architecture can be some combination of optical networking, Ethernet, and IP technologies, and these infrastructure details are transparent to the end-user, who sees a service at the Customer Edge but does not see the underlying technology being used.

Metro Ethernet technologies are not visible to customers but they are responsible for provisioning these services across their core network from the Metro Ethernet access ring. This represents a huge market for the ISP because there are many customers that have existing Ethernet interfaces, and the more customers know about their ISP and the core network, the more informed they will be about the different types of services they can receive and the problems that might happen with those services. In these situations, it is critical to think about the appropriate SLA for advanced WAN services provided to the customer via Metro Ethernet.

A generic Metro Ethernet infrastructure contains multiple blocks that provide a wide variety of services and they are all connected to the Metro Ethernet core. The core can be based on multiple technologies (e.g., TDM, MPLS, or IP services) that operate on top of the GigabitEthernet. The ISP can use SONET/SDH rings, point-to-point links, DWDM, or RPR. The connection points for the different blocks use edge aggregation devices or User Provider Edge (UPE) devices that can multiplex multiple customers on a single optical circuit to the Network Provider Edge (NPE) devices.

The Cisco Metro Ethernet Solution

The Cisco Metro Ethernet solution has specific components, such as a multi-Gigabit RPR over SONET in a dual-link topology, with RPR operating at Layer 2 and SONET operating at Layer 1. The core device is the Cisco Optical Network System (ONS) SONET Multiservice Provisioning Platform (MSPP), which provides data, voice, and video services.

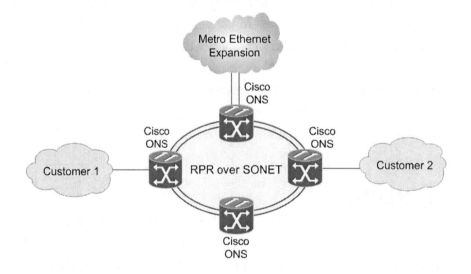

Figure 6.4 – Cisco Metro Ethernet Solution

A typical Cisco Metro Ethernet topology is presented in Figure 6.4 above. The aggregate and transport services are very flexible and they can use Ethernet or optical modules (including 10 Gbps Ethernet modules). They can support the ring topology but they can also support linear point-to-point start and hybrid topologies. The Cisco ONS MSPP device represents NPE and UPE devices located at the customer location in the form of various high-end routers and switching platforms.

Cisco offers a very scalable Metro Ethernet solution over SONET, but it can also support switched Ethernet networks for the enterprise or for the very popular IP Multiprotocol Label Switching (MPLS) networks that will be analyzed later in this chapter. This offers multiple classes of services and multiple bandwidth profiles supporting not only data, voice, and video traffic but also storage applications. The Cisco optical Metro Ethernet solution supports five Metro Ethernet Forum (MEF) services:

- Ethernet Private Line (EPL)
- Ethernet Relay Service (ERS)
- Ethernet Wire Service (EWS)
- Ethernet Multipoint Service (EMS)
- Ethernet Relay Multipoint Service (ERMS)

When selecting between all of these technologies, network designers should analyze the type of connection they need. If the company needs only point-to-point services, designers should focus on the characteristics of EPL, EWS, or ERS, whereas if multipoint services are needed, EMS or ERMS should be used. These services are covered in detail in the following sections.

Ethernet Private Line

The Metro Ethernet EPL service is a point-to-point service that uses SONET/SDH rings and provides dedicated bandwidth with no oversubscription abilities. It provides simple uptime for SLAs. Typically, the Customer Edge (CE) device is a high-end router or a multilayer switch and the line rate between customer sites can reach 1 Gbps. EPL Metro Ethernet topologies are usually used in the following areas:

- Mission-critical links on the Enterprise Network and in metro areas
- Data centers
- Support for the Business Continuity Plan (BCP) and availability solutions
- Network consolidations with multiple services

The major disadvantages of EPL are that it does not offer oversubscription and its simple SLA uptime capability.

Ethernet Relay Service

This particular flavor of Metro Ethernet, which is known as ERS, is all about multiplexing multiple services (i.e., a number of connections bundled into a single link). This is typically a point-to-point service, although it can also support point-to-multipoint connections between two or more customer sites, similar to Frame Relay. While Frame Relay uses the Data-Link Connection Identifier (DLCI) number as the Layer 2 connection identifier, ERS Metro Ethernet uses a VLAN tag, so every customer has a VLAN tag mapped to a certain Ethernet virtual connection. The Ethernet service in this situation is not transparent to the Layer 2 Ethernet frames because of the VLAN tag, which dictates the destination.

Because of its service multiplexing capabilities, ERS offers scalability for large sites over a few connections to the MAN or WAN Ethernet services. Typically, the CE device is a high-end router or an ASA device. ERS can also integrate with the existing Frame Relay or ATM solution. ERS offers the advantage of having different service tiers, so the ISP can provide several tiers of services with different cost structures based on bandwidth, distance, or class of service. The SLAs are also flexible with ERS and they include the committed information rate (CIR), the peak information rate (PIR), and traffic bursting.

With multipoint connections, the ERS technology transforms into the ERMS Metro Ethernet technology. ERS is a great solution for interconnecting routers in the Enterprise Network and for connections to ISPs for direct access to the Internet, and for providing VPN services to other branches or remote offices.

Ethernet Wire Service

EWS is another point-to-point Metro Ethernet service that uses shared provider network switched transport. It offers oversubscription services using statistical multiplexing and it provides tier service offerings that can be based on distance, class of service, and bandwidth. Because of these features, EWS allows for SLA capacity based on class of service.

The CE device is usually a high-end router or a multilayer switch. EWS also supports content networking and can provide a wide variety of services, such as the following:

- Portal services
- Monitoring services
- Billing services
- Subscriber database services
- Address management services
- Policy services
- Point-to-point LAN extensions
- Ethernet access to different storage resources
- Connectivity to the data center

EWS is a port-based service, so the carrier network is transparent to all of the customer Ethernet traffic. It also provides all-to-one bundling, which means that all of the customer packets are transmitted to the destination port in a transparent fashion, and the VLAN tags from the customer are preserved through the provider network (P network).

Ethernet Multipoint Service

EMS is the multipoint version of EWS and it has the same type of characteristics and technical requirements. In an EMS topology, the P network is a virtual switch for the customers, so several customer sites can be connected and can be offered any-to-any communication. This is very useful, especially with the rapid emergence of multicasting and VoIP services. The technology that allows this is called Virtual Private LAN Service (VPLS) and this will be covered later in this chapter.

EMS allows for rate limiting and service tiers based on distance, bandwidth, and class of service. The CE device is usually a router or a multilayer switch. Typically, ISPs will offer extensions of the corporate or campus LAN to the regional branch offices, extending the LAN over the WAN. This is a great disaster recovery solution, so it can be integrated into the Disaster Recovery Plan (DLP) or the Business Continuity Plan (BCP).

EMS is an excellent subscription service, as the P network can be oversubscribed as necessary using statistical multiplexing. From a technology standpoint, EMS uses Q-in-Q encapsulation to separate customer traffic.

> **NOTE:** A very common example of a commercial EMS solution is Verizon, which offers a Transparent LAN Service (TLS) that uses a loop-free Cisco 6500 switch topology and fiber-based GigabitEthernet links.

Ethernet Relay Multipoint Service

ERMS is a combination of EMS and ERS. This service offers the any-to-any connectivity of EMS but it also provides the service multiplexing of ERS. ERMS provides rate limiting and multiple service tiers based on distance, bandwidth, and class of service. The CE device is typically a high-end router, which is also used by the technologies discussed previously. ERMS is used to support various services, including:

- The customer Intranet and Extranet networks
- Layer 2 branch VPN connectivity
- Layer 3 VPNs (Intranet or Extranet)
- ISP Internet access
- Distributed Route Processor (DRP) and Bridge Control Protocol (BCP) solutions

VIRTUAL PRIVATE LAN SERVICE

VPLS is a point-to-multipoint or multipoint-to-multipoint technology. The primary goal of the VPLS architecture is connecting two or more CE devices, leveraging Ethernet bridging techniques. This is accomplished as an overlay on an MPLS network. VPLS is a multipoint technology that runs over MPLS P networks. VPLS is defined in two RFCs: 4761 and 4762.

General Considerations for VPLS

The P network simulates an 802.1 Ethernet bridge so that each Metro Ethernet EMS will be similar to a VLAN. What makes VPLS different from other technologies is the way that is handles issues such as discovery, communication between the peers, and provisioning. For example, if there is an outage at the P network, IP rerouting will quickly restore connectivity. VPLS functions by learning the source MAC address to the port association, as the discovery part, and then the frames are forwarded based on the destination MAC address.

At the P network, the VPLS core uses a split-horizon Forwarding Architecture (FWA) instead of STP. By using split horizon, the Ethernet frames will not be sent back to the P network device on which they were received. Another particularity of a VPLS environment is that it always floods broadcast and multicast traffic.

VPLS is used more and more as an enterprise WAN connectivity service, as it offers stability as the network gets larger. The major disadvantage of implementing VPLS is the broadcast and multicast traffic radiation between sites, as the VPLS network represents a single broadcast domain. All of the routers will typically be routing peers, so full-mesh connections may become a scaling issue. To prevent this issue, a hierarchical VPLS design is recommended, as it provides more scalability.

Hierarchical VPLS

Cisco highly recommends that ISPs implement a hierarchical VPLS (HVPLS), as opposed to a full-mesh VPLS, because HVPLS is stable and more scalable.

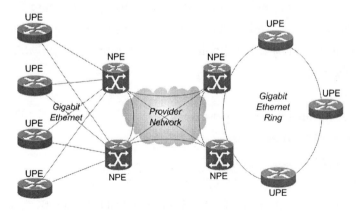

Figure 6.5 – Hierarchical VPLS

In Figure 6.5 above, NPE devices are connected to UPE devices through direct links or through a GigabitEthernet ring. To achieve scalability, only the core MPLS routers (the NPE routers) are interconnected in a full mesh. The multitude of UPE VPLS devices are connected hierarchically, so the HVPLS will partition the network into several edge domains that are interconnected using the MPLS core.

The left side of Figure 6.5 is a point-to-point topology that can be implemented using various Metro Ethernet technologies, such as EPL, EWS, or ERS. The center of the topology represents the MPLS core, and the right side represents an Ethernet MPLS edge in a ring topology (RPR or SONET). VPLS can use a variety of physical topologies as transport mechanisms between the UPE and the NPE:

- Point-to-point connections
- GigabitEthernet connections
- Ethernet rings
- Ethernet over SONET (EoS)
- Resilient Packet Ring (RPR)

NOTE: UPE is often referred to as the Customer Edge (CE), while NPE is often referred to as the Provider Edge (PE).

HVPLS offers an extremely flexible architectural model that is easier to scale than any type of full-mesh VPLS topology. It also allows multipoint Ethernet services, as well as Ethernet point-to-point Layer 2 VPNs and Ethernet access to Layer 3 VPN services. There are three major factors that affect scalability in a VPLS design:

- The challenges to scaling a full mesh of pseudo-wires (PW). A PW represents the PE devices and the number of such devices. It is similar to the OSPF DR, which is a pseudo-node in an OSPF area.
- The broadcast and the multicast aspects discussed earlier (broadcasts and multicasts are flooded to all of the ports).
- MAC address learning and the size of the MAC address table (the CAM table) on the switches.

The most important VPLS issues include the following:

- HVPLS scalability comes from meshing cheaper devices.
- There are MAC address tables for many devices and customers.
- A poor VPLS design results in non-scalability and instability.

- QoS is more difficult to implement on multipoint links than on point-to-point links.
- Customers can perform rate limiting or traffic shaping at the edge, although there will still be issues at the ISP core. Traffic manipulation ensures optimization, guarantees performance, improves latency, increases stability, and provides predictable bandwidth.
- OSPF broadcasting and multicasting can be inconsistent with VPLS.
- Flapping routers at the CE can increase CPU utilization, so fewer OSPF/EIGRP peers should be used.
- VPLS does not allow the use of IGMP snooping for multicast.

VIRTUAL PRIVATE NETWORK DESIGN

Even though the VPN concept implies security most of the time, unsecured VPNs also exist. Frame Relay is an example of this because it provides private communications between two locations, but it might not have any security features on top of it. The decision to add security to the VPN connection depends on the specific requirements for that connection.

VPN troubleshooting is difficult to manage because of the lack of visibility in the P network infrastructure. The P network is usually seen as a cloud that aggregates all of the network locations' connections. When performing VPN troubleshooting, first ensure that the problem does not reside on the devices before contacting the ISP.

The variety of VPN technologies includes the following:

- Site-to-site VPNs (or Intranet VPNs), for example, Overlay VPNs (such as Frame Relay) or peer-to-peer VPNs (such as MPLS). These are used when connecting different locations over the public infrastructure. When using a peer-to-peer infrastructure, communication can be seamless between the sites without worrying about IP addressing overlap.
- Remote Access VPNs, for example, Virtual Private Dial-up Network (VPDN), which is a dial-up approach for the VPN that is usually carried out with security in mind.
- Extranet VPNs, when connecting to business partners or customer networks.

VPNs often tunnel traffic when sending it over an infrastructure. One tunneling methodology for Layer 3 is called Generic Routing Encapsulation (GRE). GRE tunnels traffic but it does not provide security. To tunnel traffic and also provide security, IPsec can be used. This is a mandatory implementation component of IPv6 but it is not a requirement for IPv4. IPsec is also used in conjunction with Authentication, Authorization, and Accounting (AAA) services to track user activity. The main benefits of VPNs are:

- Increased security
- Scalability (can continuously add more sites to the VPN)
- Flexibility (can use very flexible technologies like MPLS)
- Cost (can tunnel traffic through the Internet without much expense)

IP SECURITY FOR VPNS

IPsec represents a suite of protocols working together to achieve different security features in IP networks. Virtual Private Networks provide connections between devices that do not literally share a physical cable. By using VPNs, networks look like they are connected but the connections between them are just logical connections. IPsec ensures data protection on top of the specific logical connections.

IPsec VPN Functionality

IPsec helps protect the information that is transmitted through the VPN and it can be one of two varieties:

- Site-to-site VPNs
- Remote access VPNs

Site-to-site VPNs provide a permanent secured connection between two locations. Remote access VPNs are used when the virtual link is not always on. This is a situation where the individual needs to transfer something for a short duration of time, up to the corporate headquarters, and then disconnect. Remote access VPN technologies are similar to dial-on-demand technologies, such as the old circuit-based technologies that functioned only after a number was dialed. The remote access connection closes after it is used, meaning it does not remain permanently open like a site-to-site connection.

IPsec is a security suite that allows for many different degrees of security to be designed and implemented. Some situations might require strict security features to be implemented, while other situations might require the security policies to be relaxed for various reasons. The most important security mechanisms provided by IPsec are as follows:

- **Data origin authentication:** Ensures that the packet was sent by an authorized user.
- **Data integrity:** Ensures that the packet was not changed or manipulated in the transit path.
- **Data confidentiality:** Ensures that only authorized users read the data, so sensitive information is not compromised.
- **Anti-reply:** Protects against DoS attacks that send the same packet multiple times.

The IPsec VPN tunnel is built in two phases:

- ISAKMP/IKE negotiation
- Data transmission using negotiated IPsec SA

The Internet Security Association and Key Management Protocol (ISAKMP)/Internet Key Exchange (IKE) negotiation phase is not very secure, as it is an initial security phase in which details about how the data will be secured are discussed. The secure VPN tunnel is built after this initial phase. ISAKMP/IKE negotiation serves as a mechanism for transferring the IPsec SAs (Security Associations, which are forms of agreements on different IKE/IPsec parameters) and is composed of two distinct phases:

- Phase 1: ISAKMP SA setup
- Phase 2: IPsec SA negotiation

ISAKMP and IKE are initial secure negotiation channels used for the initial exchange of parameters. The goals of the ISAKMP/IKE process include the following:

- Authentication of the parties and establishment of a secure negotiation channel (Phase 1, ISAKMP SA)
- Perform additional negotiation (Phase 1.5, including XAuth and Mode Configuration)
- Negotiate data protection parameters (Phase 2, IPsec SA)

In the first phase, ISAKMP uses a technology called Diffie-Hellman (DH), which can generate cryptographic keys to ensure that the communications are secure. Phase 1 can operate in two modes:

- Main mode
- Aggressive mode

Main mode takes longer to negotiate because it hides the parties' identities by performing the DH exchange ahead of time. The aggressive mode takes less time to negotiate but does not provide the same level of security as the main mode because it does not hide the parties' identities. ISAKMP aggressive mode permits flexible authentication with Pre-Shared Keys (e.g., Easy VPN).

The ISAKMP initial Phase 1 negotiation process provides several authentication mechanisms to verify the parties' identities. These mechanisms offer different degrees of security:

- **Pre-Shared Keys (PSKs):** Using this technology, hosts know the same key via an Out-of-Band messaging system. This is the least secure authentication mechanism.
- **RSA signatures:** Using this method, hosts trust a certificate authority for authentication. This is a much more secure mechanism than using PSK because a trusted third-party authority controls the process by verifying the identity of each party involved in the authentication process.
- **RSA-encrypted nonces (IOS only):** This technology uses RSA keys to hash random numbers (nonces) and other values.

Once ISAKMP Phase 1 is completed, network designers must decide how the data will be secured. ISAKMP SA determines how the secure negotiation channel will be established and the ISAKMP SA peers must agree on the following parameters:

- **Authentication method:** PSK (weak), RSA signatures (strong)
- **Encryption type:** DES (weak), 3DES (medium), AES (strong)
- **Hash algorithm:** MD5 (weak), SHA (strong)
- **Diffie-Hellman group:** 1, 2, or 5

After ISAKMP Phase 1 is completed, a secure communication channel exists between the IPsec peers, and at this moment the IPsec SA can be created. ISAKMP Phase 2 can be implemented based on two different technologies:

- Authentication Header (AH)
- Encapsulated Security Payload (ESP)

AH is rarely used in modern networks because it can only perform authentication, without securing the data. On the other hand, the ESP approach uses both authentication and encryption and is the preferred method to be used in ISAKMP Phase 2.

When designing IPsec VPNs and providing all of the criteria for Phase 1 and Phase 2, a lifetime for the entire negotiation process must be defined. ISAKMP and IPsec SAs have a definable lifetime and when it expires, the processes at Phase 1 and Phase 2 will rerun. A shorter lifetime means more security and more overhead, while a longer lifetime implies less security and less overhead. If the process is alive for a long period of time, a possible attacker has a long time to hack the connection (i.e., solve the algorithms).

The IPsec SA rekeying process can also involve Perfect Forward Secrecy (PFS), which is a technology that allows the rekeying to take place while the IPsec tunnel is in place. The PFS mechanism adds extra CPU overhead and it is used to run additional DH exchanges, so the IPsec SA keys are not derived from ISAKMP SA keys.

All of the details covered above confirm that IPsec VPNs are based on a complex suite of technologies, and for each of these technology areas, an appropriate level of security must be designed. It is important to balance the SA lifetime and the number of IPsec tunnels created against the router's ability to handle these resource-intensive processes and to always monitor the network devices to make sure their resource utilization stays within normal limits.

Site-to-Site IPsec VPN Design

Cisco invented a series of technologies to make site-to-site VPNs very secure and simple to implement. The Cisco Easy VPN technology was developed with the concept of having software running on routers that could completely automate the establishment of a site-to-site or a remote access VPN configuration. This software solution is easily operated by configuring settings in a graphical interface.

A Cisco Easy VPN server can be configured to act as the headend device and push the required VPN configuration to a remote client. This can happen on many Cisco devices, including IOS routers and firewalls. The Easy VPN server wizard is a built-in feature in the Cisco Security and Device Manager (SDM), which is the graphical interface on Cisco devices. The configuration process can be very complicated, but the Easy VPN server wizard can be utilized to configure certain features, including the following:

- Interface selection
- IKE configuration
- Group policy lookup method
- User authentication
- Group policies
- IPsec transformations

In some situations, GRE might be needed in conjunction with IPsec because IPsec ESP (used for authentication and encryption) works only with unicast transmissions. Key technologies like routing protocols rely heavily on multicast, so GRE is used for encapsulation in unicast packets.

Although GRE provides some interesting capabilities, IPsec without GRE has a much better scalability. The situation in which IPsec is used with GRE and possibly running a routing protocol over the connection adds significant overhead.

NOTE: Cisco recommends using EIGRP as the preferred routing protocol to lower the overhead on GRE-over-IPsec solutions.

GRE keepalives can be added to the solution mentioned above and this can add value to the GRE-over-IPsec design, especially when static routing is used. When using dynamic routing protocols, the keepalive mechanism does not need to be used because the dynamic protocol automatically detects a failure on a specific device.

In a GRE-over-IPsec design, multiple headend devices might be needed to scale the solution or to provide redundancy. When using multiple headend devices to achieve redundancy, routing metrics should be used to prefer one of the links over the other.

The most popular topology for site-to-site VPN solutions is the hub-and-spoke topology. Cisco invented the Dynamic Multipoint Virtual Private Network (DMVPN) as a technology that helps automate the hub-and-spoke site-to-site VPN deployment. The peers can be dynamically discovered and on-demand tunnels can be created to assist with large hub-and-spoke VPN designs.

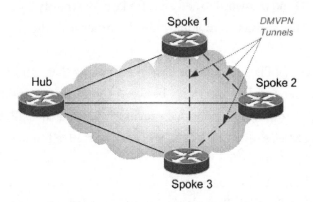

Figure 6.6 – Dynamic Multipoint VPN

The DMVPN approach illustrated in Figure 6.6 above should be used when spoke-to-spoke traffic represents more than 20% of the total VPN traffic, or when a full-mesh VPN topology design is considered. Using DMVPN tunnels, traffic is directly exchanged between peers so it does not have to pass through the hub router, thus saving valuable bandwidth and response time. DMVPN is usually used in conjunction with other protocols, such as the following:

- IPsec
- GRE
- Next Hop Resolution Protocol (NHRP)

The advantages of DMVPN from a design standpoint include the following:

- When using a full-mesh topology, the tunnels are built on demand, so at any given point, fewer active tunnels are established.
- Additional remote sites in a hub-and-spoke environment can be added without the need for additional static configuration.
- Spokes can be statically or dynamically addressed (even behind NAT devices).

The most important design recommendations regarding DMVPN are as follows:

- Use IPsec in tunnel mode.
- Use 3DES or AES for the encryption.
- When implementing Public-Key Infrastructure (PKI), the Certificate Authority (CA) should be placed in a private subnet of the hub location.
- EIGRP with route summarization for query scoping is the recommended routing technique.
- Use devices that are capable of hardware acceleration for IPsec.
- Use an NHRP ID and password to add an extra layer of security.
- Use multiple NHRP servers on multiple hubs to further scale the design.

Virtual Tunnel Interfaces (VTIs) are another Cisco technology that can be used when designing IPsec VPN. VTIs are IPsec routable interfaces between Cisco routers and they offer support for QoS, multicast, and other routing functions that previously needed GRE. IPv6 has adopted the VTI technology for building IPsec site-to-site VPNs. VTIs can be statically and dynamically configured.

Another Cisco proprietary technology used in site-to-site VPN implementations is Group Encrypted Transport (GET) VPN. When using the GET VPN approach, routers become part of a trusted grouping of VPN devices, and secure packets flow between these routers and their original IP header is preserved. This behavior eliminates many QoS and multicast issues. GET VPN simplifies the security policy and key distribution in the group of routers mentioned previously using the group key distribution model.

GET VPN is a very sophisticated technology and it uses the concept of Group Domain of Interpretation (GDOI), as specified in RFC 3547. GDOI features a Key Server (KS) and multiple Cooperative Key Servers (COOP KSs). The KS can be a Cisco router and its role is to authenticate group members and distribute security policies and required keys. The COOP KSs can be used across wide geographical distributions. The key technologies that make up the GET VPN include the following:

- GDOI
- KSs
- COOP KSs
- Group members
- IP tunnel header preservation
- Group security association
- Rekey mechanism
- Time-based anti-replay (TBAR)

Some of the most important GET VPN design advantages are as follows:

- It provides large-scale any-to-any IPsec security.
- It uses the underlying IP VPN routing infrastructure.
- It integrates with existing multicast infrastructure.
- QoS policies are consistent because of the preservation of the original IP header (IP source and IP destination address).

MULTIPROTOCOL LABEL SWITCHING VPN TECHNOLOGY

MPLS is an emerging and high-performance technology that allows the transport of packets by switching them based on special packet "labels" that are inserted between Layer 2 and Layer 3 information. This mechanism allows for a much faster forwarding process than the traditional Layer 3 forwarding process. The most important application that runs over MPLS is the MPLS VPN technology.

General Considerations for MPLS

The MPLS approach leverages the intelligence of the IP routing infrastructure and the efficiency of Cisco Express Forwarding (CEF). MPLS functions by appending a label to any type of packet. Packet forwarding through the network infrastructure will be performed based on this label value instead of any Layer 3 information, which is very efficient and allows MPLS to work with a wide range of underlying technologies. By simply adding a label in the packet header, MPLS can be used in many Physical Layer and Data-link Layer WAN implementations.

The MPLS label is positioned between the Layer 2 header and the Layer 3 header. Using MPLS, overhead is added a single time, when the packet goes into the ISP cloud. After entering the MPLS network, packet switching occurs much faster than in traditional Layer 3 networks because the MPLS label is simply swapped instead of having to strip the entire Layer 3 header. MPLS-capable routers, also called Label Switched Routers (LSRs), come in two flavors:

- Edge LSR (PE routers)
- LSR (P routers)

PE routers are Provider Edge devices that perform label distribution, packet forwarding based on labels, and label insertion and removal. P routers are Provider routers and their responsibility consists of label switching and efficient packet forwarding based on labels.

With MPLS, there is a separation of the control plane from the data plane, resulting in greater efficiency in how the LSRs work. Resources that are constructed for efficiency of control plane operations, such as the routing protocol, the routing table, and the exchange of labels, are completely separate from resources that are designed only to forward traffic in the data plane as quickly as possible.

When using CEF, the Forwarding Information Base (FIB) is a copy of the routing table information in the cache memory and it is used for quick forwarding. Using MPLS, the Label Forwarding Information Base (LFIB) is used for label-based traffic exchange. The Forwarding Equivalence Class (FEC) describes the class of packets that receives the same forwarding treatment (e.g., traffic forwarded through the ISP cloud based on a specific QoS marking).

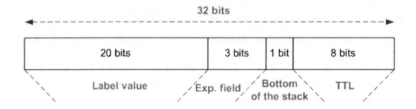

Figure 6.7 – MPLS Label Fields

Analyzing Figure 6.7 above, the MPLS label is 4 bytes in length and it consists of the following fields:

- 20-bit Label Value field
- 3-bit Experimental field (QoS marking)
- 1-bit Bottom of the Stack field (useful when multiple labels are used; it is set to 1 for the last label in the stack)
- 8-bit TTL field (to avoid looping)

MPLS VPN Operation and Design

MPLS VPN is a technology that is being used intensely in modern networks, and it has replaced traditional VPN services and is an alternative to Metro Ethernet services. MPLS VPNs are the most important technology that uses MPLS; in fact, MPLS itself was developed to serve the MPLS VPNs technology. Usually, MPLS VPN implementations require the use of a stack of MPLS labels because one label identifies the MPLS edge device and another label identifies customer Virtual Routing and Forwarding (VRF).

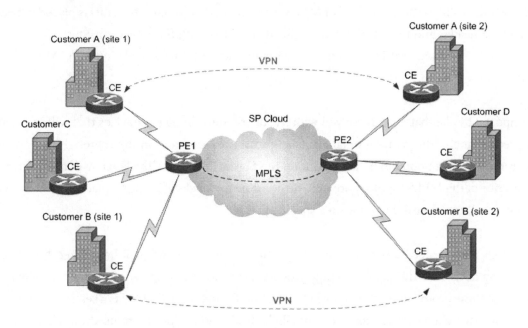

Figure 6.8 – Example of an MPLS VPN

An example of an MPLS VPN configuration is shown in Figure 6.8 above. In the center, the ISP cloud offers MPLS VPN services. The PE routers connect to different customers, and some customers occupy two sites, each connected to a different PE router. With the MPLS approach, the customers with two sites receive transparent secure communication capabilities based on the unique customer labels assigned. The ISP uses MPLS to carry the traffic between the PE routers through the P devices.

> **NOTE:** An important advantage of MPLS VPN technology is that this secure connectivity is assured, without the customer having to run MPLS on any device. The customer simply runs a standard routing protocol with the ISP and all of the MPLS VPN logic is located in the ISP cloud.

When employing MPLS VPNs, a stack of labels is used because one label identifies the customer (VPN identification) and another label initiates the forwarding through the ISP cloud (egress router location).

Layer 3 MPLS VPN technology is a very powerful and flexible option for ISPs when providing customers with the transparent WAN access connectivity they need. This is very scalable for ISPs because it is very easy for them to add customers and sites. MPLS comes in two different flavors:

- Frame Mode MPLS
- Cell Mode MPLS

Frame Mode MPLS is the most popular MPLS type, and in this scenario the label is placed between the Layer 2 header and the Layer 3 header (for this reason, MPLS is often considered a Layer 2.5 technology). Cell Mode MPLS is used in ATM networks and it uses fields in the ATM header as the label.

An important issue that must be solved with MPLS is determining the devices that will insert and remove the labels. The creation of labels (label push) is carried out on the Ingress Edge LSR and label removal (label popping) is carried out on the Egress Edge LSR. The label-switched routers in the interior of the MPLS topology are only responsible for label swapping (replacing the label with another label) to forward the traffic on a specific path.

The MPLS devices need a way in which to exchange the labels that will be utilized for making forwarding decisions. This label exchange process is carried out using various protocols. The most popular of these protocols is called Label Distribution Protocol (LDP). LDP is a session-based UDP technology that allows for the exchange of labels. UDP and multicast are used initially to set up peering, and then TCP ensures that there is a reliable transmission of the label information.

A special feature that improves MPLS efficiency is Penultimate Hop Popping (PHP), where the second to last LSR in the MPLS path is the one that pops out the label. This adds efficiency to the overall operation of MPLS, as the edge router does not have to deal with two MPLS labels.

The concept of Route Distinguisher (RD) describes the way in which the ISP can distinguish between the traffic of different customers. This allows different customers who are participating in the MPLS VPN to use the exact same IP address space. This means both Customer A and Customer B are using the 10.10.10.0/24 range and the traffic is differentiated between customers using RDs. Devices can create their own VRF tables, so a PE router can store each customer's specific data in a different isolated table, which provides increased security.

VPNv4 prefixes are carried through the MPLS cloud using Multiprotocol BGP (MP-BGP). VPNv4 prefixes are those that result after the RD is prepended to the normal prefix. Customers can be filtered from accessing certain prefixes using import and export targets.

Layer 2 versus Layer 3 MPLS VPN

The characteristics of MPLS VPNs depend on whether they are implemented at Layer 2 or at Layer 3. Network designers should understand the fundamental differences between these two technologies.

Layer 3 VPNs forward only IP packets, so the CE routers are peers of the MPLS VPN PE routers. These types of VPNs are based on Layer 3 information exchange and the ISP is involved in the routing process. This means the SLA should include information about the way the ISP is involved in the customer routing process. Layer 3 VPNs offer support for any access or backbone technology so they are extremely flexible; in addition, ISPs can offer a wide variety of advanced WAN services.

The advantage of an MPLS VPN at Layer 2 is that it supports multiple protocols, not just IP like Layer 3 VPNs do. The PE devices forward frames to the CE devices via Layer 2, so there is no peering with the ISP. The Layer 2 service allows the customers' routers to peer directly to one another without having to do this via an ISP router. The customers have control of the Layer 3 policy and the ISP offers Layer 2 VPNs as a point-to-point service, where the access technology is determined by the type of VPN being used. MPLS VPNs at Layer 2 might be a good solution for a service internetworking or carrying out conversions of Frame Relay or ATM into Ethernet to get delivery on high bandwidth links.

The major factors that help determine the need for Layer 2 or Layer 3 MPLS VPNs include control and management. The amount of control needed should be determined at the company level. This solution puts the CE router under the domain of the ISP in the SLA. In a large organization with a big pool of resources, including qualified network engineers, the Layer 2 VPN solution might be best because this offers total control of the Layer 2 policies and implementation.

Advanced MPLS VPN

The most important MPLS VPN issues and considerations include the following:

- Determining whether the routing is achieved by the ISP or by the customer. This depends on the level of control required, as mentioned earlier, and costs. A Layer 3 VPN solution can be more expensive than a Layer 2 solution. Details about the responsibilities of the ISP and the way CE devices are managed should be clearly stated in the SLA.

- Determining whether to use a single MPLS VPN provider or multiple providers to achieve redundancy and high availability. It is not very likely that two ISPs on dedicated backbones will experience a common outage, but having two ISPs will add more complexity to the overall solution. If there are two ISPs with two CE devices at every site, the design must be able to support the proper default gateway configuration with the appropriate First Hop Redundancy Protocol (FHRP).

- Determining the need for QoS and multicasting. Using a Layer 3 MPLS VPN may provide support for IP multicast, whereas operating a Layer 2 MPLS VPN may require a great amount of support from the ISP to achieve this functionality and this can be very expensive. QoS should be available from the ISP, so it is important to decide whether to include QoS parameters in the SLA. With Layer 3 VPN, the customer will typically implement QoS internally.

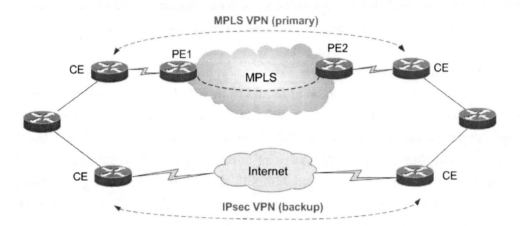

Figure 6.9 – MPLS VPN with Backdoor Route Scenario

A special scenario involves an MPLS VPN agreement with an ISP and an internal backdoor route, for example, an IPsec VPN connection through the Internet (or a GRE-over-IPsec configuration), which represents a second path between locations, as depicted in Figure 6.9 above. The backdoor connection is typically used as a failover backup route. Using BGP, this situation can be controlled in much more detail but it does become an issue if redistribution into IGP results in other external routes. As a best practice, the locations where route redistribution is implemented should be minimized. If this is performed in many locations, it could adversely impact the stability of the network.

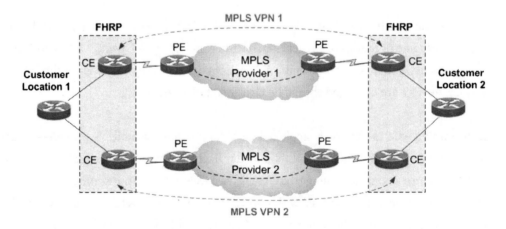

Figure 6.10 – Dual MPLS VPN Providers

As shown in Figure 6.10 above, using multiple providers to achieve failover and high availability requires carefully implementing an FHRP. This type of arrangement must be negotiated in the early phases of the contract. If using two ISPs with parallel paths between the locations, it is important to know how they will support failover. One solution is to use an FHRP, such as HSRP, VRRP, or GLBP. This should be negotiated with the ISPs before the implementation phase, as part of the contract and the SLA, as each ISP must be informed that the organization is using another parallel provider.

WAN DESIGN METHODOLOGIES

The Enterprise Edge design process must follow the PPDIOO (Prepare, Plan, Design, Implement, Operate, Optimize) methodology described previously. The network designer should carefully analyze the following network requirements:

- The types of applications available and their WAN requirements
- Traffic volume
- Traffic patterns (including possible points of congestion)

The preparing and planning phases involve analyzing the existing network to find out which technologies are currently being used for WAN, as well as the issues with those technologies, and to document the location of key hosts, servers, and network infrastructure devices.

The next phase is designing the particular topology that will be used in the Enterprise Edge module. The existing technology should be analyzed so that the most appropriate one is chosen; traffic usage should be projected; and reliability, availability, and performance should be considered. In addition, constraints (financial or related to resources) should be addressed and a solid implementation plan should be built.

When designing the Enterprise Edge infrastructure, flexibility should be kept in mind at all times. An example of design flexibility is Voice over IP (VoIP). Considering the strict requirements of this technology, it is important to ensure that VoIP can function over the designed solution at any time, even if this is not an initial requirement for the organization. Flexibility in the design of the Enterprise Edge consists of the ability to easily incorporate other technologies at any given time. Other key design criteria when considering WAN design include the following:

- Response time
- Throughput
- Reliability
- Window size
- Data compression

Reliability is another aspect that should be considered. This provides information about the health of the WAN connection and resources (e.g., whether the connection is up or down) and how often the WAN functions efficiently, as per the design criteria.

Window size influences the amount of data that can be sent in the WAN in one "chunk." Transmission Control Protocol (TCP) involves using a sliding window concept that works by sending an amount of data, waiting for an acknowledgement, and then increasing the amount of data until the maximum window is reached. In the case of a congested WAN link, everyone in the network that is sending data via TCP will start increasing the rate at which they send it until the interface starts dropping packets, forcing everyone to back off from using the sliding window. When the congestion disappears, everyone will again increase the rate at the same time until new congestion occurs. This process, called TCP global synchronization, repeats again and again and leads to a waste in bandwidth during the periods all of the hosts decrease their window size simultaneously.

Another key WAN factor is whether the traffic can be compressed. If the data is already highly compressed (e.g., JPEG images), any additional compression mechanisms will be wasted.

SELECTION CONSIDERATIONS FOR WAN SERVICES

The possibility of obtaining advanced WAN services using VPLS, Metro Ethernet, or MPLS VPN has been discussed throughout this chapter. A reliance on sales and marketing persons is not an effective approach to selecting these advanced services. Instead, it would be best to talk to the actual implementation team to get a deep understanding of the advantages and disadvantages of each technology and how they can meet the technical and business goals.

If redundancy and high availability are needed, the organization should consider connecting to two ISPs. One advantage to this configuration is that there is a large pool of technology options from which to choose. For example, if an organization was using a more traditional technology with their initial ISP, it could create a relationship with a new ISP and integrate new technology, such as Metro Ethernet or MPLS VPN solutions, along with a multitude of other services offered.

Advanced WAN services are part of agreements or different partnerships between multiple organizations that should be tied to solid risk assessment and an SLA that is closely related to various aspects, such as the following:

- Disaster recovery planning
- Business impact analysis
- Business continuity planning

It is very important to practice good security policy procedures and to consider the impact of the design decisions in the following areas:

- Dynamic routing protocols
- VLAN implementation (because many WAN services operate at Layer 2)
- QoS (covered by the ISP or by the customer)
- Multicast (what types of services are running)
- Security
- Management
- Reporting

In addition, it is important to analyze whether the advanced services are part of the standard agreement or are upgrades and what the future costs for any potential new technologies and new upgrades to these services would be.

SERVICE LEVEL AGREEMENT

A Service Level Agreement (SLA) is often considered the main contract with an ISP; however, the SLA is actually the technical aspect of the complete Service Level Contract (SLC), where the service levels are formally defined. The SLA often refers to contracted delivery times, values, parameters, and features that are negotiated, and it often describes, in plain language, what the organization is purchasing from the ISP.

General Considerations for SLAs

Many companies, vendors, and ISPs must provide SLCs to their partners or customers, and the SLA is a component of the SLC. The SLA defines specific parameters and performance measurements between devices (e.g., routers, servers, workstations, or other equipment). The SLC designates connectivity and performance levels that the ISP guarantees to the organization and that the organization guarantees to the end-users. An SLA is a common agreement of features such as the following:

- Services
- Priorities
- Responsibilities of the ISP and the organization
- Guarantees
- Warranties

SLAs might contain technical definitions, such as data rates, Mean Time To Failure (MTTF), Mean Time Between Failures (MTBF), or Mean Time To Repair (MTTR), which are predicted times to certain events in the system. All of these parameters depend on system failure and recovery definitions, as agreed to with the customer. SLAs can often be made up of smaller components known as Operating Level Agreements (OLAs). An OLA is often used internally in the organization and it describes what will be provided to the organization.

The SLA should contain measurable targets, committed information rates, and distinct levels of services defined in terms of minimum/maximum targets. The contract should also specify actions that should be taken in situations of non-compliance. The different levels of an SLA include the following:

- **Customer-Based SLA:** Defines the services offered to a particular customer.
- **Service-Based SLA:** Defines a particular service that can be offered to a customer or to multiple customers.
- **Multilevel SLA:** Includes multiple levels, each one of which has a different set of customers for the same services.
- **Corporate-Level SLA**
- **Customer-Level SLA**
- **Service-Level SLA**

The main resource regarding Cisco SLA concepts is the Cisco SLA portal at www.cisco.com/go/saa, where several white papers with information about implementing SLCs can be found:

- Service Level Management: Best Practices
- Deploying Service-Level Management in an Enterprise
- Service-Level Management: Defining and Monitoring Service Levels in the Enterprise

SLA Monitoring

From a technical standpoint, SLA monitoring can be achieved using tools like IP SLA, which is a service that allows monitoring, baselining, and optimization by generating many different types of synthetic traffic. IP SLA can be implemented on a variety of Cisco devices (IP SLA technical details were covered in the first chapter of this manual). SLA monitoring should take into consideration the metrics that define service baselines and that relate to the following:

- Ongoing diagnostics
- Comparison between different service levels and results
- Troubleshooting
- Optimization

SLA monitoring can be considered an early warning system in knowing whether there will be an outage or a service disruption from the ISP. SLA performance should be audited on a regular basis using SLA monitoring. SLA monitoring will also contribute to the continual improvement of the Information Technology Infrastructure Library (ITIL), which is a set of best practices related to IT service management.

SUMMARY

Wide Area Network technologies operate at the Enterprise Edge in the modular Cisco Enterprise Architecture model. WANs span across large geographical distances to provide connectivity for various parts of the network infrastructure. Most ISPs are well trained to ensure they can properly support not only the traditional data traffic but also voice and video services (which are more delay sensitive) over large geographical distances.

Various optical link technologies are used in large Enterprise Network infrastructures to ensure some kind of connectivity. Some of the optical networking techniques include SONET/SDH, CWDM, DWDM, and RPR.

Synchronous Optical Network (SONET) and Synchronous Digital Hierarchy (SDH) are usually considered to be similar, although there are some key differences between the two technologies. SONET is the North American high-speed transport standard for digital-based bandwidth and it is an ANSI standard. It provides incrementally increased rates that can be used on digital optical links. On the other hand, SDH is European and it is an ITU standard.

SONET and SDH are popular connectivity solutions that ISPs can offer based on customer needs. SONET/SDH uses Time Division Multiplexing (TDM) as a technique for framing the data and voice on a single wavelink through fiber. Some of the considerations that must be taken into account when new SONET connections are being purchased include:

- Details about transport usage (whether the link will be used for data or voice transport)
- Details about the topology (linear or ring-based)
- Details about single points of failure in the transport
- Customer needs
- Costs
- Implementation scenarios (multiple providers, multiple paths, etc.)
- The type of oversubscription offered by the ISP

Coarse Wave Division Multiplexing (CWDM) and Dense Wave Division Multiplexing (DWDM) are two different types of Wavelength Division Multiplexing (WDM). Both of these use a multiplexor (MUX) at the transmitter to put several optical signals on the fiber. A de-multiplexer (DEMUX) installed at the receiver will achieve the inverse operation.

CWDM transmits up to 16 channels, with each channel operating in a different wavelength. CWDM boosts the bandwidth of the existing GigabitEthernet optical infrastructure without having to add new fibre-optic strands. CWDM has a wider spacing between the channels compared to the DWDM technology, so it is a much cheaper technology for transmitting multiple gigabit signals on a single fibre-optic strand. DWDM is a core technology for optical transport networks that is similar to CWDM in many ways. However, with DWDM, the wavelengths are much tighter, so there are up to 160 channels as opposed to 16 channels with CWDM.

Resilient Packet Ring (RPR) is a Layer 2 transport architecture that provides packet-based transmission based on a dual counter-rotating ring topology. In RPR, using dual fibre-optic rings allows for a much higher level of packet survivability and availability. This is a Layer 2 technology, so either SONET/SDH or GigabitEthernet/10-GigabitEthernet can be used at the Physical Layer. RPR is a proper solution for Metropolitan Area Networks (MANs) with large organizations, and a typical RPR topology contains the following components:

- The IP backbone network
- RPR supporting routers
- RPR rings, which are at the MAN Core and Distribution Layers

RPR is an excellent way to provide oversubscription because of its bandwidth guarantees and it functions much like Ethernet in that it uses statistic multiplexing as opposed to TDM.

Metro Ethernet is a rapidly emerging solution that defines a network infrastructure based on the Ethernet standard, as opposed to Frame Relay or ATM, which is supported over a MAN. Extending the MAN technology over to the Enterprise WAN will happen at Layer 2 or Layer 3. This flexible transport architecture can be some combination of optical networking, Ethernet, and IP technologies, and these infrastructure details are transparent to the end-user, who sees a service at the Customer Edge but does not see the underlying technology being used.

A generic Metro Ethernet infrastructure contains multiple blocks that provide a wide variety of services and they are all connected to the Metro Ethernet core. The core can be based on multiple technologies (e.g., TDM, MPLS, or IP services) that operate on top of GigabitEthernet, while the ISP can be using SONET/SDH rings, point-to-point links, DWDM, or RPR. The different connection points of the blocks use edge aggregation devices or User Provider Edge (UPE) devices that can multiplex multiple customers on a single optical circuit to Network Provider Edge (NPE) devices.

The Cisco Metro Ethernet solution has specific components, such as a multi-Gigabit RPR over SONET in a dual-link topology, with RPR operating at Layer 2 and SONET operating at Layer 1. The core device is the Cisco Optical Network System (ONS) SONET Multiservice Provisioning Platform (MSPP), which provides data, voice, and video services.

The Cisco optical Metro Ethernet solution supports five Metro Ethernet Forum (MEF) services:

- Ethernet Private Line (EPL)
- Ethernet Relay Service (ERS)
- Ethernet Wire Service (EWS)
- Ethernet Multipoint Service (EMS)
- Ethernet Relay Multipoint Service (ERMS)

When selecting between all of these technologies, network designers should analyze the type of connection they need. If the company needs only point-to-point services, designers should consider using EPL, EWS, or ERS, whereas if multipoint services are needed, EMS or ERMS should be used.

Virtual Private LAN Service (VPLS) is a point-to-multipoint or multipoint-to-multipoint technology. The primary goal of the VPLS architecture is connecting two or more Customer Edge (CE) devices, leveraging Ethernet bridging techniques. This is accomplished as an overlay on a Multi-Protocol Label Switching (MPLS) network. Cisco highly recommends that ISPs implement a hierarchical VPLS (HVPLS), as opposed to a full-mesh VPLS, because HVPLS is stable and more scalable.

VPLS can use a variety of physical topologies as transport mechanisms between the UPE and the NPE:

- Point-to-point connections
- GigabitEthernet connections
- Ethernet rings
- Ethernet over SONET (EoS)
- RPR

IPsec represents a suite of protocols working together to achieve different security features in IP networks. Virtual Private Networks provide connections between devices that do not literally share a physical cable. By using VPNs, networks look like they are connected but the connections between them are just logical connections. IPsec ensures data protection on top of those specific logical connections.

IPsec helps protect the information that is transmitted through the VPN and can be one of two varieties:

- Site-to-site VPNs
- Remote access VPNs

The IPsec VPN tunnel is built in two phases:

- ISAKMP/IKE negotiation (in two subphases: ISAKMP SA setup and IPsec SA negotiation)
- Data transmission using negotiated IPsec SA

Site-to-site IPsec VPN technologies that improve VPN design and deployment include the following:

- Cisco Easy VPN
- GRE-over-IPsec
- DMVPN
- VTI
- GET VPN

MPLS is an emerging and high-performance technology that allows the transport of packets by switching them based on special packet "labels" that are inserted between Layer 2 and Layer 3 information. This mechanism allows for a much faster forwarding process than the traditional Layer 3 forwarding process. The most important application that runs over MPLS is the MPLS VPN technology.

MPLS VPN is a technology that is being used intensely in modern networks, as it has replaced traditional VPN services and is even an alternative to Metro Ethernet services. MPLS VPNs are the most important technology that uses MPLS; in fact, MPLS was developed to serve the MPLS VPNs technology. Usually, MPLS VPN implementations require the use of a stack of MPLS labels.

The characteristics of MPLS VPNs depend on whether they are implemented at Layer 2 or at Layer 3. Network designers should understand the fundamental differences between these two technologies. The advantage of an MPLS VPN at Layer 2 is that it supports multiple protocols, not just IP like with Layer 3 VPNs.

The Service Level Agreement (SLA) defines specific parameters and performance measurements between devices in a WAN environment. The Service Level Contract (SLC) designates connectivity and performance levels that the ISP guarantees to the organization and that the organization guarantees to the end-users.

SLA monitoring should take into consideration the metrics that define service baselines and that relate to the following:

- Ongoing diagnostics
- Comparison between different service levels and results
- Troubleshooting
- Optimization

END OF CHAPTER QUIZ

1. What are the most common WAN deployment topologies (choose three)?
    a. Linear
    b. Hub-and-spoke
    c. Full mesh
    d. Ad-hoc
    e. Partial mesh
    f. Random

2. In a hub-and-spoke topology, the minimum number of required connections equals the number of spokes.
    a. True
    b. False

3. What is the formula that can be used to calculate the total number of connections necessary in a full-mesh topology with "n" devices?
    a. n
    b. n*(n-1)
    c. n*n
    d. n*(n-1)/2

4. Which of the following is an optical transmission technology used primarily in North America and is based on the ANSI standard?
    a. SONET
    b. MPLS
    c. SDH
    d. ATM

5. What is the number of channels on which CWDM is transmitted?
    a. 16
    b. 160
    c. 32
    d. 128

6. SONET/SDH uses TDM for framing the data and voice traffic on a single wavelink through fiber.
    a. True
    b. False

7. What is the number of channels on which DWDM is transmitted?
    a. 16
    b. 160
    c. 32
    d. 128

8. Which of the following represents a Layer 2 transport technology that offers packet transmission based on a dual counter-rotating ring topology?
    a. SONET
    b. SDH
    c. IPsec
    d. RPR
    c. MPLS

9. Which of the following is a technology that defines a network infrastructure based on the Ethernet standard over the Metropolitan Area Network?
    a. Frame Relay
    b. SDH
    c. SONET
    d. Metro Ethernet

10. EMS is a Metro Ethernet technology recommended to be used in point-to-point scenarios.
    a. True
    b. False

11. Which of the following are Metro Ethernet technologies recommended to be used with multipoint services (choose all that apply)?
    a. EPL
    b. EMS
    c. EWS
    d. ERS
    e. ERMS

12. The ISAKMP/IKE phase is composed of the ISAKMP SA setup and the IPsec SA negotiation.
    a. True
    b. False

13. Which of the following VPLS topologies is recommended for increased stability and scalability?
    a. Full-mesh VPLS
    b. Partial-mesh VPLS
    c. Hierarchical VPLS
    d. Hub-and-spoke VPLS

14. Which of the following are the main modes of operation for ISAKMP phase 1 (choose two)?
    a. Main mode
    b. Normal mode
    c. Slow mode
    d. Aggressive mode

15. Which of the following are the main varieties of IPsec (choose two)?
    a. Full mesh
    b. Site-to-site
    c. ISAKMP
    d. Remote access

16. The MPLS label is inserted between the Layer 2 and Layer 3 information.
    a. True
    b. False

17. Which of the following is a technology that helps automate the hub-and-spoke site-to-site VPN deployment process?
    a. GET VPN
    b. DMVPN
    c. Easy VPN
    d. SSL VPN

18. In which of the following MPLS VPN types will the ISP actually be involved in the routing process?

    a. Layer 2

    b. Layer 3

    c. Layer 4

    d. None of the above

19. Which of the following MPLS VPN types has the advantage of supporting multiple protocols (not just IP)?

    a. Layer 2

    b. Layer 3

    c. Layer 4

    d. None of the above

20. Which of the following defines a technical aspect within a Service Level Contract that contains all of the formally defined service levels?

    a. Transition Contract

    b. Support Contract

    c. Service Level Agreement

    d. User Level Agreement

CHAPTER 7

Designing the Enterprise Data Center

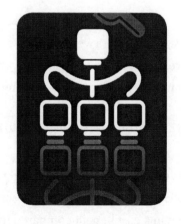

This chapter covers the following topics:

- Enterprise Data Center network infrastructure best practices
- Components and technologies of a Storage Area Network (SAN)
- Integrated fabric designs using Cisco Nexus technologies
- Network and server virtualization technologies for the Enterprise Data Center
- Designing a high availability Enterprise Data Center network that is modular and flexible

This chapter will first analyze various Enterprise Data Center design considerations, including the Core and Aggregation Layers, Layer 2 and Layer 3 Access Layers, and data center scalability and high availability. Next, it will cover SAN and Cisco Nexus technologies. The chapter will end with a discussion on the Enterprise Data Center architecture, including some considerations regarding virtualization technologies.

GENERAL CONSIDERATIONS FOR THE ENTERPRISE DATA CENTER

The data center concept has greatly evolved over the last few years, passing through many phases because of evolving technology, as illustrated in figure 7.1 below:

Figure 7.1 – Evolution of the Enterprise Data Center

At the time of their first appearance, data centers were centralized and used mainframes to manage the data. Mainframes, in turn, were managed using terminals, which are still used in modern data centers because of their resiliency, but they are quickly becoming legacy components.

NOTE: "Managing" the data in an Enterprise Data Center refers to both storing and processing data.

The next generation of data centers used a distributed processing model and introduced the client/server architecture. Business applications were installed on servers and they were accessed by clients from their PCs. This resulted in a cost benefit compared to accessing the mainframe model.

The third generation of data centers uses modern technologies (e.g., virtualization) that have further reduced costs, even though the communication equipment's performance has increased.

This approach has proven to be more efficient than the distributed processing model. In particular, virtualization has resulted in higher utilization of computing and network resources by sharing and allocating them on a temporary basis.

Enterprise Data Center Components

From an architecture standpoint, modern Enterprise Data Centers include virtualization technologies and processing, storage, and networking services. All of these features combined enable flexibility, visibility, and policy enforcement.

Major components of the Cisco Enterprise Data Center architecture framework include the following:

- **Virtualization:**
    - Cisco Nexus 1000V virtual switch for VMware ESX delivers per-virtual-machine visibility and policy control for SAN, LAN, and unified fabric.
    - Cisco Unified Computing System unifies the data center resources into a single system that offers end-to-end optimization for virtualized environments.
    - Virtualization of SAN device contents help converge multiple virtual networks.
    - All of the features above lead to simplification in the Enterprise Data Center architecture and a reduction in the TCO.

- **Unified fabric:**
    - Unified fabric technologies include Fibre Channel over Ethernet (FCoE) and Internet Small Computer System Interface (iSCSI) and they usually offer 10 Gbps transfer rates.
    - Unified fabric is supported on Cisco Catalyst and Nexus series (iSCSI). Cisco MDS storage series are designed and optimized to support iSCSI.
    - Converged network adapters are required for FCoE.
    - FCoE is supported on VMware ESX.

- **Unified computing:**
    - Cisco introduced the Unified Computing System (UCS) as an innovative next-generation Enterprise Data Center platform that converges virtualization, processing, network, and storage into a single system.
    - Unified computing allows the virtualization of network interfaces on servers.
    - Unified computing increases productivity with temporal provisioning using service profiles.

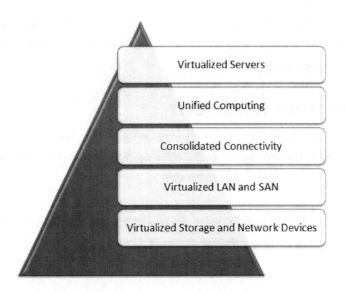

Figure 7.2 – Enterprise Data Center Topology

Figure 7.2 above illustrates the Enterprise Data Center topology. From top to bottom, the top layer includes virtual machines that are hardware abstracted into software entities running a guest OS on top of a hypervisor (resource scheduler). Unified computing resources comprise the next layer, which contains the service profiles that map to the identity of the server and provides the following details:

- Memory
- CPU
- Network interfaces
- Storage information
- Boot image

The next layer consolidates connectivity and is referred to as the unified fabric. This layer contains technologies such as 10 GigabitEthernet, FCoE, and Fibre Channel, and all of these are supported on the Cisco Nexus series. FCoE allows native Fibre Channel to be used on 10 Gbps Ethernet networks.

Next is the virtualization layer, which includes technologies such as VLANs and VSANs that provide connectivity for virtualized LANs and SANs by segmenting multiple LANs and SANs on the same physical equipment. The logical LANs and SANs do not communicate with each other. The bottom layer contains virtualized hardware that is made up of storage pools and virtualized network devices.

Server Considerations

Some very important aspects to consider when deploying servers in an Enterprise Data Center include:

- Required power
- Rack space needed
- Server security
- Virtualization support
- Server management

The increasing number of servers used means that more power is required and this leads to the need for energy efficiency in the data center. Rack servers usually consume a great amount of energy, even though they are low cost and provide high performance.

An alternative to standalone servers are blade servers. These provide similar computing power but require less space, power, and cabling. Blade servers are installed in a chassis that allows them to share network connections and power. This also reduces the number of cables needed.

Server virtualization is supported on both standalone and blade servers and provides scalability and better utilization of hardware resources, which increases efficiency. Server management is a key factor in server deployment and this can be accomplished using different products that offer secure remote management capabilities.

Enterprise Data Center Facility and Spacing Considerations

The facility, spacing, and other considerations for the Enterprise Data Center will determine where to position the equipment to provide scalability. For example, the space available will determine the number of racks for servers and the network equipment that can be installed. An important factor that must be considered is floor loading parameters.

Estimating the correct size of the data center will have a great influence on costs, longevity, and flexibility. An oversized data center will result in unnecessary costs, while an undersized data center will not satisfy computing, storage, and networking requirements, but will impact productivity. Factors that must be considered include the following:

- Available space
- The number of servers
- The amount of storage equipment
- The amount of network equipment

- The number of employees served by the Data Center infrastructure
- The space needed for non-infrastructure areas: storage rooms, office space, and others
- The weight of the equipment
- Floor load (this determines how many devices should be installed)
- Heat dissipation
- Cooling capacity (considering required temperature and humidity levels)
- Cabling needs
- Power capacity (including consumption, type, and UPS/PDU)

Physical security is another important consideration because data centers contain equipment that hosts sensitive company data that must be secured from outsiders. Factors that may affect the physical security of the equipment include fires and natural disasters. Access to the data center must also be well controlled.

Enterprise Data Center design considerations must be addressed early in the building development process and this must be carried out with a team of experts from various fields, such as networking, power, heating, ventilation, and air conditioning. The team members must work together to ensure that the systems' components interoperate effectively, providing high availability and the ability to recover network services, data, and applications. In addition, the data center must be properly designed for future use based on its limited capacity.

Enterprise Data Center Power Considerations

The power source in the Enterprise Data Center will be used to power servers, storage, network equipment, cooling devices, sensors, and other additional systems. The most power-consuming systems are servers, storage, and cooling. The process of determining the power requirements for the data center equipment is difficult because of the many variables that must be taken into consideration. Power usage is greatly impacted by the server load.

Various levels of power redundancy can affect the capital and operational expenses, based on the options chosen. Determining the right amount of power redundancy to meet the requirements takes careful planning. Estimating the necessary power capacity involves collecting the requirements for all of the current and future equipment, such as the following:

- Servers
- Storage
- Network devices
- UPS
- Generators

- HVAC
- Lighting

The power system should be designed to include additional components, such as PDUs, electrical conduits, and circuit breaker panels. Implementing a redundant system should provide protection for utility power failures, surges, and other electrical problems. When designing the Enterprise Data Center power system, the most important tasks include the following:

- Provide the physical electrical infrastructure
- Design for redundancy
- Define the overall power capacity

Enterprise Data Center Cooling Considerations

Based on the type of equipment used, careful heating and cooling calculations must be provided. Blade server deployments allow for more efficient use of space but they increase the amount of heat per server. The increased use of high-density servers must be addressed by careful data center design. Considerations for cooling must be taken into account for proper sizing of the servers. Cooling solutions for the increase in heat production include the following:

- Increase the space between the racks.
- Increase the number of HVAC units.
- Increase the airflow between the devices.

Enterprise Data Center equipment produces variable amounts of heat depending on the load. Heat has a negative effect on the reliability of the devices, including data center subsystems, racks, and individual devices, so cooling must be used to control temperature and humidity. To design a proper cooling system, environmental conditions must first be measured. Computing power and memory requirements demand more power and this leads to more heat being dissipated. The increase in device density also leads to an increase in the amount of heat generated and this can be reduced by designing proper airflow.

Sufficient cooling equipment must be available to produce acceptable temperatures within the data center. An efficient technique is arranging the data center racks with an alternating pattern of "hot" and "cold" aisles. The cold aisle should have equipment arranged face to face and the hot aisle should have them arranged back to back. The cold aisle should have perforated floor tiles that draw cold air from the floor to the face of the equipment. The hot aisles should be isolated to prevent hot air from mixing with cold air.

Other cooling techniques that can be used for equipment that does not exhaust heat to the rear include:

- Using cabinets with mesh fronts and backs
- Increasing the height of the raised floor
- Spreading out equipment onto unused racks
- Blocking unnecessary air escapes to increase airflow

Enterprise Data Center Cabling Considerations

A passive infrastructure for the Enterprise Data Center is essential for optimal system performance. The physical network cabling between devices determines how these devices communicate with one another and with external systems. The cabling infrastructure type chosen will impact the physical connectors and media type of the connector. This must be compatible with the equipment interfaces. Two options are widely used today: copper cabling and fibre-optic cabling.

The main advantages of using fibre-optic cables are they are less susceptible to external interferences and they can operate over greater distances than copper cables can. The main disadvantages of using fibre-optic cables are specific adapters might be necessary when connecting to device interfaces and they are more difficult to install and repair. The cabling must be well organized for ease of maintenance in the passive infrastructure. Cabling infrastructure usability and simplicity is influenced by the following:

- Number of connections
- Media selection
- Type of cabling termination organizers

All of these parameters must be considered in the initial data center design to prevent the following issues from occurring:

- Difficult troubleshooting
- Downtimes
- Improper cooling

Using cable management systems is essential in preventing these issues. These systems consist of integrated channels located above the rack for connectivity. Cabling should be located in the front or rear of the rack for easy access. When Enterprise Data Center cabling is deployed, space and device location constraints make it difficult to reconfigure the cabling infrastructure. Scalable cabling is essential for proper data center operation and lifespan. On the other hand, badly designed cabling will lead to downtime because of expansion requirements that were not planned in the design phase.

ENTERPRISE DATA CENTER ARCHITECTURE

Cisco has a well-proven and well-tested layered Enterprise Data Center design approach that has been improved over the last several years. The Cisco Enterprise Data Center infrastructure is used to implement even extremely large data center environments. The most important features a data center design must include are as follows:

- Flexibility
- Maintainability
- Resilience
- Performance
- Scalability

Enterprise Data Center Architecture Overview

The Enterprise Data Center architecture, as defined by Cisco, is a three-tier model that delivers scalability, performance, flexibility, resilience, and maintainability. The three tiers are the Core Layer, the Aggregation Layer, and the Access Layer, as illustrated in Figure 7.3 below:

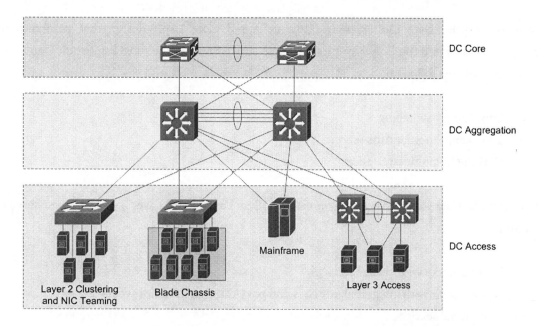

Figure 7.3 – Cisco Three-Tier Enterprise Data Center Architecture

The Enterprise Core Layer offers high-speed packet switching with 10-GigabitEthernet connections or EtherChannels with backup links. The Core Layer is the switching backplane for all of the data flows going in and out of the data center. The Core Layer is usually a centralized Layer 3 routing layer in which one or more Aggregation Layers connect. The Core Layer can inject a default route into the Aggregation Layer after the data center networks are summarized. If multicast applications are used, the Core Layer must also support IP multicast features.

The Aggregation Layer usually contains multilayer switches and aggregates a variety of network services. Other functionalities of the Aggregation Layer are as follows:

- It acts as a service module integration layer.
- It acts as a Layer 2 domain definition point.
- It provides STP processing.
- It provides redundancy.
- It provides default gateways.
- It provides security functions (firewalls, IPS, and security policies).
- It provides network analysis.
- It provides SSL offloading.
- It provides content switching.
- It provides load balancing.

Smaller Enterprise Data Centers may use a collapsed Core Layer design that combines the Aggregation Layer and the Core Layer into a single entity. Some of the most important Core Layer features include the following:

- Low-latency switching
- 10-GigabitEthernet connections
- Scalable IP multicast support

The Enterprise Data Center Access Layer usually offers Layer 2 and Layer 3 Access Layer services, including:

- Layer 2 access with cluster services
- Blade chassis with integrated switches and pass-through modules access
- Mainframe services
- Other Layer 3 Access Layer services

Typically, the Enterprise Data Center will have a three-tier design with an Ethernet Access Layer and an Aggregation Layer, with network services connected to the Enterprise Core Layer. A small- to medium-sized data center will most likely have a two-tier design that serves the server farms, where the Layer 3 Access Layer services are connected to a collapsed Core Layer that combines the standard Core Layer and the Aggregation Layer. As the company grows to an Enterprise-level organization, upgrading to a three-tier design will offer greater scalability, flexibility, and performance. Some of the benefits of the three-tier Enterprise Data Center model include the following:

- The Aggregation Layer prevents Layer 2 domain extension across the Core Layer. If Layer 2 is extended to the Core Layer, the Spanning Tree Protocol (STP) might block some paths and this situation should be avoided.
- The service modules offer an overall lower Total Cost of Ownership (TCO) because services can be shared across the entire fabric of switches.
- It decreases the complexity of the design because it reduces the number of components that must be configured and managed.
- A combination of Layer 2 and Layer 3 access models can be used and some of the newer, faster, modular platforms can be leveraged. Overall, this provides for a more flexible solution and helps to optimize the application environment.
- It offers support for clustering services and network interface card teaming (NIC-teaming). This can be combined with fault tolerance in the switches and high-availability mechanisms so the Layer 2 VLAN can be extended between the switches. This occurs at the Aggregation Layer to the Access Layer boundary.

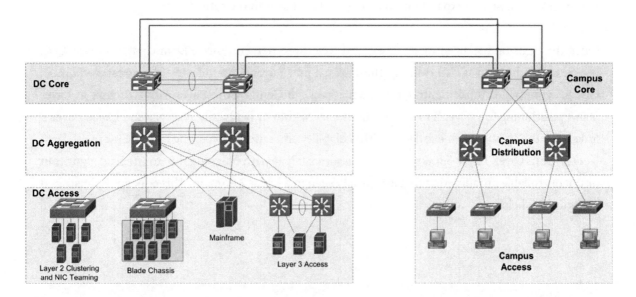

Figure 7.4 – Integration of the Enterprise Data Center Architecture into the Enterprise Campus Architecture

In a typical Enterprise Network, the Enterprise Data Center architecture connects to the Enterprise Campus architecture, as depicted in Figure 7.4 above. The connection point is at the Enterprise Data Center Core Layer, which usually connects to the Enterprise Campus Core Layer with high availability.

NOTE: The Enterprise Data Center architecture layers should not be confused with the Enterprise Campus architecture layers, even though they each might consist of a dedicated Access Layer, Aggregation/Distribution Layer, and Core Layer.

When implementing a three-tier design as described above, the network designer must decide whether a single pair of multilayer switches at the Core Layer is enough. This configuration might not support a large number of 10-GigabitEthernet ports to connect the Enterprise Data Center Aggregation Layer to the Enterprise Campus Distribution Layer switches.

Separating the Enterprise Data Center Core Layer and the Enterprise Campus Core Layer will isolate the Enterprise Campus Distribution Layer from the Enterprise Data Center Aggregation Layer because different types of policies and services might be provided at the Enterprise Campus Distribution Layer than at the Enterprise Data Center Aggregation Layer. This is important in terms of administration and policies (e.g., QoS, troubleshooting, maintenance, and security features) because there may be one team dealing with the Enterprise Campus Distribution Layer and another team dealing with the Enterprise Data Center Aggregation Layer. In addition, the possibilities for scalability and future growth should be considered. Having a separate Enterprise Data Center Core Layer makes it easier to expand into the Aggregation Layer in the future.

Once the decision has been made to expand to a three-tier Enterprise Data Center architecture, the next big decision is determining the Layer 2 and Layer 3 boundaries (demarcation points). Cisco recommends implementing the Enterprise Data Center Core Layer infrastructure at Layer 3 and positioning the Layer 2 to Layer 3 boundary within or below the Aggregation Layer. Layer 3 links offer the ability to achieve bandwidth scalability and quick convergence at the Enterprise Data Center Core Layer. Layer 3 links also avoid issues such as path blocking due to the STP algorithm or uncontrollable broadcasting that is typically seen in a Layer 2 domain. This concept is illustrated in Figure 7.5 below:

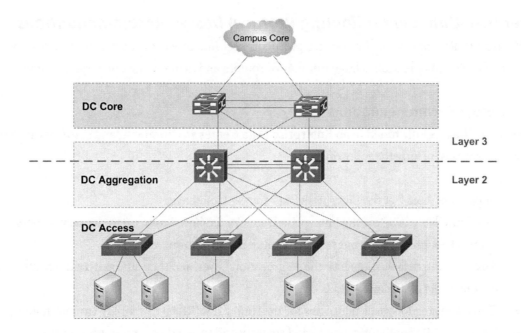

Figure 7.5 – Enterprise Data Center Layer 2 to Layer 3 Boundary

Layer 2 spanning across the Enterprise Data Center Core Layer should be avoided because all of the traffic in the data center passes through this layer, and an STP loop would bring down the entire data center.

Regarding the traffic flow across the data center, data sessions move between the Enterprise Campus Core Layer and the Enterprise Data Center Aggregation Layer submodule that holds all of the services discussed earlier, so the Enterprise Data Center Core Layer is actually combining the Aggregation Layer's traffic flows into optimized paths back to the Enterprise Campus Core Layer. In addition, server-to-server traffic (e.g., frontend to backend server traffic) will usually be contained within the Aggregation Layer submodule. However, replication traffic and backup traffic could travel between the Aggregation Layer services through the Enterprise Data Center Core Layer.

Since the Enterprise Data Center Core Layer should be designed at Layer 3, the routing protocol that will be implemented at that layer should be carefully chosen. EIGRP is Cisco's recommendation, but OSPF can also be considered, as it can be tuned to provide fast convergence times. The traffic between the Enterprise Campus Core Layer and the Enterprise Data Center Aggregation Layer should be load balanced using and leveraging the advantages of Cisco Express Forwarding (CEF). From the Enterprise Campus Core Layer perspective, there should be at least two equal cost routes to the server subnets (e.g., application servers, Web servers, or database servers). This will allow the Enterprise Data Center Core Layer to load balance the traffic flows to each of the Aggregation Layer switches using the CEF load balancing technique.

Enterprise Data Center Routing Protocol Design Recommendations

OSPF and EIGRP are two of the routing protocols recommended for data center environments because of their ability to scale a large number of routers and achieve fast convergence times.

OSPF Design Recommendations

OSPF should be carefully tuned in an Enterprise Data Center environment, and some of the design recommendations include the following:

- Implement Area 0 at the Enterprise Data Center Core Layer.
- Configure NSSAs below the Enterprise Data Center Core Layer, up to the server subnets, to control LSA propagation but still allow route redistribution.
- Advertise the default route into the Aggregation Layer, and then summarize the routes coming out of the NSSA into Area 0.
- Consider using loopback addresses for the router IDs (RIDs) to simplify troubleshooting.
- Use OSPF MD5 authentication to add security and to avoid any rogue adjacencies.

The OSPF default interface cost is calculated based on a 100 Mbps link, so the "auto-cost reference-bandwidth 10000" command should be used to set the reference to a 10-GigabitEthernet value and let OSPF differentiate the cost on higher speed links. If this parameter is not modified, all interfaces that have a bandwidth higher than 100 Mbps will be assigned the same OSPF cost (equal to 1). A workaround to this issue would be to configure manual OSPF interface costs.

The "passive-interface default" and "no passive-interface" commands should be used to suppress OSPF advertisements on all links and this process should be selectively enabled only on links that must participate in the routing process. In addition, OSPF timers can be tuned using the "ip ospf hello-interval" and "timers throttle spf" commands to allow OSPF to achieve subsecond convergence time.

EIGRP Design Recommendations

EIGRP is often simpler to configure than OSPF is, but it should be carefully implemented to avoid strange behavior in the Enterprise Data Center. Depending on the situation, other default routes may need to be filtered if they exist in the network, such as the ones coming from the Internet edge into the Enterprise Data Center Core Layer. Route filtering can be achieved using distribution lists. The "ip summary-address eigrp" command can also be used to summarize routes as they enter the Enterprise Data Center Core Layer and then pass into the Aggregation Layer.

As with OSPF, the "passive-interface default" and "no passive-interface" commands should be used to suppress EIGRP advertisements on all links and this process should be selectively enabled only on links that must participate in the routing process.

Aggregation Layer Design Recommendations

The role of the Enterprise Data Center Aggregation Layer is to aggregate Layer 2 and/or Layer 3 links from the Access Layer and to connect upstream links to the Enterprise Data Center Core Layer. Layer 3 connectivity is usually implemented between the Aggregation and Core Layers.

Cisco recommends using multiple Aggregation Layer submodules to assure a high degree of functionality and scalability. The Aggregation Layer is responsible for various services that operate in the three-layer Enterprise Data Center architecture, including the following:

- Firewalls
- IPS/IDS
- Monitoring
- SSL offloading
- Content switching
- Network analysis
- Load balancing

These services are commonly deployed in pairs using Cisco Catalyst 6500 chassis clusters and their role is to maintain the session state for redundancy purposes. By implementing this kind of architecture, the management overhead is reduced by simplifying the number of devices that must be managed.

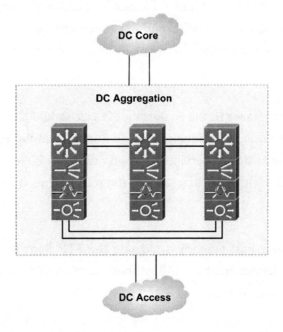

Figure 7.6 – Enterprise Data Center Aggregation Layer

As shown in Figure 7.6 above, the Aggregation Layer design is critical to the overall scalability and stability of the Enterprise Data Center architecture. All of the traffic going in and out of the data center not only is passing through the Aggregation Layer but also is relying on the services, path selection mechanism, and redundant modular architecture of the Aggregation Layer. Even though the focus is on the modular Aggregation Layer design, for the long term, the possibility of using high-density 10-GigabitEthernet line cards and larger switch fabrics should be considered.

In addition to the multiple Aggregation Layer services, STP is a primary issue, as the Enterprise Data Center Aggregation Layer will most likely contain parts that will operate at Layer 2. Using multiple Aggregation Layer services can control the size of the Layer 2 domains and limit the size of the exposure generated by one of the Aggregation Layer services failing.

The Aggregation Layer is the biggest burden to Layer 2 scalability so, according to Cisco, Rapid Spanning Tree Protocol (RSTP) is the recommended protocol to be used at this layer because of its fast convergence and additional mechanisms that are included (e.g., BackboneFast and UplinkFast). Any failure at the Aggregation Layer can be discovered very quickly, typically between 300 ms and 2 seconds, depending on how many VLANs are configured. RSTP can also be combined with features such as Root Guard, BPDU Guard, and UDLD to ensure a stable STP environment.

The Aggregation Layer will also provide the primary and secondary default gateway addresses for all of the servers in the Access Layer. Most of the time, this is accomplished using a First Hop Redundancy Protocol like HSRP or GLBP to ensure redundancy. The Aggregation Layer will also leverage some of the new virtualization and integrated services, such as virtual firewalls and security contexts in ASA security modules, virtual sensors on the IPS sensors, and server load balancing functionality.

Implementing failover techniques in the Aggregation Layer should also be considered, either in an active/active or active/standby configuration. The active/standby redundancy technique is recommended for content switching services or when dealing with old Catalyst firewall services. When using ASA modules with security contexts, the recommended approach is having active/ active failover.

Another Aggregation Layer best practice is aligning the STP Root Bridge, the primary HSRP instance, and the active service modules. All of these roles should be located within the same service context or on the same devices.

Implementing Virtual Routing and Forwarding (VRF) at the Aggregation Layer might also be a consideration. VRF can provide virtualization and management for the Enterprise Data Center design, for example, in the processing cards within a Cisco Catalyst 6500 switch where Layer 3 routing virtualization takes place. VRF can also support the isolation of the paths for MAN and WAN designs, for example, those that use MPLS at the data center.

The most important Enterprise Data Center Aggregation Layer benefits include the following:

- Aggregates traffic from the Access Layer and connects to the Core Layer
- Supports advanced security features
- Supports advanced application features
- Supports STP processing load
- Flexibility and scalability

Access Layer Design Recommendations

Just like in the Enterprise Campus design, where there is a choice between Layer 2 and Layer 3 at the Access Layer, there is the same choice in the Enterprise Data Center Access Layer (where application, Web, and database servers reside).

Some of the most important aspects that must be considered regarding the Enterprise Data Center Access Layer include the following:

- The Access Layer is the first point for oversubscription in the Enterprise Data Center design because servers will not respond to sessions and requests 24/7 at the same volume. Different mechanisms can be used to implement oversubscription, including using links bundles in EtherChannels or using 10-GigabitEthernet links.
- The Access Layer contains physical attachments to the physical servers or blades.
- At this layer, features such as clustering, NIC-teaming, and network load balancing can be implemented.

The most important benefits provided by the Enterprise Data Center Access Layer include the following:

- Provides port density for server farms
- Provides high-performance, low-latency Layer 2 switching
- Supports single-homed and dual-homed servers
- Supports mix of oversubscription requirements

Layer 2 Design

The Layer 2 design approach includes three categories:

- Layer 2 loop design
- Layer 2 loop-free design
- Layer 2 FlexLink design

Layer 2 Looped Design

The Layer 2 looped design is the most commonly used Layer 2 design and it comes in two forms:

- Triangle loop design (see Figure 7.7)
- Square loop design (see Figure 7.8)

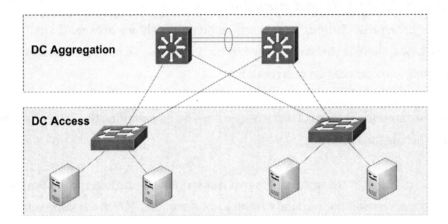

Figure 7.7 – Layer 2 Triangle Loop Design

As mentioned, one of the Enterprise Data Center Aggregation Layer design recommendation is having one of the Aggregation Layer devices offer the primary services (e.g., STP Root Bridge and active HSRP) and the other offer secondary/backup functionality. Those two devices are usually connected through an 802.1Q trunk. The triangle loop topology is one of the most popular topology design options and this involves connecting each Access Layer switch with two Aggregation Layer devices to ensure redundancy. The triangle loop design supports VLAN extension, offers resiliency with dual-homing, supports stateful services at the Aggregation Layer, and should be implemented along with RSTP, which offers quick convergence. Cisco recommends implementing additional Layer 2 features, such as BPDU Guard, Root Guard, Loop Guard, and UDLD.

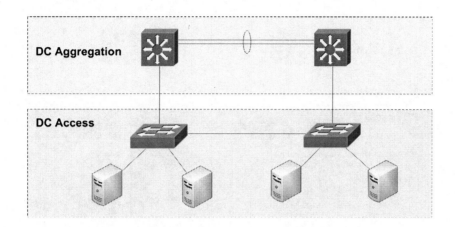

Figure 7.8 – Layer 2 Square Loop Design

One of the main differences between the triangle loop topology and the square loop topology, as shown in Figures 7.7 and 7.8 above, respectively, is the trunk link between the Access Layer switches, which will involve leveraging 10-GigabitEthernet port density on the Aggregation multilayer switches. The advantage of this option is that the square design will accommodate more Access Layer switches, so this topology design might have to be considered in an environment with many Access Layer switches. In the triangle loop design scenario, the primary Aggregation Layer device will still need to be used to offer active services (e.g., STP Root Bridge and HSRP), connecting via an 801.1Q trunk to the standby Aggregation Layer device.

Layer 2 protocols like RSTP and MSTP can be used to ensure fast convergence and additional Layer 2 features such as BPDU Guard, Root Guard, Loop Guard, and UDLD can also be used. Using the square loop design will achieve active/active failover at the Aggregation Layer, which provides great benefits. The square loop design is not as common as the triangle loop design, but it is being used more and more for Enterprise Data Center solutions.

Layer 2 Loop-Free Design

Layer 2 loop-free topologies come in two forms:

- The loop-free U topology
- The loop-free inverted U topology

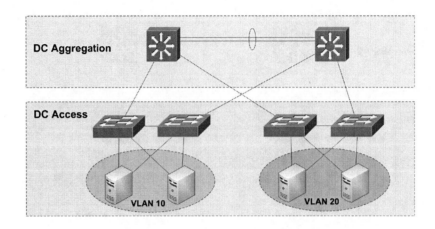

Figure 7.9 – Layer 2 Loop-Free U Topology

In a loop-free U topology, the VLANs are contained in Layer 2 switch pairs distributed across the Access Layer, as depicted in Figure 7.9 above. There is no extension outside of the switch pairs and all of the uplinks to the Aggregation Layer devices are active, so none of the ports will be blocked by the Spanning Tree Protocol. Nevertheless, STP will still be used to deal with uplink failures or configuration issues. In this type of scenario, the recommendation is to implement a fail-closed technique at the Aggregation Layer services (i.e., firewall services, IPS services, and others) that will achieve traffic black holing. This is useful in situations where one of the services fails, as this will prevent traffic from continuing to pass through to those services.

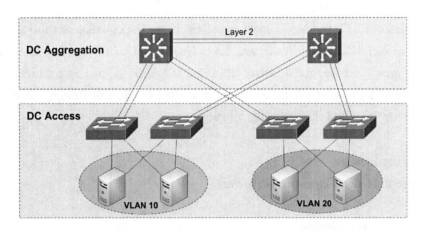

Figure 7.10 – Layer 2 Loop-Free Inverted U Topology

The difference between the loop-free U and the loop-free inverted U designs is that the first topology has a U-form design pointing up from the Access Layer switches to the Aggregation Layer devices, while the inverted topology has a U-form design pointing down from the Aggregation Layer devices to the Access Layer switches. The loop-free inverted U design is illustrated in Figure 7.10 above.

The loop-free inverted U design supports VLAN extension by having a VLAN configured on each Access Layer switch and a corresponding 802.1Q uplink that is extended between the Aggregation Layer switches. This uplink is not extended between the Access Layer switches, as there are no links between them, as in the case with the standard loop-free U design. The trunk between the Aggregation Layer switches is a Layer 2 trunk and this allows active/standby configuration and stateful communications between the services to achieve redundancy. All of the uplinks in an inverted U design are active, similar to the loop-free U design, with no STP blocking. One downside to this design type is that it presents some scalability issues when using ISL instead of 802.1Q.

Layer 2 FlexLink Design
The Layer 2 FlexLink topology is the third major design type and it is an alternative to looped Access Layer technology. FlexLink technology offers an active/standby pair of uplinks on a common Access Layer switch, so this design type involves flexible uplinks (dotted lines) going up from the Access Layer switches and connecting to the Aggregation Layer devices, as depicted in Figure 7.11 below:

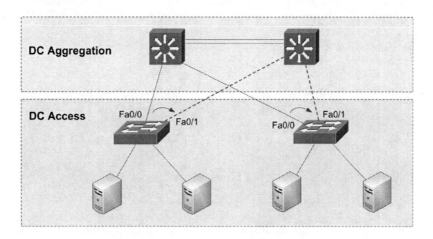

Figure 7.11 – Layer 2 FlexLink Design

FlexLinks are configured using the "switchport backup-interface <interface_id>" command on the primary interfaces (Fa0/0 on the Access Layer switches). The interface_id in this command is the secondary interface (Fa0/1 on the Access Layer switches). Only one interface can belong to one FlexLink but the interface pair can contain different types of interfaces (e.g., FastEthernet, GigabitEthernet, PortChannels, or 10 GigabitEthernet). FlexLinks automatically disable STP on the configured ports so no BPDUs are exchanged on those links.

The failover from the active to the standby link occurs in a one- to two-second time period so this technology does not provide a convergence time comparable to the one offered by RSTP. FlexLinks operate using only a single pair of links and the Aggregation Layer switches are not aware of the FlexLink configuration, so from their perspective the links are up and the STP logical and virtual ports are active and are allocated. FlexLinks are supported on a wide variety of Cisco platforms, as long as they are using IOS release 12.2 or higher. However, FlexLinks are not used very often and are an option suitable only for small- to medium-sized organizations. Since FlexLinks disable STP, the possibility for Layer 2 loops exists in certain scenarios. In addition, Inter-Switch Link (ISL) scaling issues must be considered in FlexLink environments, as opposed to situations using 802.1Q.

Comparison of Layer 2 Access Designs

The table below, which has been provided by Cisco, summarizes the main advantages of the various Access Layer designs presented previously.

	Uplinks on Aggregation Layer Switch in Blocking or Standby State	VLAN Extension Supported across Access Layer	Service Module Black Holing on Uplink Failure	Single Attached Server Black Holing on Uplink Failure	Access Layer Switch Density per Aggregation Layer Submodule	Must Consider ISL Scaling
Looped Triangle	NO	YES	YES	YES	NO	YES
Looped Square	YES	YES	YES	YES	YES	NO
Loop-Free U	YES	NO	NO	YES	YES	YES
Loop-Free Inverted U	YES	YES	YES	YES/NO	YES	NO
FlexLinks	NO	YES	YES	YES	NO	YES

NOTE: The table can be found at http://www.cisco.com/en/US/docs/solutions/Enterprise/ Data_Center/DC_Infra2_5/DCInfra_6.html.

Layer 3 Access Design

This design type involves using Layer 3 (multilayer) switches at the Access Layer, as the Layer 2 to Layer 3 boundary moves down at this level in the Enterprise Data Center architecture, as shown in Figure 7.12 below. In a Layer 3 design, the Access Layer switches link to the Aggregation Layer switches, with a Layer 3 uplink and a dedicated subnetwork. In this type of environment, Layer 3 routing takes place on the Access Layer switches first.

The Access Layer switches are connected to Layer 2 trunks that provide support for the requirements of Layer 2 adjacencies in the data center. The most important consideration when choosing this design is that the Layer 2 adjacencies are limited to the Access Layer switch ports. Therefore, VLAN extension across the data center is not possible. Using this model, Cisco highly recommends running STP, which will only be active on the inter-switch trunk ports and the server ports in the Access Layer multilayer switches.

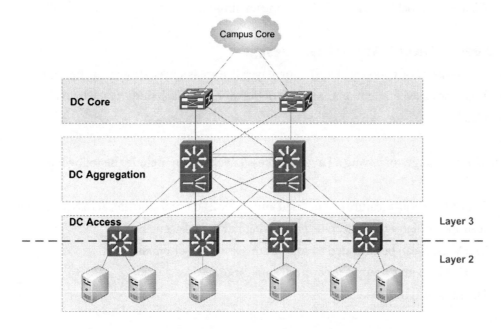

Figure 7.12 – Layer 3 Access Design

Layer 3 implementation at the Enterprise Data Center Access Layer is becoming more and more popular, especially in large organizations. Some of the most important benefits of implementing Layer 3 at the Access Layer include the following:

- Increased control of broadcast domains and the ability to limit their size.
- Minimized failure domains, offering a higher level of stability.
- All of the uplinks from the servers are active.
- CEF will be used to achieve load balancing.
- Convergence times are faster than those offered by STP.
- This design can be used when multicast IGMP snooping is unavailable at the Access Layer.

Some of drawbacks of using a Layer 3 Access Layer design include the following:

- The IP addressing scheme will be more complex, especially if moving from Layer 2 to Layer 3 at the Access Layer.
- This design typically follows a migratory pattern, meaning it is not implemented very often when the data center is first deployed. This will involve making changes to the IP addressing scheme.
- Custom applications that have hard-coded addresses are affected by this migration process.

- It might be challenging to determine all of the adjacencies when migrating from a Layer 2 to a Layer 3 Enterprise Data Center Access Layer.
- Clustering capabilities and NIC-teaming are limited.

Layer 2 versus Layer 3 Access Layer Design

The overall decision of choosing Layer 2 or Layer 3 Access Layer design in the Enterprise Data Center should be based on a complex analysis of the topology. Each design type has specific benefits and drawbacks.

Some of the advantages of having a Layer 2 Access Layer design include the following:

- The NIC-teaming feature can be used and Layer 2 adjacency occurs across a wider area.
- It supports high availability clustering using Layer 2 adjacencies.
- The VLANs can be extended to support the server requirements.
- It provides better support for custom applications.
- FlexLinks can be used.

On the other hand, a Layer 3 Access Layer design offers the following benefits:

- Easier loop management.
- Faster convergence of the network, as opposed to using Layer 2 design and STP.
- It minimizes the broadcast domains, which leads to greater stability and easier management and troubleshooting.
- It provides better support for link utilization on all of the active uplinks.

The process of deciding on a specific Enterprise Data Center Access Layer design should take the following aspects into consideration:

- The organization's needs
- Whether there is staff expertise in Layer 2 or Layer 3 technologies
- Oversubscription requirements
- Supporting and placing service submodules
- Scalability issues
- Costs (for migrating from a Layer 2 to a Layer 3 Access Layer design)

Sometimes, the ability to extend VLANs across Aggregation Layer switches with the Layer 2 option is too important and this will prevent migrating to a Layer 3 design. The convergence time of Layer

3 is often insufficient, and the ability to create tighter broadcast domains and achieve better stability sometimes cannot override the advantages of a Layer 2 solution.

Designing Blade Servers

Blade server chassis can be deployed using different models:

- Pass-through model
- Integrated Ethernet switches model

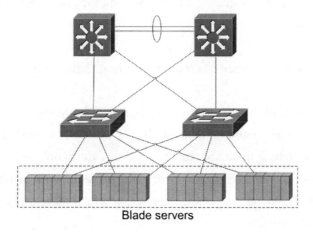

Figure 7.13 – Blade Server Pass-Through Model

The pass-through model presented in Figure 7.13 above shows external Layer 2 and Layer 3 switches for the Access Layer, and these switches are not integrated in the actual blade server farm. The blade servers connect to Access Layer switches and these switches connect to the Enterprise Data Center Aggregation Layer.

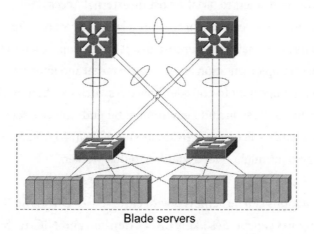

Figure 7.14 – Blade Server Integrated Ethernet Switches Model

In the integrated Ethernet switching model depicted in Figure 7.14 above, the Layer 2 Access Layer switches are integrated into the blade server chassis and the chassis connects directly to the Enterprise Data Center Aggregation Layer.

Usually, blade servers are used to replace older server farms that used towers or other types of rack-mount servers, where density is a big issue. Another situation in which blade servers are needed is when new high-end applications that require clustering are used. With blade servers, the data center managers can actually lower their TCO and save a great amount of rack space. Blade servers represent a huge area of the server market and various vendors, such as Cisco, Dell, HP, and IBM, offer this type of solution.

Implementing blade server farms presents some interesting challenges:

- Regarding administration, manageability, and control, the people responsible for the switches and the blade servers should be defined. This is especially important when implementing the integrated switching model because many times, the people responsible for data and applications are not the same as those working under the network administrator. Other issues include service considerations, change control, and how these aspects integrate within the organization's IT structure.
- Interoperability is an important issue, especially when integrating blade systems that have vendor-specific switches in the Enterprise Data Center infrastructure. IEEE standardization is now being addressed.
- Scaling STP is a challenge, as the integrated switches in blade systems are logically similar to the external rack-based switches.
- Pass-through cabling is an issue, as blade servers have the option of using a pass-through model that allows customers to use the existing external Access Layer switches to connect the servers in the blade server chassis, for reasons relating to cost or migration. The pass-through cabling model must be analyzed to ensure that it can be supported in the physical cabinets.
- Every blade server implementation has its own external and internal switch trunk connectivity options, so it is important to consider how the switch trunks and VLANs will function.
- Other matters to consider include environmental and power issues. Many servers in one cabinet or one chassis will create a great amount of heat, so water-cooled server systems or other specific systems might offer a solution to this problem.

Blade server implementations can be achieved with either Layer 2 or Layer 3 Access Layer designs. The Layer 2 design supports capabilities like VLAN extension and NIC-teaming, while the Layer 3 design can be used to achieve specific capabilities, as discussed in the previous sections. The Layer 2 implementation is more susceptible to the following issues:

- Complex STP design and link blocking issues
- Problems with oversubscription of uplinks and trunks
- A larger failure domain

NOTE: NIC-teaming, a generic term that refers to link aggregation, is a feature that occurs on the blade server chassis or on the data center servers. NIC-teaming is also called Ethernet bonding or link bundling.

The blade server trunk failover feature offers Layer 2 redundancy when deploying NIC adapter teaming (also known as link-state tracking). By implementing the blade server trunk failover feature on integrated blade switches, the link-state of the internal downstream port is bound to the link-state to one or more of the external upstream ports. The internal downstream port is the interface that connects to the blade server, while the external upstream port is an interface for the external network.

The trunk failover mechanism automatically puts all of the associated downstream ports in the error-disabled state and this behavior causes the server's primary interface to failover to secondary interfaces. This is a feature of the NICs used. Without the Layer 2 trunk failover, if upstream interfaces lose connectivity, the downstream links will not change, and this is a problem. When implementing trunk failover, STP should be enabled to ensure a loop-free topology.

Enterprise Data Center Scalability

One of the key issues with scalability involves the uplinks and oversubscription. The correct amount of uplink bandwidth on the Access Layer switches should be known. The oversubscription ratio can be calculated by determining the total number of server GigabitEthernet connections and then dividing that number by the total aggregated uplink bandwidth on the Access Layer switch. An example of this is a Cisco Catalyst 6509 switch with four 10-GigabitEthernet uplink connections, which supports 336 server Access Layer ports. A 40-GigabitEthernet uplink bandwidth for 336 server ports implies an 8:4:1 ratio.

Oversubscription ratios are extremely important because they are used to determine how long it takes to send particularly large files, as this can have a major impact on the cluster operations and server performance. If the NICs are PCI express, then a high-speed transfer bus speed and large amounts of memory will be needed. This issue will affect almost every aspect of the server implementation process. EtherChannel utilization and load balancing and its effect on active/standby and active/active server modules must also be considered. This is important because in an active/active environment, both devices must be able to process all of the traffic if one of them goes down.

Other Enterprise Data Center scalability issues include the following:

- The STP design is a huge issue because this is the feature that helps deal with a large number of VLANs in the organization and it will determine the ability to extend the VLANs across the data center. A large number of data centers may have to be consolidated into a few data centers to meet the Layer 2 implementation needs.
- Determining the need for VLAN extension in all areas of the network. Some scenarios might require access to everything from everywhere and this should be determined in the Enterprise Data Center design.
- Determining the number of necessary Access Layer switches and the total number of possible Access Layer switches supported by the Aggregation Layer. Port density is a key issue here.
- Determining whether to use RSTP or Multiple Spanning Tree (MST) as the Spanning Tree Protocol mechanism. They both have quick convergence times but RSTP is the most common. MST is usually used in ISP environments but it is not very common in the Enterprise Data Center because it has issues with some service modules (e.g., ASA in transparent mode). If STP scaling issues cannot be supported with RSTP, MST should be implemented because it supports a large number of VLANs and port instances and it is used in some of the largest data centers in the world.
- Preventing and solving scalability issues by adding Aggregation Layer services (more than two Aggregation Layer services can be used, as mentioned in previous sections).
- Performing manual pruning on trunk links to reduce the total number of necessary active logical and virtual port instances.
- Determining the optimal ratio of VLAN to HSRP instances. There is typically a 1:1 ratio of VLANs to HSRP instances and Cisco recommends having a maximum of 500 HSRP instances on the Catalyst 6500 supervisor engine 720. Sometimes, the number of VLANs will be determined by the number of HSRP instances.

Enterprise Data Center High Availability

The key to understanding Enterprise Data Center high availability is determining the common points of failure in the data center design. These points are located on the server path to the Aggregation Layer switches. If there are single-attached servers that are connected to single-attached Access Layer switches, then there will be a wide variety of failure points at the Physical Layer, and server network adapters, Access Layer switch ports, and network media must also be considered. To solve some of these issues dual-attached servers and NIC adapter teaming can be used.

Redundancy should be implemented at Layer 2 in the server farm and the following common NIC-teaming options should be considered:

- **Adaptive Fault Tolerance (AFT):** This mode involves having two network cards that are connected to the same switch, both sharing common MAC and IP addresses. One of the adapters is active and the other adapter is in a standby state.
- **Switch Fault Tolerance (SFT):** This mode involves one of the ports being active and the other port being in a standby state, with the switch using one common IP and MAC address.
- **Adaptive Load Balancing (ALB):** This mode involves one of the ports receiving traffic and all of the ports transmitting traffic using a single IP address and multiple MAC addresses.

NOTE: NICs from different manufacturers might operate differently, especially with different operating systems.

EtherChannels provide high availability and scalable bandwidth for network servers (e.g., Microsoft, Unix, or Solaris). In these situations, a combination of Layer 3 and Layer 4 port-based CEF hashing algorithms for the EtherChannel ports can be enabled using the "port-channel load-balance" command.

Another Cisco-specific mechanism that can be used to achieve high availability is Cisco Nonstop Forwarding (NSF) with Stateful Switchover (SSO) and Nonstop Routing (NSR). In implementing this solution, the service submodules do not converge if there is a supervisor failure, so dual supervisors that use Cisco NSF with SSO can be implemented to achieve increased high availability in the Enterprise Data Center Network.

STORAGE AREA NETWORKS

Storage is an issue that comes up in Enterprise environments, as networks are becoming more robust and are responsible for achieving more and more functions.

SAN Technology Overview

The main objective of Storage Area Networks (SANs) is concentrating all of the data that end-users and devices in the network need to access and separating it from the server infrastructure. SAN devices are pools of storage that everyone can access based on pre-defined rights. In this way, servers can share the storage space, thus increasing resource utilization efficiency and reducing the TCO.

Another important aspect is ensuring high levels of Input/Output (I/O) for servers and other devices, which allows seamless read and write access to the data in the same way as accessing a local hard drive.

As with every major technological area, there is some degree of SAN technology incompatibility between vendors when new generations of products are released, but the compatibility issues disappear as the technology becomes more mature. The main components of a SAN infrastructure are as follows:

- Host Bus Adapters (HBAs), which are very fast adapters that connect to the disk subsystem. HBAs connect via GigabitEthernet or 10-GigabitEthernet copper or optical links.
- The communication subsystem (this evolved from IDE and ATA connectivity to Fibre Channel communications), which allows a large number of devices to connect to the SAN at higher speeds over long distances.
- The actual storage system, which consists of an array of hard drives that can be considered "just a bunch of disks" (JBOD). Storage arrays are groups of devices that provide mass storage and the physical disk space can be virtualized into logical storage structures.

Disk arrays can be organized in various Redundant Array of Independent Disks (RAID) configurations. The most common levels of RAID are:

- **RAID 0:**
  - Functions by striping across multiple disks
  - Ensures increased performance
  - Offers no redundancy

- **RAID 1:**
  - Functions by mirroring the contents on multiple disks
  - Usually offers the same performance as a single disk
  - Offers increased redundancy

- **RAID 3:** Allows for error detection
- **RAID 5:** Allows for error correction and performance enhancement

The predecessor of SANs is Direct Attached Storage (DAS), which involves specific disks associated with each server. This solution offers limited scalability and low I/O levels and it is difficult to back up. Network Attached Storage (NAS) involves placing certain disk arrays in an IP network and accessing it via specific protocols, such as Network File System (NFS) or Common Internet File System (CIFS). NAS systems offer slow I/O rates and sometimes offer less performance than DAS systems do.

The SAN concept describes a storage network that is separate from the rest of the network, but at the same time, it must be accessed and virtualized. The technologies that make this possible include the following:

- **Small Computer System Interface (SCSI):** This is a mature technology that offers reliable communication over short distances (up to 25 meters) and has a maximum bandwidth of 320 Mbps. This is a half-duplex technology that supports a maximum of 16 devices on the SCSI bus.
- **Fibre Channel (FC):** This is a modern technology that offers higher throughput and distances than traditional SCSI connections do. FC can extend SCSI networks and it provides its own protocol – Fibre Channel Protocol (FCP) – to ensure reliable communications, which is similar to TCP. FC offers connectivity over distances up to 10 km and ensures a bandwidth of 1 to 4 Gbps. In addition, it supports up to 16 million devices (practically an unlimited number), as opposed to SCSI, which is limited to 16 devices.

Cisco invented a storage virtualization concept called virtual SAN (VSAN) that allows the creation of logical storage units from physical storage. This technology is similar to VLAN's functionality in that it allows the end-user to see only a logical space for data storage that has nothing to do with the physical storage system layout. The VSAN system handles the process of mapping to an actual physical location.

VSAN allows the overlay of multiple logical views of the storage space over the high-speed fabric environment that connects all of the storage devices. Traffic moves from one VSAN to another using enhanced ISL. The Cisco MDS 9000 family was the first generation of products that supported this technology.

Traffic moves between VSANs using Inter-VSAN Routing (IVR) as the fabric routing technology. This connects fabric environments without having to merge them and allows the sharing of centralized storage services across VSANs. IVR enables services and/or devices in different VSANs to communicate, for example, a replication service that is able to work from one VSAN to another VSAN without permitting any local device traversal.

The protocol used to route between VSANs is Fabric Shortest Path First (FSPF). This uses a link-state database, associate costs with each link, and uses a dynamic incremental version of Dijkstra's algorithm to calculate the shortest path.

SAN environments should be designed with security in mind, beyond the features offered by virtualization. The technology for securing SANs is called zoning and this adds another logical layer of security on top of a SAN or VSAN by grouping fabric devices. Zoning can be implemented in two ways:

- **Software zoning:** Based on DNS technologies; not preferred.
- **Hardware zoning:** Performs the operations as part of the SAN equipment; Cisco-preferred option.

IBM invented an old communications protocol called Enterprise System Connection Protocol (ESCP), which had a fiber option for connecting their mainframes to the storage system. IBM and Cisco developed the Fibre Connection (FICON) protocol to replace the legacy ESCP protocol (limited to 200 Mbps). FICON runs over longer distances and offers a higher throughput to connect mainframes to SANs. Cisco devices support FICON and Feature Control Policy (FCP) on the same physical infrastructure.

Another SAN-related protocol is SANTap, which defines a standard for accessing data on a SAN. This is a protocol that allows third-party storage applications to be integrated into the SAN, thus offering enhanced functionality, including continuous backup and long-distance replication. SANTap allows data to be written to a storage device so that it can be duplicated by another appliance in the fabric.

SAN Design Considerations

Some of the most important SAN design considerations involve port density and topology. Port density considerations include:

- The number of currently necessary ports
- The number of ports needed in the future
- The expected SAN lifetime

Topology design considerations include:

- Whether the data center is on a single floor
- Whether the data center is in a single building
- Whether SAN extension is required (multi-building scenarios)

Network designers should also analyze what happens when there is oversubscription for mission-critical resources. Typically, a methodology for failing over to directly attached storage must be designed in the event the SAN is oversubscribed. Another issue which should be a concern is traffic management design issues, including:

- QoS
- Bandwidth reservation
- The way different servers have different performance requirements
- Traffic choice between data centers

NOTE: To avoid traffic management issues, every application running in the data center should be tested after a migration process.

Fault isolation is another important SAN design issue and this is usually solved using VSANs. VSANs are critical for logically isolating faults in one VSAN so that it does not affect the entire SAN. Regarding convergence and stability in SAN environments, redundancy can be built in on devices and between them. In addition, the overall number of switches and trunks should be minimized to increase overall network stability and to reduce convergence times.

Some of the most popular SAN designs include:

- **Collapsed Core Layer architecture:** This design collapses the Core Layer into the Distribution Layer when using high-end Cisco devices. With the first generation of this technology, the collapsed Core Layer architecture was not recommended because of limited high availability. However, newer generations of devices allow for the collapsed Core Layer architecture in many implementations because they offer fully redundant single chassis technologies.
- **Dual-fabric collapsed Core Layer architecture:** This is the enhanced version of the collapsed Core Layer architecture, providing additional redundancy between devices. The dual-fabric collapsed Core Layer architecture can be implemented on a small, medium, or large scale. For example, in a large-scale design, there can be two Core Layer switches for four Enterprise Edge switches, with the Enterprise Edge switches having 64-Gigabit connections to the Core Layer and the Core Layer devices, supporting 256-Gigabit throughput to the storage devices.

SAN extension is a continuously growing technology area because as the distance between Enterprise Data Center components continues to increase, connectivity between SANs and VSANs that logically make them up must be provided. Traditionally, this was accomplished using CWDM and DWDM technologies but these had distance limitations that led to the adoption of modern SAN extension technologies, including:

- **Fibre Channel over IP (FCIP):** Provides connectivity over any distance between SAN systems.
- **iSCSI:** Carries the SCSI protocol over IP.

Some other new developments in SAN extension include the following:

- Tape backup acceleration
- FCIP write acceleration
- Hardware-assisted data compression over FCIP
- Hardware-based IP security encryption

CISCO NEXUS

Cisco Nexus technology was developed for the purpose of unifying the LAN and SAN infrastructures. While most data centers use separate LAN and SAN networks with separate switches and network adapters in the servers, Cisco Nexus technology allows for the implementation of a unified fabric Enterprise Data Center architecture, with a consolidated LAN and SAN network at the Access Layer, as depicted in Figure 7.15 below.

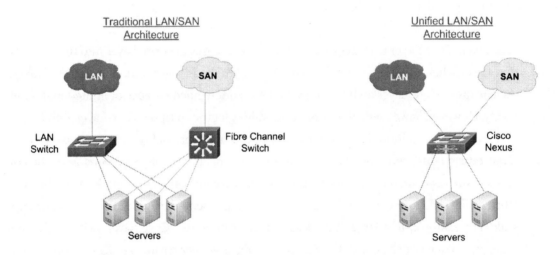

Figure 7.15 – Traditional Architecture versus Cisco Unified LAN and SAN Infrastructure

Nexus devices run NX-OS, which is based on the Cisco Storage Area Network Operating System (SAN-OS) and which operates on different platforms, including:

- Nexus 1000V
- Nexus 2000
- Nexus 4000
- Nexus 5000
- Nexus 7000
- Cisco MDS 9000
- Cisco Unified Computing System (CUCS)

The key features of NX-OS involve technologies such as the following:

- **Virtual Device Contexts (VDCs):** Although this technology has existed for some time, it offers great benefits when implementing it on robust systems like the Nexus platforms, where there is true segmentation into virtual devices. This offers complete protection against failures from one context to another.
- **Virtual Port Channels (vPCs):** This aggregation technology allows the creation of Ether-Channels to two upstream switches. Loop prevention is built in to the protocol, so the big advantage of vPCs is requiring STP and having all of the links forward traffic.

Cisco NX-OS offers continuous system operation, even in situations where there is a failure of some system within the Nexus platform. In addition, it offers the In-Service Software Upgrade (ISSU) option, which allows software upgrades on the device running in the production environment, without the need to reboot the device.

The major security enhancement in the NX-OS system is IEEE 802.1AE link-layer cryptography (128-bit AES), which offers Layer 2 protection of communication between a device and the Nexus platform. The Cisco 802.1AE implementation is also known as Cisco TrustSec. Apart from this special security mechanism, NX-OS also supports every major security feature present in Cisco IOS, including private VLANs, flooding protection, port security, and others.

The Overlay Transport Virtualization (OTV) feature in NX-OS offers a new technology for connecting remote data centers over a packet-switched network. Previous to OTV, this operation used to be achieved using VPLS technology.

The Nexus platform licensing model is very flexible and includes multiple licensing schemes:

- **Base service license (the default license):** Offers basic Layer 2 functionality, including STP, VLANs, private VLANs, etc.
- **Enterprise service package:** Offers Layer 3 functionality.
- **Advanced services:** Includes VDC, Cisco TrustSec, or OTV functionalities.
- **Transport service:** Includes OTV and MPLS features.

If a Nexus platform is purchased in a specific licensing configuration, the license can be upgraded at any time using the "install license" command. NX-OS also offers feature testing for a 120-day grace period (but only for the default virtual device context).

Some of the most important enhancements NX-OS has over IOS from a configuration standpoint include the following:

- The login process places the user directly into EXEC mode.
- Because of the platform's modularity, features can be completely enabled and disabled using the "feature" command (this also enhances security).
- Commands can run from any command mode.
- The interfaces are labeled simply as "Ethernet."
- The default STP mode is Rapid-PVST+.
- The "write memory" and "alias" commands have been removed.

Cisco NX-OS has two predefined VRF instances:

- The management VRF (the management interface is "mgmt0")
- The default VRF

Another important security feature is disabling Telnet access and using SSHv2 by default, with a mandatory username and password verification. The old password-only access mode has been removed because it did not offer any user tracking and accountability.

NX-OS booting and low-level processing is handled by a special image called "kickstart," which is completely separate from the system image. This modularity feature facilitates advanced features such as in-service software upgrades.

As mentioned, one of the enhancements of NX-OS over other Cisco platforms is the ability to run commands from any command mode because the command modes are nested and all of the lower commands are inherited as they move up the tree. NX-OS configuration modes include:

- Exec configuration mode
- Global configuration mode
- Interface configuration mode

Cisco devices are usually managed via a console port, Telnet/SSH, or Graphical User Interface (GUI). Nexus platforms offer the following management interfaces:

- **Controller Process (CP)/Supervisor:** This is the most critical interface, as it offers management and control plane access to the device.

- **Connectivity Management Processor (CMP):** This is a totally modular Out-of-Band interface that offers management and monitoring capabilities.
- **MGMT0:** This offers an Out-of-Band interface because it is in its own VRF context.
- **SSHv2**
- **XML-Based Network Configuration Protocol (NETCONF):** This allows device monitoring and configuration via XML scripting.
- **SNMP**

NOTE: Advanced GUI management of Nexus platforms can be achieved using the Data Center Network Manager (DCNM), which is a modular client-server-based GUI management system.

Cisco made a great enhancement to the supervisor engine in NX-OS devices called the Controller Processor (CP). The main features offered by the CP include the following:

- It uses modern Intel Dual-Core CPUs.
- Intra-chassis redundancy can be achieved using dual CPs.
- The CP communicates in a new architectural way compared to the classic supervisor engines used in the Catalyst 6500 series, using a QoS-aware methodology of communication called Virtual Output Queuing.
- USB ports on the CP offer enhanced functionality and actual functional file systems.
- It provides integrated diagnostics using built-in Wireshark capabilities.
- It Includes the Connectivity Management Processor (CMP), which provides remote Out-of-Band management.

Nexus platforms offer a simple, easy-to-implement, automated configuration rollback feature that allows users to take a snapshot (checkpoint) of the NX-OS configuration and then reapply it at any point without rebooting. This operates in three modes:

- **Atomic:** The checkpoint is implemented as long as no error occurs.
- **Best-Effort:** Allows the implementation of rollback and skip errors.
- **Stop-at-First-Failure:** Allows partial configurations to be applied in case of errors.

VIRTUALIZATION

Virtualization has become a critical component in most Enterprise Networks because of the modern demands on IT, including increasing efficiency while reducing capital and operational costs. Virtualization is a critical component of the Cisco Network Architecture for Enterprise.

Virtualization Considerations

Virtualization can represent a variety of technologies, but the general idea is to abstract the logical components from hardware or networks and implement them into a virtual environment. Some of the advantages of virtualization include the following:

- Flexibility in managing the system resources
- Better use of computing resources
- Consolidates low-performance devices into high-performance devices
- Provides flexible security policies

Some of the drivers behind implementing a virtualized environment include the following:

- The need to reduce the number of physical devices that perform individual tasks
- The need to reduce operational costs
- The need to increase productivity
- The need for flexible connectivity
- The need to eliminate underutilized hardware

Virtualization can be implemented at both the network level and the device level. Network virtualization implies the creation of network partitions that run on the physical infrastructure, with each logical partition acting as an independent network. Network virtualization can include VLANs, VSANs, VPNs, or VRF.

On the other hand, device virtualization allows logical devices to run independently of each other on a single physical machine. Virtual hardware devices are created in software and have the same functionality as real hardware devices. The possibility of combining multiple physical devices into a single logical unit also exits.

The Cisco Network Architecture for Enterprise contains multiple forms of network and device virtualization:

- Virtual machines
- Virtual switches

- Virtual local area networks
- Virtual private networks
- Virtual storage area networks
- Virtual switching systems
- Virtual routing and forwarding
- Virtual port channels
- Virtual device contexts

Device contexts partition a single partition into multiple virtual devices called contexts. A context acts as an independent device with its own set of policies. The majority of features implemented on the real device are also functional on the virtual context. Some of the devices in the Cisco portfolio that support virtual contexts include the following:

- Cisco ASA
- Cisco ACE
- Cisco IPS
- Cisco Nexus series

Server virtualization allows the servers' resources to be abstracted, which provides flexibility and usage optimization of the infrastructure. The result is that data center applications are no longer tied to specific hardware resources, so the applications are unaware of the underlying hardware. Server virtualization solutions are produced by companies such as VMware (ESX), Microsoft (Hyper-V), and Citrix (XenServer).

The network virtualization design process must take into consideration the preservation of high-availability, scalability, and security in the Enterprise Data Center. Access Layer control issues must be considered to ensure legitimate user access and protection from external threats. Proper path isolation ensures that users and devices are mapped to the correct secure set of resources and implies the creation of independent logical traffic paths over a shared physical infrastructure.

Server Virtualization

Server virtualization is a new area for Cisco, and it involves a more intelligent deployment of new servers and services, as opposed to the traditional approach in which a new physical server was deployed when a new application needed to be implemented.

Cisco's line of products for server virtualization is called the Cisco Unified Computing System (CUCS), and one of the major advancements Cisco introduced in this area is related to a consistent

I/O that provides uniform support for hypervisors across all servers in a resource pool. CUCS products allow advanced management and configuration of the throughput across all of the servers.

This technology supports Ethernet in all of its variations, including Fibre Channel over Ethernet. CUCS allows for a 10-Gigabit Unified network fabric with up to 40 Gbps of throughput per blade server. Cisco provides the "wire once" feature that allows for the chassis to be initially wired and then performs all the I/O changes through a GUI management system. This approach avoids any recabling issues.

The management component of the CUCS is called the Cisco Unified Computing System Manager (CUCS Manager). CUCS Manager allows the servers to be grouped in resource pools and new applications to be deployed in those pools, without associating them with any specific hardware. Moving a particular virtual machine between the server blades (for load balancing, SLA, or downtime reasons) is easily accomplished through the GUI.

Memory and CPU performance are the primary hardware factors that need to be considered in a CUCS environment, as these factors can become bottlenecks for the solution. Cisco has invented the Extended Memory Technology incorporated in some CUCS platforms that allows the mapping of physically distinct DIMMs to a single logical DIMM, as seen by the processor. This eliminated the memory bottleneck issues, as extended memory servers with a large number of DIMMs can provide hundreds of Gigabits of memory that can be mapped to a single resource.

Each server in a CUCS is physically connected to the fabric by one or more physical links. Cisco also invented a technology called VN-Link that allows virtualization of the connectivity over a single physical link, creating virtual links. The virtual machine links can be managed like other physical links, and this involves configuring VLANs, security features (e.g., ACLs), or QoS features.

SUMMARY

Cisco has a well-proven and well-tested layered Enterprise Data Center design approach that has been improved over the last several years. The Cisco Enterprise Data Center infrastructure is used to implement even extremely large data center environments. The most important features an Enterprise Data Center design must have are:

- Flexibility
- Maintainability
- Resilience
- Performance
- Scalability

The Enterprise Data Center architecture, as defined by Cisco, is a three-tier model that delivers scalability, performance, flexibility, resiliency, and maintainability. The three tiers include the following:

- Data Center Core Layer
- Data Center Aggregation Layer
- Data Center Access Layer

The Enterprise Data Center Core Layer offers high-speed packet switching with 10-GigabitEthernet connections or EtherChannel and backup links. The Core Layer is the switching backplane for all of the data flows going in and out of the Enterprise Data Center. Smaller data centers may use a collapsed Core Layer design that combines the Aggregation Layer and the Core Layer into a single entity.

The Aggregation Layer usually contains multilayer switches and it aggregates a variety of network services. Other functionalities of the Aggregation Layer are as follows:

- It acts as a service submodule integration layer.
- It acts as a Layer 2 domain definition point.
- It provides STP processing.
- It provides redundancy.
- It provides default gateways.
- It provides security functions (e.g., firewalls, IPS, and security policies).
- It provides network analysis.
- It provides SSL offloading.
- It provides content switching.
- It provides load balancing

The Enterprise Data Center Access Layer usually offers Layer 2 and Layer 3 Access Layer services, including:

- Layer 2 access with cluster services
- Blade chassis with integrated switches and pass-through models
- Mainframe services
- Other Layer 3 Access Layer services

Some of the benefits of the three-tier Enterprise Data Center model include the following:

- The Aggregation Layer prevents Layer 2 domain extension across the Core Layer.
- The service submodules offer an overall lower TCO.
- It reduces the complexity of the design because it reduces the number of components that have to be configured and managed.
- A combination of Layer 2 and Layer 3 access models can be used and some of the newer, faster modular platforms can be leveraged.
- It offers support for clustering services and NIC-teaming.

Cisco recommends implementing the Enterprise Data Center Core Layer infrastructure at Layer 3 and positioning the Layer 2 to Layer 3 boundary within or below the Aggregation Layer services. Layer 3 links offer the ability to achieve bandwidth scalability and quick convergence at the Enterprise Data Center Core Layer. It also avoids matters such as path blocking due to the STP algorithm or the downside of having uncontrollable broadcast issues that are typically seen in a Layer 2 domain.

OSPF and EIGRP are two of the routing protocols recommended for use in data center environments because of their capabilities to scale a large number of routers and achieve fast convergence times. The Layer 2 access design approach includes three categories:

- Layer 2 loop designs (triangle loop design and square loop design)
- Layer 2 loop-free designs (loop-free U and loop-free inverted U topologies)
- Layer 2 FlexLink design

The Layer 3 access design involves using Layer 3 (multilayer) switches at the Access Layer, as the Layer 2 to Layer 3 boundary moves down at this level in the Enterprise Data Center architecture. In a Layer 3 design, the Access Layer switches link to the Aggregation Layer switches with a Layer 3 uplink and a dedicated subnetwork. In this type of environment, Layer 3 routing takes place on the Access Layer switches first. The Access Layer switches are connected with Layer 2 trunks that provide support for the requirements of Layer 2 adjacencies in the data center. The most important consideration when choosing this design is that Layer 2 adjacencies are limited to the Access Layer switch ports. Therefore, VLAN extension across the Enterprise Data Center is not possible.

The overall decision of choosing a Layer 2 or a Layer 3 access design in the Enterprise Data Center should be based on a complex analysis of the topology. Each design type has specific benefits and drawbacks.

Some of the advantages of having a Layer 2 access design include the following:

- The NIC-teaming feature and Layer 2 adjacency across a wider area.
- It supports high availability clustering using Layer 2 adjacencies.
- The VLANs can be extended to support the server requirements.
- It provides better support for custom applications.
- FlexLinks can be used.

On the other hand, a Layer 3 access design offers the following benefits:

- Easier loop management.
- Faster convergence of the network compared to using the Layer 2 design and STP.
- It minimizes the broadcast domains, which leads to greater stability and easier management and troubleshooting.
- It provides better support for link utilization on all of the active uplinks.

The process of deciding on a specific Enterprise Data Center Access Layer design should take the following aspects into consideration:

- The organization's needs
- Whether the staff has expertise in Layer 2 or Layer 3 technologies
- Oversubscription requirements
- Supporting and implementing service submodules
- Scalability issues
- Costs (for migrating from a Layer 2 to a Layer 3 Access Layer design)

Data center scalability issues include the following:

- The STP design is a huge issue because this is the feature that will help deal with a large number of VLANs in the organization and it will determine the ability to extend the VLANs across the Enterprise Data Center.
- Determining the need for VLAN extension in all areas of the network.
- Determining the number of necessary Access Layer switches and the total number of possible Access Layer switches supported by the Aggregation Layer.
- Determining whether to use RSTP or MST as the Spanning Tree Protocol mechanism.
- Preventing and solving scalability issues by adding Aggregation Layer services.

- The possibility of performing manual pruning on trunk links to reduce the total number of necessary active logical and virtual port instances.
- Determining the optimal ratio of VLAN to HSRP instances.

Redundancy should be implemented at Layer 2 in the server farm; the common NIC-teaming options include the following:

- Adaptive Fault Tolerance (AFT)
- Switch Fault Tolerance (SFT)
- Adaptive Load Balancing (ALB)

The main components of a Storage Area Networking infrastructure are as follows:

- Host Bus Adapters (HBAs), which are very fast adapters that connect to the disk subsystem.
- The communication subsystem, which evolved from IDE and ATA connectivity to Fibre Channel communications.
- The actual storage system, which consists of an array of hard drives that is considered "just a bunch of disks" (JBOD).

The most common levels of RAID are:

- RAID 0 (striping)
- RAID 1 (mirroring)
- RAID 3 (error detection)
- RAID 5 (error correction)

Some of the most important SAN design considerations involve port density and topology. Port density considerations include:

- The number of currently necessary ports
- The number of ports needed in the future
- The expected SAN lifetime

Topology design considerations include:

- Whether the data center is on a single floor
- Whether the data center is in a single building
- Whether SAN extension is required (in multi-building scenarios)

Some of the most popular designs include the following:

- Collapsed Core Layer architecture
- Dual-fabric collapsed Core Layer architecture

Cisco Nexus technology was developed to unify the LAN and SAN infrastructures. While most data centers use separate LANs and SANs with separate switches and network adapters in the servers, Cisco Nexus technology allows for the implementation of a unified fabric Enterprise Data Center architecture, with a consolidated LAN and SAN at the Access Layer.

Cisco's line of products for server virtualization is called the Cisco Unified Computing System (CUCS), and one of the major advancements Cisco introduced in this area is a consistent I/O that provides uniform support for hypervisors across all servers in a resource pool. CUCS products facilitate advanced management and configuration of the throughput across all of the servers.

END OF CHAPTER QUIZ

1. What are the most important features an Enterprise Data Center design must have (choose all that apply)?
    a. Flexibility
    b. Easy to implement
    c. Resilience
    d. Scalability
    e. Supports a fixed number of servers
    f. Performance

2. One of the most important benefits of the three-tier Enterprise Data Center model is that it reduces the complexity of the design because it decreases the number of components that need to be managed.
    a. True
    b. False

3. Which of the following are Enterprise Data Center Aggregation Layer functionalities (choose three)?
    a. Mainframe services
    b. Provides STP processing
    c. Provides redundancy
    d. Layer 2 access
    e. Service submodule integration
    f. Blade chassis integration

4. Which of the following is a recommendation when implementing OSPF in a data center environment?
    a. Implement Area 0 at the Aggregation Layer
    b. Implement Area 0 across the Core and Aggregation Layers
    c. Implement Area 0 at the Enterprise Data Center Core Layer
    d. Implement Area 0 at the Access Layer.

5. Which of the following are Layer 2 design topologies (choose three)?
    a. Loop designs
    b. Circle designs
    c. Linear designs
    d. Loop-free designs
    e. FlexLink designs

6. Layer 2 loop designs can be implemented in a triangle loop or a square loop design.
   a. True
   b. False

7. Which of the following are Layer 2 loop-free topologies (choose all that apply)?
   a. Loop-free with FlexLinks
   b. Loop-free U
   c. Loop-free square
   d. Loop-free inverted U

8. Where is the Layer 2 to Layer 3 boundary located in a Layer 3 access Enterprise Data Center design?
   a. At the Core Layer
   b. At the Aggregation Layer
   c. At the Access Layer

9. Which of the following Enterprise Data Center Access Layer designs provides increased control of broadcast domains?
   a. Layer 2 loop design
   b. Layer 2 FlexLink design
   c. Layer 2 loop-free design
   d. Layer 3 design

10. The Enterprise Data Center Core Layer is the same as the Enterprise Campus Core Layer.
    a. True
    b. False

11. Which of the following are Layer 2 Enterprise Data Center Access Layer design advantages (choose all that apply)?
    a. The ability to use NIC-teaming
    b. The ability to minimize broadcast domains
    c. The ability to use FlexLinks
    d. The ability to extend VLANs according to the server requirements
    e. Easier loop management

12. The Layer 3 Enterprise Data Center Access Layer design provides faster convergence times than the Layer 2 design does.
    a. True
    b. False

13. Which of the following are the most common NIC-teaming options (choose three)?
    a. CDP
    b. AFT
    c. ALB
    d. STP
    e. ABL
    f. SFT

14. Which of the following components of a SAN infrastructure describes server adapters used to connect to the disk subsystem?
    a. SHA
    b. BHA
    c. HBA
    d. HSA

15. Which of the following RAID options provides content mirroring?
    a. RAID 0
    b. RAID 1
    c. All RAID types

16. SAN zoning can be implemented either in software or in hardware.
    a. True
    b. False

17. Which of the following are the most important SAN design considerations (choose two)?
    a. Port density
    b. Physical location
    c. SAN vendor
    d. Topology design

18. Which of the following are the most popular SAN designs (choose two)?
    a. Square topology
    b. Single layer architecture
    c. Collapsed Core Layer architecture
    d. Dual-fabric collapsed Core Layer architecture

19. Which of the following Nexus technologies allows the creation of EtherChannles to two upstream switches?
    a. vEC
    b. vPC
    c. LACP
    d. VDC

20. Which of the following is Cisco's line of products for server virtualization?
    a. Cisco Catalyst
    b. Cisco ACE
    c. Cisco UCS
    d. Cisco ASA

CHAPTER 8

Designing the E-Commerce Submodule

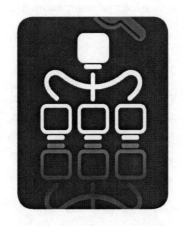

This chapter covers the following topic:

- Effective e-commerce design

This chapter will present general considerations regarding the e-commerce submodule design, including specific aspects of this process, high availability techniques, security, load balancing, and design topologies.

GENERAL CONSIDERATIONS FOR THE E-COMMERCE SUBMODULE

One of the main reasons for using the Internet is to conduct electronic commerce over large distances. The e-commerce submodule allows companies to support a wide variety of applications over the Internet, as well as Internet-related technologies.

E-commerce is a critical area for network design in modern network infrastructures because the failure of this submodule most often involves significant financial loss for the company. This is the network submodule that generates and sustains the sales process and it should be designed accordingly to avoid any outages.

The e-commerce submodule can be in the same location as the data center but it should be separated from the rest of the data center and designed with redundancy in mind. A reliable e-commerce submodule should include the following resources for the organization:

- Trained staff to handle the operating and maintenance processes
- Proper documentation and processes
- Optimal management tools

> NOTE: Many people tend to confuse the availability and reliability features in a submodule. Availability is whether a service can be used, while reliability is whether a service is working the way it should be working. An available e-commerce service does not necessarily imply a reliability service.

One of the most important design aspects regarding the e-commerce submodule is that it must be connected to the Internet through at least two providers. From a security standpoint, the e-commerce submodule should be protected using multiple layers of firewalls (also known as a "firewall sandwich") at different points in the network. This implies using firewalls between different layers.

The high degree of firewalling can be simplified using firewall virtualization (i.e., virtual contexts), which is a cost-effective solution for separating different layers. Another important technology present in e-commerce environments is server load balancing, which is used to distribute client requests across active servers. The most common Server Load Balancing (SLB) design models include the following:

- **SLB router mode:** Actively participates in the routed path.
- **SLB bridge (inline) mode:** Acts as a transparent bridge.
- **SLB one-arm mode:** Takes place in the same subnet as the servers.
- **SLB two-arm mode:** Takes place in a different subnet than the servers (this adds complexity to the configuration).

Technologies such as Policy Based Routing (PBR) or Network Address Translation (NAT) must be used when configuring one-arm mode or two-arm mode SLB.

The most common e-commerce topologies include the following:

- E-commerce base design
- E-commerce dual layer firewall design
- E-commerce SLB one-arm mode with dual layer firewall design
- E-commerce SLB one-arm mode with security contexts

A common topology for e-commerce design used to involve one firewall per ISP, with each edge path using NAT to translate inside addresses. When using this topology, a DNS should be used to achieve load balancing across the different ISP connections; the main issue with this is it does not offer a stateful failover to another path.

The modern topology of e-commerce design involves using firewalls that support stateful failover and translating addresses to a common external prefix. Cisco ASA devices can be used, as they support active/active failover by backing each other up, meaning they both can remain active at the same time.

The most sophisticated implementation for e-commerce involves using distributed data centers that allow e-commerce operations to be replicated across geographically distributed data centers. This topology protects against regional problems; in fact, one site can be taken completely offline and still have its e-commerce service available. The distributed data center design is a required topology in banking environments or in other organizations that must run critical services. Other features of this design include:

- Databases backing each other up in an active/active failover design
- The use of technologies (like Cisco Global Site Selector) that can detect and react to data center outages

After designing the e-commerce model and setting up SLB and security features, the submodule should be tuned by implementing several features:

- BGP traffic tuning, for entrance and exit optimization.
- Enhanced object tracking, featuring the ability to track a particular prefix/interface and then take an action based on that interface.
- Performance Routing (PfR), which used to be called Optimized Edge Routing (OER). This technology uses a Master Controller (MC) node that monitors several performance metrics (using IP SLA), which are corrected by managing and taking actions on Border Routers (BRs).
- Cisco Global Site Selector, which ensures the requests for information are routed to the available sites (data centers).

Another interesting technology is the Web Cache Communication Protocol (WCCP), which uses a Cisco Cache Engine to handle and distribute Web traffic (user requests) quickly. When a user requests a Web service (e.g., a page on a Web server), the router sends the requests to the Cache Engine, which will respond with a copy of the requested page, if it has the page stored locally. If the Cache Engine does not have the requested page stored, it will retrieve the page, store it, and then respond. Any future requests for that Web page will be responded to with the locally stored information.

E-COMMERCE HIGH AVAILABILITY

For many organizations, the e-commerce submodule facilitates interaction between the company and the outside world, and it is often the only way customers see the company's products and services. In this regard, companies must be able to provide applications and Web services quickly, securely, and with high availability to potential customers. Downtime in the e-commerce submodule can be catastrophic and there are many examples of companies that have failed by not providing security or high availability.

For some companies, downtime in the e-commerce submodule can cost millions of dollars, maybe on an hourly basis. Network designers should think about high availability techniques that can be used in the e-commerce design and they should take five main components into consideration:

- Redundancy
- Technology

- People
- Processes
- Tools

Redundancy

Redundancy involves having hot spares and cold spares to eliminate any single points of failure. Redundancy should be implemented in several different areas of the e-commerce solution (both hardware and software), so if one component goes down, the service is not interrupted for at least an acceptable period of time. This is accomplished using the following techniques:

- Dual devices (routers, switches, firewalls, and servers)
- Dual links between the network devices
- Multiple ISP links (multi-homing)
- Diverse paths
- Diverse geography (the e-commerce submodule components are not placed in a single location)
- Redundant data centers and facilities (warm sites, cold sites, hot sites, and mobile sites)
- Cost-benefit analysis to minimize costs and maximize functionality

Technology

Some of the technologies that help improve high availability in the e-commerce submodule include:

- Stateful Switchover (SSO) – especially in firewall systems
- Non-Stop Forwarding (NSF)
- Server Load Balancing (SLB)
- Enhanced Object Tracking (EOT)
- IP SLA
- Performance Routing (PfR)/Optimized Edge Routing (OER)
- Fast routing convergence

NSF is a Layer 3 process that works together with SSO to minimize the amount of time the network is unavailable to users, following a switchover from a primary device to a secondary device. The main goal is to continue forwarding IP packets after the route processor switchover. NSF is supported by a wide variety of dynamic routing protocols (e.g., EIGRP, OSPF, IS-IS, and BGP). If a router is running one of these protocols, it can detect the internal switchover and take the proper steps to continue forwarding network traffic using and leveraging the FIB, while recovering route information from its peer devices.

Cisco NSF with SSO is a mechanism of supervisor redundancy that is part of the IOS software and it provides an extremely fast supervisor switchover at Layers 2, 3, and 4. SSO allows the standby route processor to take control of the device once a hardware or software fault occurs on the active route processor. SSO synchronizes the following parameters:

- Startup configurations
- Startup variables
- Running configuration
- Layer 2 protocol states for ports and trunks
- Layer 2 and Layer 3 tables (e.g., FIB, adjacency tables, and MAC tables)
- Access Control Lists
- QoS tables

Monitoring content load balancers will achieve scalability and high availability by distributing the requests from the clients for services across active servers. The load balancer can provide a virtual IP address for all of its servers, and then clients will resolve that address to DNS requests. The load balancer will intelligently pass the traffic to a pool of real servers, according to configured balancing rules. SLB can rewrite source and destination MAC/IP addresses depending on the mode in which it is running.

EOT is an IOS function that uses a standalone process to track the status of objects and notify other processes when it detects a problem. This is useful for verifying end-to-end path availability and for noticing situations where the network might be transmitting traffic along a path that is actually black holing packets or experiencing traffic congestion.

PfR is a technology that detects undesirable situations along a path. It provides automatic outbound route optimization and load distribution for multiple connections by choosing the optimal exit point. PfR/OER facilitates path selection based on policies that can be measured for parameters such as loss, jitter, delay, load, and reachability.

People

The most overlooked resource for providing high availability in e-commerce submodules is well-trained engineers, who are critical in such environments. People resources should have the following skills:

- Reliable
- Communicative
- Consistent

- Skilled in creating documentation
- Skilled in troubleshooting

An organization's security policies may involve a rotation of duties so that more than one person is skilled in providing high availability solutions and managing the e-commerce submodule. This should also include good program and project management because it is very important to understand all of the hardware and software components of the e-commerce submodule and to manage different tasks efficiently. People are an important high availability resource and it is vital that the team responsible for e-commerce functionality is always aligned with services and business needs.

Processes

Processes are also very important for managing the e-commerce submodule and they should meet the PPDIOO lifecycle, the ITIL, or other framework goals. Some of the most important considerations in this component include the following:

- Creating solid, repeatable and reusable processes
- Documenting change procedures
- Implementing a good change management strategy that includes testing and rollback procedures
- Documenting all of the plans for failover and the procedures for testing in labs
- Documenting the implementation of the network
- Making constant improvements and iterations to ensure that the best strategies are in place
- Establishing good labs to test processes whenever possible and ensuring that the lab environment is a prototype of the production network
- Implementing failover mechanisms that are documented and tested
- Ensuring that every update is tested and validated between deployments
- Ensuring that any changes have as little impact on end-users as possible
- Ensuring that everybody in the organization is aware of the way changes can affect their work
- Ensuring ongoing control of operations and maintenance of systems, including auditing, monitoring, reporting, tracking, and management
- Ensuring that all of the changes are correlated with a business impact analysis and possibly a risk analysis

Tools

Some of the most important actions and tools that should be used in an e-commerce environment include:

- Performance monitoring
- Performance reporting
- Reporting on trends (observing anomalies from baselines)
- Observing traffic drops, packet loss, latency, and jitter
- Investigating case studies before launching an e-commerce solution and perhaps implementing a prototype in a lab environment
- Documentation tools, including high-level and low-level network diagrams. Documentation should be kept up to date to reflect the most recent e-commerce submodule architecture and it should include reasons for choosing a particular network design and implementation steps. All of the devices, configuration, addressing information, and virtualization aspects should be documented.

E-COMMERCE SECURITY DESIGN

Security design aspects are extremely important because of the e-commerce submodule's exposure to the Internet and to public untrusted networks and because of its access by hundreds to millions of users on the Internet. The security components should be considered during the initial acquisition because they are key elements in the e-commerce design.

The e-commerce submodule is usually placed in a server farm or a data center facility and it is connected in a multi-homed fashion to multiple ISPs. It is recommended that the submodule be secured using multiple firewall layers, a technique called a "firewall sandwich." The Web tier is often protected by a redundant firewall pair (e.g., Cisco ASA devices) in an active/standby or an active/active failover topology to ensure high availability.

Some organizations will actually use a combination of security products from different vendors to create a more secure environment. The idea behind this scenario is that different vendors have different vulnerabilities and if an attacker manages to pass through one of the security devices, it will not be able to pass through the component from a different vendor. Some interoperability issues might appear when using devices from different vendors but some companies are willing to sacrifice this to increase their network security. Another important aspect in this scenario is that organizations need people resources that have expertise in multiple vendor solutions.

Other common security options that can be considered in the e-commerce submodule design include:

- Implementing application-specific gateways.
- Leveraging features such as security contexts (virtual firewalls) on ASA devices to achieve scalability and flexibility.
- Implementing advanced features, including active/active failover.
- Deploying the firewall in routed or transparent mode.

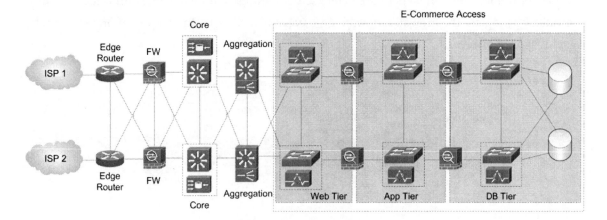

Figure 8.1 – Typical E-Commerce Submodule Design

In a typical e-commerce submodule design, as depicted in Figure 8.1 above, there are multiple ISPs connected to the edge routers (left side) that can be part of the Cisco ISR family. Firewalls are positioned behind the routers (Cisco ASA devices) in an active/standby or an active/active failover scheme, and they are connected to the Core Layer switches. Instead of using separate firewall and Core Layer switch components, some topologies might use Cisco Catalyst 6500 series chassis, which can integrate firewall modules (Firewall Services Module – FWSM) in a single enclosure. In other words, the firewall layer is collapsed into the Core Layer. The Core Layer devices might also aggregate content services modules or devices.

The Core Layer connects to the Aggregation Layer, which is made up of switches that can integrate Content Switching Modules (CSM). Moving to the right side of the topology in Figure 8.1, the Access Layer is made up of a combination of switches and IPS sensors to provide an additional mechanism of defense and a protection layer. The next layer of firewalls (the second firewall layer) can be positioned behind these devices.

The e-commerce Access Layer (LAN) is logically divided into three tiers:

- Web tier
- Application tier
- Database tier

The area containing the Aggregation Layer switches and the Access Layer devices is considered the Web tier, which communicates with the application tier through the second layer of firewalls, and the application tier connects to the database tier through another layer of firewalls (the third firewall layer). Again, the firewall sandwiching mechanism with its three layers of firewalls can be seen in Figure 8.1 above.

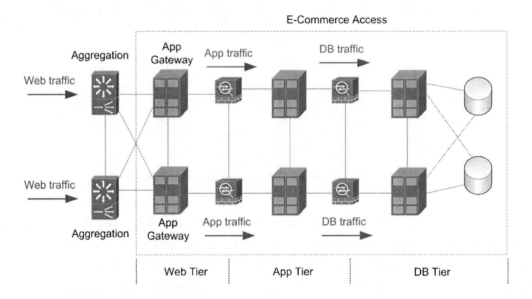

Figure 8.2 – E-Commerce Submodule Design Using Application Gateways

Once the traffic gets past the Core Layer and the Aggregation Layer into the access zone (the e-commerce LAN), in some architectures all of the traffic between the firewall layers will actually go through servers or will use servers as application gateways. The application-specific gateway methodology (see Figure 8.2 above) increases security because possible attackers must penetrate the firewall, as well as the Web server operating system, to get to the middle layer of firewalls. This method avoids operating firewalls from multiple vendors.

In the design that involves application gateways, the Web-tier servers are application-specific gateways, and the inbound and outbound connections on these servers are on separate VLANs. The ACLs on the Internet edge firewalls allow only Web and related traffic to go to these Web servers. In addition, the middle firewall layer allows only application traffic from the Web servers to the application server. If traffic needs to pass between the firewalls, a single VLAN connects both firewall layers. Private VLANs can also be included in this implementation to achieve separation, using isolated servers on secondary VLANs to create a secure scenario.

Another security mechanism that can be used involves virtual firewalls or security contexts that can be configured within a single physical device. Each context acts as a separate firewall device and has its own set of security policies, logical interfaces, and administrative domains and these can be applied to different servers in the e-commerce solution.

Virtual firewalls retain the same separation of rules and other customer features as physical firewalls do. ISPs can use virtual contexts to serve individual customers and enterprise organizations, as well as to maintain separation between Internet services and application services.

Another security consideration is the mode in which firewalls are implemented. Usually, firewalls can be implemented in two modes:

- Routed mode
- Transparent mode

Common firewalls are implemented in routed mode, with the device actually being a hop that participates in a dynamic routing protocol (e.g., RIP, EIGRP, or OSPF). Another deployment technique is transparent mode, which is similar to a bridging mode and allows for less configuration options. Firewalls in transparent mode are actually Layer 2 devices and they offer many Layer 2 security features, but not as many Layer 3 security features. Transparent firewalls can be deployed in strategic locations within the e-commerce submodule, without having to perform IP re-addressing or worry about the configuration of routing protocols. Transparent firewalls are invisible for the devices on the protected network.

E-COMMERCE SERVER LOAD BALANCING

SLB can be deployed in the e-commerce submodule to support scalability and high availability. Its function is to redirect requests for service from clients across the active servers in the Web, application, and database tiers, as shown in Figure 8.3 below:

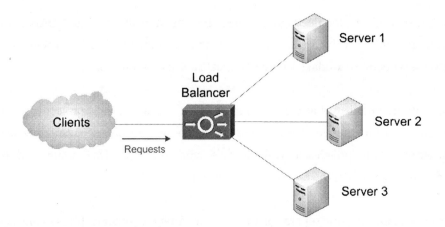

Figure 8.3 – Server Load Balancing

The load balancer will present a public IP address, also referred to as a virtual IP address, for each service (Web, application, and database). The clients resolve this virtual IP address through DNS requests. The load balancer is an intelligent engine that passes traffic to a pool of actual physical servers, and it performs load balancing and applies QoS mechanisms according to configuration rules. The load balancer will also serve as a proxy by rewriting the source and destination IP/MAC addresses, depending on the mode in which it operates. Another important functionality SLB accomplishes is monitoring server health and performance. SLB can also be deployed for failover configurations.

The SLB market is quickly evolving, and over the past few years, Cisco has had a few product lines that have offered SLB and Content Load Balancing (CLB) services, including:

- Content Services Switch (CSS)
- Content Switching Module (CSM)
- Application Control Engine (ACE) module and appliance

Some of the most common features offered by SLB solutions are as follows:

- Custom CLB and SLB (round robin, weighted round robin, least connection, weighted least connection, and others)
- Asymmetric load
- SSL offload
- DoS protection
- Firewall functionality and other security functions
- HTTP compression
- TCP offload

- Direct server return
- QoS techniques
- Content inspection
- Server health and performance monitoring
- Virtualization (similar to virtual contexts)
- Logging

SERVER LOAD BALANCING DESIGN MODELS

SLB can be deployed in the following modes:

- Router mode
- Bridge mode
- One-armed or two-armed mode

SLB Router Mode

SLB router mode is one of the most popular implementation modes. In this mode, the load balancer will route between the outside subnets (toward the clients) and the inside subnets (toward the servers). In this scenario, the services' addresses are typically globally routable public IP subnet addresses. The external subnets represent public networks, while the internal subnets represent private networks, as illustrated in Figure 8.4 below:

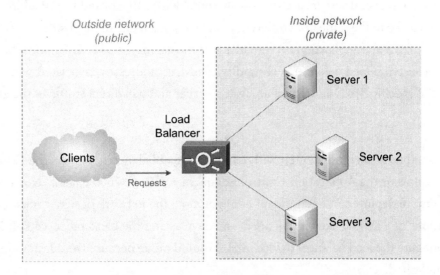

Figure 8.4 – Server Load Balancing Design – Router Mode

The load balancer device routes between the public and the private networks and the servers will use the load balancer's inside address as their default gateway. Since the replies that come back from the servers (responses to clients) pass through the load balancer and it changes the server IP address to the appropriate address, the end-users do not know there is a load balancer device in the path. This process is similar to NAT technology. SLB router mode is easy to deploy, works with many server subnets, and is the recommended mode to be used for the majority of appliance-based SLB.

SLB Bridge Mode

SLB bridge mode is also called the "inline" mode and it works by having the load balancer device operate as a transparent firewall. In this situation, an upstream router is needed between the clients and the load balancer, as shown in Figure 8.5 below:

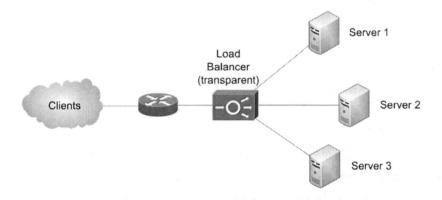

Figure 8.5 – Server Load Balancing Design – Bridge Mode

In this design, the physical servers are in globally routable IP subnets and the IP addresses on the load balancer can be in the same or in different IP subnets. Each one of the inside server farms (i.e., the Web server farm, the application server farm, and the database server farm) must be in a single IP subnet because the load balancer will modify the MAC addresses associated with the virtual IP (VIP) to the specific MAC address of a physical server and will direct traffic to the appropriate server.

This design method is seen most often with integrated load balancers, such as the Cisco Content Switching Module or the Application Control Engine in a 6500 or 7600 chassis. However, if these load balancers are deployed in a redundant configuration, the network designer must be aware of the implications of STP and how it will affect the devices and the backend servers. It is typically easier to configure the load balancer device in SLB routed mode because troubleshooting STP can be very complicated.

SLB One-Armed/Two-Armed Modes

The one-armed/two-armed modes (see Figure 8.6 below) are popular approaches as well and they involve running the load balancer device in an Out-of-Band fashion, similar to an IDS sensor that analyzes mirrored traffic from a switch. The load balancer is connected to a switch with one or two links that are not placed directly in line with the traffic, as is the case with the router and bridge modes presented previously.

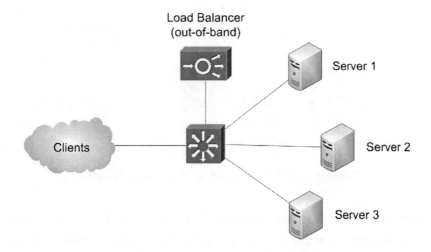

Figure 8.6 – Server Load Balancing Design – One-Armed/Two-Armed Modes

In a one-armed topology, the load balancer and the physical servers are in the same VLAN (or subnet), while with the two-armed approach, the load balancer device routes the traffic to the physical server subnet, which can also be a private subnet with NAT.

ISP MULTI-HOMING DESIGN

When connecting the e-commerce submodule to multiple ISPs, multiple design topologies can be implemented:

- One firewall per ISP
- Stateful failover with a common external prefix
- Distributed data centers

One Firewall per ISP

The most common e-commerce design topology for connecting multiple ISPs is to have a single firewall per provider. The path to each ISP will be managed by a dedicated edge router that is positioned in front of the firewalls, as illustrated in Figure 8.7 below:

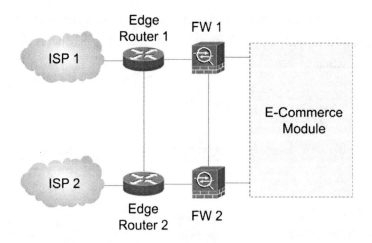

Figure 8.7 – IPS Multi-Homing – One Firewall per ISP

In some situations, edge router functionality can be managed by the firewall appliance, so only one single device has to be configured instead of a dedicated router and firewall for each ISP. An example of a device that can accomplish both functions is the Cisco ASA 5500 series.

This is a very common multi-homing approach and it is typically deployed in small sites because it is relatively easy to configure and manage. This approach uses external DNS to resolve the company site name to an address from the ISP's external address block, possibly using a round-robin approach. When using a round-robin balancing mechanism, the external users will be load balanced across the two paths to the organization's Web servers behind the firewalls. The traffic is routed to the outside of the firewall/NAT device and the edge router NAT will translate the address block provided by the ISP to the inside address of the e-commerce servers.

The major downside of this topology is that there is no stateful failover between the two firewall devices. This means that if there is a failure on an edge router or an edge firewall, some sessions will be lost and will have to be re-established with the Web servers

Stateful Failover Design

A more sophisticated approach for the e-commerce site would be to use two ISPs and a stateful failover between the edge devices (using a First Hop Redundancy Protocol like HSRP, VRRP, or GLBP) or ASA devices with active/active failover. This topology will leverage the security contexts/virtual firewalls feature on ASA devices.

The edge devices translate addresses using NAT to a block that both ISPs will advertise for the company's site. The edge routers will most likely be advertising the specific block to both ISPs using BGP.

> **NOTE:** When using BGP, it is important to implement mechanisms that will avoid having the company's site become a transit link between the ISPs.

If one of the ISPs loses connectivity, BGP will automatically failover to the other path, through the other ISP. The edge device can support stateful failover either with an active/active design or using a FHRP (HSRP is the most popular protocol in Cisco environments).

Distributed Data Centers Design

This design applies to very large e-commerce sites that offer mission-critical services, such as banks, brokerage firms, and other large organizations. The distributed data centers design goes beyond providing two chassis for failover flexibility; it involves two sites that offer high availability and lower uptime requirements for individual sites.

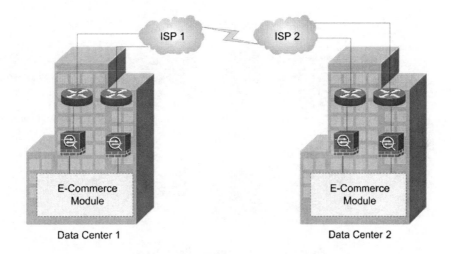

Figure 8.8 – IPS Multi-Homing – Distributed Data Centers

This design will offer total redundancy by providing a primary and a secondary data center, as depicted in Figure 8.8 above. If devices have to be taken offline at one site, all of the e-commerce operations can be switched over to the other data center. This design also protects against regional problems, like weather conditions. In a distributed data centers design, technologies such as clustering services will be used that will offer active/active hot databases instead of an active database with a mirrored hot-spare.

A good design recommendation is to use separate ISPs between the sites to ensure high availability. In some designs, the redundant sites are linked together using an external fiber WAN link or a MAN link.

INTEGRATED DESIGNS FOR THE E-COMMERCE SUBMODULE

The four most important integrated designs for the e-commerce submodule are as follows:

- Base design
- Dual layer firewall design
- SLB one-armed mode with dual layer firewall design
- SLB one-armed mode with security contexts

E-Commerce Base Design

The e-commerce base design involves a three-tier topology, with a dedicated Core Layer, Aggregation Layer, and Access Layer (which contains Web, applications, and database servers).

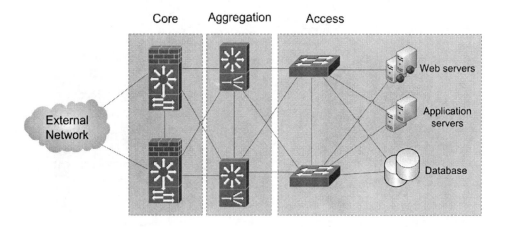

Figure 8.9 – E-Commerce Base Design

This is a fully redundant design, with each layer having devices in active/active or active/passive configuration, as presented in Figure 8.9 above. The Core Layer devices, as well as the Aggregation Layer devices, are connected through trunks (often port-channel links). The Aggregation Layer to Access Layer connection is often a trunk that carries VLANs that group the services contained in the Access Layer:

- Web VLAN
- Aggregation VLAN
- Access VLAN

The Core Layer usually contains Cisco Catalyst 6500 devices and ensures redundant connections to the ISP. The Core Layer Cisco 6500 chassis usually contains firewall service modules that move the firewall perimeter to the Core Layer, making the Aggregation Layer a trusted zone.

One of the major disadvantages of the base design topology is that it does not offer security features between the Web, application, and database zones. One way to solve this issue is to implement private VLANs.

The Aggregation Layer supports the SLB submodules, and the default gateway for the e-commerce servers is the virtual IP address on those submodules, meaning all of the e-commerce traffic will pass through the SLB submodules at the Aggregation Layer. The Access Layer switches are usually Layer 2 devices and they connect the Web servers, the application servers, and the database servers.

From a routing standpoint, static routing will mainly be used toward the Core Layer. At the Core Layer, either static routes or dynamic protocols (BGP) can be used to connect to the ISP. In the e-commerce base design, only a single firewall layer will be positioned at the Core Layer, but if there is extra funding and personnel, a dual layer firewall design can be implemented.

E-Commerce Dual Layer Firewall Design

The dual layer firewall design is similar to the e-commerce base design, with the exception of adding a firewall in the Aggregation Layer, as shown in Figure 8.10 below:

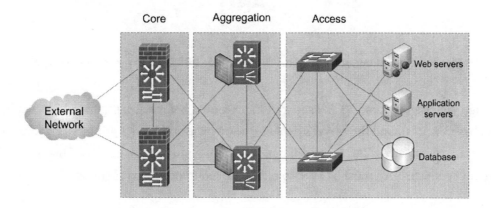

Figure 8.10 – E-Commerce Dual Layer Firewall Design

To implement the second layer of firewalls, ASA devices or dedicated firewall modules can be placed between the Core Layer devices and the Aggregation Layer switches. The second layer of firewalls can be placed either in a classic routed mode or in transparent mode, which is commonly done in modern designs.

The advantage of this solution is that it offers an extra layer of security for the backend servers in situations where the Core Layer switches are compromised and the first firewall layer is breached. In this design, the perimeter firewalls at the Core Layer provide security services and make policy decisions, while the Aggregation Layer firewalls form an internal DMZ perimeter that protects the servers. Similar to the base design, there are still content switch modules at the Aggregation Layer making SLB decisions.

E-Commerce SLB One-Armed Mode with Dual Layer Firewall Design

The SLB one-armed mode with dual layer firewall design is a modification of the dual layer firewall design that separates the content services module from the Aggregation Layer switch. Instead of using an integrated design with the load balancer device in the same chassis as the Aggregation Layer switch, an SLB one-armed topology is used, as shown in Figure 8.11 below:

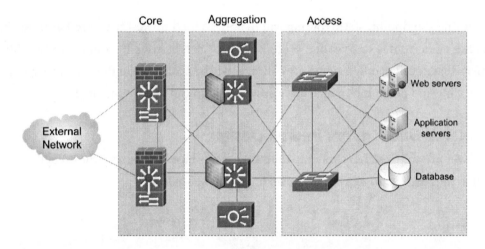

Figure 8.11 – E-Commerce SLB One-Armed Mode with Dual Layer Firewall Design

This design will use the same VLAN separation presented before (i.e., separate Web, application, and database VLANs), and the server's default gateway will still be the primary IP address on the Aggregation Layer devices. The major difference from previous design models is that policy-based routing or client-side NAT must be used to redirect the outbound server traffic.

E-Commerce SLB One-Armed Mode with Security Contexts

The e-commerce SLB one-armed mode with security contexts design is similar to the previous model, except for the way the firewalls work at the Aggregation Layer. This design provides increased convergence by running the firewall modules in transparent mode, basically functioning as Layer 2 bridges. The SLB component performs routing between the Aggregation Layer and the Core Layer.

The firewall contexts feature is leveraged on the Aggregation Layer submodules to create multiple virtual firewalls on a single physical device. Outbound traffic from the servers passes through the Aggregation Layer firewall modules, and then it is routed to the SLB component using policy-based routing, before reaching the Core Layer.

E-COMMERCE SUBMODULE OPTIMIZATION

Network designers should be aware of different methods for tuning the e-commerce submodule. The most common optimization mechanisms include:

- BGP tuning
- Enhanced Object Tracking (EOT)
- Performance Routing (PfR)
- DNS tuning and Global Server Load Balancing (GSLB)

The most important optimization mechanism that involves outside connectivity is BGP tuning, as this is the preferred routing protocol to be used with ISPs.

All of the ingress and egress traffic from all of the points in the network to the ISP should be analyzed and this should be correlated with failover behavior. With a single ISP, the Multi-Exit Discriminator (MED) BGP attribute or BGP communities can be used to communicate preferences for traffic flow from the Internet to the organization. It is important to ensure that the ISPs are always updating the route filters, and traffic monitoring and periodic testing should be performed to make sure that the prefixes have not been accidentally filtered.

Another optimization mechanism is EOT, which is a standalone process that tracks objects and gives updates on the status of the end-to-end path. This feature, available since the 12.2(15)T IOS version, lets other processes know when it has detected a problem. EOT is a good end-to-end path availability tool that can also detect congested links and situations in which the network is sending traffic on a path where black holing is occurring.

EOT can be combined with FHRPs (i.e., HSRP, VRRP, or GLBP). In this situation, the FHRPs are considered EOT clients, as this technique offers the ability to discover problems and then react to them. EOT can track multiple parameters, including:

- The line protocol
- The IP routing state
- IP routing metrics
- IP SLA operations results

NOTE: A very popular EOT implementation is combining HSRP and IP SLA tracking to influence the priority of the HSRP devices.

PfR, also known as OER, offers automatic outbound route optimization and load distribution for multi-home links by choosing the optimal exit point. PfR is an integrated IOS software feature that allows IP traffic flow monitoring, and then determines policies and rules based on several factors:

- Prefix performance
- Link load distribution
- Link cost
- Traffic type

When implementing PfR, one or more border routers will have to be configured so that they communicate with the router selected to be the Master Controller (MC). The MC makes decisions about the proper outbound traffic to use based on the configured policy. PfR follows a cycle that contains multiple phases:

- Learn
- Measure
- Apply policy
- Enforce
- Verify

Another way to tune e-commerce services is to offer DNS-based choices for the best destination for each client using the GSLB protocol. Cisco Global Site Selector (GSS) is a product that provides global server load balancing. Companies that offer Web and application hosting services typically need network devices that have the ability to perform extremely complex routing to multiple redundant geographically dispersed data centers. These devices must provide fast response times, failover protection, and disaster recovery.

Cisco GSS leverages global content deployment across several distributed and mirrored data center locations. If a user requests a connection to a website, GSS will offload the DNS servers by taking over the DNS resolution process. The GSS can transmit DNS requests at thousands of requests per second, and it can improve the existing DNS infrastructure by offering centralized domain management. GSS provides real-time global load balancing across two or more data centers, and it enhances global data center selection processes by offering user-selectable global load balancing algorithms. GSS is scalable, as it supports hundreds of data centers or SLB devices. It is also a great disaster recovery tool because it offers traffic re-routing in the case of total failure.

SUMMARY

For many organizations, the e-commerce submodule facilitates interaction between the company and the outside world, and it is often the only way customers see the company's products and services. In this regard, companies must be able to provide applications and Web services quickly, securely, and with high availability to potential customers. For some companies, downtime in the e-commerce submodule can cost millions of dollars, maybe on an hourly basis. Network designers should think about high availability techniques that can be used in the e-commerce design and they should take the following five components into consideration:

- Redundancy
- Technology
- People
- Processes
- Tools

Redundancy involves having hot spares and cold spares to eliminate any single points of failure. Redundancy is needed in several different areas of the e-commerce solution (both hardware and software), so if one component goes down, the service is not interrupted, at least for an acceptable period of time.

Some of the technologies that help improve high availability in the e-commerce submodule include:

- Stateful Switchover (SSO) – especially in firewall systems
- Non-Stop Forwarding (NSF)
- Server Load Balancing (SLB)
- Enhanced Object Tracking (EOT)
- IP SLA
- Performance Routing (PfR)/Optimized Edge Routing (OER)
- Fast routing convergence

The most overlooked resource for providing high availability in e-commerce submodules is well-trained engineers, who are critical in such environments. People resources should have the following skills:

- Reliable
- Communicative
- Consistent

- Skilled in creating documentation
- Skilled in troubleshooting

Processes are also very important for managing the e-commerce submodule and they should meet the PPDIOO lifecycle, the ITIL, or other framework goals. Some of the most important actions and tools that should be used in an e-commerce environment include:

- Performance monitoring
- Performance reporting
- Reporting on trends (observing anomalies from baselines)
- Observing traffic drops, packet loss, latency, and jitter
- Investigating case studies before launching an e-commerce solution, and perhaps implementing a prototype in a lab environment
- Documentation tools

Security design aspects are extremely important because of the e-commerce submodule's exposure to the Internet and to public untrusted networks and because of its access by hundreds to millions of users on the Internet. The security components should be considered during the initial acquisition because they are key elements in the e-commerce design.

The e-commerce Access Layer (LAN) is logically divided into three tiers:

- Web tier
- Application tier
- Database tier

Server load balancing is deployed in the e-commerce submodule to support scalability and high availability. Its function is to redirect requests for service from clients across the active servers in the Web, application, and database tiers.

SLB can be deployed in the following modes:

- Router mode
- Bridge mode
- One-armed or two-armed modes

When connecting the e-commerce submodule to multiple ISPs, multiple design topologies can be implemented:

- One firewall per ISP
- Stateful failover with a common external prefix
- Distributed data centers

The four most important integrated designs for the e-commerce submodule are as follows:

- Base design
- Dual layer firewall design
- SLB one-armed mode with dual layer firewall design
- SLB one-armed mode with security contexts

Network designers should be aware of different methods for tuning the e-commerce submodule. The most common optimization mechanisms include:

- BGP tuning
- Enhanced Object Tracking
- Performance Routing
- DNS tuning and Global Server Load Balancer

END OF CHAPTER QUIZ

1. What are the most important high-availability components that must be considered within an e-commerce design (choose four)?
   a. Flexibility
   b. Redundancy
   c. Vendors
   d. Tools
   e. Processes
   f. Technology

2. E-commerce submodule downtime can cause an extremely high financial loss for some companies.
   a. True
   b. False

3. Which of the following e-commerce submodule components should be designed with redundancy in mind?
   a. Only devices and internal links
   b. Only devices and ISP links
   c. Only internal and ISP links
   d. Devices, and internal and ISP links

4. Which of the following is a technology that works together with SSO to minimize the amount of time the network is unavailable to users, following a switchover from a primary to a secondary device?
   a. HSRP
   b. EOT
   c. NSF
   d. BGP

5. Which of the following is an IOS technology that tracks the status of various objects and notifies other processes when it detects a problem?
   a. SSO
   b. HSRP
   c. QoS
   d. NSF
   e. EOT

6. The e-commerce submodule can be operated with minimal people resources.
   a. True
   b. False

7. Which of the following is a technology that provides automatic outbound route optimization and load distribution for multiple connections by choosing the optimal exit point?
   a. SSO
   b. NSF
   c. HSRP
   d. PfR
   e. EOT

8. Which of the following are important tools that should be used in an e-commerce environment (choose three)?
   a. Performance monitoring tools
   b. Performance reporting tools
   c. VPN management tools
   d. Documentation tools

9. Which are the common layers in a typical e-commerce submodule (choose three)?
   a. Core
   b. Presentation
   c. Aggregation
   d. Access
   e. Session

10. The advantage of implementing a multi-vendor security solution is increased security enforcement, as a possible attacker will have problems breaching multiple firewall operating systems.
    a. True
    b. False

11. Which of the following are common e-commerce submodule tiers (choose all that apply)?
    a. Web
    b. Application
    c. Session
    d. E-commerce
    e. Database

12. A typical e-commerce design contains no firewall layers.
    a. True
    b. False

13. Virtual firewalls are also known as:
    a. Fake firewalls
    b. Security contexts
    c. Transparent firewalls
    d. Redundant contexts

14. What are the most common firewall deployment modes (choose two)?
    a. One-armed mode
    b. Inline mode
    c. Routed mode
    d. Two-armed mode
    e. Transparent mode

15. Which of the following represents a device that is usually deployed in e-commerce sub-modules to redirect requests for service from clients across the active servers?
    a. ASA
    b. Aggregation Layer switch
    c. Server gateway
    d. Server load balancer

16. SSL offloading and HTTP compression are common features of SLB devices.
    a. True
    b. False

17. What are the most common SLB deployment modes (choose four)?
    a. Router mode
    b. Three-armed mode
    c. Two-armed mode
    d. DMZ mode
    e. One-armed mode
    f. Bridge mode

18. Transparent SLB deployment mode is also called:
    a. Bridge mode
    b. Routed mode
    c. One-armed mode
    d. Two-armed mode

19. Which of the following parameters can be tracked using the Enhanced Objet Tracking (EOT) feature (choose three)?
    a. Distance between sites
    b. Number of interfaces participating in a routing protocol
    c. IP routing metrics
    d. IP routing state
    e. Line protocol

20. Performance routing determines policies based on which of the following factors (choose three)?
    a. Link load distribution
    b. Prefix age
    c. Link cost
    d. Device type
    e. Traffic type

CHAPTER 9

Designing Advanced Security Services

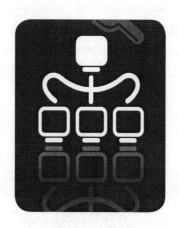

This chapter covers the following topics:

- Firewall designs
- NAC appliance designs
- IPS/IDS designs
- Remote access VPN designs for the teleworker

This chapter begins by presenting general network attacks and countermeasure concepts. Next, it will analyze specific design recommendations and issues for various enterprise-level technologies, including firewalls, NAC, IPS, and VPN. The last part of the chapter will cover security management and policy issues.

NETWORK ATTACKS AND COUNTERMEASURES

From a design standpoint, security is one feature of risk management that must be included in the overall business policy. Every organization must determine the acceptable levels of risk and vulnerabilities, and these should be based on the value of the corporate assets. Organizations should also define the risk probability and the reasonable expectation of quantifiable loss in case of a security compromise.

One aspect of risk management is risk assessment and this is the driving force behind an organization's written security policies. Network designers play a key role in developing these security policies but they do not implement them (this will be the role of another team).

When a network designer is in the process of attack recognition and identifying countermeasures for those specific attacks, the designer should consider and plan for the worst situations because modern networks are large and they can be susceptible to many security threats. The applications and systems in these organizations are often very complex and this makes them difficult to analyze, especially when they use Web applications and services.

Figure 9.1 – High-Level Security Components

As shown in Figure 9.1 above, the network designer should be able to guarantee to the company the following important system characteristics:

- Confidentiality
- Integrity
- Availability

These three attributes are the core of the organization's security policy. Confidentiality ensures that only authorized individual users, applications, or services can access sensitive data. Integrity implies that data will not be changed by unauthorized users or services. Finally, the availability of the systems and data should result in uninterrupted access to computing resources.

Threats to Confidentiality, Integrity, and Availability

Before a network designer offers security consultancy services (i.e., risk assessment or business impact analysis) the designer must understand the real threats to the network infrastructure. Different categories of threats to confidentiality, integrity, and availability include the following:

- Denial of Service (DoS) and Distributed Denial of Service (DDoS) attacks
- Spoofing (masquerading)
- Telnet attacks
- Password-cracking programs
- Viruses
- Trojans and worms

These threats must be analyzed in the context of the Enterprise Campus design submodules they affect and the exact system component they target.

Denial of Service Attacks

The main purpose of a DoS attack is to make a machine or a network resource unavailable to its intended users. In this particular type of attack, the attacker does not try to gain access to a resource; rather, the attacker tries to induce a loss of access to different users or services. These resources can include:

- The entire Enterprise Network
- The CPU of a network device or server
- The memory of a network device or server
- The disk of a network device or server

A DoS attack will result in the resource being overloaded (e.g., disk space, bandwidth, memory, buffer overflow, or queue overflow) and this will cause the resource to become unavailable for usage. This can vary from blocking access to a particular resource to crashing a network device or server. There are many types of DoS attacks, such as ICMP attacks and TCP flooding.

An advanced form of DoS attack is the DDoS attack, which works by manipulating a large number of systems to launch an attack on a target over the Internet or over an Enterprise Network. To manage a DDoS attack, hackers usually break into weakly secured hosts (e.g., using common security holes in the operating systems or applications used) and compromise the systems by installing malicious code to gain full access to the victim's resources. After many systems are compromised, they can be used to launch a massive simultaneous attack on a target that will be overwhelmed with a very large number of illegitimate requests. The difference between a DoS attack and a DDoS attack is illustrated in Figure 9.2 below:

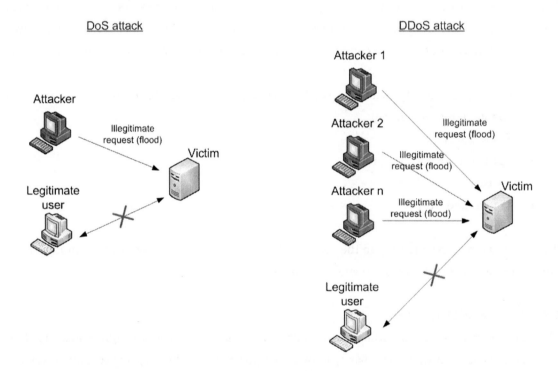

Figure 9.2 – DoS versus DDoS Attacks

NOTE: The process of sending illegitimate requests by the attacker to a network resource is also called flooding.

Spoofing Attacks

Spoofing (or masquerading) attacks involve a process in which a single host or entity will falsely assume (spoof) the identity of another host. A common spoofing attack is called the Man in the

Middle (MITM) attack (see Figure 9.3 below) and it works by convincing two different hosts (the sender and the receiver) that the computer in the middle is actually the other host. This is accomplished using DNS spoofing, where a hacker compromises a DNS server and explicitly changes the name resolution entries.

Another type of masquerading attack is ARP spoofing, where the ARP cache is altered and thus the Layer 2 to Layer 3 address mapping entries are changed to redirect the traffic through the attacker's machine. This type of attack usually targets a LAN.

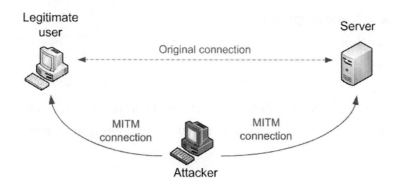

Figure 9.3 – Man in the Middle Attack

Telnet Attacks

Programs like Telnet or FTP utilize user-based authentication but the credentials are sent in clear text (i.e., unencrypted) over the wire. These credentials can be captured by attackers using network monitoring tools and they can be used to gain unauthorized access to network devices.

Other related threats in this area are generated using old unsecured protocols like rlogin, rcp, or rsh that allow access to different systems. These unsecured protocols should be replaced by protocols like Secure Shell Protocol (SSH) or Secure File Transfer Protocol (SFTP).

Password-Cracking Programs

Password-cracking software is very easy to find nowadays and the programs can be used to compromise password security in different applications or services. They work by revealing a password that has been previously encrypted with weak encryption algorithms (e.g., DES). One way to prevent password cracking from happening is to enforce the organization's security policy by:

- Using strong encrypting algorithms (e.g., AES).
- Choosing complex passwords (a combination of letters, numbers, and special characters).
- Periodically changing passwords.

Viruses

A virus is a generic term for any type of program that attaches to individual files on a targeted system. Once the virus appends its original code to a victim's file, the victim is infected, the file changes, and it can infect other files through a process called replication.

The replication process can spread across hard disks and it can infect the entire operating system. Once a virus is linked to an executable file, it will infect other files every time the host file is executed. There are three major types of viruses, defined by where they occur in the system:

- Master Boot Sector (MBR) viruses
- Boot sector viruses
- File viruses

MBR and boot sector viruses affect the boot sector on the physical disk, rendering the operating system unable to boot. File viruses represent the most common type of viruses and they affect different types of files.

Another way to categorize viruses is based on their behavior, such as:

- Stealth viruses
- Polymorphic viruses

Stealth viruses use different techniques to hide the fact that a change to the disk drive was made. Polymorphic viruses are difficult to identify because they can mutate and they can change their size, thus avoiding detection by special software. When using these virus detection programs, the recommendation is to make sure they are updated as often as possible so they are capable of scanning for new forms of viruses.

Trojans and Worms

Trojan programs are comprised of unauthorized code that is contained in legitimate programs and performs functions that are hidden to the user. Worms are other illegitimate pieces of software that can be attached to e-mails, and once they are executed they can propagate themselves within the file system and perform unauthorized functions, such as redirecting user traffic to certain websites.

Network Device Vulnerabilities

An important vulnerable area in the network infrastructure, considering the attacks presented above, is where network devices reside. The targeted devices can be part of any network module and layer, including Access Layer devices, Distribution Layer devices, or Core Layer equipment. Since network devices (e.g., routers, switches, or other appliances) provide embedded security features, they must be secured from intruders.

The first thing to control is physical access. Critical equipment should be placed in locked rooms that can be accessed only by authorized users, preferably via multiple authentication factors. Network administrators must follow security guidelines to avoid human errors. Finally, network devices must be hardened, just as hosts and servers are, by applying the following techniques:

- Enable only the necessary services
- Use authenticated routing protocols
- Use one-time password configurations
- Provide management access to the device only through secured protocols, such as SSH
- Make sure the devices in the operating system are always patched and updated so they are protected against the latest known vulnerabilities.

Network Infrastructure Vulnerabilities

Network infrastructure vulnerabilities are present at every level in the Enterprise Architecture model and the attacks aimed to exploit these vulnerabilities can be categorized as follows:

- Reconnaissance attacks
- DoS and DDoS attacks
- Traffic attacks

Reconnaissance is a military term that implies scoping the targets before initiating the actual attack. The reconnaissance attack is aimed at the perimeter defense of the network, including the WAN network or Enterprise Edge module. This type of attack includes activities like scanning the topology using techniques such as:

- ICMP scanning
- SNMP scanning
- TCP/UDP port scanning
- Application scanning

The scanning procedure can use simple tools (e.g., Ping or Telnet) but it can also involve using complex tools that can scan the network perimeter for vulnerabilities. The purpose of reconnaissance attacks is to find the network's weaknesses and then apply the most efficient type of attack.

As a countermeasure to these reconnaissance attacks, NAC can be used, including hardware and software firewall products, and the devices can be hardened to ensure that they are using only specific ports, specific connections, and specific services.

DoS and DDoS attacks are meant to compromise the connectivity and availability to or from the network and can be categorized into the following types:

- Flooding the network with poisoned packets
- Spoofing network traffic
- Exploiting application bugs

Countermeasures that help protect against DoS attacks include using firewall products and ensuring that the network operating systems are updated regularly, to include the latest patches. Cisco has a very useful feature in its IOS and firewall products called TCP Intercept, which can be used to prevent SYN flooding attacks that are used against websites, e-mail servers, or other services. This feature intercepts and validates TCP connection requests before they arrive at the server. QoS mechanisms can also be used to filter certain types of traffic.

Because DoS attacks affect the performance of network devices and servers, many large organizations oversize their resources to gain additional bandwidth, backup connections, and redundancy. When DoS attacks occur, these extra resources can compensate for the negative effects of an attack without critically affecting internal services. The downside to this approach is the cost factor.

Application Vulnerabilities

The applications and individual host machines are often the ultimate target of the attacker or the malicious user. Their goal is to gain access to permissions so they can read sensitive data, write changes to the hard drive, or compromise data confidentiality and integrity.

Attackers try to exploit bugs in the operating system (for servers, hosts, and network devices in the OS) and abuse vulnerabilities in various applications to gain access to the system. Some applications are very vulnerable, mostly because they were not properly tested and were launched without advanced security features in mind.

After gaining basic access to a system, attackers will use a tactic called privilege escalation that will provide them with system administrator privileges by exploiting vulnerabilities in certain programs and machines. Once they get administrator access, they can either attack the entire system or read/write sensitive and valuable information.

Countermeasures against application and host vulnerabilities include using secure and tested programs and applications. This can be enforced by requiring applications to be digitally signed and using quality components from different vendors. Hosts can be hardened using a variety of techniques to ensure that the machine is locked down and only the appropriate services and applications are used. Firewall and virus detection techniques should also be used and updated often.

Another useful countermeasure is minimizing exposure to outside networks, including the Internet, even though many attacks come from inside the organization. As organizations get larger, increased attention must be given to the human factor and to inside threats. Network administrators, network designers, and end-users should be carefully trained to use the security policies implemented in the organization.

DESIGNING FIREWALLS

As discussed in the previous chapter, firewalls can be deployed in multiple modes, including routed and transparent, and most of them can be virtualized into security contexts that provide cost-effective solutions.

Virtual Firewalls

The virtual firewall is a security context and it is a way to partition a physical firewall into multiple logical devices, each with its own configuration. This is similar to having multiple standalone firewalls but without having to buy separate devices. When defining security contexts on a device, the old configuration will be saved in the appropriate file and the new virtual firewalls will each have dedicated configuration files. Security contexts are distinct and independent firewalls in the sense of having their own attributes, such as the following:

- Security policies
- Assigned interfaces
- NAT rules
- Access Control Lists
- Administrators

Each virtual firewall has a system configuration that can be modified through the administrator context, which is created automatically when converting from single-mode to multiple-mode. The administrator context is just like any other virtual firewall, with the exception that it is the one used to access the system and configure it. Typically in the design, the VLANs are linked to security contexts and most firewalls allow for multiple VLANs to be assigned to a single security context.

Some of the technologies that are not supported on common virtual firewalls include:

- IPsec VPN
- Secure Sockets Layer (SSL) VPN
- Dynamic routing protocols

Another important concept in virtual firewall design involves resource classes. When configuring an ASA device, all resources are available to all security contexts, by default. This can be modified from the administrator context that allows the creation of new contexts and the assignment of resources to each of them. These resources can be grouped into resource classes and these can be easily managed and assigned to security contexts from the administrator context.

Active/Active Failover Firewalls

The active/active failover mechanism used on firewall devices leverages the virtual context feature. The best results are obtained when the two devices configured with active/active failover have an identical platform and operating system. The two firewalls must be connected with a failover state link and this can be accomplished in three ways:

- **Single physical link:** Both the failover and stateful information are transmitted on this link.
- **Dual physical links:** The failover information is exchanged on one interface and the stateful information (maintaining the TCP connection and the translation rules) is exchanged on another.
- **Dual redundant physical links:** These act as a single logical link that carries both the failover and stateful information between the firewalls.

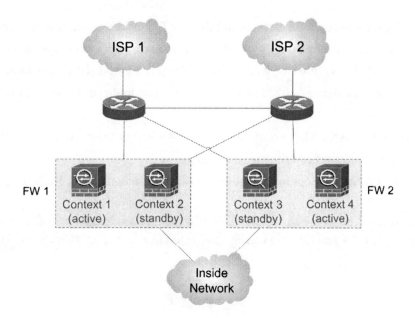

Figure 9.4 – Active/Active Failover Firewall Deployment

Although the two devices are identical, either firewall modules or ASA devices, the security contexts feature will be leveraged. As depicted in Figure 9.4 above, this is accomplished by defining two security contexts on each firewall that will accomplish the following functions:

- Context 1 is the active firewall for the left device (FW 1).
- Context 3 is the standby firewall for the left device (FW 1).
- Context 2 is the standby firewall for the right device (FW 2).
- Context 4 is the active firewall for the right firewall device (FW 2).

This scenario provides two virtual firewalls, with the physical devices each being partitioned in one active and one standby context. Contexts 1 and 3 in Figure 9.4 are logically grouped across the two physical devices, just like Contexts 2 and 4 are. In many situations, the security contexts feature will serve only as a mechanism to create active/active failover configurations, but on high-end devices, this functionality can be used for both creating active/active topologies and assigning a set of VLANs to each virtual firewall.

Private VLANs

Private VLANs (PVLANs) can be an option for adding an extra security layer in the Enterprise Campus module or the data center submodule, especially in the e-commerce submodule. A PVLAN is a way to take a VLAN and divide it into more logical components, which allows groups of servers or individual servers to be isolated, quarantining them from other devices.

To build a good trust model between servers and the DMZ, consider separating the servers so that if one of the servers is compromised (e.g., by a worm or a Trojan attack), it will not affect other servers in the same subnet. PVLANs function by creating secondary VLANs within a primary VLAN. The secondary VLANs can be defined based on the way the associated port is defined on the switch:

- **Community VLANs:** They communicate with devices in the same community VLAN and with promiscuous ports on the primary VLANs.
- **Isolated VLANs:** They communicate only with promiscuous ports on the primary VLANs.

NOTE: Promiscuous ports are those that allow the sending and receiving of frames from any other port on the VLAN and they are usually connected to a router or other default gateway.

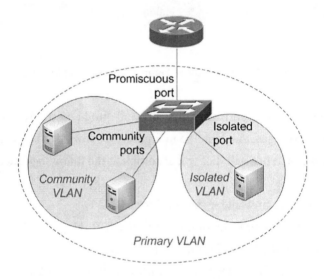

Figure 9.5 – Private VLANs

As illustrated in Figure 9.5 above, the primary VLAN usually represents the server farm and this can be divided into secondary VLANs for private traffic flows. Secondary VLANs are logical VLANs within a VLAN and they are similar to subinterfaces on a physical interface. Community ports can communicate with ports configured with the same community or with promiscuous ports but they cannot communicate with ports from other communities or with isolated ports. On the other hand, isolated ports can communicate only with the upstream promiscuous ports to reach the default gateway.

Implementing PVLANs is a good way to connect and secure server farms (secondary community VLANs) and isolated servers (secondary isolated VLANs). A major advantage of using PVLANs is that no additional STP instances are created when secondary VLANs are defined. Using the classic model of dedicated VLANs, each newly created VLAN would imply adding an extra STP instance, which would increase the management overhead. PVLANs can also be trunked across multiple switches in complex environments to span across the data center infrastructure.

If PVLANs are trunked across switches, VTP (VLAN trunking protocol) will not be supported. Configuring the switches for PVLANs requires operating in transparent mode and manually adding all of the VLANs on the switches.

Zone-Based Firewalls

A zone-based firewall policy is an IOS feature that can leverage the existing ISR routers by configuring firewall functionalities on them, as opposed to using dedicated ASA devices or firewall modules. Cisco Zone Based Firewall (ZBF) functionality was introduces in Cisco IOS 12.4(6)T as an evolution from traditional firewall implementation, which was an interface-based model (the "ip inspect" command can be applied on an interface in the inbound or outbound direction). The limitations imposed by the traditional firewall implementation led to the development of zone-based firewalls, which work by following these steps:

1. Create security zones.
2. Place an interface or multiple interfaces into each security zone.
3. Create unidirectional zone pairs to define relationships between zones.
4. Apply a modular, flexible, granular policy (using class maps, policy maps, and service policy) to the zone pairs.

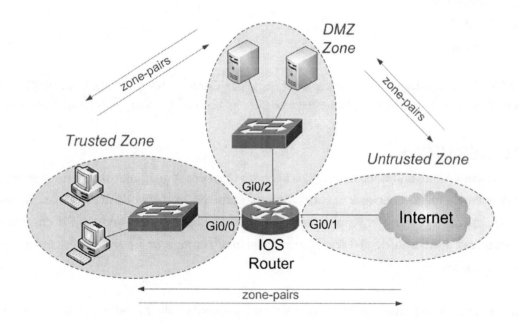

Figure 9.6 – Example of a Zone-Based Firewall

Analyzing Figure 9.6 above, a few security zones (i.e., Trusted, Untrusted, and DMZ) have been created and interfaces have been placed into each zone (i.e., Gigabit0/0 in the Trusted Zone, Gigabit0/1 in the Untrusted Zone, and Gigabit0/2 in the DMZ). After defining the zones and assigning interfaces, unidirectional zone pairs can be created to enforce policies for traffic passing through the three defined zones:

- Trusted to DMZ
- DMZ to Trusted
- Trusted to Untrusted
- Untrusted to Trusted
- DMZ to Untrusted
- Untrusted to DMZ

After the zone pairs are defined, different policies can be applied to them, and once the modular policies have been created and the zone-pair relationships have been defined, other interfaces are placed into that zone and the policy applies to it automatically. Using zone-based firewalls no longer requires having just one ACL per interface per direction per protocol to provide security policies.

Zone-based firewalls provide major advantages because they use a modular configuration structure (similar to modular QoS), including:

- Modularity
- Flexibility
- Granularity

NOTE: Zone-based firewalls have replaced the older Context Based Access Control (CBAC) firewall technology that was implemented using the "ip inspect" command on various interfaces.

NAC SERVICES

Cisco Network Admission Control (NAC) is a service that tries to guarantee that various endpoints are compliant with the network security polices enforced by network devices (i.e., firewalls, switches, or routers). Cisco NAC provides access to compliant devices and then it ensures that non-compliant devices are denied access, are placed in quarantine, or are given restricted access to certain resources.

NAC is an important part of the Enterprise Network's security policies and it focuses on two main areas of security enforcement:

- Security of operating systems
- Security of applications that run inside the operating systems

The NAC products consist of two general categories:

- The NAC framework, which is a system that provides security for network environments (LAN, WAN, WiFi, extranet, and remote access)
- The NAC appliance

The NAC framework is a system that provides security for network environments (e.g., LAN, WAN, WiFi, extranet, and remote access) in which hosts are trying to gain access to the network by providing credentials, typically using EAP (Extensible Authentication Protocol) or 802.1x.

The Cisco NAC solution consolidates all of the functionalities of the NAC framework into a single network appliance that will recognize users, devices, and roles in the network. After this step, it will evaluate whether systems are compliant with the security policies and will enforce these policies by blocking, isolating, and repairing the non-compliant machines.

One of the first design decisions involves selecting the location in which the NAC solution will be implemented. The following aspects should be considered in this decision process:

- **Choosing between a virtual and a real IP gateway:** The most common deployment option is the virtual gateway mode, where the network access server functions as a standard Layer 2 Ethernet bridge but with extra functionality. This option is used when the untrusted network already has a Layer 3 gateway (e.g., a router). When using the real IP gateway mode, the network access server operates as the Layer 3 default gateway for the untrusted managed clients. In this mode, all traffic between the untrusted and trusted network goes through the network access server, which can apply IP filtering, access policies, and other traffic management mechanisms. The Cisco network access server can also perform actions such as DHCP or DHCP relay when acting as a real IP gateway.

- **Choosing In-Band or Out-of-Band deployment mode:** This decision involves choosing whether the traffic will flow through the network access server.

- **Choosing a Layer 2 or a Layer 3 client mode:** In Layer 2 mode, the MAC addresses of the client devices will uniquely identify these devices; this is the most common client access mode. It supports both virtual and real IP gateway operation modes, either In-Band or Out-of-Band. In Layer 3 client access mode, the client is identified by its IP address and the device is not Layer 2 adjacent to the Cisco access server. Any Cisco access server can be configured for Layer 2 or Layer 3 client modes, but it can only be configured to operate in one mode at a time.

- **Choosing a central or edge physical deployment:** The edge deployment model is easier to implement and it involves the access server being physically and logically in line with the traffic path. This model only leads to more complexity when more access closets are added. The central deployment mode is the common mode option and it involves the access server being logically in line but not physically in line. In other words, the VLAN IDs must be mapped across the access server when it is in virtual gateway mode.

According to the aspects detailed above, the following NAC design models can be considered:

- Layer 2 In-Band virtual gateway
- Layer 2 In-Band real IP gateway
- Layer 2 Out-of-Band virtual gateway
- Layer 3 In-Band virtual gateway
- Layer 3 In-Band with multiple remote sites
- Layer 3 Out-of-Band

The modern Cisco NAC solution includes the Identity Service Engine (ISE), which uses Cisco network devices to extend access enforcement throughout a network and consists of the following components:

- **Policy administration and decision component:** Cisco ISE.
- **LAN policy enforcement points:** Cisco Catalyst switches, ASA devices, or ISR routers.
- **Policy information component on the endpoints:** Cisco NAC Agent, Web Agent, Cisco AnyConnect client, or native 802.1x supplicants.

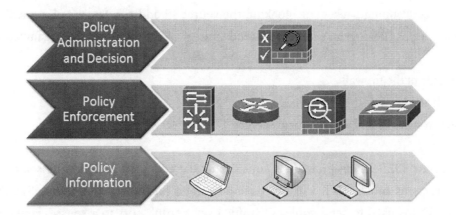

Figure 9.7 – Cisco ISE Components

ISE (see Figure 9.7 above) offers the following benefits:

- Improved visibility and control over all user activity and devices
- Consistent security policy across the enterprise infrastructure
- Increased efficiency by automatic labor-intensive tasks

DESIGNING INTRUSION PREVENTION SYSTEMS AND INTRUSION DETECTION SYSTEMS

The major difference between Intrusion Prevention Systems (IPSs) and Intrusion Detection Systems (IDSs) is that IPS devices operate in line with the traffic, while IDS devices receive only a copy of the traffic so they can analyze it. Cisco offers a wide range of products that offer IPS/IDS functionality in Enterprise Networks, including:

- Cisco 4200 and 4300 series IPS sensor appliances
- Cisco AIP-SSM modules for ASA devices
- Cisco IDSM modules for Catalyst 6500 switches
- Cisco ISR routers with IOS IPS functionality

Intrusion detection, even though it is an old technology, is still used because there are still places where sensors are running in line with the traffic. Having a promiscuous mode (an IDS) device that captures and analyzes traffic (e.g., in the DMZ) is still a valid approach in modern networks and the underlying security policy will be the same, whether or not IDSs or IPSs are deployed.

The actions taken by a device in a promiscuous mode include sending alerts, alarms, log messages, or SNMP traps. On the other hand, by adding an inline sensor, the device will take more aggressive actions, such as dropping packets or blocking the source IP address. Sensor placement is a very important aspect, as IPS devices should be placed strategically throughout the organization:

- Outside of the firewall
- Inside the firewall
- On the same VLAN as the critical servers (DMZ or server farm)

A very important IPS/IDS design issue is considering the effect the design will have on network traffic. Promiscuous mode (IDS) will not have any effect on the traffic because Switched Port Analyzer (SPAN) is used to send copies of traffic over a trunk port to a sensor. However, when deploying IPS solutions, it is very important for the device to be able to process all of the traffic that flows on that particular segment, because all of the traffic passes through the IPS device.

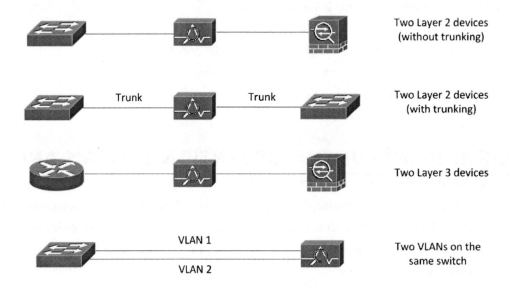

Figure 9.8 – IPS Deployment Models

When placing the IPS sensor on the Enterprise Network, there are several options to choose from, as depicted in Figure 9.8 above:

- **Two Layer 2 devices (without trunking):** This is a popular Enterprise Campus design, where the sensor is placed between two Layer 2 devices (a Layer 2 switch and a transparent mode firewall). The IPS can be between the same VLAN on two different switches or it can be between VLANs with the same subnet on two different switches.

- **Two Layer 2 devices (with trunking):** This is similar to the previous model with the difference of having a trunk between the two devices. This is a common scenario that provides protection for several VLANs from a single location, with the sensor being placed on a trunk port between switches. The sensor can protect a pair or a larger group of VLANs.

- **Two Layer 3 devices:** This design model involves placing the sensor between a Layer 3 switch or a router and a firewall that is running in routed mode (two Layer 3 devices in the same subnet). This deployment option is common in the server farm submodule, the Enterprise Campus module, and the e-commerce submodule. This is much easier to configure since the integration takes place without actually having to touch any of the other devices, unless the IPS module is integrated in another device.

- **Two VLANs on the same switch:** This model involves sensor bridging VLANs together on the same switch by bringing packets in on one VLAN and sending them out on another VLAN. This is a common scenario with ASA devices.

Some of the challenges with deploying IDSs and IPSs include:

- **Asymmetric traffic flows:** Usually, the network packet flows are symmetric, meaning they are taking the same path through the network in both directions (from the source to the destination and from the destination to the source). However, many newer network designs do not have symmetrical traffic flows, as they are engineered to take advantage of all of the links in the network, especially the low-cost links. Asymmetric traffic flows exist so that voice traffic can follow a different path than data traffic, and this is a common issue with the emergence of any-to-any traffic and VoIP services. This problem should be carefully managed and network designers should be aware of traffic patterns that can influence IPS sensor deployment.

- **High availability issues:** Problems might occur if in-line placed sensors go down, especially when they are configured in a failed close deployment type, meaning any hardware failure will block all of the traffic. IPS devices must be carefully placed in the network and configured with high availability in mind (active/active or active/standby) to avoid major service outages in the network.

- **Choosing an appropriate IPS device:** A wide variety of IPS devices can be used, including Cisco ISR routers, ASA devices, Catalyst 6500 modules, or dedicated 4200/4300 appliances with different features and port densities. Special care must be taken when virtualizing IPS services because this adds more complexity, as virtual sensors have different features that depend on platform and licensing models.

- **Choosing the appropriate management and monitoring solution:** Complex IPS deployments need robust management and monitoring solutions, like Cisco Security Manager (CSM).

- **Regularly updating IPS signatures:** Something that sets IPS sensors apart from other security devices (like firewalls) is that signatures must be automatically updated on a regular basis. It is critical for the network operations team to ensure that new signature definitions are regularly downloaded and installed on the IPS device to keep up with evolving threats and vulnerabilities.

ADVANCED VPN

The most common VPN solutions deployed in modern networks include:

- SSL VPN
- IPsec VPN
- DMVPN
- GET VPN

Secure Sockets Layer VPN

Secure Sockets Layer (SSL) VPN is also referred to as Web-VPN, even though Cisco does not use this term any more. Understanding SSL VPN deployments is of great importance for network security designers, as this technology can be configured either on Cisco ISR routers (as part of the router IOS) or on Cisco ASA devices.

SSL VPN is a technology that provides remote access through a gateway that offers many different features, access methods, group configurations, and group policies. End-users can access the gateway from a wide variety of different endpoints. From a design standpoint, network designers need to understand the different access methods, including:

- Clientless access
- Thin client (port forwarding) access
- Full tunnel access

Clientless access mode involves the user accessing corporate resources through a Web browser that supports SSL certificates on different operating systems (e.g., Windows, Mac OS, or Linux). The user does not need to install any software client, as it has access to Web-enabled applications and file sharing services (using NFS or CIFS). The gateway performs address and protocol conversion, content parsing, and rewriting.

The thin client access method behaves differently than the clientless access mode in that it uses a Java applet and performs TCP port forwarding so other services can be used in addition to Web-enabled applications. TCP port forwarding with static port mapping extends application support beyond Web-enabled applications, so SSH, Telnet, IMAP, POP3, and other protocols can be used.

The full tunnel access mode offers extensive application support and user access by downloading either the Cisco SSL VPN Client or the newer Cisco AnyConnect Client. The VPN clients can be loaded through Java or ActiveX and they can operate in two modes:

- Users can run it in workstation memory for the lifetime of the session and then clear off the machine when using public workstations.
- Users can install the VPN client permanently on a system, if they have administrator permissions.

Full tunnel access mode offers the most access of all access methods because it supports all IP-based applications, not just TCP or HTTP as clientless access mode does. This functions much like IPsec remote access VPN.

The next issue network designers must analyze involves the places where the VPN devices and the firewalls will be installed. Unlike traditional designs, which include separate VPN and firewall devices, in modern networks the VPN concentrator and firewall are usually integrated into the same platform, such as an ASA device.

The most common SSL VPN design types are as follows:

- The parallel design
- The inline design
- The DMZ design

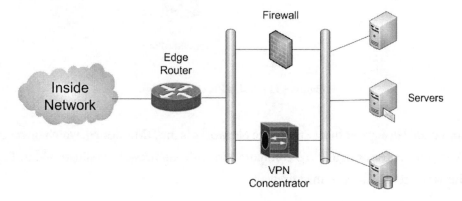

Figure 9.9 – SSL VPN Parallel Design

As depicted in Figure 9.9 above, the parallel design places the firewall logically in parallel with the VPN appliance, behind the edge router. The enterprise servers and services will be placed behind the VPN/firewall layer. The exact design depends on the submodules in use (e.g., e-commerce, WAN services, etc.); however, the firewall policies need to limit traffic that comes into the VPN termination device.

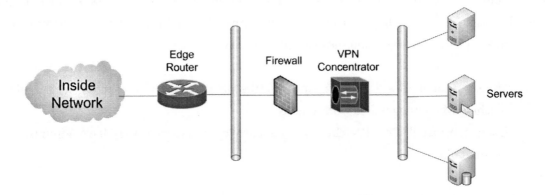

Figure 9.10 – SSL VPN Inline Design

With the inline option, the SSL VPN gateway/concentrator and the firewall are also placed behind the router and in front of the servers, but the difference from the previous model is that the firewall and VPN devices are placed in line, as depicted in Figure 9.10 above. This is a viable option that is suitable for small- to medium-sized businesses.

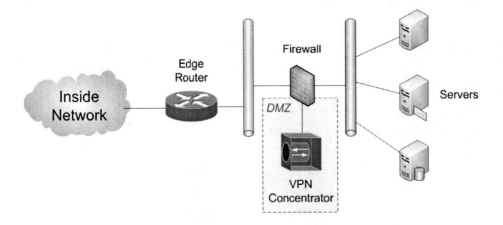

Figure 9.11 – SSL VPN DMZ Design

The recommended design for most Enterprise Networks is the DMZ design, which involves placing the SSL VPN concentrator in a DMZ configuration with the firewall, as illustrated in Figure 9.11 above. This is the classic three-armed firewall.

NOTE: The SSL VPN design topologies presented above can be applied to IPsec VPN solutions as well. The firewall and VPN concentrator can also be integrated into a single platform, like the ASA appliance. Either way, the firewall logically comes before the VPN gateway.

From a routing standpoint, the most common option is the one in which internal routers (placed behind the external firewall) use static routes for the address blocks that point to the private interfaces of the headend device. If there are a large number of intranet networks behind the headend device, static routes become difficult to manage, so using Reverse Route Injection (RRI) should be considered. RRI automatically allows injecting static routes and pushing them to remote clients as part of the policy.

Another issue security network designers should think about is the IP addressing mechanisms to be used in a VPN solution. Statically configured IP pools can be used on headend devices or DHCP services can be leveraged, either inside the network or in a DMZ. When using DHCP, the recommended method is to associate a dedicated scope of DHCP addresses to the VPN headend devices.

Large enterprise organizations may want to use a Remote Authentication Dial-In User Service (RADIUS) server or Lightweight Directory Access Protocol (LDAP) services to allow users a single sign-on. If the user device uses a clientless access method (via a Web browser), the headend device will proxy ARP on behalf of all of the local subnet IP addresses, so the client will receive the traffic from the headend interface IP.

Site-to-Site IPsec VPN

IPsec VPN is an overlay on the existing IP network, so the VPN termination device (e.g., ASA device, FWSM module for Catalyst 6500 switches, or IOS router) needs a routable IP address for the outside Internet connection. Scaling large IPsec VPNs in large organizations is a challenge and network designers must find solutions to scalability, sizing, and performance issues.

To choose the VPN concentrator performance, first analyze the traffic that it must support, which depends on the level at which the solution is implemented. This can include teleworker VPN termination devices, small business devices, or high-end enterprise headquarters devices, according to the Cisco recommendations summarized below:

Location	Model
Teleworker/Small Business	ASA 5505
Small Branch	ASA 5510, ISR 1900
Medium Branch	ASA 5520, ISR 2900
Enterprise Branch	ASA 5540, ISR 3900
Enterprise Headquarters/Data Center	ASA 5550/5580 Cisco 7600/6500

Site-to-site IPsec VPN is an overlay solution that can be implemented across multiple types of networks:

- **Peer-to-peer:** Using this topology provides connectivity between two sites through a secure tunnel.
- **Hub-and-spoke:** This design is a very popular topology that can include VPN solutions on top of Frame Relay networks or DMVPN solutions.
- **Partial mesh:** This can include VPN topologies over Frame Relay or DMVPN solutions.
- **Full mesh:** Full mesh VPN topologies can be expensive and can include Group Encrypted Transport (GET) VPN solutions that can be used to solve some of the any-to-any private broadcast requirements.

Some of the most popular designs for placing the VPN devices on the network include:

- Parallel design
- DMZ design
- Integrated design

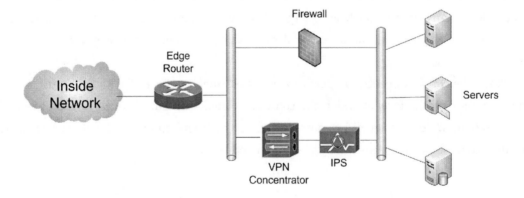

Figure 9.12 – IPSec VPN Parallel Design

The parallel design, depicted in Figure 9.12 above, implies placing the firewall and the VPN concentrator between the edge router and the Enterprise Campus module. The VPN device also connects to the IPS sensor, which usually has redundant connections to the LAN switch. The main advantages of this solution are it is easy to implement and it provides a high availability scenario that can include active/active or active/standby failover mechanisms. Another advantage is the lack of a centralized location to perform logging and content inspection. The major disadvantage is that the IPsec decrypted traffic is not inspected by the firewall.

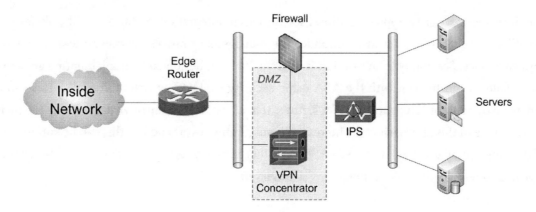

Figure 9.13 – IPsec VPN DMZ Design

A very common solution is to put the IPsec concentrator into a DMZ on a particular firewall interface, as shown in Figure 9.13 above. The advantage of this solution is that the IPsec traffic is decrypted and inspected by the firewall. The disadvantages of this design are it provides moderate scalability and increases the configuration overhead and complexity. In addition, the firewall performance requirements may impose some throughput restrictions because it analyzes all of the decrypted traffic.

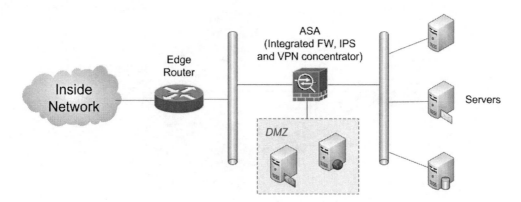

Figure 9.14 – IPsec VPN Integrated Design

With the explosion of ASA solutions, many organizations are integrating the VPN and the firewall on a single platform (see Figure 9.14 above). The only difference from previous designs is that all of the security services listed below are integrated within a single ASA device:

- Firewall services
- IPS services
- Site-to-site and remote access VPN termination services

This integrated security approach allows for an easier integration of the firewall policies with the VPN and IPS policies. It also simplifies the management process because there is only one physical device. Scalability in this design is an issue that can be solved by implementing an active/active failover mechanism with the ASA using security contexts or virtual firewalls. This can be enhanced by additional higher-end ASA features that allow for IPS sensor virtualization. The major disadvantage of this approach is the increased configuration overhead but this can be solved using GUI configuration tools, such as Cisco ASDM. In this design type, the ASA device can also connect a DMZ submodule that hosts public-accessible servers.

Dynamic Multipoint Virtual Private Network Design

Cisco invented the Dynamic Multipoint Virtual Private Network (DMVPN) as a technology that automates the hub-and-spoke site-to-site VPN deployment. The peers can be dynamically discovered and on-demand tunnels can be created to assist with large hub-and-spoke VPN designs. In using DMVPN tunnels, traffic is exchanged directly between peers so it does not have to pass through the hub router, thus saving valuable bandwidth and response time. This design is illustrated in Figure 9.15 below:

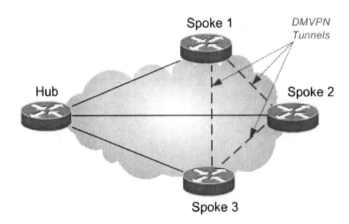

Figure 9.15 – DMVPN Design

DMVPN creates a dynamic mesh, where the number of tunnels is actually lower than in a full-mesh design because the tunnel relationships are created and disabled automatically between spoke devices over a DMVPN cloud. DMVPN involves less configuration on the hub device because it relies on a couple of protocols that work together to allow the spoke sites to dynamically find the public spoke's IP address using one of two protocols:

- Next Hop Resolution Protocol (NHRP)
- Multipoint GRE (mGRE)

In many modern networks, the spoke sites are connected using DSL and cable low-cost subscriptions, where the ISP dynamically assigns them IP addresses. DMVPN can automatically create tunnels between these sites, even though many devices are behind NAT or PAT.

DMVPN should be used to avoid having all of the traffic between spokes pass through the hub device. With DMVPN, unicast traffic passes through the automatically created tunnels across the VPN cloud, while the multicast traffic is still going through the hub. The major advantage of using DMVPN is not worrying about scalability, as dynamic peer discovery and the generation of on-demand tunnels can be leveraged.

Some common recommendations when designing DMVPN solutions include the following:

- Using tunnel protection mode to use IPsec protection in tunnel mode
- Using 3DES or AES for encryption and confidentiality
- Using digital certificates instead of Pre-Shared Keys, as this provides more scalability and using a trusted third party simplifies the process of adding additional spoke (branch) sites
- Deploying hardware acceleration to minimize CPU overhead
- Implementing high availability at the hub site (i.e., multiple NHRP and backup servers)

Virtual Tunnel Interface (VTI) is another new technology that is often used when implementing DMVPN solutions. VTIs avoid using crypto-maps to secure the VPN topology. The VTI interface is actually a routable interface that can be used to terminate the IPsec tunnel and in this situation a dynamic routing protocol (like EIGRP) can be used to accommodate multicast and broadcast traffic and determine interesting traffic.

Some of the advantages of using VTIs include the following:

- Multicast and routing support
- QoS support

- Simplified hub configuration (no more crypto-maps and ACLs)
- Increased scalability
- The ability to define static or dynamic VTI interfaces (dynamic interfaces are suitable for large enterprise designs)
- Simplified IPsec/VPN interoperability with other vendors

Group Encrypted Transport VPN Design

With the rapid deployment of multicast processes, audio, video streaming, and any-to-any communications (like VoIP), it is important to have a secure solution that does not rely on an overlay VPN or on building tunnels. When using the GET VPN approach, routers become part of a trusted grouping of VPN devices and secure packets flow between these routers with their original IP header preserved. This behavior eliminates many QoS and multicast issues. GET VPN simplifies the security policy and key distribution in the group of routers mentioned before using the Group Key Distribution Model (GKDM). The GET VPN design concept is illustrated in Figure 9.16 below:

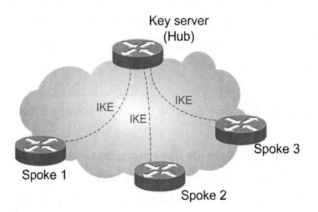

Figure 9.16 – GET VPN Design

GET VPN works on a topology where the key server is positioned at the hub site and it uses a technique that allows the original IP header to be preserved, copied, or reused, without encapsulating it. GET VPN is well suited for IPsec or MPLS VPN networks, which are getting more and more popular, and it works by leveraging the keying protocol, which is actually an IPsec extension. GET VPN technology is a perfect example of the extensibility of IPsec and it enforces IPsec as a framework, as the protocol used by GET VPN is called Group Domain of Interpretation (GDOI).

The key servers at the hub site automatically manage different types of keys (e.g., TEK or KEK), and secure communication channels are established with the spoke sites without using tunnels. The remote sites can register or refresh their keys with the closest server in the group and the re-keying process is performed on a regular basis, according to the IPsec policy and the security association validity period.

The most important advantages of using GET VPN include the following:

- It does not use tunnels.
- It easily supports any-to-any communication.
- It allows for replication using multicast.
- It is a very secure solution because it uses AES as the traffic encryption mechanism.

SECURITY MANAGEMENT

A network designer's main responsibilities include defining the network and security architecture, but the actual implementation of security mechanisms and the deployment of security solutions is another team's responsibility. From a design standpoint, the network designer should focus on security management concepts, and the CCDP candidate should understand the reasons for network security, including the systematic approaches to managing security.

Cisco invented the concept of the Self-Defending Network, which describes the network infrastructure and the services used to respond to attacks while maintaining availability and reliability. Networks should be able to absorb attacks and remain operational so that the organization's productivity will not be affected.

Security Threats and Risks

Efficient security mechanisms must be able to successful address threats to the organization and mitigate risks. One feature that characterizes successful security is transparency to the end-user. The security manager is responsible for maintaining the balance between strict security policies and productivity and collaboration. If the security rules are too tight, the end-users' experience might be affected and the employees might not be able to fulfill their tasks easily. On the other hand, if the security rules are too permissive, the end-users' experience might improve but the network will be more vulnerable to attacks.

The network designer should create a secure environment for the organization by preventing attacks while ensuring that these features have as little effect on an end-user's productivity as possible. A network security implementation must include the following actions:

- Block outside malicious users from getting access to the network
- Allow system, hardware, and application access only to authorized users
- Prevent attacks from being sourced internally
- Support different levels of user access using an access control policy
- Safeguard the data from being changed, modified, or stolen

As mentioned, network threats can be categorized into the following types:

- Reconnaissance
- Unauthorized access
- Denial of Service

Reconnaissance is the precursor of a more structured and advanced threat. Many of the worms, viruses, and Trojan horse attacks usually follow some type of reconnaissance attack. Reconnaissance can also be accomplished through social engineering techniques, by gathering information using the human factor. There are several tools that can be used for reconnaissance, including port scanning tools or packet sniffers. The goal of a reconnaissance attack is to gather as much information as possible about the target host and network, and then use that information to gain unauthorized access and launch an attack or exploit a system or host by reading or modifying confidential data. Unauthorized access might relate to operating systems, physical access, or any service that allows privilege escalation in a system.

Another type of threat is Denial of Service, which is the process of overwhelming the resources of different servers or systems and preventing them from answering legitimate user requests. The affected resources can include memory, CPU, bandwidth, or any other resource that can bring down (crash) the server or the service. A DoS attack denies service using well-known protocols, such as ICMP, ARP, or TCP, but attackers can also perform a more structured and distributed DoS attack using several systems to overwhelm an entire network by sending a very large number of invalid traffic flows.

Vulnerabilities are the measurements of the probability of being negatively influenced by a threat (reconnaissance attack, unauthorized access, or DoS attack). Vulnerabilities are often measured as a function of risk and this might include:

- Risk to data confidentiality
- Risk to data integrity
- Risk to the authenticity of systems and users
- Risk to the availability of networking devices

The level of security risks (vulnerability to threats) must be assessed to protect network resources, procedures, and policies. System availability involves uninterrupted access to network-enabled devices and computing resources, which minimizes business disruptions and loss of productivity. Data integrity involves making sure that data can be seen by authorized users and will not be modified in transit (i.e., data that leaves the sender node must be identical to the data that enters the receiver node). Data confidentiality should ensure that only legitimate users see sensitive information. Confidentiality is used to prevent data theft and damage to the organization.

The risk assessment process involves identifying all possible targets within the organization and placing a quantitative value on them based on their importance in the business process. Targets include:

- Any kind of network infrastructure device (switches, routers, security appliances, wireless access points, or wireless controllers)
- Network services (DNS, ICMP, or DHCP)
- Endpoint devices, especially management stations that perform In-Band or Out-of-Band management
- Network bandwidth (which can be overwhelmed by DoS attacks)

Security Policy Mechanisms

The Cisco network designer may or may not have a role in creating the corporate security policy. Every organization, regardless of size, should have some form of written security policies and procedures, along with a plan to enforce those policies and a disaster and recovery plan.

Figure 9.17 – Cisco Security Policy Methodology

As shown above in Figure 9.17, when initially developing a security policy, Cisco recommends a methodology that consists of the following steps:

1. Risk assessment
2. Determine and develop the policy
3. Implement the policy

4. Monitor and test security

5. Re-access and re-evaluate

Risk assessment involves determining what the network threats are, making sure the entire network is documented, and identifying the current vulnerabilities and the countermeasures that are already in place. The second step involves determining and developing a security policy, which should be based on a wide variety of documents, depending on the organization. The policy should take into consideration the company's strategy, the decision makers and their obligations, the value of the assets, and prioritization of the security rules.

After the policy is developed, it should be implemented from a hardware and software standpoint. This implies putting into place all of the mechanisms involved in the Cisco SAFE blueprint (this will be covered in detail later in this chapter) and applying these to the Enterprise Campus infrastructure module and submodules. The next step is to monitor and test the security plan, and then re-evaluate it and make changes that will improve the policy.

This methodology closely relates to the PPDIOO design methodology presented earlier. The security policy documentation can be different for each organization and can be based on different international standards. Some common written documents include the following:

- Security policy
- Acceptable use policy
- Personnel policies and procedures
- Access control policy
- Incident handling
- Disaster recovery plan

The security policy is a general document that is signed by the management of the organization and it contains high-level considerations such as the company's objectives, the scope of the security policy, risk management aspects, the company's security principles, planning processes (including information classification), and encryption types used in the company.

The acceptable use policy and the personnel policies and procedures cover the ways in which individual users and administrators use their access privileges. The access control policy involves password and documentation control policies, and incident handling describes the way a possible threat is handled to mitigate a breach in the organization's security. The disaster recovery plan is another document that should be included in the security policies and it should detail the procedures that will be followed in case of a total disaster, including applying backup scenarios.

When documenting the security policy, the components may be divided into the major security mechanisms that will be applied in the organization, including:

- Physical security
- Authentication
- Authorization
- Confidentiality
- Data integrity
- Management and reporting

Physical security is often ignored when documenting the security policy. It implies physically securing the data center and the wiring closets, restricting access to the network devices (including the LAN cabling and the WAN/PSTN connection points), and even securing access-to-endpoint devices such as workstations and printers.

Authentication implies making sure the individual users that are actually accessing particular objects on the network are who they claim to be. Authentication is used to determine the identity of the subject and authorization is used to limit access to network objects, authorizing them based on their identity. Confidentiality and data integrity define the encryption mechanisms to be used, such as IPsec, digital signatures, or physical biometric user access. Management and reporting involve auditing the network from a security standpoint, logging information, and auditing users' and administrators' actions. This can be supported by the use of Host Intrusion Detection Systems (HIDSs) to ensure that the network servers can detect attacks and protect themselves against those attacks.

Network Security System Lifecycle

Security is one of the main responsibilities of a design professional and this includes a solid knowledge of security policies and procedures. The security policy is a key element in securing network services, offering the necessary level of security and enhancing network availability, confidentiality, integrity, and authenticity. The network security system lifecycle is illustrated in Figure 9.18 below:

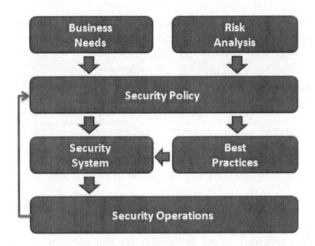

Figure 9.18 – Network Security System Lifecycle

The security policy is a small part of the larger network security system lifecycle that is driven by an assessment of the organization's needs and by comprehensive risk analysis. A risk assessment may also need to be performed, using penetration testing and vulnerability scanning tools.

The security policy contains written documents that include:

- Guidelines
- Processes
- Standards
- Acceptable use policies
- Architectures and infrastructure elements used (e.g., IPsec or 802.1x)
- Granular areas of the security policy, such as the Internet use policy or the access control policy

The security system can include the following elements:

- Cisco ASA devices
- IDS and IPS
- 802.1x port-based authentication
- Device hardening
- Virtual private networking

These security system elements are chosen based on a set of guidelines and best practices. The entire process defines the organization's security operations, which involves the actual integration and deployment of the incident response procedures, the monitoring process, compliance with different standards, and implementation of security services (e.g., IPS, proxy authentication, and zone-based firewalls). The diagram presented in Figure 9.18 is an iterative process. Once the security operations are put into place, the process can pause and the organization's needs can be reassessed, leading to changes to the security policy. The network security system lifecycle is an ongoing framework and all of its components should be periodically revised and updated.

Security Policies and Procedures

The security policy is the main component of the network security system lifecycle and it is defined per RFC 2196 as a formal statement of the rules and guidelines that must be followed by the organization's users, contractors, and temporary employees and by anybody who has access to the company's data and informational assets. It is a general framework for security implementation and it covers the different areas of the organization using a modular approach.

One way of approaching the security policy is by examining the modular network design of the organization and developing a separate policy for each module or a single policy that will include all of the modules. The modular approach is also recommended when performing risk and threat assessments.

The security policy also creates a security baseline that will allow future gap analysis to be performed to detect new vulnerabilities and countermeasures. The most important aspects covered by the written security policies and procedures are as follows:

- Identifying the company's assets
- Determining how the organizational assets are used
- Defining the communication roles and responsibilities
- Describing existing tools and processes
- Defining the security incident handling process

A steering committee will review and eventually publish the security policy after all of the component documents are finalized.

Cisco has introduced a four-step process that defines the security policy methodology that is part of the network security system lifecycle, as shown in Figure 9.19 below:

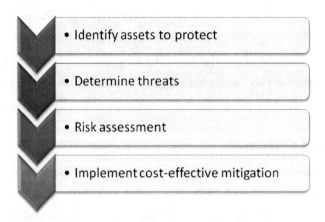

Figure 9.19 – Security Policy Methodology

The first step is to identify and classify the organizational assets and assign them a quantitative value based on the impact of their loss. The next step is determining the threats to those assets, because threats only matter if they can affect specific assets within the company. One company may assign a higher priority to physical security than to other security aspects (e.g., protecting against reconnaissance attacks).

Next, a risk and vulnerability assessment is performed to determine the probability of the threats occurring. The next step is performed after the security policy is published and it involves implementing cost-effective mitigation to protect the organization. This defines the actual tools, techniques, and applications that will mitigate the threats to which the company is vulnerable. The last step, which is often skipped by many organizations, involves a periodic review of the security policy and documenting any changes to the policy.

Many organizations have templates for developing the security policy and some of the common components include the following:

- **The acceptable use policy:** This is a general end-user document that defines the roles, responsibilities, and allowed processes, software, or hardware equipment. For example, certain file sharing applications or Instant Messaging programs can be forbidden.
- **Network Access Control policy:** This policy contains general access control principles that can include password requirements, password storage, or data classification.
- **Security management policy:** This policy summarizes the organization's security mechanisms and defines ways to manage the security infrastructure and necessary tools (e.g., CiscoWorks or Cisco NAC).

- **Incident handling policy:** This document should describe the policies and procedures by which security incidents are handled. It can even include emergency-type scenarios like disaster recovery plans or business continuity procedures.
- **VPN policy:** This dedicated policy covers the virtual private networking technologies used and the various security aspects that concern them. Different policies may be applied for teleworkers, remote access users, or site-to-site VPN users.
- **Physical security policy:** This involves physical security aspects like access control (e.g., badges, biometrics, and facility security).
- **Training and awareness:** Ongoing training and awareness campaigns must sustain the organization's security policy and this is especially applicable to new employees.

There are two driving factors behind the security policy:

- The organization's needs and goals
- Risk assessment

Network security requires a comprehensive risk management and risk assessment approach that will help lower the risks within acceptable levels for the organization. These acceptable levels will vary from organization to organization. The risk assessment process will lead to the implementation of the components included in the security policy. A risk assessment will also be accompanied by the cost-benefit analysis, which analyzes the financial implications of the mitigation (control) that will be put into place to protect specific assets. For example, money should not be spent protecting certain assets from threats that are not likely to occur.

The risk assessment process involves three components:

- Severity
- Probability
- Control

These three components should explain what assets will be secured, their monetary value, and the actual loss that would result if one of those resources were to be affected. The severity and the probability aspects refer to the probability and impact of a certain attack on the organization. The control aspect defines how the policy will be used to control and minimize the risks.

The three components are used to develop a risk index (RI), which uses the following formula:

RI = (severity factor * probability factor) / control factor

where:
- Severity represents the quantitative loss of a compromised asset
- Probability is a mathematical value of the risk actually occurring
- Control is the ability to control and manage that risk

For example, the severity factor may have a range of 1 to 5, the probability factor may have a range of 1 to 3, and the control factor may also have a range of 1 to 3. If the severity factor for a two-hour DoS attack on an e-mail server has a value of 3, the probability factor has a value of 2, and the control factor has a value of 1, then the calculated RI equals 6. This calculation should be applied to different areas of the network and should take into account different types of threats.

Another characteristic of risk assessment is that it is an ongoing process that will undergo continuous changes due to new technologies emerging. The security policy must be updated to reflect these infrastructure changes. There are four steps to the continuous security lifecycle:

1. Secure
2. Monitor
3. Test
4. Improve

Figure 9.20 – Risk Assessment Security Lifecycle

Referring to Figure 9.20 above, securing implies using authentication and identification techniques, ACLs, packet inspection, firewall techniques, IDS and IPS technologies, VPNs, or encryption. The next step is monitoring the processes using SNMP or SDEE. Ongoing vulnerability testing should be provided, along with penetration testing and security auditing, to ensure the functionality of each process. The last step is an iterative process that helps improve different areas based on data analysis, reports, summaries, and intelligent network design.

Trust and Identity Management

Trust and identity management is another key part of the Cisco Self-Defending Network initiative. This is a critical aspect for developing secure network systems. Trust and identity management states who can access the network, what systems can access the network, when and where the network can be accessed, and how the access can occur. It also attempts to isolate infected machines and keep them off the network by enforcing access control, thus forcing the infected machines to update their signature databases and their applications.

Trust and identity management has three components:

- Trust
- Identity
- Access control

Trust is the relationship between two or more network entities, for example, a workstation and a firewall appliance. The trust concept will determine the security policy decisions. If a trust relationship exists, communication is allowed between the entities. The trust relationship and the level of privilege can be affected by different postures (e.g., an outdated virus signature database or an un-patched system).

Devices can be grouped into domains of trust that can have different levels of segmentation. The identity aspect determines who or what accesses the network, including users, devices, or other organizations. The authentication of identity is based on three attributes that make the connection to access control:

- Something that the subject knows (password or PIN)
- Something that the subject has (token or smartcard)
- Something that the subject is (biometrics, such as fingerprint, voice, or facial recognition)

The domains of trust can be implemented on a Microsoft Active Directory and they can be based on the Cisco design methodology. In large organizations and across the Internet, certificates play an important role in proving user identity and the right to access information and services.

Access controls in enterprise organizations typically rely on Authentication, Authorization, and Accounting (AAA) services. AAA solutions can use an intermediate authenticator device (e.g., a router, switch, or firewall) that can leverage some backend services, like Cisco Access Control Server (ACS) or various RADIUS or TACACS+ servers. Authentication establishes user or system identity and access to network resources, while authorization services define what users can access.

The accounting part provides an audit trail that can be used for billing services (e.g., recording the duration of a user's connection to a particular service). Most of the modern Cisco devices can act as authenticators and can pass user authentication requests to RADIUS/TACACS+ servers.

Secure Connectivity

Secure connectivity is another component of the Cisco Self-Defending Network that works in close relationship with the trust and identity management concepts described above. This implies using secure technologies to connect endpoints. Examples include the following:

- Using IPsec inside the organization and over the insecure Internet
- Using SSH to replace insecure technologies like Telnet for console access
- Using SSL/TLS (HTTPS) secure connectivity using Web browsers
- Using solutions from ISPs, such as MPLS VPNs

The primary goal of trust and identity services when combined with secure connectivity is infrastructure protection. From a Cisco standpoint, this can be accomplished using a wide variety of integrated hardware security features, such as the following:

- Cisco ASA devices, including the 5500 family (ASA 5510, 5520, 5540, and so on)
- Routers using IOS security feature sets that include basic firewalls, zone-based firewalls, IPS functionality, IPsec VPNs, DMVPNs, or SSL VPNs for Web-based clients.
- Cisco Catalyst switches with firewalls, IDSs, or VPN modules and other Layer 2 security features (e.g., 802.1x port-based authentication). The Cisco Catalyst 6500 series switch is a modular switch that supports a wide variety of service modules that help enhance network security. Examples of these modules include Cisco Firewall Services Module (FWSM), Cisco Intrusion Detection System Services Module (IDSM-2), and the Cisco SSL Services Module.

NOTE: 802.1x is also known as Identity Based Network Services (IBNS) in terms of Cisco products.

Threat Defense Best Practices

Some of the best practices for protecting the network infrastructure through trust and identity include the following:

- Using AAA services with the Cisco ACS server or other RADIUS/TACACS+ servers
- Using 802.1x

- Logging, using Syslog and SDEE (Security Device Event Exchange – the protocol used by Cisco IDS/IPS sensors to send information to the management stations) to create comprehensive reports
- Using SSH instead of Telnet to avoid any management traffic crossing the network in clear text
- Using secure versions of management protocols, such as SNMPv3 (authenticates the client and the server), NTPv3, and SFTP
- Harden all network devices by making sure that unnecessary services are disabled
- Using authentication between devices that are running dynamic routing protocols
- Using the Cisco one-step lockdown feature on network devices to harden them
- Using ACLs to restrict management access, allowing only certain hosts to access the network devices
- Using IPsec as an internal (encrypting management or other sensitive traffic) or external (VPN) solution
- Using the Cisco NAC solution, which ensures that the network clients and servers are patched and updated with the newest antivirus, antispam, and antispyware mitigation tools in an automated and centralized fashion

SUMMARY

The network designer should be able to guarantee to the company the following important system characteristics:

- Confidentiality
- Integrity
- Availability

Before a network designer offers security consultancy services (e.g., risk assessment or business impact analysis), the designer must understand the real threats to the network infrastructure. The different categories of threats to confidentiality, integrity, and availability include the following:

- Denial of Service (DoS) and Distributed Denial of Service (DDoS) attacks
- Spoofing (masquerading)
- Telnet attacks
- Password-cracking programs
- Viruses
- Trojans and worms

Firewalls can be deployed in multiple modes, including routed and transparent, and most of them can be virtualized into security contexts to provide cost-effective solutions. The virtual firewall partitions a physical firewall into multiple logical devices, each with its own configuration. This is similar to having multiple standalone firewalls but without having to buy separate devices. Security contexts are distinct and independent firewalls in the sense of having their own attributes, such as the following:

- Security policies
- Assigned interfaces
- NAT rules
- ACLs
- Administrators

The active/active failover mechanism used on firewall devices leverages the virtual context feature. The best results are obtained when the two devices configured with active/active failover have an identical platform and operating system. The two firewalls must be connected with a failover state link and this can be accomplished in three ways:

- **Single physical link:** Both the failover and stateful information are transmitted on this link.
- **Dual physical links:** The failover information is exchanged on one interface and the stateful information (maintaining the TCP connection and translation rules) is exchanged on another.
- **Dual redundant physical links:** These act as a single logical link that carries both the failover and stateful information between the firewalls.

Private VLANs (PVLANs) are an option for adding an extra security layer in the Enterprise Campus module or data center submodule, especially in the e-commerce submodule. A PVLAN divides a VLAN into more logical components and this allows groups of servers or individual servers to be isolated, quarantining them from other devices.

A zone-based policy firewall is an IOS feature that can leverage the existing ISR routers by configuring firewall functionalities on them, as opposed to using dedicated ASA devices or firewall modules. Cisco Zone Based Firewall (ZBF) functionality was introduces in Cisco IOS 12.4(6)T as an evolution from traditional firewall implementation, which was an interface-based model (the "ip inspect" command can be applied on an interface in the inbound or outbound direction). The limitations imposed by traditional firewall implementation led to the development of zone-based firewalls, which work by following these steps:

1. Create security zones.
2. Place an interface or multiple interfaces into each security zone.
3. Create unidirectional zone pairs to define relationships between zones.
4. Apply a modular, flexible, granular policy (using class maps, policy maps, and service policy) to the zone pairs.

Cisco Network Admission Control (NAC) is a service that tries to guarantee that various endpoints are compliant with the network security polices enforced by network devices (e.g., firewalls, switches, or routers). Cisco NAC provides access to compliant devices and then it ensures that non-compliant devices are denied access, are placed in quarantine, or are given restricted access to certain resources. NAC products are categorized as follows:

- The NAC framework, which is a system that provides security for network environments (LAN, WAN, WiFi, extranet, and remote access)
- The NAC appliance

One of the first design decisions involves selecting the location in which the NAC solution will be implemented. The following aspects should be considered in this decision process:

- Choosing between a virtual and a real IP gateway
- Choosing In-Band or Out-of-Band deployment mode
- Choosing a Layer 2 or a Layer 3 client mode
- Choosing a central or edge physical deployment

The modern Cisco NAC solution includes the Identity Service Engine (ISE), which uses Cisco network devices to extend access enforcement throughout a network and consists of the following components:

- **Policy administration and decision component:** Cisco ISE.
- **LAN policy enforcement points:** Cisco Catalyst switches, ASA devices, or ISR routers.
- **Policy information component on the endpoints:** Cisco NAC Agent, Web Agent, Cisco AnyConnect client, or native 802.1x supplicants.

The major difference between Intrusion Prevention Systems (IPSs) and Intrusion Detection Systems (IDSs) is that IPS devices operate in line with the traffic, while IDS devices receive only a copy of the traffic so they can analyze it.

Cisco offers a wide range of products that offer IPS/IDS functionality in Enterprise Networks, including:

- Cisco 4200 and 4300 series IPS sensor appliances
- Cisco AIP-SSM modules for ASA devices
- Cisco IDSM modules for Catalyst 6500 switches
- Cisco ISR routers with IOS IPS functionality

Sensor placement is a very important aspect, as IPS devices should be placed strategically throughout the organization:

- Outside of the firewall
- Inside the firewall
- On the same VLAN as the critical servers (DMZ or server farm)

Some of the challenges in deploying IDSs and IPSs include:

- Asymmetric traffic flows
- High availability issues
- Choosing an appropriate IPS device
- Choosing the appropriate management and monitoring solution
- Regularly updating IPS signatures

Secure Sockets Layer (SSL) VPN is also referred to as Web-VPN, even though Cisco does not use this term any more. Understanding SSL VPN deployments is of great importance for network security designers, as this technology can be configured either on Cisco ISR routers (as part of the router IOS) or on Cisco ASA devices.

SSL VPN is a technology that provides remote access through a gateway that can offer many different features, access methods, group configurations, and group policies. End-users can access the gateway from a wide variety of different endpoints. From a design standpoint, network designers must understand the different access methods, including:

- Clientless access
- Thin client (port forwarding) access
- Full tunnel access

The most common SSL VPN design types are:

- The parallel design
- The inline design
- The DMZ design

Site-to-site IPsec VPN is an overlay solution that can be implemented across multiple types of networks, including peer-to-peer, hub-and-spoke, full mesh, or partial mesh. Some of the most popular designs for placing the VPN devices on the network include:

- Parallel design
- DMZ design
- Integrated design

Dynamic Multipoint VPN (DMVPN) creates a dynamic mesh, where the number of tunnels is actually lower than that of a full mesh design, because the tunnel relationships are created and disabled automatically between spoke devices over a DMVPN cloud. DMVPN involves less configuration on the hub device because it relies on a couple of protocols that work together to allow the spoke sites to dynamically find the public spoke's IP address:

- Next Hop Resolution Protocol (NHRP)
- Multipoint GRE (mGRE)

With the rapid deployment of multicast processes, audio, video streaming, and any-to-any communications (like VoIP), it is important to have a secure solution that does not rely on an overlay VPN or on building tunnels. When using the Group Encrypted Transport (GET) VPN approach, routers become part of a trusted grouping of VPN devices and secure packets flow between these routers, with their original IP header preserved.

A network security implementation must include the following actions:

- Block outside malicious users from getting access to the network
- Allow system, hardware, and application access only to authorized users
- Prevent attacks from being sourced internally
- Support different levels of user access using an access control policy
- Safeguard the data from being changed, modified, or stolen

Vulnerabilities are measurements of the probability of being negatively influenced by a threat (e.g., reconnaissance attack, unauthorized access, or DoS attack). Vulnerabilities are often measured as a function of risk and this might include:

- Risk to data confidentiality
- Risk to data integrity
- Risk to the authenticity of systems and users
- Risk to the availability of networking devices

END OF CHAPTER QUIZ

1. Which of the following security characteristics should be guaranteed to any enterprise-level organization (choose three)?
   a. Low cost
   b. Confidentiality
   c. Availability
   d. Free upgrades
   e. Integrity

2. Which of the following are valid network threats (choose all that apply)?
   a. DoS attacks
   b. OOB attacks
   c. Spoofing
   d. Viruses
   e. Routing
   f. Trojans

3. The main purpose of a Denial of Service attack is to make a network resource unavailable to its intended users.
   a. True
   b. False

4. What is the term used to describe the process of sending illegitimate requests by an attacker to a network request?
   a. Spoofing
   b. Logging
   c. Query
   d. Flooding

5. Which of the following are valid types of vulnerability scanning (choose three)?
   a. ICMP scanning
   b. SNMP scanning
   c. Syslog scanning
   d. BGP scanning
   e. TCP scanning

6. Which of the following are attributes that are specific to each security context within a firewall (choose three)?
   a. VPN configuration
   b. Security policy
   c. NAT rules
   d. Dynamic routing protocols configuration
   e. Access Control Lists

7. Which of the following features are NOT supported by common virtual firewalls (choose all that apply)?
   a. IPsec VPN
   b. Access Control Lists
   c. NAT rules
   d. SSL VPN
   e. Assigned interfaces
   f. Dynamic routing protocols

8. Which of the following are valid firewall failover link configuration methods (choose three)?
   a. LLDP
   b. Single physical link
   c. Virtual link
   d. Dual physical links
   e. Dual redundant physical links

9. Which of the following are valid private VLAN port roles (choose three)?
   a. Isolated
   b. Promiscuous
   c. Voice
   d. Community
   e. Independent

10. Which of the following private VLAN port types is usually connected to a router?
    a. Isolated
    b. Promiscuous
    c. Voice
    d. Community
    e. Independent

11. Which of the following is the first step in the zone-based firewall configuration process?

    a. Creating zone pairs

    b. Placing interfaces into security zones

    c. Creating security zones

    d. Configuring the modular security policy

12. Which of the following technologies is the zone-based firewall solution predecessor in terms of IOS firewall solutions?

    a. SNMP

    b. RIP

    c. CBAC

    d. CEF

13. The zone pairs in a zone-based firewall solution are bidirectional.

    a. True

    b. False

14. Which of the following is a network service that tries to guarantee that various endpoints are compliant with the network security policy enforced by network devices?

    a. SNMP

    b. RIP

    c. RTP

    d. NAC

    e. NTP

15. Which of the following is NOT a valid NAC deployment model?

    a. Layer 2 In-Band real IP gateway

    b. Layer 3 Out-of-Band

    c. Layer 4 In-Band

    d. Layer 2 Out-of-Band virtual gateway

    e. Layer 3 In-Band with multiple remote sites

16. Which of the following is a modern Cisco NAC product?

    a. ISP

    b. ISE

    c. IPS

    d. ISA

17. Which of the following are components of a generic NAC solution (choose two)?
    a. NAC framework
    b. NAC router
    c. NAC monitoring server
    d. NAC appliance

18. Which of the following is the dedicated Cisco IPS sensor appliance family?
    a. 4200/4300
    b. 6500
    c. 7200
    d. 3800

19. Which of the following are the most common SSL VPN deployment models (choose three)?
    a. Parallel design
    b. Inline design
    c. Out-of-Band design
    d. DMZ design
    e. Campus design

20. Which of the following devices can integrate firewall, VPN, and IPS functionalities?
    a. ISR router
    b. Catalyst switch
    c. ISE
    d. ASA device

Quiz Answers

Chapter 1: The Cisco Enterprise Architecture Model

1 – b, e	6 – c	11 – b	16 – b
2 – d	7 – b	12 – b	17 – a
3 – b	8 – a	13 – c	18 – c
4 – c	9 – a, c, d	14 – a	19 – b
5 – b	10 – e	15 – d	20 – a, c

Chapter 2: Advanced Enterprise Architecture Model

1 – d	6 – d	11 – c	16 – a, b, c, f
2 – b, c, e	7 – b	12 – a	17 – a
3 – b	8 – a, c	13 – a	18 – a
4 – a	9 – d	14 – c	19 – c
5 – e	10 – b	15 – c	20 – b

Chapter 3: Designing Advanced IP Addressing

1 – c	6 – b	11 – c	16 – a
2 – d	7 – b	12 – a	17 – b
3 – a	8 – a, c, e	13 – a, c	18 – a
4 – b	9 – d	14 – b	19 – a
5 – a, c	10 – a	15 – a, b, d	20 – d

Chapter 4: Designing Advanced IP Multicast

1 – b	6 – d	11 – e	16 – b
2 – c	7 – b	12 – a	17 – c
3 – a	8 – a	13 – a	18 – a
4 – a, d	9 – b, c, e	14 – a	19 – d
5 – d	10 – b	15 – b	20 – c

Chapter 5: Designing Advanced Routing Solutions

1 – c	6 – a	11 – c	16 – a
2 – c	7 – b	12 – b	17 – d
3 – a	8 – a, c, d	13 – c	18 – c
4 – d	9 – d	14 – b	19 – b, d
5 – d	10 – a	15 – b	20 – a

Chapter 6: Designing Advanced WAN Services

1 – b, c, e	6 – a	11 – b, e	16 – a
2 – a	7 – b	12 – a	17 – b
3 – d	8 – d	13 – c	18 – b
4 – a	9 – d	14 – a, d	19 – a
5 – a	10 – b	15 – b, d	20 – c

Chapter 7: Designing the Enterprise Data Center

1 – a, c, d, f	6 – a	11 – a, c, d	16 – a
2 – a	7 – b, d	12 – a	17 – a, d
3 – b, c, e	8 – c	13 – b, c, f	18 – c, d
4 – c	9 – d	14 – c	19 – b
5 – a, d, e	10 – b	15 – b	20 – c

Chapter 8: Designing the E-Commerce Submodule

1 – b, d, e, f	6 – b	11 – a, b, e	16 – a
2 – a	7 – d	12 – b	17 – a, c, e, f
3 – d	8 – a, b, d	13 – b	18 – a
4 – c	9 – a, c, d	14 – c, e	19 – c, d, e
5 – e	10 – a	15 – d	20 – a, c, e

Chapter 9: Designing Advanced Security Services

1 – b, c, e	6 – b, c, e	11 – c	16 – b
2 – a, c, d, f	7 – a, d, f	12 – c	17 – a, d
3 – a	8 – b, d, e	13 – b	18 – a
4 – d	9 – a, b, d	14 – d	19 – a, b, e
5 – a, b, e	10 – b	15 – c	20 – d

Lightning Source UK Ltd.
Milton Keynes UK
UKOW010040090413

208863UK00003B/55/P